To
Terry –
may God
bless your when
and by your reading
Freedom's Tree –

Ken Lippincott
1-25-2015

FREEDOM'S TREE

KENNETH LIPPINCOTT

WESTBOW®
PRESS
A DIVISION OF THOMAS NELSON
& ZONDERVAN

This is a work of fiction. All of the characters, names, incidents, organizations, and dialogue in this novel are either the products of the author's imagination or are used fictitiously.

WestBow Press books may be ordered through booksellers or by contacting:

WestBow Press
A Division of Thomas Nelson & Zondervan
1663 Liberty Drive
Bloomington, IN 47403
www.westbowpress.com
1 (866) 928-1240

Because of the dynamic nature of the Internet, any web addresses or links contained in this book may have changed since publication and may no longer be valid. The views expressed in this work are solely those of the author and do not necessarily reflect the views of the publisher, and the publisher hereby disclaims any responsibility for them.

Any people depicted in stock imagery provided by Thinkstock are models, and such images are being used for illustrative purposes only. Certain stock imagery © Thinkstock.

Scripture taken from the Holy Bible, NEW INTERNATIONAL VERSION®. Copyright © 1973, 1978, 1984, 2011 by Biblica, Inc. All rights reserved worldwide. Used by permission. NEW INTERNATIONAL VERSION® and NIV® are registered trademarks of Biblica, Inc. Use of either trademark for the offering of goods or services requires the prior written consent of Biblica US, Inc.

ISBN: 978-1-4908-5813-5 (sc)
ISBN: 978-1-4908-5814-2 (hc)
ISBN: 978-1-4908-5812-8 (e)

Library of Congress Control Number: 2014919109

Printed in the United States of America.

WestBow Press rev. date: 12/12/2014

DEDICATION

Freedom's Tree is dedicated to my bride of fifty-two years, Karen Rose Lippincott. Karen has not only encouraged me to write and finish what I started forty-eight years ago, but she also served as my muse in this my first novel. Her assistance with editing proved especially valuable as was her reading from a woman's point of view. The main character bears her name and reflects her strength and character. Though both bruised and flawed like the characters in the novel, my wife and I are partners. She, more than any other reader, will appreciate what the novel represents. God blessed me the day we married and continues to do so as we partner through life together like two cracked pots. We pray that the beauty of Jesus shines through those cracks.

ACKNOWLEDGEMENTS

Special thanks to our daughters, Kristin Anne Becker and Krystal Rene Thomas. My lovely daughter Kristin reminded me to keep writing that she and her family were waiting to read my book and that I should write with that audience in mind. My darling daughter Krystal gave me the gift one Christmas of transferring my manuscript from yellow pad and Apple 2E computer to a word document. Both daughters and their children regularly asked how I was progressing and when would my book be finished. Finally, in January, 2014 I set all projects aside and finished! Thank you, daughters dear.

I also thank our good friend and artist, Kathryn Calahan, for contributing artwork.

CONTENTS

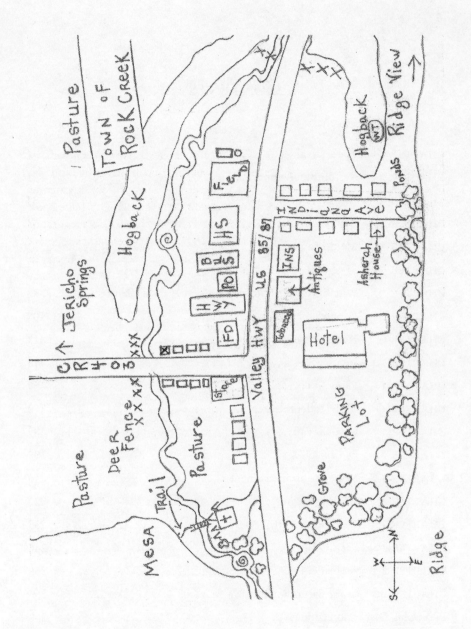

Preface

Have you ever wondered what God wanted you to do next? Are you at a point in your life where you know you don't have too many more years left to live and you are concerned about finishing well? I sought answers to both questions. My answer came as a question. What were you to do that you haven't done? Finish the book was my reply. As a result, what follows is my best effort to fulfill God's request of me. Really, it was a command, but it didn't sound like one when he spoke to me in a gentle, personable voice. He followed by reminding me that he had given me a dream about a scene with a tree. I had made an oil painting of the scene, which I hope you will be able to see eventually. There's more to my story.

I had the dream forty-eight years ago, when I was attending college at Colorado University Denver Center. Studying to become a teacher, I crammed as many classes in each semester as I could handle. I was in a hurry, because I made $200 a month at minimum wage, while my wife made $275. My motivation was to do right and support my wife, so we could have children and become a family. Regardless, I would work on the book periodically, and then put it down only to pick it up again later. Learning that Hemmingway had been known to rewrite a conclusion a hundred times, I thought it noble to draft and revise. That became a trap for me.

Four years ago I retired after being a public school teacher and administrator for forty-three years. I also served as a bi-vocational pastor for three small churches. As a teacher, I coached and sponsored a variety of student organizations and clubs. My wife, Karen, and I worked within the church as well with students and adults. We managed to spend a wealth of hours battling for community causes, especially after retirement. Along the way I've been broken physically with heart disease and diabetes largely due to working decades under stress. Today, August 27, 2014, I have lived one day more with heart disease than without it. God has gifted me with thirty-five plus years that I figure he gave me, in part, to finish this assignment. In January this year I wrote two-thirds of *Freedom's Tree*. It was stress free and joyous. I can't say the same for the revision and editing, which became stressful. I compared it with grading the 65,000 five hundred word compositions I figure I graded over the years, while teaching primarily ninth and tenth grade English.

Teaching really has been a blessing and aid to my writing. Teaching *Romeo and Juliet, Julius Caesar, To Kill a Mockingbird, The Hobbit,* and *The Natural* influenced my literary thinking. Teaching composition and strategic reading to thousands of students did the same for my own writing. But, what influenced me the most was experiencing the Arthurian Legend with my students. What I really did was teach children, who are now all adults. Some are in their sixties and retired before I did! All the kids my wife and I influenced through school and church groups knew I was writing a book. When I see them, you can imagine what they ask me. The book is finished! Another has been started, a third is planned.

Here are three concepts they will remember from my classes. Like J. R. Tolkien and C. S. Lewis, I have created my own world, a fictitious valley comprised of some of my favorite geologic and geographic features from around Colorado where I present my dramatic re-enactments. I use scripture with each chapter title as a lens for the reader to use in reading each chapter. My characters have been developed through what I called two rails of a train track. One rail is the testimonial track: what the character says and does, what others say and do in response to the character, what the author tells about the character, and the character's friends and enemies. The other rail is the motivational track: why a character does what he or she does (motivation), choices the character has, decisions the character makes, and how the character solves problems. Do the ends justify the means or the means justify the ends? When you read *Freedom's Tree*, I hope you will view the characters using the rails of this track. Note the questions at the end of the book.

I hope my former students from 1967 thru 2010 will realize that sometimes I was praying for them as I walked the aisles of my classroom and as I sat looking at them from the front of the classroom quietly perched upon my stool. I needed prayer as I was grading their papers, mostly essays!– Mr. Lipp

The Arrival

CHAPTER I

*"Have I not commanded you? Be strong and courageous.
Do not be afraid: do not be discouraged, for the LORD
your God will be with you wherever you go." Joshua 1:9*

Within bruised and flawed, without modest, now slender, and refreshingly wholesome, Karen Gustafson softly sang "Greater is he that is in me! Greater is he that is in me! Greater is he that is in me, than he that is in the world." Again, she soloed, eyes closed while visualizing the church choir back home joining her with vigor. No other passenger heard her, and tears swelled in her pale blue eyes. Soft facial features flushed with color like a ripening peach. From her Bible again she softly mouthed, as she read: *You, dear children are from God and have overcome them, because the one who is in you is greater than the one who is in the world. I John 4:4.* Briefly, calm returned within that she displayed outwardly by a knowing smile. The message renewed her strength and resolve. With her right hand, she brushed back once long, blond tresses recently given way to an ear length bob fashioned by her own hands. Like an arrow from a quiver, Karen shot an arrow of prayer when she uttered, "Help me, Jesus!"

The scale of Karen's inner struggle tipped toward trusting the Lord. Reassured, she changed her tune and softly sang over and over again, "You are my rock, my firm foundation. Whom shall I fear, whom shall I fear?"

Comforted she closed her study Bible and placed it on the seat beside her. Picking up her new crossword puzzle book, she tilted her head to the left and gazed out the window at the canyon wall with creek rushing below. With confidence yet not in herself, she meditated, praying silently, Father, please hold me. I know you love me, but I'm afraid. I want to trust you, rest in you, but I am afraid. I try to let go of my fear, the past. Had the child really killed herself? Oh, Lord, set me free. Karen's heart ached and her inner scale shifted in the opposite direction.

Later, Karen read clues to her puzzle. Four down: another name for Phoenician. Canaanites, she wrote. The next clue read: Led God's people into the Promised Land. Moses! No, Moses doesn't fit, she thought. Let's see what

1

intersects: a primary battle in the Promised Land. Oh, she concluded, that's got to be Jericho. So, the other answer is Joshua. She read twelve-across: large fortified room behind the city gate. She remembered the answer from Sunday school. The Canaanites, enemies of God's chosen people, built a large room behind their city gate. When attacked, the Canaanites could control an enemy breeching the gate. While troops fought invaders below, reinforcements waited on a wide ledge above. If invaders began to win the battle, reinforcements dropped down from above to turn the tide.

Humming, Karen's attention shifted outside the window to the steep river canyon below, past the driver in front, and across the aisle to the imposing rock wall near the bus windows. At first oblivious of other passengers, the scene held her gaze. Totally awesome, she nearly spoke aloud. And then she thought how could such a small creek carve such magnificence? What persistence, what long-suffering effort, what resolve would it take for man to create such beauty, such ruggedness? This beautiful canyon with a grand mesa high to the west could symbolize real life. Karen reflected that circumstances and relationships carve into us, erode away parts, and lay bare often what we preferred not be exposed. How rude! How life like!

Next looking at the passengers before her then back across the aisle to the rock wall, Karen wondered how many fellow passengers hurt. Are we all wounded? How many know where to go for healing?

Interrupting Karen's gaze, white letters on a green highway sign flashed before her eyes announcing Rock Creek three miles, Jericho Springs eight miles, and Ridge View seventeen miles. Taking the cue, she looked center aisle over the driver's shoulder and observed the highway. She saw only rock wall barrier, front and right, and treacherous canyon below and left. Around another curve, the bus dipped then climbed a resistant incline. A quarter mile stretch of straight and level road offered yet a different perspective. The narrowness of the canyon imposed the illusion of a box where both sides merged and differences appeared non-existent. Above and left water flowed from a forested mesa, and wind blew the precipitation against bus windows clouding her view. To the right of the bus, a ridge without trees gave way to a clear vista of plains beyond. Karen's stomach churned with the bends and curves as the bus swayed right then left, down a slope, across a bridge, past the waterfall, slowing then, through the narrows, and around one last curve.

"Here we are Friday, August 1, 1980, Colorado Day in beautiful downtown Rock Creek, a naturally moistened garden spot!" the driver shouted, "Entrance to the valley, historical landmarks, Rock Creek Valley Museum, the Stage Stop Hotel, our destination for lunch at Rock Creek's finest and only restaurant."

Karen connected the scene with the clue, she recorded vestibule in twelve across, and then closed her puzzle book. Vestibule: where the Canaanites encountered the enemy.

Slowing to a near halt, the driver made a hard right into an unpaved parking lot, and then forced the wheel left so the bus came parallel to hitching posts in front of the Stage Stop Hotel. Braking to a halt, the driver depressed the air brake, pulled down the emergency brake, switched off ignition key, and stood before his passengers to open the bi-fold door next to him. Tongue in cheek, with exact enunciation the driver shouted, "Hold on!"

Passengers rising and already in the aisle hesitated at the driver's admonition, as he said, "Hear me now, little lambs, I don't want you to go astray; I can't go looking for you! You have a thirty-minute lunch break. It's 11:30 a.m. We beat the noon rush. I have a standing order at the Stage Stop for the Rocky Mountain Cheeseburger Deluxe. The cook usually makes extras ready to go. Ask the waitress, Sarah, about cold sandwiches, too! She usually has shaved ham and turkey, and roast beef, and all kinds of breads. But if you don't want to sit in the restaurant, the gas station across the highway has some of those terrible packaged sandwiches. Their steamer oven doesn't work too well, but they also sell packaged lunchmeat too. So, you have some choices. Make your selection but be back on the porch at the Stage Stop by twelve o'clock noon. Meanwhile, I'll take care of this little lady getting off here, and then I'll get some diesel across the street. Enjoy yourselves, little lambs!"

Having had his say, the driver opened the bi-fold door. Those in line exited and paused as the fragrance of fresh baked bread wafted toward them, while a few gathered themselves together in the aisle and moseyed to the front. Across the aisle and two seats ahead of Karen, only a young mother and child remained seated and waited as others departed the bus. Opening their sack lunch, the mother pulled out what she called Mickey Mouse specials. Offering the peanut butter and grape jelly sandwich, the mother said, "Take this Son. I pressed some Mickey Mouse specials."

Following the driver's good humor, remaining passengers vacated the bus in seconds. Some competed with others by bounding up porch steps into the hotel. Six crossed the highway and headed directly toward the gas station and its convenience store, barely checking for oncoming traffic on US Highway 85/87 business loop. One woman and a man walked straight for exterior bathrooms on the north side of the building without checking to see if a door key was needed to enter. Both needed keys. Apparently not wanting to wait, a man with a full beard sprinted to the trees beyond the store parking lot to a creek south of the crossroad and under a bridge. His tan trench coat flapped behind him. The driver's watch kept ticking.

Outside the bus, Morris Goodenough, the driver, checked his watch and said, "11:34 a.m. Twenty-six minutes to take off." Only Karen waited for Morris to get her luggage from the storage compartment. Continuing his oration, "Now, Miss, if I can see your ticket to confirm your luggage."

Already prepared Karen handed Morris her one-way ticket and four baggage identification stickers. "Sure," she said and added, while walking, "I have two boxes and two suitcases, camel-brown matching Samsonite. You placed them in back of this side storage compartment."

"Thank you, Miss...." Morris said as he checked her name, "Miss Karen Gustafson? Yes, four items with tag numbers TW4448 through TW44451." Not distracted Morris waved toward honking from the driver of a red Ford F250 truck parked just behind the Trailways bus. "You say you have two boxes and two suitcases?" Morris continued as he opened the rear compartment. "Luckily, they're here together. I do a good job packing, first, the suitcases, next the boxes."

"Hey, Morris!" shouted a rancher now outside the truck, "If you have time, I'll see you inside. Bring your calendar. We need pulpit supply a couple of times at church before Thanksgiving, and the folks enjoy your teaching."

"Will do, hey, Adam, have you been following the Bears? Randy Bass is on a tear again. He hit four taters outta the park one night in '79 and he's got the homerun stroke going again this year," Morris said enthusiastically.

"Denver's doing well this year, not as good as last year, but I liked it better when we were the Yankees' triple A affiliate. But, I'm still suffering from the Steelers winning the Super Bowl."

"First team to win four Super Bowls. Beat the Rams 31-19," chided Morris as he performed a victory dance.

"Our Broncos just didn't get the job done this year, but they have been fun to watch," concluded Adam.

"Inside, Adam, ask Sarah where she has me seated. I've got a Rocky Mountain Cheeseburger Deluxe with my name on it. Order me a diet cola, okay?" rotund Morris responded.

Walking toward Karen and Morris, the tall, lanky, and handsome rancher paused, nodded toward Karen, doffed his wide-brimmed, charcoal Stetson then barely uttered an okay. Not looking, apparently not wanting to be noticed, she ignored his gesture. In a youthful display, the rancher pranced up the porch steps like the Marlborough-Country man. A lilt in his step and energized, he uttered, "Humma, Humma, that's one fine young woman, modestly dressed and lovely. There's a beauty, her countenance-just wonderful! Boy, do I feel silly!"

With both feet stomping the ground in a cloud of dust, a little boy held what remained of his Mickey Mouse special in one hand and a Bible in the other. "Andrew," his mother called, "Not so fast! You wait for me!"

Clutching her purse with both hands in front at her waist, Andrew's mother approached Morris and Karen, who were startled by the little boy's arrival. Coming closer the young mother anxiously wrestled the Bible from her son's hand. She asked Karen, "Miss, my son found this Bible where you were seated. It's yours, isn't it?"

Appreciative, Karen responded, "Yes, thank you, I would be lost without it. Thank you very much!"

"You must be a Christian. I am too. I mean a person doesn't carry a Bible

4

around, let alone read it on a bus, unless they are one. Besides, I can see it in your eyes. You have a godly presence about you."

"What a nice compliment. I hope you are accurate," smiled Karen.

"Oh, I am! I have a favor to ask."

"How could I refuse?"

"Will you keep us in your prayers, Andrew and me? We need prayer."

"Why, what is it? How may I pray for you?" answered Karen kindly.

"Actually, I should be very happy. I am, but scared silly at the same time. Andrew and I are going to Ridge View. Andy's father and I are getting back together. Well, actually, we did at the beginning of the summer, and then Rob got a job transfer. We separated again. I mean not like how we were, but we still are. We've decided to give our marriage another try. But, I worry. It is so easy to hurt and be hurt. Like how Elvis sang, 'I'm all shook up'."

Andrew added, "Yeah, I get my dad back! And we're going to live in a new place. Pop already has a house for us and everything! I get to have ducks and chickens and rabbits and a dog and a cat, and I don't know what else, but it's going to' be great 'cept I have to go to school in a few weeks, after Labor Day, Mom said."

Laughing the women hugged one another, while the driver helped one other passenger with his one small suitcase. This passenger, a rather large man, picked up his suitcase and walked behind the bus and across the street where he disappeared. His work completed, Morris joined them, and he robustly said, "I couldn't help but overhear. May I join you? I'm a prayer warrior, too. Prayer ends the shakes!"

"What a coincidence," noted Karen with discernment.

"Go ahead Miss Gustafson. You start. I'd say the Lord's timing is just perfect. He has us here right now for this purpose," proclaimed Morris the bus driver and pulpit supply.

Both women nodded with consent. Andrew joined in eagerly. Tears poured forth from his mother's eyes, while she laughed and prayed, "Father, how merciful you are. You brought me two of your people to help!"

"Okay," began Karen, "what's your name?"

"Ruth Browning. This is my son, Andrew. Andrew, when he's in trouble or being mature, Andy when he's my nice little boy. My husband's name is Robert, Robert Browning but no relation to the poet. Well, we wish there was, but there isn't … Rob does write great letters …"

Interrupting, Karen began, "O Lord, how precious this would happen right now, right here. Thanks for reminding us you know where we are and what we are doing. Thanks for using me and our driver, too. Thanks for this mother and child and the man who is waiting for them. We ask you to prepare his heart to receive them tenderly. Thanks for this encouragement that you are restoring their marriage. We ask that you bring a complete healing to this marriage. And, abba, Daddy, please provide them time to be fully restored."

Morris added a hearty, "Amen."

Andrew chimed in, "Me, too."

The boy and the bus driver exchanged hand slaps. The women embraced.

"I hope to see you again," said Karen to Ruth, "because I may be moving here myself."

"Great! That's settled. I have a new home, new friends, and new chance in my marriage. Lord willing, all will work out," said Ruth enthusiastically.

"It is God's sovereign will. He purposes for marriages to prosper. He hates divorce," professed Morris, as an encouragement.

"Amen," they said in unison.

"Well, folks, I have my lunch waiting for me, and it is almost noon. Good day, Miss Gustafson," Morris said quickly, as he scampered up the stairs to the porch and into the hotel.

Turning to go, Ruth added, "It's true you know. I knew you were a Christian the moment I saw you. I see the beauty of Jesus in you, and I got goose bumps. Good-bye, new friend. I look forward to a chance to know you."

Beaming now after such affirmations from Ruth, Morris, and her Lord, "You guys just made my day. What a new beginning in Rock Creek! Let's see how the Lord tops this," pronounced Karen as she clutched her Bible and reached for her luggage.

Ruth followed Andrew back on the bus. "Come on, Ma! Do ya have another Mickey Mouse special?"

Behind Karen a gentle man said, "Excuse me, may I help you?"

Walking toward her with a sales pad and an open carton of books in one hand, a middle-aged man took hold of one of her suitcases. Without waiting for an answer, he climbed the stairs before Karen could respond. From the porch he said with an infectious smile, "I'll leave this just inside the doorway."

Startled, Karen picked up one box and tucked it under her right arm, then grasped the handle of the remaining suitcase in her left hand and started up the stairs.

From behind, Andrew picked up the remaining box, and said, "I'm right behind you, Miss Karen. Mama said to help you. Said she saw tears on yer face. She said you came here to fix a broken heart. Did ja? How do you break a heart, Miss Karen? How ya fix one? Glue?"

Andrew, the boxes, the suitcase, and Karen merged at the lobby door. Forgetting what the gentle man said, they stumbled over her other suitcase. Laughing but regaining her balance, Karen dropped everything in a heap. Andy exited slamming the door.

"I'll be with you in a minute, Miss," said the clerk from behind the counter, "just set your things by the maze plant or on the other side by the telephone booth, while I finish with Mr. Powell."

Suitcases in hand, Karen pushed the boxes aside with her feet across the hardwood floor to the east wall of the hotel lobby near the dining room entrance.

6

Next to the maze plant in a large brass pot, she plopped into an overstuffed, brown, leather chair with a high back and ornate, wooden arms. She noted there was no carpet anywhere in the lobby and left of the stairwell before the bar entrance was one closed door with a restroom sign fixed to it. Dreamily, she rested as if asleep, while wondering how a Rocky Mountain Cheese Burger Deluxe might taste. The hotel clerk forgot her. Chatter disturbed her, as bus passengers filled the lobby, passed through from the dining room, and clomped across the hotel porch, and down to the parking lot. Many waved at her as they passed by. Morris and Adam, the rancher, passed quickly without noticing Karen.

In moments Karen alone remained. She heard only the clattering of dishes from the kitchen, laughter from the bar behind the west wall, and the roar of the bus engine starting in the parking area. Moving to the windows and pulling the curtain aside, she looked in hope of catching Ruth's eye or perhaps that of Adam Claymore, the tall and lanky rancher wearing the black Stetson hat, red long sleeved checkered shirt, western cut blue jeans, and polished brown cowboy boots. Before leaving Karen watched as a strange looking man emerged from the undergrowth of the trees beyond the gas station. Hurriedly, he crossed the highway at the intersection, coat tails flapping behind him. He banged on the bus door with the palm of his hand before Morris opened it for him.

"Curious," Karen said aloud, "his trousers are sopping wet, but not his tan trench coat."

Once the late arrival sat down safely, Morris accelerated the mighty diesel, turned the steering wheel with a rigorous tug left to pull the bus away from the hotel, then right just as hard. As if there would be traffic, Morris looked both ways. The bus entered onto the Valley Highway, a business loop off U. S. 85/87, and into a hunter's paradise. It was rush hour at Rock Creek.

From the bus Ruth watched Karen at the hotel window and hoped they would be friends. She needed a friend, especially a Christian stronger than herself. Clasping her hands, she brought them to her mouth and over her nose prayerfully. "Lord," she whispered, "I'm scared to death. Rob waits for me. What's ahead for us?"

Ruth watched from the bus window next to her as Morris guided the bus north into a valley between two parallel ridges drained by the creek that flowed through the canyon.

"My, gosh, Miss, I'm sorry. I forgot all about you. Some desk clerk I am. Won't you please register, before I get distracted again?" the mousey haired woman said with a laugh. She walked from behind the counter toward Karen and continued, "Here let me help you."

Taking hold of Karen's luggage, the desk clerk escorted a smiling Karen to the registration desk, and then said, "Did I say something funny? Sometimes I can be a complete scatter brain."

"No, I was startled. It seems I keep getting startled today. Maybe I need to walk backwards, and then I can meet people without embarrassing myself." They both laugh.

"Please complete the registration form. Will you be staying for one night or longer?"

"I called in a reservation about a week ago."

"Excuse me. We don't get many reservations, so I'm sure someone recorded it here," the clerk said.

Reaching for a folder, the clerk continued, "Wow! Two for today and you must be Karen Gustafson. One week's lodging. The other one is a man, Paul Smith. He was supposed to be on the bus too."

"I didn't notice."

"Well, anyway--say, did you get lunch? I'll bet we still have some sandwiches, if you didn't. Sarah usually has a couple of extras, but today she might not with the entire crowd in town for the parade in Jericho Springs. Would you like me to see what we have left?"

"That would be great. I'd like to take a sandwich to my room. I need a nap. Bus rides wear me out. What's the parade for?"

"Colorado Day, August 1," the desk clerk reported, "but I've never seen it. I'm kinda new here."

"Reminds me of a song, I love a parade," Karen began to sing.

"O...kay," the clerk said with a smirk, "Be right back. You finish the song and the form, please."

Karen finished singing, completed the form, waited briefly, and then removed a book from a display carton on the counter. Recognizing the author, Karen thumbed through it scanning chapter headings.

"This is all we have left. It's roast beef on wheat, okay?"

"Great! Are these books for sale?"

"Oh, sure, we just got them. I thought I'd give them a try. What do you think? Mr. Powell, he left them here on consignment. He is so nice! He asked me how he could pray for me, and he gave me a catalog with music in it too! Mr. Powell is a real gentleman. Want to buy that book?"

"*The Hobbit* by J. R. Tolkien, he is a good author. If he wrote it, you can count on it being good. Sort of like his friend, C. S. Lewis. Also, I'm impressed by Dr. Dobson and newcomer, Chuck Swindoll. He just wrote *Three Steps Forward, Two Backward*. It has to do with surviving under pressure."

"Who?"

"Oh, they're some of my favorite authors. You can bet their books are good. Same way with the music of Amy Grant. She's barely out of her teens."

"Never heard of her," said the clerk.

"'My Father's Eyes'. Do you listen to Christian radio?"

"I don't think we get it here. I read in the newspaper where a group is raising money to get an antenna here. Or maybe it's called a translator. That way we could pick up the Denver and Colorado Springs radio stations. Someone donated two gold nuggets to get things started!"

"Real, gold nuggets?" asked Karen, "Are there gold mines here?"

"More like rocks, I mean it's hard to imagine. I haven't seen any ads to tour gold mines. I've heard of people still having gold coins but not nuggets. It's like they dug them out of the ground or something or from the creek."

"It's hard to imagine gold nuggets still lying around, and it's hard to imagine life without Christian radio," then Karen hesitated, "Can I put this on my bill?"

"You bet. I'm glad you like it. I haven't read Christian books other than the Bible. I don't recognize those authors. And I didn't know there was so much available. There must be ten whole pages in Mr. Powell's catalog. I just like the idea of these books being close to me while I work. I need reminders."

"Me, too, when I finish, I'll share it with you."

"I'd like that! Sorry, no elevator and I can't help you up the stairs. I gotta help in the kitchen. Your room is 218, second floor, up the stairs, then down the hall on the left. You have a good view. Out back there's trees other side of the back lot and the hogback. Rooms aren't great, but at least the mattresses are... or so I'm told."

"Thank you. I'll want to hike the hogback later. How late do you serve dinner?" asked Karen.

"Well, the bar opens at four and closes at midnight. I guess you won't be in there. We serve dinner from 4:00 to 8:00 p.m. during the week, 10:00 p.m. Friday and Saturday. The gas station stays open 'till midnight. People gas up down-the-road-a-piece after hours. Menu specials are on the chalkboard there. Friday and Saturday nights, it's pretty good. I'm off the desk at eight, if you need anything. You'll find a bathroom at the end of each hall. They're generic. My name is Hannah. Welcome to Rock Creek, vestibule and gateway to the valley. That's my official duty. Only I'm supposed to give the welcome and tell my name first thing instead of the last," Hannah said, smiled, and added, "I don't think I forgot anything."

Counting the wooden stairs each time, Karen made three trips to carry her suitcases, boxes, and lunch to room 218. Between trips Hannah gave Karen soap and shampoo, a face cloth, and two towels, one small and one large. At the last landing on her last trip up the stairs, Karen counted her steps out loud, "At last, 218, 219, on and on, 240. Lord, let me make it to my room and onto my bed."

Entering her room, Karen set everything on the floor in the center and looked around. To her right a single bed with a gray blanket and one pillow with a blue pillowcase filled the corner. On her left, one old oak chair and a three-drawer dresser occupied the west wall. Above the dresser she studied herself in a dusty mirror on the wall and wondered what the rancher and the book salesman thought when they noticed her. Continuing counterclockwise, she noted a closet door flanked the chair. In the center on the floor, a faded blue or gray throw rug spanned between bed and dresser while straight ahead before an open window, a lamp with a broken shade perched on a small wooden table. No pictures, no wall coverings, no bathroom. A thin nail in the wall over the single bed indicated where a picture used to hang. Content to have a place to rest, she sat on the bed, laid down, and quickly fell asleep, but first thought that she shouldn't have cut her long blonde tresses. Karen had arrived…out of the box canyon and into the cloistered vestibule.

Unnoticed, the last bus passenger entered the hotel lobby and stepped directly into the telephone booth. His had been a planned entrance. He had already explored the convenience store across the highway, only after he had walked through the church parking lot with a cemetery behind it. Crossing a foot bridge that spanned a creek, he had proceeded north following a footpath to another bridge on County Road 403. Pausing under the bridge before climbing the slope to the road above the creek, he had studied concrete slopes leading to both crawl spaces. Though he had lingered below, he climbed the steep creek bank, as if it were effortless, and suddenly appeared on the road above, which startled passengers in a late model sedan. He caught up with the automobile at the convenience store and entered in. All conversation halted, as those inside watched him meander throughout the store. As quickly as he had appeared, he exited the store, crossed the highway and hotel parking lot, and then bounded up the stairs to the hotel porch, and entered the nearly empty hotel lobby with stealth.

Placing a quarter in the coin slot, he made his call, "Yes, hello, this is Paul Smith calling John. If he is not available immediately, tell John I have been to Quail Point, have arrived in Rock Creek, and have registered at the Stage Stop Hotel. No, don't disrupt his other telephone call, I will call him in a day or two and will proceed as planned. Thank you, Amanda, goodbye."

As if mesmerized, Hannah registered Paul Smith, and at his request, assigned him to the most distant available room from the lobby, room 319. Paul asked for and received directions to the room by way of a stairwell not being used by the woman who had just registered. As a result, he left the hotel lobby, and walked east around the building, where he ascended an exterior stairwell to the third floor and entered room 319.

Another stranger had entered the vestibule successively, as if it were part of a grand design.

RESTORATION BEGINS
CHAPTER 2

"Restore us, O God; make your face shine upon
us, that we may be saved." Psalm 80:3

Immediately north of the town of Rock Creek, two hogbacks marked the eastern border of the Rocky Mountains by spanning the length of Rock Creek Valley. Running parallel to one another with a valley between them, the one to the west hugged the foot of the mountains to Jericho Springs where it appeared to cradle the town, and then met the other near the town of Rock Creek. The other meandered north to south helping to form the ridge leading to endless plains beyond. Both uplifts continued hogback formations spanning beyond Colorado borders.

One uplift in Colorado, the Dakota Ridge, began at the Wyoming border where US Highway 287 had been laid to guide travelers over strike valleys made from erosion of the hogbacks. They have channeled run off over clay and limestone deposits to the Poudre River in Fort Collins and have continued to Raton Pass before entering New Mexico. With narrow ridges and sharp descending slopes, hogbacks have been displayed intermittently to Boulder where impressive Flatirons marked the landscape with sharply tilted sandstone mass. Near Morrison, Dinosaur Ridge had displayed dinosaur tracks as the sedimentary rock had been tilted nearly upside-down. Farther south the Garden of the Gods had been graced with a series of hogbacks in response to mountain making forces creating Pikes Peak. Kissing Camels, Three Graces, and Cathedral Spires were fine specimens.

Here in Rock Creek Valley, less dynamic hogbacks resembled their namesake and appeared more like a hog if it were lying on its back with feet pointing upward from thick and meaty thighs. Rock Creek flowed between these geologic oddities with the highway east of the creek to where Highway 96 formed a T with the Valley Highway, US 85/87 business loop. At that intersection two tributaries of Rock Creek merged and the Valley Highway continued west of the creek. The highway crossed a bridge over the water and proceeded north for the length of the valley to Ridge View, the town at the north end of Rock Creek Valley. Only here, just north of the town of Rock Creek, two elongated mounds of earth sharply crested where uplifted rock nearly merged and created the appearance of a fortress wall around Rock Creek. Out and onto the plains, the valley opened displaying fertile meadows close to Rock Creek, then gave way to grazing land toward the ridge east at the valley's edge. The hogbacks separated only to come closer again at the north end of the valley. Up creek two tributaries drained into the main flow of water. One entered east at a break in the hogback and continued north along the base of the ridge. An intermittent series of wetlands followed south between the hogback and the ridge to the great plains east. The other tributary, a mountainous watershed bounded by twin peaks of Mt. Huajatolla, flowed from the west through Jericho Springs to the junction of the Valley Highway and Colorado 96. Close to Jericho Springs, the valley became more fertile. Peonies grew wild and perked one's senses in their blooming season. Bright pink blossoms and a captivating fragrance immediately created a positive first impression for sojourners passing in and out of Jericho Springs. What would taint such loveliness?

North to Ridge View the Trailways bus travelers passed through the valley without incident. Gradually, the valley, plains, and ridge met and leveled out at a modest waterfall. Below the waterfall a garden scene unfolded for a brief distance. Above the waterfall the wind picked up and seemed constant. From there, wayfarers saw without obstruction, and in the morning the spectacular sunrise would illuminate shades of yellow and gold on the landscape, which matched the radiance of the sunset looming over the mountains in the evening.

Though the bus ride to Ridge View lasted less than twenty minutes, Ruth Browning replayed her recent past without her husband, Rob. At first she shriveled inside herself, withering in the reflections, but then she unfolded, as she coped with the thoughts and memories. Scars had cut deeply. She and her son, Andrew, suffered greatly during Rob's absence, both financially and emotionally. Loneliness became a depressing enemy. She shunned suicidal thoughts fearing the temptation to just end everything. Remembering Rob's harsh words and physical roughness, a knot returned to her stomach, hives swelled on her arms and neck. Itching remained constant, pestering, biting, and spreading venom. She felt panic then wrestled with the torment, the betrayal. Now before the moment of answered prayer, a plague of bitterness invaded. Old insecurities flooded her thoughts. While hungering for Rob's affection, she dreaded facing him now. Scratch marks and red, elongated lumps of swollen flesh revealed how her emotions had been rived by inward anxiety and dismay. Just lovely, Ruth thought, "Wait 'till Rob sees me like this; so much for romance."

"Help me Jesus!" Ruth breathed. Immediately, scripture answered her plea, "Oh yes, *My grace is sufficient for you, for my power is made perfect in weakness*; *2 Corinthians 12:9*. I think that's from second Corinthians chapter twelve, verse nine. Yes, I'm positive." The swelling and itching persisted, but confidence began to displace panic. With time, anxiety would flee as healing followed forgiveness and restoration. At least Ruth believed it would.

Ruth believed God would restore lost time for her and Rob to become one again. She believed their marriage would strengthen, commitment would deepen, and a new resolve would withstand future tests. Looking at her swollenness, Ruth opened her purse searching for at least one ointment she had purchased to sooth discomfort.

If Rob could see inside Ruth's purse, he would roar with laughter. Often he jested with her and told friends how she could find everything in her purse. She had heard him say that if it wasn't for the size of it, Ruth would have a kitchen sink in there. Once after moving across Colorado, Rob bought her a nearly new clothes washer. He needed foot levelers to balance it. She pulled four levelers from her purse. She had removed the levelers from their old washer before moving from their previous apartment. Another time Rob needed a y-connector for an outside hose faucet. Ruth had one in her purse she had purchased recently at a garage sale.

Now Ruth needed something to rub on her throbbing skin. Reaching in her purse, she found an ointment and hemorrhoid cream. Previously, both produced temporary relief but not enough. When they hadn't worked effectively, Ruth had asked her aunt for a remedy. Ruth's aunt had told her to get a good antacid, and then rub it on her hives. Several bottles of antacid had provided some relief but not enough. Ruth remembered that cigarette tobacco had once taken the hurt out of bee stings. Once she had removed tobacco from one of her uncle's packs of cigarettes, had chewed it, and with a look of disgust, had pressed it onto one swollen hive. Again, no results had occurred. Being a farmer, her Uncle Paul had recommended udder cream. Works real well on cows, her Uncle Paul had said and laughed. It sure ought to work on you, little lady! It hadn't. A six dollar tube of anti-itch cream and some fancy oil had helped a little. Finally, and she had some in her purse, she remembered taking a double dose of hay fever medication. It had worked. Finding a bottle of it in the bottom of her purse, Ruth swallowed four pills. Relief arrived eventually.

Leaning back in her seat by the bus window and gazing outside, again Ruth watched the fence posts fly by. She recalled all the books on marriage she had read, advice given her by well-meaning people, and how she had prayed and kept a daily journal. She knew God loved her, really loved her. She saw his involvement in her life and listened for his inaudible voice. She trusted that God cared for Rob too. Thoughts had entered her mind, and she received knowledge that she needed to focus on who she was and to work at being the woman God wanted her to be, the wife Rob needed her to be. God wanted her to put him first, not second to Rob. She no longer asked God to change Rob but to change her. She had pleaded for Rob, for God to have mercy on him and to bring Rob close to him. She remembered how she had confessed that it was hard for her to let go of Rob and to not want to fix him herself. But, Ruth had finally let go.

Ruth became content and aware that God knew her thoughts, her selfishness, and her ambivalence, as well as her genuine desire to trust and serve him. She trusted restoration would happen, but she knew she could make it on her own with God and without Rob, if she had to. Ruth didn't want to, but she knew God would give her the strength to persevere. God had reminded Ruth about Lazarus, how Jesus called Lazarus out of the tomb, and how Lazarus had come out from the dead. Lazarus had responded. Then God had told her in her thoughts that he would do the same with Rob. And Rob had come home.

A few weeks later Rob had applied for a job transfer doing outside work with the utility company in Ridge View. The transfer had been approved. Within weeks he had rented a small house with outbuildings and a pasture about two miles south of Ridge View on County Road 403 to Jericho Springs. Trying to soothe Ruth's fears with assurances, he had said driving home was just like in the song, over the river and through the woods. Rob had said it would be their promised land just the west side of Rock Creek. Then he had said there may be giants in the land of plenty, but together we can take 'em. Rob had! And Ruth loved his plan and was willing to follow him in spite of his not consulting her before making the decision.

The Brownings had realized they could not run from their problems. They would be taking some problems with them to Ridge View. Rob and Ruth had agreed to solve their problems in a new place, a place away from old temptations and influences unsuccessfully resisted in the past. Now, he had resolved to flee from evil. She had known she too needed to leave the convenience of having Mom and Dad ever ready to come to her defense, so often at Rob's expense. Now, Ruth needed to stand up for herself, not alone but with God and her husband together on one team.

Ruth summarized her commitments. She believed her commitments reflected how God had instructed her through the lead of the Holy Spirit. They reflected her beliefs and attitudes that were in line with God's plan for her. She recalled studying what the Bible said about divorce and never found any examples of a woman divorcing a husband. If a husband would become rightly aligned with God, there would be no need for divorce. She relished the words instructing the husband to love his wife and in so many ways too! Ruth had found that God's instruction to the women mentioned nothing about loving the husband, but instead called the wife to respect her husband. Guessing that when the husband loved the wife, she concluded the wife just naturally loved the husband in return. She believed God abhorred divorce and expected marriage partners to work at resolving their differences, under the Lordship of Christ and through the leading of the Holy Spirit. She compared her thoughts with scripture and tested her own thinking and the voice within. Ruth remembered instruction that honest communication tempered by love was important, as was dialogue. Dialogue went beyond discussion. She recalled that in discussion both persons presented their positions, and the couple made compromises. In dialogue spouses presented their position, and then the two prayed and sought a third position as a couple. Ruth realized the task would become a search for what was best for them, together.

Understanding an active prayer life was necessary, Ruth summarized that she must do her part and not target on changing Rob. Her prayers had been focusing on her getting in line with being the woman God wanted her to be, the woman her husband needed her to be, and the mother Andy needed her to be. The words of her mother contradicted Ruth's conclusions. Mom had told her to never let a man walk all over her, to make certain she got her way at least fifty percent of the time, and to take care of herself. Mom had thrown side issues in Ruth's face about divorce being acceptable if a husband had left his family. Remaining conflicted, she still did not know how to answer her mother. Ruth just referred to scripture and prayed for her own understanding.

Ruth had wanted to give herself, her time, and affection to Rob to such an extent that he had complained about being smothered. She naturally had responded with thoughts questioning how he could feel that way after all she had done for him. The sacrifices! Then hurt and humiliated, Ruth had withdrawn and followed her mother's advice to the point of bitterly demanding her way and withholding affection.

Rob had said Ruth gave mixed messages, and often he didn't know where she was coming from. Usually, he had responded with anger and frustration and sometimes a physical threat, but he had never really hit her or beat her. He did lightly punch her arm, and then had grabbed her roughly. They never had an all out fight. He had made certain of that. When either threatened violence, he had left the house. And he did leave for almost a year, well really eight months. It just seemed to both of them that Rob had been gone forever.

Ruth had spent the time Rob was gone first by withdrawing, followed by mourning, and then by being angry. Finally, in the midst of wanting to hurt herself, she had confessed her helplessness and hopelessness to the Lord. God gave Ruth his word through scripture; she had felt his closeness; and peace returned as she had turned the situation over to him. Then she had started to focus on what she needed to do not how Rob needed to change. A quiet confidence had returned, but her inner struggle continued, as Ruth had battled against bitterness, her old habits, memories, and fear.

Now Ruth spoke confidently that her marriage would be restored and more. She knew things would not be rosy, the road without bumps, or that she could keep Rob happy by physically satiating all his desires. She had read enough books on lovemaking but knew a marriage could not be rebuilt on sex alone. It wouldn't hurt though, she determined. Issues left unprocessed had remained harmful, as had memories of her pain caused by Rob leaving her and Andrew, and of his betrayal. Time would heal hurts, so would their working together and not against one another. With certainty, she hoped their marriage would be strengthened, victorious, with the enemy defeated, as they would take back surrendered ground. Now she waited for her beloved, her man, father of her child, the one person she wanted to grow old with. By the time Ruth reviewed what she had learned she was exhausted.

As the sign post had awakened Karen when she was about to enter Rock Creek, another sign now alerted Ruth of her entrance to Ridge View. She hardly noticed the surroundings. Ruth just kept looking for the bus terminal, her husband's face, to see if he were smiling.

A few blocks into town on Main Street, Morris wheeled the bus to a stop at the Ridge View Transportation Center, a combination railroad depot and bus terminal, where the Rio Grande Railroad and Trailways Bus Line shared the facility. Historical records at the museum in Rock Creek told how pony express riders hastily changed horses at what was now Ridge View. The transportation center continued as a junction for travelers entering the Rock Creek Valley or heading for metropolitan centers north and east across the plains. Many colorful stories particular to Ridge View laid dust covered waiting to be rediscovered. Most would make the residents proud.

Eagerly, Rob Browning waited. Tall and blond with sun tanned skin surrounding dark blue eyes and smiling mouth, Rob nearly startled Morris with his hasty approach to the stopping bus. Andy not only bounced up and down in the seat but also knocked the hat off the man seated in front of him. With Andy's apology spoken, he and his mother struggled to see Dad. Rob was smiling; still Ruth's Mr. Wonderful. With heart pounding, she noted his obvious effort to make himself presentable. Though mid-afternoon, he must have exchanged work clothes for white shirt, dark blue sweater vest with a v-neck, blue gray dress slacks and black, wing tipped shoes, freshly polished. Ruth thought to herself, "I wish I had been there to shower with him. How handsome my man is. How much I've looked forward to this moment."

Six other passengers smiled with approval as they watched Ruth and Andy's enthusiasm for Dad as they exited the bus. Ruth and Andy made way to the door. Although still angry with his father, Andrew anxiously awaited to learn how Dad would greet him. Andy leaped from the second step into his dad's waiting arms. All resolve to be distant vanished, when Andy's daddy held him. Andy quickly decided he could be angry later, if he still wanted to.

Healing would take time. Andrew blamed himself for his parents' separation. Many nights Andy had awakened his mother by crying and questioning why his daddy didn't come home anymore. In the midst of sobs, Andy had asked his mother what he had done wrong. Other times he had accused his mother of being a bad Mommy, otherwise Daddy wouldn't have left them. Those thoughts would come back again, as the healing began and the family processed things together. But Andy would never feel abandoned again. Daddy would not leave them again. Instead a time would come for Andrew to leave Mom and Dad. Instead of it being a moment of betrayal, that future time would be an ending and a new beginning with all three starting a new phase of life.

In the midst of the bus terminal surrounded by luggage and six other passengers, the Mom hugged and kissed her husband and son. The Dad hugged and kissed his wife and son. And the Son just hugged and kissed. Three together were in a hug fest.

With more passengers to deliver north on the Valley Highway, Morris interrupted this intact family and asked for their luggage tickets, so he could finish unloading. Laughing with tears flooding their eyes, Ruth and Rob let go of one another and set Andrew down. Ruth began to search her purse.

Rob asked, "Is the kitchen sink in there?"

"No, but I might have some levelers!" Ruth responded, which brought more laughter from the Brownings and the onlookers. Ruth dramatically pulled out the baggage claims for three suitcases and handed them to Morris. As the Browning's scurried to leave the transportation center, Morris and all the remaining bus passengers witnessed the family and smiled.

Leaving the bus station, Ruth said, "Rob, my father will ship several boxes filled with household supplies next week, unless you prefer to replace everything."

"I'd love too!" Rob announced with a gleam, "And I have a hunch you'll have a lot of ideas as soon as you see our place. Wait 'till you see our new car. I traded the pickup for a low mileage '72 Chevy Impala station wagon and a '69 Ford Bronco. They're in good shape too. I thought it was time we had real family cars. We will need the four-wheeler for mountain adventures. They're plated and insured too, just like I'm supposed to do. And Ruth, we have no car payments. They're free and clear too."

Looking at Ruth, Rob said, "That's just one change Ruth. No more driving without insurance. No more my having my pickup and you at home without transportation. No more depending on your mom to haul you around."

Ruth smiled and nodded agreement.

"Come on let's blow this pop stand. I can hardly wait to get you home. But, we need to stop at the grocery store. When we get home, I have to change clothes and get back to work," exclaimed Rob.

Holding her critical tongue, Ruth smiled, took Andy by the hand, and carried the one suitcase Rob hadn't picked up. She thought progress had been made, yet Rob had chosen their home and cars without consulting her. In her heart Ruth promised she wouldn't stuff her thoughts and emotions. She would deal with them soon and not allow anger to fester, which had been her past practice and Rob's too. She followed him to the exit and noticed the bearded man in the tan trench coat leaving before them with one suitcase in hand.

Beaming before Ruth in the parking lot just outside the bus terminal, Rob announced playfully, "Your chariot awaits you, Madam. Your chauffeur has your steed all polished and gassed to carry you to the neighborhood Piggly Wiggly Grocery Store. But let's hurry, I can't wait to get you home."

"Then to the grocery, fair prince. Make haste for this lady is bone weary and eager to view our castle and the grounds of our estate."

"Daddy," interrupted Andrew, "do we have a castle? Where do we put the ducks and the chickens and the rabbits? Do the ducks swim in the moat? When do I get a dog and cat? Can they live in the house? What do I feed them?"

"Mom! Put dog and cat food on the grocery list. What do rabbits eat? Birds too? We need bugs, Mom, like in the book where the chickens ate all the grasshoppers or like Daddy's story about where he grew up and the invasion of army worms. Where do I get army worms 'n how much are they?"

"Whoa, Son, slow down," said Rob. Looking at Ruth, Rob caught her piercing glance and knew he had better talk with her. "We best talk about all that. I've already gone too far buying the cars and renting the house without your mom seeing them," he said, and added, "The next purchases will be ones we decide as a family. We'll talk tonight or tomorrow at breakfast. Since tomorrow is Saturday, I don't have to work and I'd like to introduce you to a blond friend of mine at the feed store. You see, Ruth, I've been doing some reading too, and there is much I want to share with you."

"Sounds good, I want to be optimistic," said Ruth smiling pensively, then thinking to herself, Lord how am I going to keep from just caving in and going back to being a doormat. I have loved him so much. The thought came to her that because you love him so much you are going to be his equal. From man's side woman was made, so she would be his partner, so he could put his arm around her tenderly.

Hurriedly, Rob opened the rear door to the light blue station wagon and put the suitcases inside. He unlocked the passenger side front door, opened it for Ruth, reached around to unlock the rear door, and gracefully moved aside while motioning for his lady to enter. With more grace, Ruth sat on the bench seat, folded her dress under her, and thanked her kind gentleman. Andy giggled.

Dad opened Andy's door, as his son locked his arms around his Dad's leg. "Daddy, I missed you. Are we really going to be a family again?"

"Yes, Son, your daddy's home," Rob said as the dad lifted son with a hug and gently set him in place. "I wish I had something to strap you in place. I don't want you, my treasure, to fall out," Dad said, smiled, and closed the door.

"Ah, Dad," said Andy faking disappointment.

In minutes the Browning's arrived at the grocery store on the west end of town. The family selected their purchases with haste. Rob urged they only buy for tonight and Saturday breakfast. He told Ruth and Andy that Saturday's agenda included a whirlwind shopping tour beginning or ending with a return to the grocery store. The family managed to go through the checkout line without waiting. Rob loaded the groceries in the station wagon, while Ruth and Andy got situated. On the way out of town, Rob stopped at the Rock Creek Valley Feed and Lumber Store across from the Cozy Corner Café. He explained he had to deliver a message for a friend of his named Irv Moss. In and out within minutes, Rob continued driving out of town on County Road 403, the primary route south and west to Jericho Springs from Ridge View.

As Rob said earlier, they traveled two miles over the meadow and through the woods to a bridge over Rock Creek. Halting to a stop before passing over, he told Ruth he liked to view the valley from the bridge. Ruth edged forward on her seat to get a better view. Andy followed suit and peered out the driver side rear window.

It was Andy who made the discovery. "Daddy is that where we live?"

"Yes, Son."

"Rob, where is it?"

"Down where the meadow meets the woods is our house. I've got the Bronco parked in the outbuilding on the right. I hope you like it."

"Daddy, Daddy! Are the chickens and ducks and rabbits and dogs and cats and what else Dad: are they down there?"

"No, not yet," Rob glanced over to Ruth and continued, "That's on tomorrow's agenda, if it is okay with your mother."

"Hey, you guys, you're kind of rushing things. Give a girl a break. We're going to have some understandings before we get into the livestock business," said Ruth, while thinking that at least Rob considered her feelings before taking care of that project. Ruth repeated, "There's going to be some understandings."

"Well, come on," said Rob, "I've been dying for you two to see our place. I think you'll like it. Let me continue the tour. This will be like one of those bus tours where the driver describes the sights, while driving along."

Both passengers stiffened and nodded affirmatively.

"Here is the bridge over Rock Creek. See the rocks. See the water, crystal clear and not very deep this time of year. Notice how rugged the creek bed and walls are. It doesn't look like it now, but with more water and no bridge, this creek would be quite a barrier to the other side, sort of a line of defense. I haven't seen a place where a covered wagon could easily cross over Rock Creek, except east on the plains. Maybe further down in the valley. A lot of water can pass through here and has. On the left, what is below our house is the flood plain. Just below the bridge, not even a hundred feet, is a waterfall and what appears to be a modest basin that holds the water before it continues down creek. I haven't been there, but I'm told it's a garden spot. You can barely catch a glimpse of it, if you go the other way on this road."

Andrew piped up, "Can we go there when we get out of the car, Mom?"

"Not today, but soon Son. We have plenty of summer yet to explore things."

"Ahhh, Mom, you were thinking the s word weren't you. Ahhh!"

"The s word? What's that? I know it's not sex."

"School, Rob. Andy isn't in a hurry to start school. Besides that's after Labor Day."

The tour continued to their house, where Rob unloaded everything with

Andy's help, and Father and Son ushered Mother into their new home. Rob gave a quick tour of the house and explained he had made a commitment to his boss to go back to work after picking them up at the bus stop.

"Sorry, honey. I feel like I should be with you right now to put things away and stuff, but I've got unfinished business that has to be done by sundown. Here are the keys to the station wagon. I'll take the Bronco. It's parked in our garage. You know where town is if you want."

"Rob, it's okay. Andy and I will do just fine. We'll make do with what's here. Town is for tomorrow. Maybe it's even better for us to discover things here by ourselves. Besides, from the looks of things, I'll be busy tidying up."

"Mom, can I go see outside?"

"Fraid not, stay here. You and I are going to have some quality time together."

"That means work, Dad. Mom says it like that so I'm supposed to think it's special. Dad! Don't laugh!"

"Okay, but help your mom. I'm really looking forward to tomorrow. I've thought a lot about you being here. This is the kind of place I wish I had gotten to live in when I was your age. It won't be long before you get to really enjoy living outside of town. Mom knows. Farming's in her family."

Rob changed clothes and announced, "Got to go, see you later."

At the door, "Wait a minute, buster. You don't get out of here so easy." Into his arms Ruth rushed. The embrace lingered.

Andy beamed with tears. "Gosh! I suppose there's gonna be huggin and kissin 'round here."

"You bet. This isn't the last of it, sweetheart," Rob said to Ruth in a tough guy, James Cagney impersonation. "See you after sunset, sweetheart."

Having made his exit, Rob drove the Bronco from the outbuilding garage, waved goodbye as he passed by the front door, and drove back to the county road leaving Ruth struggling to hold Andy from running after him.

Onto the road Rob hurried toward the bridge, out of the woods, and past the meadow. Moments later he looked to see just how much of the waterfall and basin he could see from the county road. From this distance Rob witnessed a man standing in the middle of the basin near the waterfall. The man held tan colored clothing above his head, while walking back and forth through the water.

"That's weird," said Rob while approaching the bridge. Without pausing he crossed over to the other side of Rock Creek, passed over the ridge and down the plains into the town of Ridge View, where he exchanged the Bronco for his company utility truck.

Friday afternoon passed quickly for Ruth Browning. Andy worked. He contributed unusually well to help his mom make this house their home. Memories of the recent past motivated Andy to do his part to make a happy family. Fortunately, Andrew's enthusiasm gave way to an afternoon nap thanks to his helpful efforts to add polish to a less than tidy household.

Guilt clouded Ruth's response to Andy's helpfulness. Ruth viewed him coping with life situations unjustly thrust upon him by immature parents who truly loved him and each other.

Andrew's response to surviving the crisis stimulated him to action. Andrew wanted to make his world a better place. Rather than sitting back and waiting for handouts to pacify his longings for comfort, Andy became a helpful contributor.

Ruth hoped this would continue. She did not know yet, but her son would be noted for such character as a hallmark of his manhood. As an adult Andrew would be known as one whose light so shines before others that God, his heavenly Father, would be glorified by the witness of those who would see Andrew's good works and would praise God for Andy's example not only as a father and husband, but as a member of the community and his church. But that would be a time to come when Ruth's American dream had come true and well after the walls of Jericho came tumbling down.

Andy awakened from his nap before sunset. Ruth felt good about Andrew and her efforts to clean their new home and organize it more to her liking. Shopping list completed, clothes unpacked and put away, walls and floor lightly scrubbed, windows washed, exhaustion displaced the excitement of their reunion. Ruth desired a break. She sensed the need to pray. Mom and Son decided to hike to the bridge in hopes of seeing the sun set on their new valley. Ruth longed to gain Rob's approval of a job well done.

Ruth and Andy hiked to the bridge by way of the road in case Rob passed by, so he could join them. He didn't. Instead the boy and his mother reached the bridge with no one around to notice or record their presence. The man in the tan trench coat had long since passed by without incident. Only the coming shadow of dusk marked their travels beyond their driveway, along the road, and to the bridge northeast on County Road 403. Since the sun seemed to recline behind the mountains, shadow passed over them and reached the valley's ridge, as they arrived at the bridge at dusk. Ruth and Andy prayed and gave thanks not only for where they now lived but also because their family was united. Separation had exposed their flaws and each was bruised by the others.

Rob arrived as they concluded their prayer. His return after work was answered prayer. Tired Mom and Son climbed into the green and gold '69 Ford Bronco. Small talk proceeded, but Mom tired and Dad understood. With right arm around her, Rob snuggled with her briefly. She shared the events of the day on their ride back to the house. He told her about his afternoon and of the man holding tan clothing over his head at the waterfall and pond. Andy told his dad that he would really like to see the pond tomorrow. Dad promised that a trip to the pond would be soon. First, the family needed to go shopping early on Saturday morning and do whatever chores Mom wanted completed. Mom looked startled at Dad's consideration. Being startled had been the theme for the day for several people.

The Browning family ate a quick dinner of creamed tuna on white rice with once frozen peas on the side and tapioca pudding for dessert. Rob smothered his dinner with Ruth's home-made salsa. Without doing the dishes, the Browning's prepared for bed on their first night together in their new home. Husband and wife made love, which brought comfort and tears of joy. Though careful not to disturb their son, muffled sounds and conversation from the bedroom of Andy's parents' ushered in a sense of well-being for Andy. Although Andy had a restful late afternoon nap, he not only slept peacefully throughout the night for the first time in a year, but he also made it through the night without wetting his bed.

INVASION BEGINS

CHAPTER 3

*"For though we live in the world, we do not wage
war as the world does." 2 Corinthians 10:3*

Wakening with stiffened neck and shoulder, Karen turned on the lamp in her room. Massaging her neck, she noticed the Friday evening sunset. Gorgeous, she thought to herself, then aloud, "What a beautiful orange and blue sunset." Looking out the window behind the hotel to the back of the parking lot, she heard the noise of a dumpster lid closing. She watched the cook take a long drink from a bottle he then returned to his hiding place near the dumpster. Karen decided it would be fun to hide his bottle in another place. Wouldn't he be surprised, she thought? Noise from the bar suggested Friday night would be a drunken one for many at the Stage Stop Hotel.

Beyond the trees to the right, one antelope passed through the shadows to the crest of the ridge. Then passed another and one by one a single file of antelope followed the first north along the cliff then turned east onto the plains. Captivated by their regimentation, Karen counted. One hundred, then two and the last passed by following the steady stream of pronghorns. Never have I seen so many wild animals together in one herd. This must be a hunter's paradise, Karen thought.

Dusk now, Karen's gaze returned to the skyline. Her thoughts reviewed the day: calling her parents at their home in Colorado Springs; riding the bus to the Rock Creek Valley from her apartment in Quail Point; Adam, the rancher; her new friend, Ruth Browning and her son Andy; Morris Goodenough, the bus driver and prayer warrior; Hannah the desk clerk; Mr. Powell the gentle man and Christian book salesman, as well as the other people she met, including the bearded man in the tan trench coat.

Looking at the sunset, Karen prayed for those she had met and for the people in the valley. Next, she prayed aloud for herself, "Here am I Lord, just your little girl easily frightened and intimidated. But Father your word says you have plans for me, that I am to prosper in your ways. Your word tells me to be bold and courageous, so Lord I present myself to you just as I am. Thank you for loving me.

In Jesus name, Amen." Karen picked up her new book and began reading about a Halfling called out of his comfort to go on a great adventure.

Usually after a fruitless episode in town, the engine of the red Ford F250 truck screamed up the mesa road toward Claymore Flats relentlessly pushed by the driver. Tonight was different. Adam rambled along disinterested and mumbling to himself. He had lost his temper at an emergency meeting at the high school called by Dr. Maurice Wood, the assistant superintendent of schools. Adam cursed a group of students when he left. At the prior week's meeting, the same students mocked him. Once again they had mocked him about being a childless, bald headed, old geezer who needed to mind his own business.

Reflecting on the comments brought a double sting. Baldness had come early. Adam coped with that. Most often he didn't think about his baldness, nor let joking bother him. Usually he gave a come-back like saying that baldness shows sign of superior intellect. Superior brains had pushed the hair out or some other attempted wit. This had not been joking. Their comment injured their target. Being childless meant more. These high school kids weren't old enough to remember that Mary Claymore died in the birth of their son, John Paul. Mother and Son had died ten years ago today in the delivery room. These high school kids heard of Adam's sorrow from their parents or another adult. The teens had been trained to deliver the stunning blow from home or even in school.

Instead of driving intently, Adam drove with distraction. Discouraged, he doubted his effectiveness as Chairman of the Rock Creek Valley School District Accountability Committee. He recognized that what happened had been a power play by the assistant superintendent to railroad his agenda, while feigning the need to meet a deadline. Since they had met the prior week and had little notice of this meeting, barely half the committee attended. Others were unable to meet at such a ridiculous time. His efforts to prevent the meeting had failed. He had received an insensitive and uncaring response. Key school figures couldn't attend either. John Alden, principal of the high school, was out of town attending a state department conference. Most of the counselors attended a meeting with county health department officials about something referred to as an adolescent health clinic or some sort of counseling project. Feeling defeated, resigning from his position seemed attractive. Why be subjected to such rude and senseless behavior? He could easily join a group planning a tax payer revolt to force the school district into change. Working within the system had not worked he thought. He wondered what it would take for the schools to become more accountable to the public. Also, Adam wondered about the meaning of an adolescent health clinic.

Adam had warned local authorities about their godless actions and decisions. The Adolescent Health Clinic proposal; sex education that taught how to use contraceptives; values clarification curriculum that included transcendental meditation and mind control techniques; situational ethics with no absolutes;

proposals to replace classical literature with ethnic and feminist material not as electives but as the required course of studies, and outcome based education. And now, alternative lifestyles. What's worse was the timing. These issues should have been dealt with in the spring, not just before school started.

Aloud Adam said, "They go too far. They mention that abstinence is the best policy. Then they say, 'But if you are going to have sex, here is how you use a condom.' That's like telling a bank robber not to rob a bank, then teaching him how to use an Uzi. I could have punched that idiot counselor. Her stupid comment that kids are going to do it anyway, that they are societal victims. Baloney! We don't want teenagers destroying their lives in the heat of passion, she said. My foot! They need to keep their pants on! In the heat of passion! More like a couple of dogs in heat. What person, young or old, would be likely to stop and put on a condom in the heat of passion? If they already lack control, they weren't going to stop and use a rubber! These people are insane. They have a different agenda! For sure they lack the common sense of decency."

Adam's tirade ended as he arrived at the top of the mesa, where the Holy Spirit brought scripture to mind: *The wrath of God is being revealed from heaven against all the godlessness and wickedness of people, who suppress the truth by their wickedness, Romans 1:18.* Adam stopped his truck in the center of the road, turned on his dome light, and then removed his Bible from the vest-pocket of his jacket and a yellow highlighter from the glove compartment. Finding Romans 1:19 Adam began reading the remainder of chapter one, and he chose to highlight certain phrases. Skipping through the passage, *since what may be known about God is plain to them, because God has made it plain to them. For although they knew God, they neither glorified him as God nor gave thanks to him, but their thinking became futile and their foolish hearts were darkened. Although they claimed to be wise, they became as fools. ...God gave them over in the sinful desires of their hearts to sexual impurity for the degrading of their bodies with one another. They exchanged the truth about God for a lie,* Adam paused then continued with verse twenty-six, *...God gave them over to shameful lusts...just as they did not think it worthwhile to retain the knowledge of God, so God gave them over to a depraved mind, so that they do what ought not to be done...evil, greed and depravity... envy, murder, strife, deceit and malice. They are gossips, slanderers, God-haters, insolent, arrogant and boastful; they invent ways of doing evil; they disobey their parents; they have no understanding, no fidelity, no love, no mercy. ...they know God's righteous decree that those who do such things deserve death, they not only continue to do these very things but also approve of those who practice them."*

"Man is that on target or what?" Adam voiced, and then it came to him. "Do you suppose these programs are already in place for this year? I bet curriculum has already been purchased and someone is covering their butt to make certain the school board or the administration has followed procedure to use public input."

Adam turned across the road to think further and watched the setting sun.

He switched off the engine and slumped over the steering wheel. Adam's self instruction continued as he thumbed to the book of *Titus* beginning with *1:9*... *"He must hold firmly to the trustworthy message as it has been taught, so that he can encourage others by sound doctrine and refute those who oppose it. For there are many rebellious people, mere talkers and deceivers...They must be silenced, because they are ruining whole households by teaching things they ought not to teach...and that for the sake of dishonest gain...rebuke them sharply."*

Watching the shadow from the sun setting behind the mountain, Adam called out to the Lord that he was all alone on the committee. It seemed he was the only one willing to take a stand to defend what was right and to speak against what was wrong. The other committee members, who thought like him, shared that they feared reprisal on their kids or that they had relatives employed in the district. They believed they would be pressured. Maybe they already had been pressured.

Adam thought what would I do if John Paul had lived and was a student at school? How would a child of mine react to having a father who caused the school people trouble? Adam pounded the steering wheel shouting, "Wait a minute, who works for whom? Father, I know Maurice Wood is likely to retaliate to my opposing him. I ask you give me wisdom to respond to what he might do himself or have others do. Father, let your truth and justice prevail."

Angrily Adam shouted to God, "Father break down the walls triumphantly! The enemy holds us captive. Bring Joshua and Caleb! Let Rahab give them safety! Be glorified in this land I pray."

Righteously invigorated, Adam switched on the engine like a snorting bull ready to charge, backed up in a cloud of dust, and whirled the truck around toward home on the road to Claymore Flats while spraying dirt and stone like an exploding shotgun blast.

From the west was sounded, "Cough, cough, sputter, cough, sputter, boom. Cough, cough, sputter, cough, sputter, boom. Cough, cough, sputter, cough, sputter, boom," choked the six cylinder, gray 1953 Chevrolet short bed truck. Laboring up the incline on the only road headed west out of Jericho Springs, again it sputtered. The scruffy old man braked to a stop at an overlook on the horseshoe bend of the winding dirt road above the town below. A blue cloud followed the truck to a halt; the smell of oil permeated trees and bushes. The passenger exited the cab.

The bearded man in a tan trench coat waved goodbye and echoed a thank you to the speechless driver. The truck continued its sputtering assent up the side of Mt. Huajatolla. This solitary figure, a bearded man in a tan trench coat, briefly watched the progress of the old truck with the moniker, "The Gray Whiz," scratched on its side fender. He watched until The Gray Whiz passed out of sight following the canyon of the west tributary of Rock Creek. It's destination, a saw mill on a meadow in a clearing above, where the scruffy old man had cut slab to load in the short bed of The Gray Whiz. Later he would haul it down the mountain to sell as firewood in the valley. The old man bagged some saw dust he would sell to a garden shop for compost, and saved the rest to compress as wood pellets for wood stoves and fireplaces.

Several hundred feet above, a scar remained as evidence of a tremendous rock slide on the south side of the northern peak. The scar outlined the distinguishable image of a white lamb to some observers. Others claimed it was a goat footed satyr or salamander. Museum records testified that original sojourners saw the scar as a white buffalo. Still others claimed the image was nothing other than a blank spot on the mountain side, and a minority could see each point of view depending on where they were standing when looking. All were fascinated by the mountain's flaw.

Residual effects of the ancient slide had prompted a series of smaller slides, which combined to decrease the intermontane basin above. Another altered the flow of the west tributary of Rock Creek a decade ago, which caused litigation over property boundaries and ownership of land and mineral rights. From the overlook by the hairpin turn on the mountain road, keen observers determined where the slide recently had filled in an area between the mountain side and a lonely volcanic miniature topped by a magnificent tree. The miniature, like a sentry, had protected the town below from damaging effects of the slide. To the casual, less astute onlooker, all the formation below appeared to be the result of the rockslide on the west side of Jericho Springs. It created a citadel on the west side of Jericho Springs that could be viewed by most of the valley. As if reclaimed, the volcanic mound as a citadel no longer appeared as a little orphan miniature alienated from Mt. Huajatolla with its twin peaks.

The west tributary of Rock Creek cascaded between Mt. Huajatolla, the slide deposit, and the citadel. On the south side of the citadel, hot springs formed a series of pools that once were part of Rock Creek. Now they remained as the former creek bed. Only night air and seepage from West Rock Creek cooled the tepid water, which formed a trickle compared to the volume before the rock slide. At dusk steam helped create eerie vapors encircling this part of Jericho Springs with fog chilled by the approaching night air.

Above heated pools in the citadel's center, a hollow displayed the dry image of a hot springs pond. Magma had created the pond as it had advanced through the core then retreated leaving a plug short of the top of the formation. When seepage from a much more active Rock Creek became heated, the pressure caused water to rise within the cavern and up into the pond. Vapors now discharged meagerly from what had once been a favorite bath of Ute medicine men. Unnoticed and rarely visited, the once favorite bath laid unused, no longer appreciated for its restorative, healing powers. Below a gold filled cavern awaited discovery.

Straining to see and discern, the bearded man in the tan trench coat tried to couple the vision below him with memory to no avail. No longer could he see what he thought he knew. "Is it because of the dusk? Do I need the sun to see what is below? He wondered. "I don't remember!" he pleaded to an unresponsive audience of rock, trees, and mountain critters. The slide hid what once was. Rock Creek no longer split pine forest with an intrusion of ancient deciduous trees. Only one mammoth Live Oak remained on the mountainside rim of the former hot springs pool in the center of the citadel. Once it overshadowed all below. Voluminous foliage had created a shadowy canopy of protection from summer's searing sun for bathers. Now the tree stood alone. No foliage. No acorns. No bathers. No shade. No refreshing water. Only barren limbs remained above ground and below roots dangled inside the cavern as if trying to grasp more of the precious gold.

Below the citadel, the man in the tan trench coat could only see the roof top of the deserted building. In the dark he decided he would make his descent, but now at dusk he gave thanks for lodging below. He watched as the cloak of darkness enveloped the sloping landscape from Rock Creek uphill to the ridge in the east. For an instant, the sun appeared to stop. Motionless, he held his breath listening to the sounds around him and to the thoughts within. Watching, he saw only partially. Words of thanks sincerely affirmed his attitude of praise. The bearded man wearing the tan trench coat waited for nightfall to cloak his descent.

In the east a sojourner would soon appear on the ridge and discover the view from a different angle but with similar appreciation. As if reclining comfortably in an easy chair to reflect on his beloved, friend sun settled back behind twin mountain peaks. With a hush the haze of dusk settled on once sunlit peaks and valleys sketching the horizon. Though sunbeams momentarily illuminated picturesque hillsides, clouds of vapor entered gently blocking their path. Once proclaiming individuality, trees formed a continuous forest blanket. Pink and purple mountain shadows replaced stark features of Mt. Huajatolla, Breast of the Earth, and mystery disguised the truth below.

Timers clicked and lights turned on! Headlights, house and streetlights, floodlights on billboards and church steeples resisted the night and pushed back the darkness. Parking lots, gasoline bays, convenience stores turn on with a come-and-get-it message. Liquor stores, fast food express lanes, motel marquees, post office depositories shined with a buy it here, put it there statement. As one candle, Jericho Springs flickered at the base of Huajatolla signaling to travelers the presence of light in darkness.

Highway travelers dotted the landscape north and south, but like an alien in a foreign land, one lonely pair of headlights partially illuminated aged pavement east on Colorado Highway 96. Barely noticeable and apparently unimportant side road reflectors designated the five mile marker and flashed by in a blur. To the crest, over a hill, into open range, the driver now relaxed the foot feed. Gradually down toward East Rock Creek, field mice and chipmunks scampered off the road avoiding the oncoming truck. A porcupine escaped a wheel, as did two adolescent skunks cavorting into the barrow ditch alongside the roadway. On a mission the driver slowed to admire deer sucking in their fill at the creek yet alert for an unpredictable response to his intrusion. Quickly, heads snapped to attention, eyes reflected beams from his headlights, cool waters dripped from soft mouths eager for more refreshing liquid. With his passing, startled and indignant mule deer resumed their evening ritual. Back and forth ears twitched fully aware of man with the roar of his engine and wake of exhaust. Speeding now the intruder interrupted a raccoon family fishing expedition, passed beyond Rock Creek, and crossed through new mown meadow. With engine laboring, our traveler accelerated up a sharp grade bending north to chase the last of day's light, to the point of the ridge, then left across asphalt ribbon stopping at what had become his favorite turnout. Barely in time to catch fleeting moments, he skidded to a stop. Sundown on Huajatolla, Breast of the Earth, dusk on the Rock Creek watershed.

"Ah, this makes the trip worth it," the sojourner said out loud to himself, while lightly slapping the dashboard. With transmission in neutral, he set both the emergency brake and turned off the ignition switch leaving his keys in place, then depressed the clutch and shifted his tranny to reverse protecting against forward movement on the slight downhill slope. Moving business papers aside and grabbing ever ready binoculars from the glove compartment and two sizeable sedimentary rocks from under the bench seat, our driver exited the truck, his traveling companion, to observe this treasured scene.

Rocks rightly placed in front of rear wheels. Binoculars positioned. "What a Bronco sunset, blue sky and orange clouds! No wonder Denver football fans claim God loves the Broncos best!" he shouted to all creation around him. Only the stars above and the insects below winked.

Usually on a Friday evening and only if the sun were setting on the mountain and dusk in the valley, he stopped here to admire this postcard scene. He relished taking a last look, but not in the winter when hazardous conditions threatened tragedy. In the winter he knew an early afternoon departure was necessary to escape tragedies accompanying whiteouts on the snow blown plains. By winter overnight lodging became a necessity, and often he was fortunate to trade Bibles and books for a bed to sleep through the night.

Routinely, he faced west and watched the sunset from east on the ridge. He glanced northward to the end of the valley. He studied the path of the Valley Highway back again from the north to the south where the road exited the valley at the canyon. From the ridge he had seen that the Valley Highway paralleled the Rockies' front-range to the west, like a dangling black ribbon. The main tributary of Rock Creek meandered out of the mountains and briefly flowed south past Jericho Springs before curving northward between two chains of hogbacks. Conversely, East Rock Creek, a lesser tributary, flowed from the north and past Ridge View where it crossed south under the highway bridge and became bordered by the ridge where the sojourner stood. East joined West Rock Creek near the junction of Colorado 96 and the Valley Highway.

The sojourner turned and faced away from the mountains where he saw how the Great Plains began their descent to the east from the ridge. Turning toward the mountains again, he marveled that usually at the base of the front-range, foothills created a gentler slope to the valley below, but here there was no extension to the formidable shape of the mountain. Force pressured earth plates more here than elsewhere partially due to the construction of Pikes Peak. Geothermal powers lurked angrily below. Unusual hogbacks displayed perpendicular sheets of sedimentary rock layers mixed with intrusions of igneous rock a few miles north, east, and south of Jericho Springs, Colorado. Layers of basalt rock revealed evidence of a lava flow. What was once the rock of ocean floor now beckoned skyward like a chorus of uplifted rock appeared as praying hands. East, and like waves approaching sandy beaches, strings of hogbacks with steep crests bordered the uplifted rock. Only then was the soil allowed a peaceful appearance where violent uplift gave way to the meandering level plains.

Shifting his gaze to the south, purposefully ignoring what was before him to save it for a last look, our sojourner imagined God's hand molding earth like a ball of clay. South must be where squeezed clay oozed between God's index finger and thumb to create a formidable mesa to provide forest and lakes for spectacular fishing, a refuge for deer and elk, and to make the river flow onto the plains. Only a county road to Wolf City sometimes carried a river of traffic over the mesa during high school football season. Winter storms swept south below the peaks along the front-range but stopped at the mesa where clouds literally dumped their payload on the mesa and in the river valley below. During winter storms, the Valley Highway traffic stopped where the mesa met the ridge to the plains. Then only water escaped the valley usually under frozen sheets of ice.

Now relishing what remained, our traveler fixed his gaze to the center and back on the mountain. As if admiring the shape, so as to find a particular spot, he began at the north peak then rested downward detailing what he could still see. Below the precipice, a hallowed space, one blemish he saw. There on the right peak, he imagined the concave, where a giant scoop had been used to form an ice cream ball of earth. Instead of filling a cone, earth landed with a plop and became the citadel on the west edge of Jericho Springs or so he speculated. Here he looked, was drawn, more intently focusing his binocular lens. Vapors rising, it was too late with not enough light at this distance to make out the image of the once magnificent tree.

"But it is there," he spoke disappointedly to the night air, "so much for now. On with what needs be done." And he began to worship and pray out loud, intermittently singing praises with uplifted hands and quoting scripture as the Lord brought verses to mind.

The sojourner replayed his day, the stops before entering each town with prayers to invoke God's guidance, God's answers, the book sales and deliveries he had made, conversations with new and old acquaintances, things he had overheard and what he had seen. He remembered that reading the weekly newspaper, the *Outcry*, had been more positive than his late lunch at the Cozy Corner Café at the north end of the valley. He recalled scanning the society column by Rose Alden, wife of John Alden, Principal of the Jericho Springs Junior/Senior High School, minutes from the school board and city council meetings, and the weekly calendar of events announcing a Tuesday school board meeting in Rock Creek and Thursday city council meeting in Jericho Springs. With interest he had read two follow up articles. The first was about a missing teacher who may have witnessed the alleged murder of one Gloria Jones. The school board agenda included the proposed hiring of a replacement for the missing teacher. The second article elaborated about a Jericho Springs City Council agenda item to condemn the Blair House, a property belonging to a couple named Blair so long as they remained guardians for a child that ran away fifteen years ago. The Blair's died, so the property reverted back to original owners, who had not been located. Valuable mineral and water rights were at stake. Without finishing the article, he had shifted to reviewing notes about area worship services. The sojourner asserted, "One day, Father, they will invite me here!" More humbly before the close, he thanked God for the peace and joy gifted him. Interceding he asked his abba daddy to blanket mercy, forgiveness, righteousness, and healing over these people in Rock Creek Valley.

With rocks in hand, he climbed back into his truck and calmly drove away from his favorite vista and headed northeast at a relaxed pace. Noticing the time on his watch had passed 8:00 p.m., he sang "Tis So Sweet To Trust In Jesus", and congratulated himself as if speaking to someone else in the cab saying, "Kip Powell, Mr. Sojourners' Company, it has been a good trip." With moist eyelids, "Thank you, Lord, for man prospers at your will and discretion."

North, south, west, and east—a concert of prayer had covered the roadways leading to and from the valley. The walls of the city shook!

As if the order to advance had been given, the bearded man in the tan trench coat made his descent unseen from the road above the Blair House in Jericho Springs. Carrying one suitcase he entered the dilapidated building below the citadel by forcing his way in through a door with boards nailed across it to block entrance. Only the suitcase gave evidence of his being a traveler. He found what he hoped to be a comfortable space, laid down, and slept with the suitcase as his pillow and the tan trench coat as a blanket. Its lining served as a cushion beneath him. Thermal long-johns and mid-length tube socks replaced twice soaked clothes, which he hung over several doorknobs to dry. The bearded man in the tan trench coat dreamed the dreams of a wanderer seeking to find a way home, while across the valley in Rock Creek another traveler emptied her suitcase.

With both bags on her bed and two boxes on the floor, Karen stopped reading and decided to put her things away. She unpacked, sorted her clothing for temporary storage, and placed everything in its place, with clothing in the dresser, coat and suitcases closeted, Bible on nightstand with the J. R.Tolkien book, and toiletries on top the dresser. Picking up both boxes, she thought about how she had decided what to pack. She had stored most of her belongings with her mom and dad in Colorado Springs, but she had retained her apartment in Quail Point. Mom had wanted her to vacate her apartment and stay with them, but Dad had understood her need to leave and find her bearings. Knowing she could only take a few extra items with her, Karen had remembered her dad's advice to take her ten most valued things. Pop had said that making such a decision will help you sort things out and decide what is important.

Since her Bible and clothing weren't included in the count, Karen had become selective in making her decision. Unpacking she removed the contents: first the photo album; letters from Mom and Pop while she was at Calvary Bible College; her placement file and teaching credentials; the single action, twenty-two caliber, Frontier model pistol and holster belt with plenty of ammunition for target practice, which had been a gift from her father on her sixteenth birthday. She slid the pistol from the holster, spun the bullet chamber, and expertly twirled it first in her right hand and then in her left before returning it to her holster. Next she gently removed a box of stationery; her diary; the 35mm camera with wide angle lens, loaded and ready for use; one, small jewelry box; Great Grandmother Gustafson's crucifix taken from Karen's bedroom wall; and last, a cabin shaped birdfeeder from Mom. Karen put the crucifix on the wall above her pillow where a picture had been hung; the pistol and jewelry box in the top dresser drawer underneath her undergarments; and the diary on the table so she could write later. With hopes she would want to use the camera, she placed it on the table with the diary, and took out her credentials and college placement file for use Monday when interviewing for the teaching position. Keeping the camera and diary on the lamp table, but putting everything else back in the box and into the closet, Karen left the cabin shaped birdfeeder in the center of the room on the throw rug.

Hungry, Karen gathered her key and purse plus the empty plate from lunch, locked her door, and walked downstairs for dinner barely noticing the man, a new arrival, at the other end of the hallway. He exited the back door, climbed the outside stairwell to the third floor to enter room 319, as she descended the front stairwell to the dining hall, passed the bar, and walked through the lobby. Sitting near the window, she consumed a hamburger smothered with chili con carne, cheddar cheese and onions on rye toast. Surprisingly, it was quite tasty. Still she added salsa, then after taking another bite, she realized she had made a mistake. "More water please," she said to the waitress who hurried by her. Waiting and looking around, she recognized the cook she saw by the dumpster, decided the waitress must be Sarah, and noticed a man passing through the lobby from the stairwell to the bar. Briefly, Karen wondered if he had been the man she had seen in the hallway minutes earlier.

As if bored the waitress returned to Karen's table, set the water down with Karen's bill, and said, "Want some dessert? We have some great homegrown apple pie."

Karen declined, paid for the meal, confirmed the waitress was Sarah, and then thanked her for fixing her sandwich at lunch. Exchanging pleasantries, she returned to her room where she discovered the birdfeeder and the rug were no longer center in the room but obviously had been pushed toward the table. Discounting the change, she thought she must have moved things when she had left for dinner. Karen didn't notice what was missing, took off her clothes, got into bed, made notes in her diary, and read about Bilbo Baggins well into the night only to fall asleep hours later with the bedside lamp still on. Protectively, the little light illuminated the dark and warned that someone might be watching what happened out of doors.

EXPLORE

CHAPTER 4

"Send some men to explore the land of Canaan..." Numbers 13:2

As Friday had ended with God's people praying north, south, east, and west, Saturday morning began with some of his people exploring the land. Adam, Karen, the Brownings, and the bearded man in the tan trench coat set out to explore and discover what they could about not only the land, but also about themselves. It was not without risk.

Sound sleep escaped Adam Claymore Friday night. Dreams of the hospital delivery room and the deaths of both his wife and his son on Colorado Day had invaded his sleep. His torment had increased when reminders came of what was and what should have been. He awakened and tried to change the script of his dream to no avail. He thought of the high school students who had taunted him. He asked God for forgiveness and received the reminder that the children were lost and he should not expect better of them. He prayed for them and forgave them, which removed him as an obstacle to their forgiveness. He gave his tormentors over to the Lord, surrendered against seeking any revenge he might seek, and prayed for their salvation. Sometimes Adam rebuked his tormenting dreams knowing Satan wanted to pester him with memories of the deaths of his wife Mary and son John Paul. When the dreams came to Adam like torment, too often an early death seemed a friendly option for him. It wasn't that he contemplated taking his life; it was more like finding ways to lose himself and giving up on having an intimate personal life. Loneliness had become an unwanted companion, a wily enemy. To compensate, he worked and fled from intimacy. Often he worked the ranch ten and twelve hours daily during the week, but left the weekend work to his men. When he wasn't working, he tried to lose himself doing good things in an unappreciative community that called him a workaholic. He spent himself on church work as a deacon with an unresponsive congregation that had lost its bi-vocational pastor. Occasional sermon preparation lifted his spirits temporarily, until reminders of worshipping with Mary flooded his memory. Nothing filled the void and loss of intimacy. Occasionally, he had dated but had found no one compared favorably with Mary. He found no relief for his wounded heart. Realizing his emotions and actions had been a question of lordship, he committed to ask Christ to reign over this area of his life. Adam knew he could not cope with the torment and loss of his wife and son on his own.

Saturday morning Adam rode out on his favorite mare at dawn on Claymore Flats saying nothing to his men and carrying a side arm slung on his left hip and a Winchester in the saddle breech. The mare's foal followed with Saguache close behind. This morning the black Gordon Setter with dark brown tinting the front of his forelegs pursued Adam's fellowship to the point of annoyance, yet no matter what Adam said or did to him, Big Foot's loyalty remained one constant encouragement. Besides, Adam thought, Big Foot had proven himself before when searching the mesa for sign of black bear, especially when part of the herd grazed in the mountain meadows. Adam's heart led him to the east side of the mesa, where his bride and son remained buried in a plot in the Claymore Cemetery. Adam had hoped his yearning would subside. It had not.

Morning had come earlier west in the valley for the bearded man in the tan trench coat than for Karen or the Brownings. The old house at the base of the prehistoric volcanic mound stood conspicuously above the rest of the town. Sun rays caught it first as the shadow descended down Mt. Huajatolla. The giant Live Oak without leaves became starkly revealed before the town received direct sunlight.

With filtered rays piercing his eyes through dust covered windows, the sun brought light to the house revealing its innards. The man had slept on the floor in the piano room to the left of the front door. A dusty bed sheet covered the old upright piano. Sheet music and song books lay under the lid of the piano bench lid. Wishing he could play, he knew sounds of music would give him away by announcing an intruder had come to the neighborhood. Inspecting the piano bench surrounded by the old bay window, he peered out the windows toward the houses across the street. A sloping sidewalk, cracked by tree roots, led from the old mansion to the black wrought iron fence at the street. He wondered who lived in the houses across the street. Left to speculation, he next tested each of two wicker rockers, and then exited the piano room to inspect the rest of the old house.

A foyer connected the piano room with its twin on the south side of the front door. Here the intruder uncovered a day bed. Moving around the room, he blew dust off an antique, oak dresser with three drawers and hand carved scrolls on the edges. He sat in one wooden chair to discover if it were sturdy. Studying the shape of the room, he wondered how a false wall and stairwell could be place on the side to the south, which would allow secretive passage to the floors above and below the room. Creaking sounds announced that it was the floor not the chair that might need attention. In fact, he thought that both rooms needed nothing more than a thorough cleaning and some paint.

A long corridor led from the rear of the foyer to the back of the house. On the right he discovered a large formal dining room with coved ceilings, its furnishings cloaked with dust covers. Across the hall walls of built in bookcases lined a reception room. Correctly, he guessed it doubled as a study in recent years. Midway down the hall, an oak stairwell led to a second then third floor. Below the stairwell a door opened to a basement. He continued down the hallway to investigate the kitchen that spanned the width of the house. It connected with a large dining room and a bathroom, which had a free standing bathtub and a shower with a wrap around curtain. He concluded the shower had been added to the original fixture. Across the hall from the dining room, a small furnished apartment with a kitchen and bathroom had probably replaced a large master bedroom.

In the rear where the intruder entered last night, an enclosed and empty porch spanned the width of the house opposite the kitchen. He noted large windows had replaced wire mesh screen on the porch's exterior walls. Now he secured the back entry door to avoid detection, but the dusty floor still bore evidence of his footprints. Throughout the first floor, dusty brown disgraced once elegant wallpaper and floorboards creaked everywhere as he passed. Ornate stairwell trim and wooden staircase spindles needed both a cleansing and oil treatment to restore both moisture and finish. In fact the mansion needed oil to heal it.

The intruder didn't inspect the basement but did climb the stairs to the second then third floors. To his surprise both floors looked like college dorms. Buffet rooms without a kitchen or bath lined both hallways. Each room mirrored the others, except those in each of the four corners. Baseboard hot water heat accompanied an unused and old fashioned radiator heating system that had not been removed. A light layer of coal dust covered the walls and ceilings, which had probably resulted from burning coal in the fire places of each corner room. Above the closed-in, first-floor porch, an open balcony with white wooden railing now disgraced the second and third floors, where former residents had sat and enjoyed picturesque surroundings. Now the front exterior, second and third floor balconies, were stacked perilously with mounds of boxes and clothes. The stench from the rot permeated the front of the house upstairs. Mold and mildew rotted clothing and the wooden floor on each front balcony. Gaping holes from missing floor boards discredited the mansion and extracted its one time glory. Holding his nose, he sadly surveyed the mess and wondered if the side and rear porches had suffered as much as the front porches.

He made a mistake. On the street below, a woman riding a hunter green, mountain bike stopped and noticed him. At least the woman believed she saw someone. Our intruder darted back inside and hoped he'd not been seen. The cyclist rubbed her eyes, looked again, and then mounted her foot pedals to continue her bicycle ride. His question remained unanswered. Had she seen him and if she had, what would she do? The cyclist peddled her bike into the driveway of a house down the street and disappeared.

Though hungry, he did not risk further exposure. Instead he returned to the old library in the study where he examined book after book, pulling each from its place on the shelf, and then returning each to its original location. He stored his suitcase in the first floor apartment, removed the dusty mattress cover from the double bed, and looked for mouse droppings. He found none. In spite of the musty odor, he rested on the bed and decided to forage for food after sundown. A nap seemed in order, and he slept a peaceful sleep.

The clatter of the dumpster lid banging against its back side awakened Karen Saturday morning at the Stage Stop Hotel in downtown Rock Creek. She heard someone swearing about breaking down cardboard boxes and doing food prep for morning breakfast. She assumed she had heard the cook angrily going about his morning chores. Throwing back her bed covers with resolve, she stretched then dangled her feet over the side of the bed, looked at the birdfeeder, turned off the table lamp left on all night, and peered outside the open window at the new day. Leaning out of the window and deeply breathing in the crisp morning air, she captured the fragrance of both fresh baked bread and roses. Doubting the possibility, Karen repeated her action and concluded she had indeed smelled roses.

Karen continued observing the out of doors and noted that here at daybreak, the morning had defeated the night, yet darkness indeed lingered in Rock Creek. The ridge and canopy of tree cover shielded the town from the morning sunlight. Beyond the hogback north of town, night's shadow withdrew from the mountain toward the creek below. The difference between how the mountain appeared at sunrise and sunset registered in her mind. Sunlight exposed the truth about the mountain, while dusk allowed illusions of hidden specifics. Karen wished she had her car to explore the peaks and valleys.

Karen had gazed at the geography with admiration, but then shifted her focus back again to see if she correctly identified the instigator of her rude awakening. Too late, she noted. He had already gone back inside. She noticed something else. Similar to a Canaanite city vestibule, she detected a two foot wide ledge just outside her window. Looking upward from her window, she spied a three foot wide catwalk spanned the length of the third floor hotel rooms. Both catwalks appeared to continue around both ends of the building. While each floor could be accessed from the hotel lobby on the west end, the floors were accessed from the outside on the east by a metal stairwell. What she didn't see was that metal railing had been attached to the third floor catwalk and that on the southern front of the Stage Stop Hotel, the metal railing provided a balcony for each room. Near the highway a pitched roof covered the single story bar, while on the eastside, a pitched roof covered the hotel offices and storage room. The exterior metal stairwell connected the hotel to the office and storage area with an awning that covered a walkway between them. In case of a hallway fire, metal ladders descended to the second floor catwalk from both ends of the third floor ledge. The difference was that on the west side the ladder reached the ground in the back parking lot, while on the east, the ladder extended to the front parking lot and could also be accessed at the front porch, which spanned the entire front entrance. In case of an emergency, the ladders provided an escape route from outside the building to the ground below.

Karen's arms tingled with an uncomfortable chill causing her to close the window. She noticed it lacked a lock lever. Wondering how she could secure the window, she decided to get a hammer to pound a nail in each side above the lower section of the window frame. At least the window would be secured, but she would not be able to open the window without removing the nails. From her purse she retrieved paper and pen to prepare a note to leave with the desk clerk about the window. In the note Karen asked the management to replace the missing lever.

Next, Karen wrote a morning prayer in her diary and placed it on the dresser. Deciding to shower after her morning walk, she put on a burgundy sweat suit, white ankle socks, and white, cross trainer, athletic shoes. She stroked a brush through her hair, quickly combed out some tangles, and picked at a zit on her chin that she had discovered while looking in the mirror. Turning around Karen stumbled over the birdfeeder in the center of the throw rug.

Picking it up, Karen decided she would hang the birdfeeder first thing, once she rented her own place. Examining its log cabin shape, she remembered her mother had said that she kept her birdfeeder hanging outside her kitchen window. Mom Gustafson watched the birds, while washing the dishes. Mom had said it really helped at times when she felt like flying away. The birds offered distraction and a brief escape, as hope displaced discouragement.

From the convenience store across the highway just south of an intersection, Karen decided to buy packages of sunflower seeds to pour down the filler hole. The cabin's chimney hid the filler hole on one side of the roof. When filled, she planned to set the birdfeeder on the catwalk outside her window. "Why wait?" she said, "Bird watching seems very appropriate."

Taking her room key, camera, and Bible, but leaving her purse, Karen locked the room. Desiring some exploration, she walked east down the hall past rooms 217, 219 to her right and 220 on her left to the stairwell between the main building and the offices and kitchen storage, which was covered with a pitched roof identical to the west side of the building. From the second floor landing, Karen discovered more stairs led down the stairwell to the parking lot. Below, she saw the end of the front porch and noted that a three foot opening in the porch railing allowed access to a fire escape ladder that both extended to the parking lot and also to the third floor balconies. Karen confirmed that the two foot catwalk of the second floor extended around the building where a second floor frontage had been attached to the catwalk. The frontage consisted of a sloping roof over half the porch. At the end of the porch a facade had been attached and bore the hotel sign, Stage Stop Hotel.

Just left of the stairwell and down the steps from the side of the porch, Karen stepped onto a foot path leading away from the hotel in two opposite directions. One path led north to a row of houses behind the hotel. The other led east into the trees then south below the ridge toward the canyon. Choosing the southern route, she crossed behind the parking lot noting tall mounds of river rock that could hide anyone using this route to enter or exit the hotel. One could also walk to the houses behind and north of the hotel without using the side street. Following a fragrance of roses, Karen walked south and east of the highway to the mouth of the canyon.

Tracing the scent, Karen emerged from the forest at the canyon. Here the forest created a canopy over the Valley Highway high enough not to threaten semi-trucks. As a sentry, a winter storm gate stood ready to halt highway traffic into the canyon. On both sides the entrance of the canyon, rose bushes climbed three times her height. Above the climbing roses, wild Wood Roses grew amongst the rock the height of the mesa. She paused, took pictures, and admired the ruggedness of the canyon's rock walls. Mist from the waterfall chilled her face. Karen found two old fashioned nails with square heads amongst the rock at her feet and placed them in her pocket.

No traffic passed by. Karen heard only the rush of water, wind rustling leaves in the grove of birch trees, and songbirds beckoning to her from trees lining the footpath across the highway. In response she crossed over and saw four houses and a gas station at a distance. Smoke rose from wood stoves accompanied by breakfast odors of bacon, sausage, coffee, and fresh bread. Chimney smoke joined mist that had been gently powered by the canyon breeze. The morning breeze changed direction and both mist and smoke lazily enveloped the trees. Along the footpath, she strolled to a lane leading toward the houses by the highway. To her surprise the path led her to a white wooden chapel in a hollow. White trunked birch trees surrounded it. With her 35mm camera, Karen captured the setting with multiple pictures.

Walking to the front door, Karen marveled at how more rose bushes climbed the mesa wall. She peered through one stained glass window. An old fashioned offering box with only a trace of paint on the lid stayed fixed to the window sill. Curiously, she opened the box and promptly closed the lid upon discovering its empty contents. She tried the locked door. It didn't open. Noting the foundation corner stone, she discovered the church's 1880 origin. The bell still hung in the steeple. Although mowed grass had crept into the parking area, the building and grounds had been maintained by people that must truly love their church. "The light of this church may flicker but it lives," Karen concluded with delight.

Karen hoped to attend services here tomorrow. Behind the narrow, white frame building, she explored a coal shed now filled with wood. One rusted wheel barrow with freshly oiled handles stood on its nose against a well used chopping block. Beyond the white picket fence behind the white coal shed, a cemetery quietly offered some local history. Here the breeze stopped and the haze of smoke and mist densely gathered. No birds chirped.

Ancient wooden markers and old upright stones dominated the graveyard, yet there were also many newer grave markers laying flat in freshly mown lawn. Karen spent an hour, then two, noting the names and the dates. Several markers included Bible verses, statements about the person's character, and how each died. She recognized the frequency of some families—William and Elizabeth Claymore 1880's—their "yes meant yes", Hiram and Rebecca Claymore 1900, with a generation listed nearly every twenty years, then a cluster of Claymore's during the late '30's and early '40's. Next, she found none beyond the 1940's. Other frequent sir names included Wood, Braley, McNaughton, Blair, Sentry, Parson and Jaramillo. Toward the back of the well kept cemetery, faded wood marked older graves. Karen wondered what mysteries would be told if grave markers could reveal the story behind the remains of each buried person.

Surprisingly, the path continued through the cemetery. Karen followed it to a footbridge that crossed Rock Creek. On both ends dogwoods formed a dense arch and their scent enveloped the bridge. A tall cottonwood tree bordered the east end of the bridge. The path continued as a trail on the other side and lead upward to the top of the mesa, while it also led in the opposite direction to County Road 403. Raspberry bushes dominated the left side of the trail to the mesa, while wild strawberry plants were prolific to the right of the trail and up the path to the mesa ridge. The footpath leading away from the mesa appeared to follow the creek to the road, which cut between the mesa and the uplift standing next to a strike valley. Up creek leading to the road, the creek wall became less imposing and receded to half its height at the foot bridge, which allowed flood waters to flow into the fields west of the creek.

In the center of the footbridge, Karen studied the Word for her morning devotion and did a word search on water. Focusing on Psalms, she read: *That person is like a tree planted by streams of water, which yields its fruit in season and whose leaf does not wither-whatever they do prospers. Psalm 1:3.* Next, she prayed and gave thanks to God for being sovereign and sustaining her. Her thoughts wandered back to her arrival, when she watched the man in the tan trench coat return to the bus dripping wet. Identifying with him, she prayed that he would find what he had been seeking. Earnestly, she also prayed for her new friends, Ruth and Andy and their husband/father. Also she prayed for Hannah the desk clerk, Sarah the waitress, Morris the bus driver, and then Karen prayed for the cowboy, who looked like the Marlboro Country man, at least until he took his hat off.

Hearing sounds of people active in town, Karen returned to the Stage Stop Hotel for breakfast. Hungry after her walk, she devoured two eggs, hash-brown potatoes smothered with green chili, four sausage links, two buttered tortillas, black coffee, a small glass of freshly squeezed and unstrained orange juice, plus a giant tumbler of ice water. Filled to the brim, she left the dining hall, stopped at the front desk to deliver her note to the management about the window lock, rang the bell for attention, then left the written message on the counter under the bell. No longer waiting for acknowledgement, she climbed the stairs to her second floor room. Although tempted to nap, Karen showered and changed clothes in the bathroom at the end of the hallway.

Returning to her room from the bath, Karen dressed for an afternoon's exploration of the rest of the town. She hoped to climb both the hogback and the ridge. She marveled at her own sense of adventure and thought how unlike her to take the time for herself to be out exploring instead of grading papers, calling parents, and preparing lesson plans. "But, that is what summers are meant for," she spoke aloud, "a time for teachers to regain sanity and restore a desire to teach children." Karen needed both. Besides, her father told her to take a good look at the community when considering a job.

Opening the room's only window, Karen climbed onto the catwalk and looked below. She noticed a man walking from back of the hotel onto the footpath and then toward the rear entrance of the last house on the right. The house faced a side street north of the hotel. Having circled behind the hotel and passing below her, a late model, black Cadillac with golden wire-wheel covers stopped in the parking lot behind the first building facing Highway 85/87. She climbed back into her room and watched as a young boy emerged from the Caddy, passenger side front door. After knocking on the back door, the boy cautiously opened the door and entered the building. Light revealed nothing, but she heard laughter and thought she could smell cigar smoke. Within minutes the youngster returned to the Caddy carrying a brown leather briefcase. In no hurry, the driver let the luxury car idle from the parking lot toward the front of the hotel where Karen could no longer see it.

Hastily, Karen again climbed out her window onto the catwalk ledge and made her way toward the roof over the bar in time to watch the Caddy head west down the county road next to the convenience store. It continued across the bridge and left town coasting between the mesa and uplifted rock.

Two men exited the same building as had the boy. One walked behind the hotel onto the footpath to the house at the end of the street behind the hotel, where he also entered through the rear door. The other man crossed the highway and entered the convenience store. Hoping not to be discovered, Karen crept back to her room and crawled in through the window, which she closed. She hastened through the hall and down the stairs skipping an occasional step. She stopped at the lobby door and peered out the window toward the store across the street. Karen could not see the man in the convenience store but decided to go there anyway.

As Karen descended the steps from the porch, the man she had been watching exited the convenience store. He walked directly toward her. Holding her breath and beginning to sweat, she waited for traffic to pass heading south into the canyon. Each faced the other from opposite sides of the road. His gaze lasted

41

longer, as he tried to recognize her. Embarrassed, she avoided his eyes. Crossing the highway at the same instance, the man paused in the middle of the highway to light a cigarette, while taking a closer look at her as she passed by. He turned with admiration, saying something suggestive under his breath, and then walked with a swagger across the hotel parking lot and into the lobby. She realized he was not the man she had seen in the second floor hallway yesterday. The realization sent a chill up her spine. Karen worried if she had been seen on the hotel catwalk by those at the tobacco store.

Undaunted, Karen continued her walk to the convenience store, entered, and scanned the inside at first looking for a newspaper. She found the Denver Post and a copy of the weekly newspaper on a magazine rack featuring girly magazines, children's comic books, and some decent magazines. Feeling anger rise from her chest to her neck and face, she hoped not to telegraph her attitude. For now she wanted to conceal her disdain and hostility from the cashier. Instead, Karen wanted to appear unaffected by the pornography, so as not to make a scene or expose her reaction.

Taking her time and sensing the gaze of the cashier on her back, Karen scanned the newspaper and read about an agenda item for Thursday's city council meeting. It was about litigation surrounding a house about to be condemned. In spite of people claiming to be distant relatives, no clear ownership had been established, yet mystery seemed to surround the details. Continuing to read as she walked, she meandered around three aisles, while she noticed and examined different products. Book racks displayed more porn and new age titles. One side of an aisle provided a rental library of video movies with an adults' only section, while the other side featured candy and chips. Two more aisles displayed camping supplies, toiletries, breakfast foods, canned goods, cleaning supplies, and an automotive section with oil, gas treatment, gallon containers of windshield solvent, snow brushes, and automatic transmission fluid, types A and F. A refrigeration unit at the rear of the stored cooled soda pop, dairy products, beer, and a small selection of cheap wine. At the rear of the store, Karen entered the generic bathroom and immediately was repelled by a condom dispenser also displaying telephone numbers and obscene messages scratched into its sides.

Exiting the bathroom Karen finished her tour around the store by picking up two eight ounce packages of low sodium sunflower seeds, a package of chewing gum, a sixteen ounce cola, a hoagie sandwich from the dairy case, and the weekly newspaper. She lingered at a bulletin board to read an assortment of advertisements, business cards, and announcements from throughout the valley. Reading the messages she learned about different agencies, meeting dates for organizations, and adult education classes including yoga, palmistry, and meditation. Additionally, she learned the school district conducted an adult education program at the high school in Jericho Springs, and she wondered if all the adult education programs could be coordinated. No message announced anything remotely Christian. Karen concluded the bulletin board advertised everything worldly, perverse, or pagan in the valley. It didn't. Some things weren't announced.

Reluctantly, Karen approached the clerk, who attempted to increase her purchase by saying, "That all Miss?"

"Yes, thank you."

"Lottery tickets, Quick Picks?"

"Nope."

"Cigarettes?"

"Nnnnnno."

"You ever try these panatelas? Or are you looking for something… stronger?"

After Karen gave her one more no thank you, the woman told Karen that she was trying to quit smoking too. Then she ignored Karen's comment about never having smoked and asked Karen if she was staying at the hotel. Karen did not respond but took her change and left.

Instead of returning to the hotel, Karen made a double left north to the street the Caddy traveled to leave town. She read the street sign, County Road 403 and began walking west on the roadway. Walking past the volunteer fire station, three houses across the road on her right and a boarded up grocery store and four houses on her left, she continued to a bridge covering the creek. Another sign labeled it, Rock Creek. Midway across the bridge, she stopped, scanned Rock Creek south to the mesa and canyon, and took note of a footbridge, then scanned back to the bridge noting backyards to four houses and the area behind the convenience store. Turning around north, she discovered an area beyond the buildings across the county road. It was a wooded area north behind the old high school up the road. Across the creek and left, the uplift of a hogback ended with nearly a ninety degree angle perpendicular to the roadway. Like a stockade fence, the crest of the hogback rose above a twenty foot mound of eroded debris for another eighteen feet. As the wall west of the creek, the hogback led north from County Road 403 parallel to the creek. It bent slightly eastward where it almost joined another hogback behind the hotel and a row of houses on a side street north of the hotel. More than twenty yards upstream, Karen noticed a point where the water massed and churned like a whirlpool before continuing downstream. The water did the same south of the footbridge.

Before leaving the bridge, Karen searched County Road 403, eyeing its western passage between the uplift and a grand mesa. At the narrows, deer fence, three sections eight to ten feet tall, blocked passage in the meadow. Next to the fence, a cattle guard interrupted the pavement and prohibited livestock from entering the town. She recognized where frequent flooding characterized this location as debris blanketed a flood plain east and west of the narrows. Karen concluded regular flooding of the meadow must have occurred east and west of the deer fence.

Briefly, peering again at the houses south of County Road 403, Karen detected nothing out of the ordinary. The houses stood at attention as members of an old, small town. Continuing her investigation she climbed down to the east bank of the creek under the bridge. Below both sides of the bridge, she discovered an opening under the roadway large enough for a person to lie in. Up creek, she climbed her way over rocks and brush to the churning mass of water fifteen feet wide and thirty feet long cluttered naturally by boulders and carelessly with debris. Not able to see its depth, she dared not to enter the creek, but spent a few moments in contemplation. Karen wondered where the man in the tan trench entered the water, and she concluded this was not a safe place.

Climbing up the bank of the creek, Karen walked north through the woods where she came to a fenced area north of the fire department building. Behind the fence were dump trucks, a road grader, a front end loader, and several additional trucks. One truck had a plow blade attached to it. Another fence divided the area in half. The other half stored postal vehicles and old mail boxes. Walking around the fence perimeter toward the highway, she passed through an unpaved parking lot belonging to the highway department trailer, but extending to the north end of town. Realizing this was where the bearded man in the tan trench coat had emerged from the woods yesterday, she wondered if he had fallen into the churning mass of water. She questioned whether or not he had deliberately entered the water. No, Karen thought, why would anyone take such a risk?

Karen proceeded north on the roadway past the highway department trailer and into the post office. Curious, she inquired about general delivery services. She stood at a counter by the window and peered across the street at the Stage Stop Hotel porch and up the street a short distance at the store beside the hotel. Huajatolla Tobacco, Vending, and Juke Box Company had been identified by the sign above the doorway and plate glass window that extended the remaining width of the blond brick building. She could see that a sign painted on the south side of the building advertised an auto parts store in Ridge View. Next to the tobacco store stood two other buildings that she wanted to investigate. North of the buildings, she could barely see a white house with what appeared to be faded yellow trim facing the side street. A chain link fence surrounded the back and front yards. Karen could not yet see that three children, one girl and one older and one a younger boy, played in the back yard squirting each other with water pistols, as they circled around a smoldering ash pit.

Everything appeared normal, Karen thought normal except the Caddy and men that earlier had been in the parking lot behind the store. Continuing her walk, she strolled past Quonset huts that sheltered a fleet of yellow school busses surrounded by chain link fence. Next, she walked in front of the three-story, Rock Creek School, her destination and purpose for being in town. A sign posted in a marquee on the frontage informed that the Rock Creek Valley School District occupied the second floor, and that the third floor housed the Rock Creek Valley Museum. Ground level windows revealed a lower level floor, which housed a storage area in the front and also a senior center in the rear accessed from a north side entrance. Below the lower level, dark catacombs hid school records, community artifacts, athletic trophies, and other relics not included in the museum displays. A wealth of secrets waited there to be unearthed and revealed. Like a buttress, four massive red brick pillars supported an open balcony over the entry way. Six bottom floor windows, three on each side of the entry way, contained bottle glass squares in rows five high and six long. Each glass square measured a half foot length and width. Upper floor windows formed a series of window frames with sets of glass panes a yard square with two panes wide and three panes long for each window frame. Five sets of frames bordered each side of the entry way. Over the entrance three rows of yard square windows formed an outline of a large tic-tac-toe game board. The Masonic cornerstone dated the building 1880. The red brick school apparently had endured hard times remarkably well. On Monday morning Karen would be interviewing here with the Director of Human Resources for a senior high school science and social studies position.

Since the high school had been repurposed, an old football field north of the school remained unattended. As an eerie remnant of past glory, sagging goal posts and brown turf with patches of tangled weed silently portrayed past activity. More than once a powerful kicker had successfully cleared the uprights and placed a football into the creek beyond the field. Also, a lone pole topped with a rectangular frame once provided spectators with scoreboard details. Eight foot chain link fence now guarded the field. Protruding at a forty-five degree angle from the top of each fence pole, three strands of barbwire connected angular extensions implying more of a prison than learning or playing atmosphere. Two sets of wooden bleachers with flaking white paint flanked the sides of a tower with a crow's nest next to where football games had been announced. A comparatively large white building with an asphalt roof of green shingles provided spectators with restrooms and a concession stand. Black mold covered the back side and mildew the inside of the building creating a stench that carried to the administrative offices by powerful north winds. Behind the bleachers and concession, a parking lot separated the football complex from the creek. Open field remained between both sides of Rock Creek to the hogback at the narrows north of town.

Across the street from the football field stood another imposing hogback where the town's water supply had been stored in a tank on a mighty white tower. On the tower, Rock Creek had been painted in two locations proudly announcing the name of the town. Opposite the school building, two business buildings and Indiana Avenue bordered the Valley Highway. The first building housed both an insurance and real estate company, while the other featured antiques. Both appeared identical and duplicated the outward appearance of the tobacco store down the street. The insurance company bordered the last house on the northeast corner of the side street, Indiana Avenue, where the children played in the backyard. Next to the side street a billboard advertised Asherah House: Bed and Breakfast at the end of the street. Turn here, it said, for an enjoyable night's rest and a delicious breakfast.

Immediately beyond the football complex and parking lots, both creek and highway nearly merged where passage had been narrowed by uplifted rock on the left and right. Normally, eroded uplifts would have created a larger strike valley, but here at the narrows, rushing water ravaged sedimentary deposits channeling silt though the narrows between the two hogbacks, and depositing debris left and right of the highway to the canyon. In flood stages, the water had backed up before the canyon and spilled over the creek bank into pasture land toward Jericho Springs. Winter storm gates stood ready to halt highway traffic leaving Rock Creek and traveling north. Right of the storm gate and extending to the hogback to the east of the creek, deer fence completed the barrier north of town at the highway.

Above the road on top the hogback and parallel to the deer fence and storm gate, the Rock Creek water tower perched before hogback crest as a sentry. Pigeons cooed from the tower. Karen climbed the steep slope at times on all fours to maintain footing. On top she resisted climbing both the ladder of the water tower and the eight foot crest of the hogback. Instead she enjoyed a crisp breeze on this elongated mound above the town. From here she used her camera to preserve a picture of the setting and then she counted the buildings below. Five houses bordered each side of Indiana Avenue and then the hotel. The last house on each side of the street rose three stories high. Left of the three stories, continuous clusters of mountain birch separated rows of houses from the ridge just east of the mound. Near the base of the mound where she stood, more ten foot deer fence blocked passage to or from Rock Creek. Below she noticed a footpath emerged from a thicket south of the hotel and its rear parking lot. The footpath continued through backyards on both sides of Indiana Avenue to the deer fence. Although the path continued, the fence blocked passage. North of the fence a series of ponds formed a marsh with cattails and willows separating the standing water. Karen figured this was where the antelope watered the night before. Though blocked by the deer fence, the footpath became a trail up and over the ridge east of the marsh.

Karen counted more roof tops. A total of ten houses bordered Indiana Avenue. She added three more to her count for the tobacco, antique, and real estate/ insurance office buildings east of the Valley Highway and five more west of the highway including, the concession stand, school, bus barn, post office, highway trailer, and volunteer fire depart. The hotel, convenience store, seven houses that bordered County Road 403, plus the boarded-up grocery store, four houses and one garage roof south of the convenience store made a total of thirty-four rooftops. Adding in the church in the glen, thirty-five buildings, some uncounted sheds, and one cemetery made up the sum total of Rock Creek, excluding mountain laurel, birch, cottonwood, and oak trees plus one creeping willow tree.

With further inspection Karen noted Rock Creek's fortress appearance. Each of four entrances could be barricaded. Winter storm gates blocked the highway when necessary. A cattle guard halted livestock entering town on County Road 403, and a deer fence closed the space below. East the ridge formed a wall. To the south the rugged creek canyon and mesa physically limited passage. The cattle guard and uplifted rock functioned the same way as the ridge and mesa on the west, while the hogback connected with the northern storm gate and deer fence.

Karen wondered whether Rock Creek was a fortress, a stronghold, or a refuge? Does it stand guard as the sentry to the valley? Is it a sanctuary? Or is it positioned as a vestibule, as in biblical times? The Canaanites built a city surrounded with walls. Behind the city gate, they built a vestibule with two stories. Above the first level, a walkway surrounded the open area below. If an enemy broke through the city gate, those inside could still control the battle. As the enemy entered, the defenders engaged them below. To maintain superior advantage, the defense dropped additional troops onto the floor of the vestibule below as needed. Archers attempted to slay the attackers in the narrows of the city gate complicating enemy entrance. Such strategy halted invasion forces, unless they could successfully scale the walls. Hot oil and more archers resisted that tactic.

North along the hogback, the valley opened up revealing ample pasture land on both sides of Rock Creek. Both Ridge View and Jericho Springs appeared in the distance, as did the road leading west into the mountains, south onto the mesa, and east over the ridge. As a physical science teacher, Karen contemplated all she saw by enjoying the rich diversity of the geologic features in the river valley. She wondered what a study of local history would reveal. Hopefully, she would have such opportunity to investigate beginning with the museum in Rock Creek. Sitting down at the southern base of the water tower, she emptied her bag from the convenience store and ate her snacks and drank her cola. Karen thumbed through the weekly paper.

Across town above on the mesa, the sun reflected on something metallic gold that caught her eye. Karen guessed the location was near where the footpath reached the top of the mesa from the footbridge below. "And there beckons tonight's adventure!" Karen declared.

Finishing her cola, sandwich, and snacks, Karen made an uneventful descent from the mound into the woods below and walked back to the hotel following the footpath. She determined not to be noticed, if possible, and avoided meeting anyone along the path. In the woods she picked up a large stone to use to pound nails gathered earlier at the entrance to the canyon. She would use it to pound the nails into her window frame. Karen felt even greater need for security now and decided to return to her room and learn more about the valley by reading the local newspaper.

Karen began to enter the hotel at the east side stairwell when she heard shouting and commotion inside the kitchen. Instead of going upstairs, she crept around to the kitchen back door and listened. From inside Karen heard someone had accused Sarah, the waitress, and Hannah, the desk clerk, of stealing Friday night's receipts. The cook came to their defense to no avail and was maligned. The wrath turned to the cook, as the accuser bewailed and slandered him, too. The women shouted back in his defense. Someone struck another. Women cried out sobbing that neither they nor the cook would cheat the accuser. More commotion then Hannah ran out the back door, passed Karen, and quickly ascended the stairwell behind her. Karen watched Hannah's assent, and then turned around when she heard the screen door slam again. This time Sarah ran out the door and sprinted up the footpath toward Indiana Avenue. Karen began to retreat, not knowing what to expect next, when a man wearing an apron came out the door backward. He fell off the porch onto the parking lot. His nose bled, and he shouted obscenities at his assailant. The cook threatened to kill the man that beat him.

In response two other men laughed at him saying he wouldn't have the guts or be able to find his way out of a bottle. They told him they couldn't believe he was a McNaughton. On cue the cook picked himself up, hurriedly walked to the dumpster, and looked for his bottle. His search became intense with lust. While Karen felt compassion for the man, she dared not say anything and unnerved she slowly climbed the stairs while shaking badly. She did not see the other hotel guest from room 319, who had witnessed all that transpired from the third floor landing of the stairwell. Dressed in black with short black hair and eyes, he retreated to his room where he waited until darkness enveloped the town before leaving the hotel to explore the town further.

Karen entered her room and heard sobbing from the next room. Immediately, she entered prayer and called upon the Lord to bring healing to those hurt by the words and actions downstairs. She asked that the truth be revealed and that the thief be exposed. Also, she pled for her own safety and for God to intercede so she could soon resolve her circumstances. This, Karen thought, is not a nice place.

Sobbing quieted next door. Taking the stone out of a plastic bag from her pocket and gathering her Bible off the dresser top, Karen searched deeper in her pocket for the nails she picked up earlier in the day. Finding them she put the rock and nails on her lamp table and her Bible on her bed. Remembering she wanted to fill the birdfeeder with sunflower seeds, she removed both packages from the convenience store bag and sat them on the bed. Retrieving the log cabin birdfeeder from the floor, she removed the chimney from the filler hole, opened the two packages of sunflower seeds, and poured them into the feeder. Opening the window, she set the feeder out the window on the edge of the catwalk, and then scanned the area. She didn't notice that something blocked the seeds from exiting one side of the birdfeeder cabin porch. Boisterous talk from the bar and restaurant not only disturbed her but also children at play in the backyard of the white house with the yellow trim by the road. As if responding to a fire drill at school, the disrupted children stopped their game and rushed to the back door of their home. As if the unruly noise startled the woman in room 216, she turned on her radio, and Karen heard some country western singer moaning about being lonesome and lost. How appropriate Karen thought.

Grasping the square headed nails in her hand, Karen's determination tempered the anger still within her. She hated violence yet could have easily resorted to it in response to the emotional abuse below. The incident stirred memories of what she had left behind, memories she hoped to process while away from her parent's home in Colorado Springs and her apartment in Quail Point. She hungered for freedom from the pain of memories and rebuked vengeful thoughts that entered her head. She had forgiven her offenders but had not been healed of their damage. In her anger she did not sin, yet she succeeded in hammering the nails into the window frame with an extra measure of clout to the thrust of the rock upon the nail head. Finally, Karen relaxed.

Sitting on her bed, Karen read articles in the weekly paper about the Tuesday school board meeting, Wednesday prayer meeting at the local church, Thursday city council meeting, the missing school teacher, and death of a young woman, who had lived at the Asherah Bed and Breakfast on Indiana Avenue. One article told about the city council meeting on Thursday night. One paragraph explained the planned condemnation of a house in Jericho Springs. She wondered why the house would be condemned and why it would hold so much interest. Next she read a brief explanation about a runaway teenager who had something to do with the issue. Wondering what had happened to the young male heir who had run-away from home, she felt convicted that the girl who took her life in Quail Point had been a runaway of sorts to escape her circumstances. Unfortunately, the girl had chosen a permanent solution to a temporary but difficult situation. Karen wondered why her former student hadn't chosen adoption for her unborn child.

Outside peculiar sounds disrupted her reading. Cough, cough, sputter, cough, sputter, boom. And again—cough, cough, sputter, cough, sputter, boom. Karen laughed and more positively said aloud, "What is next in this place of crazies! Without a doubt I'm not going to be able to wallow in self pity here."

Although Karen wished she could easily climb out the window to investigate, she resisted the urge to take the nails out of the window frame. She stepped back from the window in time not to disturb the first visitors to her cabin outside her window. Two pigeons from the water tower made the initial discovery and feasted upon the seeds. Karen watched them take their fill. Storm clouds moved into the valley, and the sunny day became chilled and darkened in the early evening.

"Fly away birds. Come back and visit another time. If you are lucky, there will be unsalted seed in my little cabin of a birdfeeder."

"Coo, coo."

"You're right," Karen mused, "I'm going coo, coo!"

Remembering the coughing sound, Karen wanted to see the automobile making the noise. She grabbed her Bible from the dresser top, left the room locking the door, and wandered downstairs into the lobby of the Stage Stop Hotel.

Noticing her note remained under the bell on the counter, she reclaimed it, dinged the bell, paused only briefly, then crossed the lobby and exited down the stairs and across the parking lot. With Bible in hand, Karen crossed the highway, while watching a scruffy old man climb into the cab of an old pickup truck by the last house on the west side of County Road 403 next to the lane leading to the church in the glen. He drove by Karen, waved with a toothless grin, and then turned left on 403. At the bridge the driver accelerated and the truck began its refrain of cough, cough, sputter, cough, sputter, boom.

Karen swatted at the blue haze in the gray truck's passing and walked down the lane toward the church in the glen. She circled the church and saw where the toothless man left a load of wood in a rickety shed. Joining the footpath, she followed it through the cemetery, admired the tree with thick branches at the bridge and crossed over the foot bridge, and onto the flood plain. She paused at the base of the mesa and prepared to climb to the top. Taking a breath and not looking behind, she began a strenuous climb. She likened her effort to *Pilgrim's Progress* and affirmed having a burden on her back that made this climb nearly impossible. Steeper than the hogback yet gentler than the creek wall, the narrow path bore evidence of other travelers having passed by perhaps to feed upon the wild strawberries. Fewmet lined the passage. Some of the deer dung remained fresh, while other decomposed alongside the trail. On top the mesa, Karen's effort earned the reward of a different view as she scanned the valley below. But that dims compared to the discovery awaiting her tonight and tomorrow.

MAKING A MEMORY
CHAPTER 5

*"...Go home to your own people and tell them how much the Lord
has done for you, and how he has had mercy on you." Mark 5:19*

On the north end of the valley, Ruth awakened first Saturday morning and instantly had headed for the kitchen to prepare breakfast. At the grocery store yesterday, she only purchased for last night's dinner and this morning's breakfast. Her choices were expensive. She made certain Rob did not see what she selected. When she had ordered him away from the checkout stand, he had indulged her knowing her intentions. Out of character she had planned this meal to be unforgettable. Ruth had pledged to herself that breakfast would be sumptuous, enough to leave an indelible imprint on Rob's mind.

Rob wakened to the fragrance of good things cookin'. Andy stirred as well. Entering the kitchen, Rob gazed at his woman. She had been such a delight the night before. Thinking of her long suffering toward him and their restored marriage brought tears to his eyes. Rob marveled now at Ruth's enthusiasm in the kitchen, her sense of timing in bringing all the items to the table piping hot.

"Hey," said Rob.

"Good morning! Come here, you honey-hunk of burnin' love! Now you can see what I'm fixin' for you, Rob."

"Hmmm, good things from the kitchen, love."

Wearing blue jeans and a long sleeved, red checkered flannel shirt, Andy burst into the kitchen, while tripping on untied shoelaces. Andy slid to his chair like a baseball player stealing a base would rise on the base ready to advance with an errant throw. Getting up and sitting down in seemingly one motion, Andy began his typical series of non-stop questions ended with his asking, "How soon do we leave for town?"

"Hold on Son. We have some things to talk about before we get started," said Rob who added, "Besides you and I are going to do the dishes after breakfast."

"Daaaad!"

"Get used to it. That's a change in the Browning household. The men are going

51

to help more. It's a manly thing? Besides I hear it pays dividends to do the dishes," Rob replied with a smile.

Ruth turned, grinned at Rob, and said, "I don't know what you have been reading or who you have been listening too, but keep it up."

With that Ruth graced the table with a pound of lean, thin sliced bacon cooked but still soft; buttermilk pancakes with bananas and walnuts mixed into the batter; a hot pitcher of maple syrup; a carton of sour cream; and hash brown potatoes with cheddar cheese scattered on top. Ruth followed with a "special recipe" omelet filled with mushrooms, artichoke hearts, scallions, Swiss cheese, and green chilies. Ruth poured a small glass of fresh squeezed orange juice for both Rob and Andy. In unison Rob sipped from a mug of strong Columbian coffee, while Andy took a gulp of milk from a blue plastic tumbler. Together they emptied their small glasses of orange juice.

Remembering a new found priority, Rob interrupted the meal with prayer. The prayer included appreciative words about the well planned meal. Rob praised Ruth for creating something wonderful to eat.

Early in their marriage, most everyone had attested to Ruth's culinary skills. Rob took genuine pride in having a good cook for a wife. Privately, his friends acknowledged Ruth as the best cook in their group. That reputation had slipped the last couple of years or so ago, as had his sensitivity toward helping around the house. Now both husband and wife privately committed to be more sensitive to the needs of the other. He intended for mealtime to be a family event, a time of building memories not only in eating but also in the fellowship and sharing together. Rob figured his job was to set the standard.

Finishing the meal Rob held true to his pledge. He washed, while Andy dried the dishes. This time, Ruth finished a second cup of coffee and took pleasure in their grateful attention.

"All done," said Rob, and then added, "Let's plan a little before we start the day."

Ruth responded with, "What's on the agenda?"

"Getting the ducks and the chickens and the dog and cat and feed and what else Dad?"

"Well, we have a snag there. When I stopped last night, Whitney said they wouldn't be getting any more baby chicks or ducklings. He had some on order, but he already sold them. Whitney did check with his friend Irv Moss, who has three adult ducks he will give to a good family. Irv also has someone I want you two to meet."

"Rob, who is it?"

"Now, hold on, it's a surprise and don't pressure me. You know how hard it is for me to keep a secret."

"Dad, who is it? Huh, huh, huh!"

"Whoa now, if it is what I suspect, we need to get some understandings in place before we get started. I'll bet whoever or whatever it is has to be fed, watered, and cleaned up after. If it's a pup, it stays outdoors."

"It is!"

"Aw, Mom, couldn't it sleep in my room?"

"No, from the get-- go, he stays outdoors."

"She."

"She?"

"The Princess Freda Louise."

"Sounds like she has good breeding, Rob, depending on what kind of dog she is, we may need to do something to make sure the ducks are safe."

"What do you mean, Mom?"

"Some dogs will kill most everything on a farm. Sometimes that's good. Most often, it's not."

"When is it not good, Mom?"

"When you want to have ducks!"

"I want to have ducks."

"Then first order of business is for us to do as Mom said. We build a coop for the ducks to live in, and we put a good wire fence around it. Freda isn't the only predator we will have to watch out for. Since Freda is a pup, we will need to make certain she is safe with a good place to sleep," summarized Rob.

"And real nice dishes to eat out of?" asserted Andy

"And dishes," Mom agreed with a nod.

The family planned how they would change the outbuildings to accommodate the ducks and the Princess Freda Louise. On paper, Rob designed a coop and pen. Together, Mom, Dad, and Son negotiated their purchases and agenda for the day. Laughter and humor set the tone. Each listened to the other. No one made disparaging remarks. The family explored ideas without rejection. Together, they began to create a memory.

The Brownings decided to buy four sheets of plywood measuring four feet by eight feet, roofing shingles and three inch nails, one fifty foot roll of chicken wire, two eight foot dowels, one role of asphalt roofing, one bale of straw, one five gallon bucket, six bags of pre-mixed concrete compound, eighteen two by four by eights, one long handled shovel, one short handle shovel, one spade, six four by four's ten feet long, one small bucket of tar, one bag of wood chips to make a bed for the puppy, one child's wading pool with a four foot diameter. Andy wanted a bigger wading pool, but Rob convinced him a four foot pool would be big enough for three ducks to swim in. Besides Rob told Andy it needed to fit inside the pen around the coop. They agreed they couldn't call it a chicken coop, because they wouldn't have any chickens for a while. They talked about calling it a duck pen or duck coop, which became "da'coop." In unison they scrapped the idea. Mom and Dad assigned Andy the job of naming the coop that was not a coop.

The family also worked out an agenda to go grocery shopping, pick up the mail at the post office, purchase a newspaper, select curtains at the dime store, eat lunch at the Cozy Corner Café, and then stop at the feed and lumber store to adopt the Princess Freda Louise. Rob officially concluded the family council meeting complaining how Ruth and Andrew twisted his arm to find out about Freda.

"Oh Dad," replied Andy, "This is the bestus plan of all." Ruth pinched herself and smiled.

The Brownings cleaned up and made themselves presentable for an excursion to the city albeit a short one. Rob and Andy greeted Ruth at the front door with their light blue Chevy station wagon. Rob accelerated the 327 cubic inch engine, and they remarked about the thrust of the old car with the four barrel carburetor. The Chevy skidded to a halt where the driveway met County Road 403. The paper carrier hailed them from an old green Toyota station wagon with a large dent in the passenger's side rear door. A fish emblem distinguished the rear hatchback.

Rob greeted Ken Bond and his two daughters, Krystal and Kristin. Since the local paper was published on Wednesday, Rob registered to receive the *Outcry* and a daily and Sunday subscription to the Denver Post. Ken informed Rob that Kristin threw the papers out the passenger side front window, while Krystal folded them in the rear compartment. Only Dad got to drive. Rob learned Kristin was nine and Krystal seven years old, the same as Andy. Ken also invited the Brownings to attend worship services at the Baptist church in Jericho Springs. Rob committed to attend not for tomorrow but the following weekend. Again Ruth pinched herself. Ruth asked about mid-week services to which Ken urged them to attend the Wednesday evening prayer meeting. Without her asking, Rob nodded an affirmative.

The Brownings continued their trek to town and stopped first at the grocery store. Ruth noted an ad to redeem grocery coupons for triple their face value. It caused a flashback memory of an argument she had once with Rob about her not being frugal. She resolved to clip coupons and eliminate one of his long standing complaints. He made an unplanned stop at the liquor store and came out with a twelve pack of Coors Beer, Extra Gold. Ruth shivered but resolved to see how Rob handled drinking. Andy watched his mom.

The Brownings arrived at their next stop, the dime store, where Ruth purchased curtains. She hoped to have a sewing machine some day. Rob and Andy chose a child's blue wading pool with Loony Tunes cartoon characters on the side wall. They stopped at the post office, picked up mail, and arrived at the Cozy Corner Café for an early lunch. While seated in a booth by the street-side window, Rob and Ruth heard distressing gossip from people seated at the counter next to them. The Brownings felt ill at ease with the coarse talk. Ruth squirmed wishing Andy had not heard what was said. They pretended not to listen and gave no indication of doing so. Customers watched the Brownings. While Rob paid the check and purchased the recent copy of the local weekly newspaper, Andy and Ruth thumbed through a counter display of books. Ruth recognized some of the authors, and tugged on Rob's coat to get his attention. Though irritated with how Ruth interrupted him, Rob endured Ruth's distraction.

"Ruth, what is it?"

"Look at this."

Rob took the book and asked the clerk to wait, that there might be something to add to their bill.

"*Making Memories*, this is what I've been talking about. Having talks around the kitchen table and planning for vacations and stuff, or just having conversations. This has all kinds of projects and activities to do as a family," commented Rob.

"And ways to bring Christ into the center of them," added Ruth, "Buy it please."

And he did.

And Ruth smiled.

Waiting behind the family in line to pay, the customers from the counter continued their embarrassing conversation. Surprised at the lack of consideration, the Brownings left in disgust and walked across the street toward the lumber yard. On the way, Rob and Ruth agreed not to discuss what they heard at the Cozy Corner Café until later when they got home.

The Rock Creek Valley Feed and Lumber Store survived hard times in the valley long before it became a feed and lumber store. The boom and bust cycle of mining; the Great Depression; the World Wars, Korea and Vietnam; the turbulent '60's; the energy crisis of the '70's; and recession politics had taken their toll. As this building passed to new generations of owners, business focus changed.

Originally, the building had been the livery for mounts ridden by pony express riders headed for Rock Creek. Later the McNaughton family, who now owned the land and buildings, purchased much of the valley west of the creek to run cattle. When miners became settlers, McNaughton interests switched from ranching to land development. Jericho Springs became a city. The population center shifted there from Rock Creek and its fort. Ridge View incorporated later and became the valley's transportation center for gold mining, timber, and cattle ranching interests. Next, the McNaughton's officially added Lumber to the store's name.

Rock Creek, the valley's original town, eventually declined. In the early years, Rock Creek had been a trading post for trappers and other frontiersmen. East of town buffalo hunters drove bison over the ridge to their deaths below and traded the hides at the post. During Indian wars that accompanied the discovery of gold, the U.S. Army conscripted the trading post and fortified the structure to protect settlers and miners from so called area savages. With the advent of farming and ranching, Rock Creek became the end of the line for stage coach service. The military demolished the fort, except for what remained as the Stage Stop Hotel. Since it is land locked by the canyon, ridge, mesa, and hogbacks, Rock Creek remained a stronghold and fortress of sorts. So-called savages were not of Native American heritage, nor had they ever been.

In spite of the changes, the McNaughton's' controlled most of the valley. Historically, very little has happened without their blessing. People still guard what they say about a McNaughton. Often resident gossips had earned harsh consequences when forgetting they were gossiping with kin of a McNaughton. This included area Native Americans. An early McNaughton married the child or grandchild of a Ute chieftain and sired several children with distinct Indian features and red hair.

Occasionally, opposition surfaced when new people moved into the valley, older families knew better. New people often tried to do things their way instead of the McNaughton way. Most adopted the traditions and practices of the status quo, the McNaughton's method of doing things. Few old families resisted intermarriage with the McNaughton clan. Sometimes intermarriage brought peace with the clan. To speak against or challenge a McNaughton still resulted in harsh, unwanted consequences. More than one cemetery plot held the remains of a man or woman killed in a gun or knife fight with a clan member. In spite of this prestige and power, the McNaughton clan had leaned toward honesty and fair play. Generally, they had been known as pleasant and friendly people, yet protective of their own to a fault.

Whitney "Red" McNaughton greeted the Browning family at the lumber company door. Red looked Ruth over and complimented Rob on his nice looking family. Rob smiled and cautioned Ruth about Whitney's reputation as a lady's man. Whitney took Rob's statement as a compliment and proudly grinned.

"Don't you worry a bit, Mrs. Browning, one thing about us McNaughtons is that we have a great fondness and appreciation for a good woman. I mean this in the most honorable sense. It's a family tradition. Great, great, Grandpa Lou was so appreciative, it's said he took many a Ute woman as wives. I heard he bought an Arapahoe girl from one of the Ute chiefs, but wore her out and she ran off after only a couple of months with him."

The Brownings joined Whitney in laughter, as did other customers, who had been eavesdropping.

Regaining composure Whitney said, "I suppose you've come to get my girlfriend and the ducks Irv left for you. Anything else you need today?"

"Matter of fact we have some building to do. Since you don't have any chickens or baby ducks for us, I guess we better stick to building our chicken coop."

"The Palace!"

"What's that, boy?" asked Red.

"The Palace, my dad said I could name the chicken coop, so I named it the Palace."

"You mean like for royalty?"

"The ducks will be neighbors of the Princess Freda Louise, so they have to live in a Palace."

"Makes sense to me," said Whitney with a smile, "for sure you folks better build the Palace before you get your other birds. By next spring we will order you some special birds to live in the Palace. Bet they'll lay golden eggs! With your son's imagination, you just may find some golden eggs."

"I'll bet with the price of feed, that would be a just return," added Ruth.

"That reminds me," said Rob, "you better add twenty pounds of cracked corn to our order."

Whitney took the order, looked it over, and asked, "You're building a chicken coop with a fence around a yard and you want to have a door, so you can lock the ducks inside, right?"

Rob nodded agreement and quizzed, "Have I forgotten something?"

"I'd say you need two hinges and a handle for your door and a heavy duty stapler and about two hundred staples to attach the chicken wire to fence posts. You probably need more two by fours if you are building a frame at the top and bottom of the fence. What about nesting boxes? Chickens are particular, but ducks lay eggs anywhere. You need to have your nests well above the floor for laying hens. You need some one by six's and one by twelve's. Straw is good enough for ducks."

"How about adding two one by twelve's, eight feet long. Two one by six's, eight feet long and six more two by four by eights," concluded Rob, but he wondered if staples would be strong enough. "Are you sure staples will be strong enough?"

Whitney nodded affirmatively, and then added, "Someone would have to purposely attempt to get through the fencing, but I'm pretty sure staples will do the job."

"Okay," Rob said, "if they don't hold, I'll be back to get something else."

"And now, I'll get my little girl." With authority, Whitney commanded his helper to fill the Browning's order and to bring out the three white ducks Irv Moss had left for Rob.

After waiting for the order to be filled, Rob, Ruth, and Andy inspected the merchandise and nodded hello to other customers. Andy discovered the tack and quizzically looked at his mom. Shaking her head Ruth responded with a distinct non verbal no, followed by an equally distinct but spoken, "No horses. I haven't heard of horses laying golden eggs, not even in fairy tales!"

Flashing his broad smile, Whitney emerged from the store room with a sizable ball of white fur held in his large hands. Whitney held the pup at her neck, eye to eye before him, while a spongy pink tongue scraped across his reddish beard repeatedly in rapid fire.

"Here she is folks, The Princess Freda Louise, daughter of Duchess, twice Rock Creek Valley Grand Champion.

On cue Freda turned to face the Brownings, struck a pose, and then wiggled in Whitney's huge hands. A picture of excitement and pent up energy, the little girl slobbered hello to Andy. As Whitney handed Freda over to Andy, he took Freda in his arms and caressed her.

"Dad, Freda's beautiful!"

"Rob, she's one of the ugliest dogs I've ever seen!" exclaimed Ruth.

Whitney laughed, "The Princess Freda Louise is something special. If her colors were reversed, you would have a hard time buying her.

"What do you mean, Whitney?"

"What Whitney means, Ruth, is this pup will be destroyed today, if we don't take her. A white boxer is a throwback to the English Bull. See her smashed in face and bowed legs. Freda would have been okay if the brindle spot over her eye was white and the rest of her body brindle. She's a runt and her lower jaw protrudes terribly. Even though Freda comes from royal blood lines, my friend, Irv Moss, wouldn't want her bred. She would tarnish the lines. We could get papers on her, but she is of no value."

"Rob's right, Ruth, seems sad but that's her fate. Irv protects the blood lines, but his heart is tender. He wanted to keep her for a pet but that doesn't work when you have a lot of other dogs to worry about. I guess an extra mouth to feed makes enough difference. What do you think? She's yours at no charge."

Ruth took Freda from Andy and held her above her head. Ruth said, "Well little girl, you may be ugly, but you are too precious to be destroyed."

On cue Freda peed with excitement.

Whitney laughed, "After that display of control, I better tell you quickly that her mother, the Duchess, is two time Grand Champion in Dog Obedience. County Champion! I hope that is encouraging!"

"Agreed," Rob added, "Good thing she's a girl. Ruth would have strangled her!"

"Wow, Mom! A royal champion! We have a champion in the family now!"

"Well, good luck folks. I see Ellis has your order ready. I hope you can load it in your station wagon. If not, you can make another trip," Whitney said, then speaking directly to Ruth, "Mrs. Browning and Andy, it is a pleasure to meet you two. Bring Freda around to see me sometime, will ya?"

"You bet, once she learns more control, royal demeanor!" declared Ruth.

"Thank you, Mr. Whitney," added Andy, then choking with emotion, "I'll take real good care of the Princess. Mom's gonna show me how. I never had a dog before. Never had anything great as Freda. I would almost trade the baseball card collection Dad gave me for her if I had it here and it was okay with Pop. Oh, except for third baseman Mike Schmidt of the Phillies. He's my Dad's favorite player. Dad watched him play ball at Veterans' Stadium in Philadelphia. Oh! Oh! I forgot Dad said the Killer was the greatest. Dad said Harmon Killebrew was the bestus to play baseball and a real gentleman. I don't know why, but my dad does!"

Ellis led the Brownings to the loading dock and helped them unload their groceries from the station wagon in order to load it again with building and pet supplies. The four foot by eight foot plywood boards had to be tied to the luggage rack, but the rest of the building and feed supplies fit behind the front bench seat. Groceries and other purchases flanked the construction materials. The family inspected the three ducks with delight. Ellis introduced Donald, Daisy, and

Quackers to the Brownings. Andy had his mom hold Freda, while he struggled with Quackers. She quacked continuously and was not satisfied until returned to the cardboard box with Donald and Daisy. When questioned by Andy, Ellis explained that Donald was a boy duck and that if Donald were a wild duck he would have green feathers covering his head to reveal he's a boy, but Daisy and Quackers would lay eggs. Secured behind the packages with the box lid folded down, Donald and Daisy quieted down; however, Quackers continued her refrain. The Brownings thanked Ellis for his help and waved goodbye to Whitney. They left with The Princess Freda Louise perched on Andy's lap. Each front paw wrapped around opposite sides of Andy's neck, while Freda rested her head on his right shoulder. As expected, Andy asked his parents if he could grow feathers, but if he couldn't he thought a Mohawk haircut would be needed to prove he is a boy.

Before Ellis returned inside the store, a man approached him. He was one of the men who had been talking at the counter in the Cozy Corner Café. He greeted Ellis, "Hey, Ellis!"

"Hey, yourself, Mr. Bailey."

"Is Red here today? I need to talk to him."

"Yup, he's probably gone to the store room to sort supplies. We have an order coming in Monday."

"Thanks, Ellis, who were the folks that just left in the loaded down station wagon?"

"That's the Brownings. I hope they don't bust a spring"

"They look like a nice family. Where do they live?"

"They're new. Live the other side of the bridge on 403. You know, where the creek leaves the plains and flows down the falls from the ridge into the valley. He's the new guy runnin' the line crew for the utility company. Red said he's all right, so he must be."

"Is he related in the valley?"

"Don't know, but the boy said his dad was from Philadelphia, so I don't think so. Say, why not introduce yourself, you would like them, Sheriff."

After returning home and unloading the station wagon, the Brownings prepared to construct the coop and fence to secure the ducks from Freda. Rob gathered his tools, while Ruth and Andy put away the groceries and other supplies. Rob laid out the lumber and wire near the out building and entertained Freda. Rob stored Freda's feed in the livestock shed and made her a bed of wood chips and shavings bought from Whitney. Shortly, Andy bolted from the house and joined his dad. Ruth followed eagerly.

The Brownings followed their design for The Palace with Rob digging holes for the fence posts, while Andy hauled water and poured it in the wading pool that Rob had already set in the ground. Mom opened cement bags. Rob sawed the posts to length, while Ruth prepared the cement mix in a five gallon bucket. Andy held the posts in place, while Rob poured the cement around the posts centered in the holes. Ruth smoothed the mixture, while Freda chewed rigorously on Andy's pant legs.

Once the posts were set, Andy finished filling the plastic duck pond, while Rob and Ruth framed the coop and made stairs for its entrance. Mom and Dad cut pieces for the coop to length. Dad hammered nails through two by fours into the posts, while Mom held the board's other end on the next post. Andy filled the plastic bucket with wood scrap, then collapsed in feigned exhaustion before he finished and pleaded for help. "Dad, how much water does a duck have to have before a duck can do its duck thing?"

"Only to the top of his quacker!"

"Where is his quacker, Dad?"

"In the saltine box, silly."

"Well, that's a fine kettle of duck soup you two!" chided Mom.

"Dad, do you think Mom knows where a duck keeps his crackers," asked the Son.

"Only if we bought some from the grocery store," speculated Dad.

"This? This is duck soup?" summarized Mom.

"Then do I need more water?" asked Son.

"You need much more water. It looks like I should have gotten a hose at the store," concluded Dad.

The Brownings continued and grew sillier as they enjoyed one another's company and the pleasure of creating something they had planned together. With a circular saw, Rob had cut the coop sides and floor to size and shape, made half a pitched roof, and nailed the coop to the side of the building just behind a side door. Two dowels joined front to back, and formed two long perches for future chicken inhabitants. He left an open space at the rear, so the coop could be cleaned out. With the roof, sides, and flooring in place, he turned to the inside construction. He made two shelves from one-by-twelves and installed them several feet above the floor. On these he placed wooden nesting boxes, and then cut and installed a detachable covering for where he left space in the floor for cleaning the coop. Next, he attached the steps and finished by nailing forest green asphalt shingles to the roof. Rob instructed Andy in spreading straw, while Rob assembled a door and attached it to the entry way. Ruth added the final touch by hammering a nail through a small piece of wood used as a door lock.

"Pop! Sound a drum roll!" commanded Ruth.

"Baaaroooooomm!" Rob sounded and proclaimed, "Presenting 'The Palace', constructed by the Browning Family."

"Andy, bring Donald, Daisy, and Quackers," Rob added, "and Ruth, please get something for feed and water. I'll get water."

"Dad, we're not done. It doesn't have a sign."

"Son, that will be your job this week."

"Huh?" questioned Andy.

"To make a sign, we forgot that part of our plan."

"Rob, between you and Whitney, I'm amazed we forgot anything. I'm more amazed no one got mad or lost their temper. I'm more than amazed. You've made me so happy," added Ruth as she ran to the house with tears streaming down her face.

"What's wrong with Mom, Dad? I thought she said she was happy."

"It's a mother thing, Son. And I'm just learning how to deal with tears. Sometimes tears from a woman will make a man do things he normally wouldn't do. Sometimes tears will make a man be quiet when he should say something. Sometimes tears will frustrate a man so much he will say or do something he regrets later. The woman will think he's mad at her and he may think so too! But what's really happening is that the man doesn't know what to do. So he acts angry. No. It's more like he is mad. Sort of like out of his head, exasperated because he doesn't really know how he feels. He just knows that somehow he hurt the one he loves the most and doesn't know what to do next. A man can be the greatest problem solver and be totally incapacitated by his woman's tears. It's just a pitiful thing, Son! Exasperating!"

"Oh, I know that word. Mom said I exasperate her a lot."

"That's men and women, Son. We exasperate each other, sometimes on purpose. And when we do, it's because we don't like being bossed or corrected, or we don't like being wrong about something and we get even."

"Pop."

"Yes, Son."

"Can I ask you a question?"

"Yes, I think you just did."

"Well, yeah, but here's another. Pop, we built the Palace and put a door on it, and we made some stairs, and put a water pool in the ground, and set up fence poles. But, Dad. how are we gonna keep the ducks inside the pen when we haven't put any wire on the fence posts?"

"Pretty tricky, I'll have to admit."

"Am I missing something here?"

"Ask your mom soon as she gets back. Now go get the ducks, but don't let them out of the box."

All three returned with feed, water, bowls, ducks, and Freda. Mom explained to Andy that cement had to set up and dry before any additional tension could be placed on the posts. They introduced Freda to the ducks and scolded her immediately for chasing them. Rob put the ducks in the coop and then shut and locked the door. The Brownings stood back with arms around each other's waist and shoulders. They admired their handy work. They called it a day.

"Is that the dinner bell, Mom?"

"Not quite dinner, Son, but soon. Are you hungry?"

"Yes, I so hungry I could eat a ..."

"A duck, a chicken?"

"We aren't ever gonna' eat our ducks or our chickens when we get them. Say it isn't so, Dad, Mom!"

"Hmm, we better think that over. We're going to eat eggs though. No argument about that," clarified Dad.

"Rob, do you know what I would like to do after dinner?"

"Yes, honey, I do. You are just dying to watch television and have a can of beer. Just leanin' back, real relaxed and sippin' a beer. Right?"

"Dad, is this one of those zasperations?" asked Andy.

"What's that, you two?" questioned Ruth.

"Man talk, honey. Man talk. I'll tell you about it after dinner. We need to talk about what we heard at the Cozy Corner Café too. Now, what is it you would like to do?"

"If it's not too late, I'd like to walk to the creek. You know by the bridge, where the water fall is. I'd like to take a towel with us and walk over there and put my feet in the cool water and just soak them."

"Too bad you don't have your bathing suit. We could just wear our swim suits and bathrobes or better yet we could go skinny dippin!"

"Yahoo, Mom! Let's go skinny dippin!"

"Rob, I can see it now. We're going to have a little nudist on our hands."

"I can see it now too, honey, and you will be beautiful," added Rob with an appreciative grin, ear to ear. Then they entered the house with Rob singing, "Tonight, tonight."

A memory was made.

MYSTERIES
CHAPTER 6

"And we know that in all things God works for the
good of those who love him, who have been called
according to his purpose." Romans 8:28

Early Saturday evening several yards from the edge of the mesa on Claymore Flats, a park bench stood perched over looking Rock Creek near the trail from the valley. Concrete held it firmly in place. After the arduous climb to the top of the mesa, Karen sat admiring the valley and viewed land west of the uplifted rock for the first time. In the distance a dirt road began where County Road 403 entered the town of Jericho Springs. It headed south to the mesa and west into a mountain valley where she noticed an odd scar on the mountain. She recognized it resulted from a rockslide and formed the distinct shape of a lamb. Lush meadow spanned the landscape where Rock Creek had often flooded the plain. In the town of Rock Creek, flood waters occasionally spilled over the creek bank primarily west of the high school and into the orchards south of the bridge over CR 403. Mountain tributaries also sometimes spilled water east of Jericho Springs. One creek drained the mesa watershed and channeled water from the mountain valley above Jericho Springs. Both met near Jericho Springs. She speculated both could flood the pasture land between Jericho Springs and the town of Rock Creek. Karen guessed a hundred head of cattle grazed leisurely in open range from deer fence and cattle guards west of Rock Creek to Jericho Springs.

The sun began setting as evening shadows started reclaiming the countryside. Dark brooding storm clouds entered the valley from the north bringing a wintry chill to the late summer air. Already the temperature made a rapid decent. Knowing little time for exploration remained before dark, Karen left her Bible on the park bench and briskly walked to the edge of a forest. She saw golden sunlight still reflecting from an object in the woods.

Observing her route to discover the golden gleam in the forest, Karen realized the mesa was also open range. She discovered several large bulls dotted a meadow south by what must be where the waterfall emptied into the canyon. Sensing potential danger Karen hurried into the trees knowing that the cool but gentle wind carried her scent and might disturb the dullards at the water. Immediately, Karen discovered another much smaller graveyard, than the cemetery surrounding the church below the mesa. Wrought iron fencing embraced few graves. One in particular captured Karen's sight.

Karen read a marker with a golden placard that created the reflection she had seen earlier from the hogback north of town: Mary McNaughton Claymore, born on Colorado Day, August 1, 1945, and died August 31, 1970, at age 25. The inscription: Beloved Wife and Best Friend. Next to her stone laid that of an infant: John Paul, Son of Adam and Mary Claymore, born and died in childbirth, August 31, 1970. The inscription: Safe with Jesus by God's Grace. The engraving on each marker portrayed the resurrected Christ triumphantly waiting with outstretched arms.

Other markers identified more Claymores. James Franklin Claymore, Father. Bessie Braley Claymore, Mother. Victoria Jaramillo Claymore, Grandmother. Willis Blair Claymore, Grandfather. Karen realized the connection with the rancher she met with Morris, the bus driver, Friday morning and also with most of the graves in the cemetery at the church. Adam Claymore was related to all buried here in one way or another. She wondered about the details of the rest of Adam's story and about his beloved wife, his best friend. When she realized Friday morning would have been his wife's birthday, her heart turned tender toward Adam Claymore, a man who honored his wife so richly. How sad she thought that he had lost his young wife and newborn child on the same day. She wanted to inspect more standing stones, but sadly left the forest. Karen grieved for Adam.

Shadows from the mountains had darkened the forest and meadow to the edge of the mesa as dusk captured the valley. Karen returned to the park bench oblivious of the nearness of the bulls. She sat, watched the growing shadow, and prayed, as if he sat with her on the bench. "Father, how marvelous you are in all your majesty that you would choose me to be yours. Thank you for the provision of your son, Jesus, as payment for my sins and redemption for my life. In return this day and each day, Father, I give my life back to you to be of service in building your kingdom. Father, grant me the privilege of reflecting the beauty of Jesus in me. Enable me to be an agent of healing to hurting people, like Adam Claymore, Hannah, Sarah, and Ruth Browning. Let me be a beacon of light in a darkened land. Make me a seeker of your truth. Heal me Father of my wounds and restore to me the pleasure of relating to people without fear of hurt in trusted relationships."

Karen paused for a moment, listened, and then continued her conversation, "Father, today I have learned much about the town below. Things I do not like and I know you abhor. Evil has a stronghold there, a fortress Father, but you enable your people to be overcomers. Father, I know not what is in store for me, but I trust you have plans for me and they are designed to make me prosper in your ways. Father, I ask you in the name of Jesus to tear down the walls of that fortress and others like it in this valley. Break down the strongholds, so your people may enter in and seize the land for you. Father in praying for this, I don't know if I will get a job here or not, but I am here for one week. I ask you to make clear to me what I should do while I am here. Then Father, grant me the strength to serve you in this land. Let me be a source of kindness, gentleness, oh Holy Lord! How precious you are. Thank you, sweet Jesus. How I look forward to worshipping you in that little church tomorrow morning."

City walls shook. Hope would bloom, healing would begin, and by God's grace and mercy forgiveness would be given person to person, and relationship would be restored and repaired. In response, sap surged to limbs of the Live Oak on its north and east sides.

Darkness settled in and Karen trembled momentarily, anxiously knowing the path she must descend. A cold nose touched Karen's neck startling her to attention, as she surmised a bull had discovered her and made his presence known. Instead it was that of a colt, who had found her and gently said hello. He bolted away from her at her anxious response and disappeared into the forest.

"Oh, how precious, I wish you would have stayed here. I'm sorry I scared you little horse. I see not everything around here is evil."

On that thought Karen moved to the edge of the mesa and looked below. Shadows distorted the features of the trail downward. Gray storm clouds blanketed the valley sky. Nearly out of sight, Karen glanced backward to where the cemetery hid in the forest. She saw a black image low to the ground. Fearful and with just reason, Karen thought the image she had seen was a bear and made rapid descent down the trail from the mesa to the path below. Caught in fear, Karen did not see the horseman nor his black Gordon setter named Big Foot.

At the creek by the water fall, Adam thought he'd seen a vision. His heart had pounded. The willowy shape on the park bench overlooking Rock Creek had taken his breath away. The figure had sat like Mary sat. That was why he had built the bench. Mary had loved to watch the sunset and though the town of Rock Creek had often brought sadness, she had a missionary's heart for the few people there. Mary had favored attending services at the little church in the glen, as did Adam's grandmother Victoria. The Jaramillo's had been early settlers in Rock Creek. In fact, Grandpa Jaramillo's family came to the valley because of the fort. He had been a non-commissioned officer, who married one of the valley girls and built the church, while serving in the Cavalry.

Adam had ridden into the woods with Big Foot to observe the woman and not disturb her. The fact she had sat there enjoying the view endeared her to him. His heart had tugged in his chest when approaching the gravesite, then had eased its pull as he watched. Unfortunately the foal had approached the vision and disturbed her. She left hurriedly climbing down the trail to Rock Creek.

With Big Foot outdistancing him, Adam rode to the bench as Big Foot had a head start from the edge of the forest. At the bench Adam climbed down from the mare and retrieved the Bible the woman had forgotten. He read the inscription: "To Karen Gustafson on the Day of Your Baptism and 12th Birthday---May 30, 1964. May you always look to the Word to light your pathway. With love, Mom and Dad." After he had figured the math, Adam said, "She's 28 and I'm 39. I wonder if she would consider me too old."

With Bible in hand, Adam climbed back onto the saddle, placed the Bible in his saddle bag, and watched his vision come to life below as Karen walked across the field to the cattle guard on County Road 403. "Stay there lovely lady, and somehow I will find you tomorrow. Oh Lord, may it be so. Father, you are in charge of circumstances and you bring hope in the midst of my sadness," Adam prayed. Although wintry clouds had entered in, Adam galloped off toward home freed from depression, his spirits lifted. Big Foot and the foal trailed behind.

Once regaining her composure, Karen had completed her descent but did not cross the foot bridge by the cemetery. Instead she had walked through the field between the mesa and County Road 403 to where the cattle guard protected the town from straying cows and steers. At the bridge Karen looked back to where she had come from and said aloud, "How quickly my courage is challenged. How quickly I see how I am easily panicked with fear of the unknown. Not by my strength, but by his alone. I should call my parents for prayer support to overcome what might lie ahead."

Karen scampered from the bridge in time to escape the arrival of several cars and trucks that crossed the bridge, stopped momentarily at the stop sign, then crossed the highway, and halted in the parking lot of the Stage Stop Hotel. Lively music echoed from the bar, and she began to get a taste of Saturday night in Rock Creek. Once inside the hotel, Karen hurried to her room not wanting to return downstairs yet at the same time very hungry.

In Jericho Springs near the road above the three story house and the tall oak tree, hunger had overcome a need for shadows, bringing danger in lieu of safety. The bearded man in the tan trench coat risked exposure and left the safety of his hiding place. He exited the back porch door then secured it. With him, he carried his suitcase filled with dirty clothes. Since he had been on the road for more than a week without a chance to cleanup, a bath seemed a welcomed but unlikely prospect for now. Washing his clothes necessitated use of a laundromat in town, unless he wanted to beat them on a rock in the mineral pools. He considered that option and discounted it, but a bath there later was a must. He needed a good meal and wanted something other than his usual meal in a can. Though low on cash, he felt like rewarding himself. He needed to read the local newspaper too. Rather than go directly into town, he made a circuitous route out from back door and around the volcanic mound to the right and over protruding roots from the mammoth Live Oak above him. He paused here knowing no one could see him, peered briefly at the trunk of the tree, imagined he saw a Christ figure there in the bark, then kicked one root and surprisingly found green life under the exterior root bark. Had he turned left at the mound he would have been seen from the street by the cyclist.

"How dry the ground," he murmured, "and warm the rubble on the slope of the mound." He wondered when the tree began to grow, as he trudged up the slope with the tree temporarily out of view, while looking for but finding no acorns amongst debris. Behind him trees on the street curb were dwarfed in comparison. Though they reached twenty feet and more skyward, the mound matched their height and the oak soared beyond the cone of the mound. Before him basalt rock and loam allowed a variety of grasses, but not much prospered on the northwest side of the mound. What might grow competed with the network of roots from the once mighty Live Oak.

Suitcase in hand, he ascended boulders west of the mound where he stopped eye level just above the base of the tree. Just above ground, the tree divided into four separate but connected trunks, each situated north, south, east and west. With sadness he studied the lifelessness of the mighty oak. This tree lost its health a long time ago he thought. Leafless, infested with insects, lifeless with so many dead branches. What few acorns still clung to the ends of branches seemed shriveled. He wondered if it would help to clear out the dead, to prune it. He wondered if there would be any chance for it to recover and come back to life. With the mineral water not too far away, he wondered why the tree did not prosper. Why had the fruit shriveled?

"Maybe it just needs a lot of water," he said aloud, as he began to climb over the boulders and earth from the landslide. It took a half hour climbing this route, but he doubted he had been seen. Beyond the debris from the landslide, he climbed to the curve of the dirt road leading up the canyon. At the top he stopped where he had descended the night before, and then walked down the road to town. He avoided Main St., until he crossed several side streets. A patrol car slowed as it passed, and he looked away pretending not to notice it. The man in the tan trench coat held his breath, until the deputy turned left up Main St. The man in the tan trench coat had second thoughts about having come to town but it was too late and he was too hungry to reconsider his strategy.

A couple of blocks north on Main Street, he found a laundromat where he bought soap and bleach from a vending machine. Inserting dollar bills in a changer, he received plenty of change to wash and dry his clothing. He sorted whites from colors, and deposited everything in three machines. Adding bleach to the machine with underwear only, he removed his sneakers and tossed them in too. Twenty eight minutes passed. He emptied the washers and put everything in one dryer, except the permanent press clothes. Those he put in separate dryer and gave them the correct setting. Later he neatly folded his clothes and returned them to his suitcase.

The bearded man in the tan trench coat left the laundromat, crossed the street to the corner Walgreens Drug Store where he purchased bar soap, shampoo, toothpaste and brush, a can of shaving cream, bottled water, three meals in a can, and a package of five disposable razors, single edge variety. He also bought the current copy of the weekly newspaper, the *Outcry*.

Back across the street, he stopped at Bustos Authentic Mexican Restaurant and enjoyed a plate of beef enchiladas smothered with green chili, covered with sharp cheddar cheese then bordered by tomatoes and lettuce. Refritos and rice filled what space remained. He added extra onions and spread a side of guacamole evenly over the enchiladas. He squirted hot salsa on his creation sparingly. Unlimited diet cola and ice water made it all slide down. He completed his feast with an order of three sopapillas. With precision he placed a pat of butter and emptied a packet of honey inside each sopapilla, then rotated each to insure honey and butter reached every corner. Topping off his dessert, he liberally sprinkled a combination of sugar and cinnamon from the jar on the counter where he sat. He emptied the napkin dispenser as he relished his feast.

The sheriff had parked his patrol car down Main Street from the restaurant, but the bearded man in the tan trench coat exited the restaurant out a side door to a now familiar sound. He walked further down the side street and stopped at another door to read the sign of John Law, Attorney at Law. Next he turned around and headed for Main Street, when he spotted the old woodcutter. He waved to the driver of the pickup truck at the corner, who willingly stopped to pick him up. They passed the sheriff, who took note and exited town to the sound of cough, cough, sputter, cough, sputter, boom. Cough, cough, sputter, cough, sputter, boom.

The grizzly old man smiled knowingly with a twinkle in his eye, still said nothing, stopped at the hair pin turn above the tall oak tree without being asked, waved as his passenger exited, and motored off into the night, not waiting for but getting an appreciative thank you. Cough, cough, sputter, cough, sputter, boom!

It was dusk and storm clouds began gathering. Shadows blanketed the slope. The bearded man in the tan trench coat gave thanks in prayer for his safe keeping before making his descent to the old mansion. On the outskirts of Ridge View and after another good time together over dinner with the dishes washed and dried, the Browning's took towels and the Princess Freda Louise to the creek, below the falls, just beyond the bridge. Dusk settled in during their walk and shadows foretold the coming arrival of a cool if not cold evening. Storm clouds invaded the valley and the sky darkened with the invasion.

"Looks like this will be a brief soak, Ruth."

"What do ya mean, Dad?" asked Andy.

"Storm clouds are moving rapidly into the valley and soon the night air will be chilly. Depending on whether or not we get rain, the temperature will drop twenty or thirty degrees pretty quick."

"Rob, where's the creek?" asked Ruth.

"Should be just over this hill, let Freda run, Andy. Put her down."

"She'll get lost," responded Andy anxiously.

"Freda's smarter than you think, Son, even at her age. She won't wander far if she does, but keep your eye on her. She should like the water but watch after her there too. And you too! I don't know how deep this is, except," he said then paused.

"Except what, Rob?" inquired Ruth.

"Well, nothing to be concerned about, 'cept we are out in the country and neighbors aren't that close."

"And?"

"Yeah, Dad, tell us more. Are there Indians or bears or skunks or lions or what else Dad?"

"Wait, you are exasperating me," hesitated Rob.

"Oh! I know what that means. Mom, I'm zasperating Dad. Makin' him craaaaazy!"

"Man talk?" asked Ruth.

"Yeah, man talk, but listen now. When I left to go back to work yesterday afternoon, I saw a man in the creek. He must have been in the pool below the falls up to his waist. He was holding something over his head. It looked like his clothes, something brown or tan."

"You mean somebody was skinny dipping in our creek, Dad. Mom, a skinny dipper and we missed him."

"Thank heavens!"

"Exactly, we are out here pretty much alone, and we need to use our heads. We need to be careful. Things aren't as safe as they use to be. It wasn't that long ago that people here in these towns didn't bother to lock their doors when they left their homes. They would leave and not worry about someone disrespecting their property. Break-ins were unheard of."

"Gosh, Dad, this must have been a special place."

"That's not that unusual, Andy. Most small towns use to be like that. Everybody knew one another. Often they were all related. Anyway, it's how they were raised. People respected one another. Stealing was unusual. Everybody worked and knew how hard somebody else worked to get what they had."

"Yeah, today, too many people get without working. These are the times of entitlements. Too many people think the world owes them a living and the government makes it easy not to be responsible and not to work. Everybody is a victim!" explained Ruth.

"How do ya mean?" asked Andy.

"Well, today a man can drink himself silly, get sick, not work and skip out on his responsibilities. Then the government steps in, gives his family an entitlement, while the man leaves the home. He gets disability. His wife and children get ADC, food stamps, housing allowance, and I don't know what all else. Then the government and the psychologists claim the guy can't help himself. He has a disease and can't get well. He is a victim and it's not his fault he's a drunk. His wife is told to divorce him. If she drinks too or if there is fighting in the house and someone gets hurt, then the children are taken from the parents."

"I don't get it, Dad. How is it a disease when the man does it to himself?"

"I don't know. And I don't like paying taxes to support someone else being irresponsible. It's un-American."

"Yes it is! And the American government perpetuates the problem instead of really helping. In a way the government wants to keep people dependent on it and to look to the government as their savior. I guess I always liked what President Kennedy said about everyone needing to add to, to help make this a great land, instead of having the government pay their way," said Ruth.

"What's the answer, Dad?"

"The truth, Son?"

"Yup, I don't want to be like that!"

"The answer is something I learned, while I was gone from you two."

"What?"

"A man needs to be a man, but more, a man needs to turn his heart to God and like that Christian radio program, a man needs to turn his heart toward home."

"How's he do that, Dad?"

"Here's what I learned. See a man was a little boy and got older. Along the way he gets bumps and bruises. Often ones he causes himself. That makes hurts on the inside of him that don't really heal. They fester. He sort of puts them in a file cabinet where they are on account."

"What's wrong with that?"

"The Bible says we are to keep a short record of accounts. That means we shouldn't hold things against people. We need to clean out the file cabinet by forgiving people and by asking others for forgiveness. By asking God for forgiveness and asking God to heal us. That takes time, but we can forgive right away. Fact is God wants us to have a life style of forgiveness," explained Rob.

"Is that it?" asked Andy.

"Nope, but one more thing, a man needs to tell God, he isn't who or what he wants to be. He only needs to confess he can't change on his own. The man needs to ask God to help him be the man God wants him to be and the husband his wife needs him to be and the father his son needs him to be."

"Is that what you did, Rob?" asked Ruth.

"Yes, dear, I cleaned out the file cabinet. I confessed a lot of sin and kept asking God to show me more. He did, and I was ashamed. I asked for forgiveness. God forgave me, then told me I needed to let go of my guilt too. Jesus is the sacrificial lamb and the scapegoat. He died for my sin and my guilt. My job is to turn from sin and live for Jesus. The best way I can do that is to be who God wants me to be."

"Rob, when did this happen?"

"This was when I first moved here earlier this summer. I went to church in Rock Creek, when I was staying at the Stage Stop Hotel. That's also how we came to rent this place. I made a friend going to the church there. His name is Adam Claymore. He is really a deacon at the church but has to do a lot of the preaching and teaching. Adam discipled me. He said he's not perfect at all, but that the Lord's been leading him. Anyway he owns the mesa south of Rock Creek and a lot of land in the valley. Somehow Adam is related to Whitney McNaughton. Adam owns this land, but he has Whitney rent it for him through a real estate office in Rock Creek. Adam has had a lot of persecution and slander directed toward him. Ridicule too. He says that is all part of being a Christian, spiritual warfare."

"Rob, the Lord told me much of the same. In his word he impressed me that if you did not come back, he would be as a husband to me. That his grace is sufficient. I made the mistake of putting you on a pedestal. I thought my way to him was through you and having the perfect family. So, I did a lot of things my way to create the perfect family, the perfect marriage. Rob, Jesus died for me. He loves me. I mean really. I didn't know that before. Not really. God told me that he loves you more than I do and that I needed to trust him no matter what. He told me to take the plank out of my eye. He told me to focus on being the woman he wants me to be and the mother Andy needs me to be. And Rob, I love you so much I want to be the wife, the lover, the friend you need me to be."

"Aw, Mom, are you guys gonna kiss? Is this what I have to look forward to? A bunch of kissin' all the time?" whined Andy.

And they answered him, and he grinned, the smile of someone who felt safer.

The Brownings played in the water and Freda joined in. For awhile they ignored the gathering storm clouds, but then the air became chilled and they toweled off the refreshing water.

Before leaving Rob lead his family in prayer. They prayed for families in the valley. Andy prayed that the men be men. He asked God to help him be the boy God wanted him to be and the boy his mama and daddy needed him to be. Rob asked for them to forgive him for having been such a jerk. With a smile Ruth told him that he had been a jerk, but now she was glad and quoted Romans 8:28. Mother and Son gladly forgave the head of their household, and Rob wept and Ruth and Andy joined him.

And the walls to the stronghold shook!

The Brownings talked further as they walked home. Rob told Ruth that Adam Claymore had told him to call him if anything funny or strange ever happened to him personally or to his household or automobile. Rob said he had asked Adam what he meant. Adam told him that he would know what he meant if something did happen. Rob said Adam is related to the first families and he's sort'a like the Lone Ranger, a good man trying to make things right. Anyway, Ruth's discernment activated, so she welcomed the time when Freda would grow up. Remembering their discussion at the feed and lumber store, Ruth thought that it is better for Freda to be an ugly dog, one capable of inspiring fear!

The Brownings walked home before the night chill enveloped the valley, relaxed awhile, and went to bed without watching television or reading the weekly newspaper—Rob and Ruth forgot to talk about what they heard at the Cozy Corner Café. Ruth did call home, talked with her parents, and arranged for her dad to forward things on the bus. Dad had agreed and asked if they could drive up with more. Rob suggested Labor Day, so they could spend some time together. That night Andy slept well without wakening in a puddle of his own making...

Mom Gustafson had told Karen that she watched birds feasting at her own feeder, especially when she wanted to fly away. The activity and freedom of the birds functioned as a diversion. Mom fantasized about traveling, and her daydreams rewrote the script of life circumstances she faced.

Pop really didn't understand this philosophy, but he made certain Mom had plenty of bird seed. Pop Gustafson, more likely, charged in directly trying to grapple with life. He equated life to a wrestling match. Pop would say that you might get pinned and you might pin the other guy. At first you might not succeed, but you had three periods to get on top of things and score the most points. Even a superior opponent could make a mistake and be pinned. The important thing was to get up, then be prepared for your next match. Pop had said a person's character wasn't revealed in never making mistakes; a person's character was revealed in how the person functioned after making a mistake. He said we have to seek and give forgiveness, and then allow God to heal our emotional and spiritual wounds. If we trusted him, he would heal us and use us to build his kingdom. Pop said God used broken people, who have learned to depend on him instead of their own resources. Karen smiled and remembered that her father would add that God used broken people, cracked pots, and that the light shined through the cracks.

Contemplating both philosophies, Karen looked out the window of her room at three pigeons feeding, two on the left side of the log cabin shaped birdfeeder and one on the right. She noticed sunflower seeds were plentiful on the left side, but something blocked the other. Struggling to remove the square headed nails she had pounded into the side of the window frame; Karen gave a forceful jerk upon each then opened the window and reached to pull the feeder inside. With a start and gasp, she noticed several men entering the rear of the tobacco store. She recognized one as the man who beat the cook earlier. Several cars occupied most of the space behind the hotel. The black Cadillac with the golden wheels stood out. A couple walked arm in arm on the footpath to the Asherah House on Indiana Avenue. Although he wore his street clothes, the cook sat next to the dumpster chugging his booze. The cook saw Karen and she saw him. He saluted with his bottle. It was early, but a band started playing in the bar and the speakers magnified the sound. Karen withdrew to the security of her room with the birdfeeder in hand.

The couple, which Karen watched in the parking lot, walked into the Asherah House Bed and Breakfast through the rear entrance. The men in the tobacco store began a serious game of poker. One man operated a chalk board with numbers on it, while a second one gathered information from telephone calls and gave it to him. Still another man stayed glued to a computer with a modem and occasionally printed data. A woman wearing a blond wig prepared a table for dinner and joked with anyone who would pay attention to her. More cars arrived and found space in the rear parking lot.

Sheriff Bailey cruised through Rock Creek, then stopped at the mouth of the canyon and parked. He waited for awhile, surveyed the town, and then left his cruiser, where it could be seen by motorists traveling north and south. The presence of the sheriff's cruiser functioned as a deterrent only to speeding motorists.

Karen sat on her bed, pulled the birdfeeder chimney out of the filler hole, saw nothing unusual, and then examined the porch on the right side of the log cabin feeder. Paper blocked access of seed supply to the porch. Sunflower seeds pressed against the paper that blocked the windows. She shook the feeder and freed some seed. Taking a pencil from her purse, she removed the blockage and examined it. Someone had written a message on the paper and stuffed it through an open window above the porch. She read it thinking her dad had played a joke on her to get her to return home. Laughing she dashed downstairs and placed a collect call. Karen was supposed to have called her parents yesterday but had not, so her mom and dad would be expecting her telephone call.

Mom Gustafson answered the phone with delight in hearing Karen's voice followed by a few moments where Karen's mother poured out news, gossip, and then questions like a one way telegraph. Karen waited patiently to get a word in edgewise, then spoke quickly.

"Mom, you guys are characters. I just found my note. Of all people, you knew I would eventually get birdseed and use my feeder."

"Karen, what on earth are you talking about?"

"The note, I found the note. You know, in the birdfeeder."

"What note are you talking about?"

"With the distinguished handwriting, the one I would read that would cause me to want to come home real fast."

"Maybe you better read it to me."

"You didn't write a note?"

"No, but maybe your dad did. He is having a real hard time worrying about how you are dealing with things."

"He is?"

"Yes, dear, he works at not holding on to you and that is tough for him to do. I can just imagine what he is going to be like when you get married. Heaven help your future husband. That's one reason we have prayed for him since you were born with hopes God would grow a man after his own heart. Dad loves you very much, honey. And so do I. You can always come home."

"Maybe Dad did write the note. Put him on the telephone, will you."

"Dad's not here now, honey. He'll be back in a half hour. He said he'd be back at 8:00 p.m. sharp."

"Oh...."

"Listen, have you eaten yet?"

"No."

"Well, get a bite to eat and call back when you are finished."

"Okay, Mom,, I am kind of hungry. I love you, Mom."

"I love you too, honey. I hope you get some good home cooking. Don't forget, call collect. Dad will want to talk to you. Knowing him, I'll bet he has played a joke on you. Good bye, dear."

"Good bye, Mom."

Sheriff Bailey walked past the woods and the lane to the church, paused at the neatly stacked wood delivered to the last house on the street, and strolled down the street to the convenience store. Bailey counted the cars he saw in the front parking lot, looking for any he didn't recognize. Next, he entered the convenience store and talked with the clerk while thumbing through one of the girly magazines. Bailey asked for and obligingly received a free pack of cigarettes, then left with the magazine, the *Outcry* weekly newspaper, and the cigarettes. The sheriff walked back to his cruiser, deposited all but the cigarettes in his cruiser, locked it and crossed the highway, and walked into the woods. Hurriedly, the sheriff followed the footpath to the hotel and beyond into the Asherah House on Indiana Avenue.

Karen had chosen a window seat at a table in the hotel dining room, where she could watch both the parking lot and convenience store. She had seen the sheriff, but lost sight of him, when he crossed the highway. From her previous exploration, she knew he could come into the hotel without being seen. The waitress recognized her and waved but continued her flirtatious conversation with four men at a table, while bending low to serve their meals. They all seemed to like her and were very familiar with each other, but one noticed Karen and waved. Sarah followed with a wave to Karen. Reluctantly, she waved back intended for Sarah only. One man asked Sarah to do something and nodding affirmatively, Sarah sashayed toward Karen's table. Men watched Sarah move in her tight white slacks and pink angora sweater with no sleeves and a scooped neck draped loosely over her.

"Sorry for the delay. I'm working on a big tip. You understand. I'll probably get a date too. You can too," stated Sarah, the waitress.

"Excuse me?"

"The gentleman who waved at you, he would like to buy you dinner. He's a lot of fun. Sells insurance and tips real well. You could get a date with him," Sarah further explained.

"No, thank you."

"You are staying here aren't you? I mean you do have a room."

"I'd like to order. At least I think I do."

"Okay, sorry. Thought you might be interested. It gets lonely here at night. A lot of girls stay here and end up enjoying some night life, especially on Saturday night. The bar will fill up later too."

"I'm sure everyone has a good time."

Under her breath Sarah quietly admitted, "Not always," then she added, "I need to tell you we are running behind in the kitchen. There's a meeting going on we have to fix dinner for. Sorry."

"How long of a wait?"

"Hopefully, just a half hour."

"I'll come back."

"You really need to place your order now. It gets worse as the evening wears on. People looking for action come to the Stage Stop."

"I see what you mean. What's good?" Karen responded.

"Tonight, try the spaghetti with the meatballs. That's what I had. I guarantee it will be ready in a half hour. Guaranteed," said Sarah with a genuine smile.

"Okay, and, Sarah, I don't mean to be a snob or anything, but I'm not the type who dates someone I don't know." Karen informed.

"Oh, you'd get to know him real fast, real well."

"I think you know what I mean."

"Hey, no problem, I'm sorry I insulted you, but if you change your mind, let me know. You're cute enough. And they would like you."

The hair stood on the back of Karen's neck. If it wasn't for the fear she felt, she might have verbally blasted Sarah. Next, a question came to Karen, should she really expect anything different from Sarah? All things considered, probably not she concluded. But that didn't change the offense, nor did it affect how Karen felt and needed to respond for herself and Sarah.

Before leaving, Karen watched Sarah sway over the table like a trainer mesmerizing a cobra, then Sarah expertly brushed against the man who wanted a date while whispering in his ear. He laughed, enjoyed the attention, and waved toward Karen.

Karen gave no acknowledgement, left, and took a seat in an obscure corner of the lobby. In her anger, she did not sin.

Cars, trucks, and multi-purpose vehicles arrived and left the convenience store. The cashier kept busy and a young man assisted her by stocking the cooler periodically, pushing a broom, mopping up spills by the soda dispenser, and helping people find what they wanted.

A brisk business followed. People stopped, pumped gasoline, bought cigarettes and beer or wine. Often customers walked to the back of the store to use the bathroom. Others pumped gasoline, rented movies, gathered things from the dairy case, picked up snacks, and also went to the back of the store to use a bathroom. Sometimes people just stopped by and purchased a newspaper, a candy bar, or a fountain drink. A lot of people just went to the back of the store.

A middle aged woman wearing a blond, Dolly Parton type wig entered the Stage Stop Hotel, crossed the lobby with a strut, entered the desk clerk's space, and then appeared at the counter to relieve Hannah, the desk clerk from Friday. Hannah nervously received instructions from the old bombshell and left directly. Without hesitating, Hannah promptly ascended the stairs.

Three young women dressed in tight blue jeans and halter tops opened the lobby door, giggled while waiting for their escorts, then linked arms with three men, who appeared to be in their thirties. No one carded them when they entered the bar. Meanwhile, Karen realized the new desk clerk had been eyeing her, while filing long, red finger nails as if bored. Karen glared back, and the woman looked away in boredom. Checking her watch, Karen noted thirty minutes had almost passed. Curious, she walked to the bar and looked in. Although it was only 8:00 p.m., patrons filled both booths and tables. Most bar stools remained empty, yet glasses partially filled with beer were scattered along the counter. To the right two men played a bowling game, where they slid what looked like a hockey puck down the table top alley under bowling pins suspended from above the alley space. The teeny boppers bouncing in their halter tops watched them. Next to the bowling machine, a foursome played pool. West of the horseshoe bar in the center of the room, the band took a break, couples left the dance floor, while someone selected more recordings on the juke box by the bandstand. Karen counted two men for each woman. Groups of men stood around together, while a few couples sat in booths. Occasionally, a couple would ascend the stairs and apparently were already registered at the hotel.

Several women sat alone and attracted attention from several men, both individually and in groups. Goose bumps stood out on Karen's arms and a chill seemed to flow over the full length and breadth of her body, as she realized the bartender had been eyeing her. She left promptly and entered the dining room. It was past 8:00 p.m., and Karen wanted to eat quickly and call her dad.

Smiling, Sarah promptly served Karen, paid her no further attention, left the check, and scurried back to the men with whom she had been flirting. While eating, Karen watched more cars and trucks parking in the lot outside. Some people crossed the highway to the convenience store. Several came out with packaged goods, a few with snacks, and some with apparently nothing. Others came directly inside. Quite a few stayed on the porch just standing around or sitting at outdoor tables. She noted that some even registered at the desk and ascended the stairs to their rooms. Most went to the bar. Most carried no luggage. Soon the desk clerk turned people away, and Karen could hear her telling travelers to go on to Jericho Springs or Ridge View. Blondie chided one man telling him she had told him, if he wanted any action, to make reservations for tonight. She told him to wait in the bar. Karen became more nervous and anxious to call her dad. Finishing her meal, she left payment for her check and tip, left the dining hall, and hurried to the telephone booth in the corner of the lobby. Karen closed the bi-fold door, grateful for the relative privacy.

Pop Gustafson answered the telephone on the first ring and began talking without checking to make certain Karen was on the other end.

"Hello, Daddy."

"Hi, Daughter Dear, your mother told me you called and asked if one of us had left a note in your birdfeeder. I didn't. She didn't. What's happening?"

"It's what the note says, Dad. And this place is weird."

"Well, tell me what it says. What's the mystery? And why do you say the place is weird, the town or the motel?"

"The note, I'm staying at the Stage Stop Hotel. The note said get out of town, while you still can."

"What?"

"The note said…"

"I heard what you said. That's peculiar. Are you okay?" Pop said with frustration, "When did you find the note?"

"I'm okay, Dad. Please settle down. I knew this would anger you if you didn't write the note as a joke. I'm all right. I found it tonight when I came back from a walk. Earlier I got some sunflower seeds, filled the feeder, and put it out on the window ledge outside my window," explained Karen.

"Didn't you notice the note when you filled the birdfeeder?" asked Karen's dad, "Do you mean someone crawled onto the window ledge and stuffed a note in the feeder?"

"I don't think so. It was rolled up. It wasn't wrinkled."

"How so?"

"I think someone put the note inside before I put the seeds in the birdfeeder. The note must have been rolled up and put in the feeder. It partially unrolled before I put the seeds in. There were no seeds on one side of the porch. You know my feeder is the shape of a cabin with a porch and rail on each side. That's where the seeds come out and the birds can get to them. If someone stuffed the note inside after I filled the birdfeeder, some seed would probably have been left on the porch. The note would probably be a little wrinkled. It isn't wrinkled and there weren't any seeds on the porch."

"You mean someone came into your room and put the note in the bird feeder."

"Yes."

"Are you sure it didn't happen before you left home. One of your friends?" asked Dad.

"No, nobody came over. Nobody said good-by, but you and Mom."

"Nobody?"

"No, not one. Once I packed it, I sealed the box with strapping tape. If someone wanted to get into the box, they couldn't without making a mess. It had to be after I unpacked."

"After you were in your room?"

"Yes, Dad, now help me think. It doesn't matter where or when. What do I do now?"

"You call the police. Is there a police station in town?" Dad exclaimed.

"Not here. I hiked all around town today. There's nothing here but the hotel, some houses, the school district offices, and a store across the highway. Oh, there's also a little church across the street like the ones we saw in Elk Mountain and on the road to Laramie from Fort Collins."

"What you are saying is that you were gone from your room a lot today and a lot of people probably saw you out and about," concluded Dad.

"I guess you're right. There isn't even a television here."

"You mean in your room?" asked Dad.

"Not in my room or here in the lobby."

"Where are you? What kind of place are you staying at? Can you check into another motel?" Dad asked with growing anxiety.

"There's nothing else, but a bed and breakfast. I don't think it's any better. I'm calling from the hotel lobby."

"You...don't have a phone in your room?" inquired Dad.

"No! Listen, Daddy, I'm okay. I probably left my room unlocked and something happened. Or maybe the cleaning lady did it."

"Was your room cleaned today?"

"No, I doubt they provide daily service. I share a bathroom with the other residents."

"Then you really are staying in a hotel. Not a place where most of the clientele changes daily," concluded Dad Gustafson.

"I don't know, but I have my interview on Monday. I know, it's probably someone else who has applied for the job and they want to eliminate the competition." Laughing, Karen added, "I'll check the bus service and see when I can get out of here. I haven't paid for the room yet, so I can let them know I'm leaving earlier than I planned. I'll talk to the management in the morning."

"Have you told anyone else?"

"The only people I have talked to were on the bus. Oh, and the desk clerk and a waitress. I might be able to talk to the desk clerk."

"If this place is weird like you said, you may want to tell someone else."

"Like who?"

"You mentioned a church. Assuming they have services tomorrow, go there and talk with the pastor. He should help. And call the sheriff's department."

"Good idea, Dad."

"Then let's pray, and you go to your room. Lock your door and your window. Move the dresser in front of the door and get your pistol. You do have your pistol with you don't you?" asked Karen's father.

"Yes, Father, I put my pistol in the dresser."

"Well, get it, load it, and put it under your pillow. Or at least have it close by. Hang the holster over a bed post like in the western movies. If anyone messes with you, they're messing with a crack shot. A twenty-two is a small caliber, but the way you shoot, you don't need much pop. Let's pray."

Father and daughter prayed. Daughter didn't tell her dad about seeing a man in the hallway, nor did she say anything about the window without a lock. She had solved that problem anyway with the nails in the window frame, and she had committed to try to find the sheriff. Both father and daughter became calm and confident. They said their goodbyes. Daughter promised to call before going to church and early Sunday evening. Dad promised not to upset her mom, then reminded Karen to call him in the morning. Karen hurried to her room, but did not see the sheriff return to his cruiser and leave Rock Creek.

Karen looked out her room from her one window. Storm clouds blocked the moonlight. One light over the back door of the kitchen partially brightened the parking lot. Another did the same from the rear of the tobacco store. Few street lights dotted the town. Other than light from a scattering of houses, darkness cloaked the town. The back porch light at the bed and breakfast signaled a welcome.

Karen wondered how to contact the sheriff. Earlier she had seen him enter the Asherah House, but she did not know if he was still there. Since she was using the telephone in the lobby, she had not seen him leave. If he returned to his squad car, she did not know. She thought about just walking over to Asherah House, knocking on the front door, then saying to whoever answered the door-- what is it you folks are doing over here anyway? Well, she could she thought, but that probably wouldn't produce the response she wanted. Perhaps she could go downstairs and look around the dining room or the bar, but thought better about that. Next, she considered walking about town in hope of finding him. Since he had parked at the mouth of the canyon, she could take the footpath to the car. If the sheriff were there, she could talk with him or leave him a note. How about checking the telephone book, then calling and asking to have a deputy dispatched. She could do that. Facing people downstairs or in the parking lot were rejected, she did not want to leave her room unattended at night. She did not want to be in a position of coming back to her room alone and possibly facing someone inside. Confronting someone unknown in the darkness of her room terrified her. That had been childhood's nightmare. She shuttered. Karen could climb out her window and look around town for the sheriff from the rooftops.

First getting her jacket from her closet, Karen checked the dresser for her pistol like her dad asked, looked inside the top drawer and saw the barrel end of her holster covered with her underwear. With assurance she easily pushed the dresser across the room, as wheels rolled on golden casters. Karen wedged the dresser firmly between the door and her bed, and then sat cross legged on the bed deep in thought.

Back home her dad had said Karen should take the ten things with her she most valued. The pistol and birdfeeder remained tied for first place. They represented her mom and dad. Mom shared with Karen how the birdfeeder pacified occasional desires to flee from herself and her marriage to a new life or just to escape pressures momentarily. The log cabin with side porches to hold the seed attracted desired visitors, mostly sparrows.

Karen removed the square headed nails blocking the window frame, silently opened the window, stepped out on to the catwalk, and closed the window behind her. She pocketed the nails for return use. Figuring no one could enter her room from the hallway, she thought she would hear if someone was at the window. Tiptoeing stealthily to the west side of the building, she watched the back door of the bed and breakfast on Indiana Avenue, and then squatted in an open space on the side. She strained to see the mouth of the canyon. A streetlight beamed on ground once occupied by the sheriff's cruiser. She looked at the parking lot and noted that the sheriff was not there, nor did he appear to be at the convenience store or in the parking lot behind the tobacco store. Karen felt another chill.

People milled around in front of the hotel. Couples pressed one another against their autos. Passion warmed car windows, and the cool night air frosted the glass. The convenience store continued non-stop business. Light appeared at some houses and off in others. Cloud cover increased and hid the light of the moon and stars.

Karen wondered when the note could have been put in the birdfeeder. Since someone wanted to leave her a message, why had someone stuffed it down inside the log cabin where it could be undetected? She had been out of her room Friday afternoon, then again in the evening. Her camera and diary weren't missing. They were back on the lamp table in front of the window. Last night she had unpacked and put away what little bit she had with her. She had bathed at different times with no predictable routine. The man in the hallway? And the other man that she had seen on the highway? Drinking outside, the cook had waved at her. Could he have thought she was someone else? Was it any one of several times when she was hiking around? She had left and thought she locked the room each time. Since she could not lock the window, someone could have entered through the window when she was not there. New arrivals went upstairs when she was eating. Earlier today she had heard the lodger next to her crying. Or what about her note to have the window fixed? Foolishly, she had left it on the counter where anyone could have read it. That really was foolish under the best of circumstances. She should have been more patient, more assertive, more responsible she judged. She replayed Friday and Saturday again, then again. It disabled her, and her thinking froze mid-thought. Her mind spun then lulled, until she became debilitated. Finally, Karen remembered coming back to her room finding the birdfeeder and throw rug pushed up against the table. Bingo! That had to be it.

Karen had left the feeder in the center of the rug in the middle of the floor. Someone had come in her room, unplugged the chimney, put the note inside, replaced the chimney, then positioned the log cabin on the rug, and shoved the rug and the birdfeeder against the table where she would notice it was out of place. That rang true, but why? She wondered and asked aloud, "Why go to such an extent to leave a note, but risk her not finding it? And what does the note really mean?"

A window opened. It closed. From the west side of the hotel, Karen stood up, rubbed her knees briefly, moved to the exterior wall, and inched toward the catwalk. With her left eye, she peered around the corner in time to watch a man, she thought, had stumbled over the log cabin feeder. Catching his balance, he swore and kicked at it, but stopped short. Already the noise may have given him away. Hurriedly, the dark figure fled along the catwalk, away from Karen, down the fire escape ladder, and into the woods. She listened and watched. Karen witnessed no movement but heard a rustling of branches against clothing in the woods beyond the footpath.

Karen wondered, "Did he go left or right? Is he waiting and watching to see if he was followed?" Karen waited but heard nothing. She wondered, "Should I follow? Which room did the person come out of? Since he stumbled over the birdfeeder, it was this side of my room. Hannah sleeps in room 216. I have no idea who is in 212 and 214. No lights are on."

Karen edged down the catwalk to her window, opened it, and entered her room. Someone watched unseen and relieved from the woods. She closed the window, regained control, and decided it is good for her to have people know she was in her room. Better for her to telegraph her presence, then she could set a snare and ambush someone wanting to enter. Karen turned on the lamp, which illuminated her room and penetrated the darkness.

Karen hung her jacket in the closet, decided to get her pistol from her holster, but had to move the dresser from where she had wedged it between the bed and the door. One bedpost blocked the drawer from opening. Before she could move the dresser, someone walked down the hallway, then stopped at her door.

A man knocked softly and asked, "You in there?" He waited and asked louder, "Hannah, you in there? Open up will ya?"

Karen made no response and wondered if she should tell the man he had the wrong room, to try next door in room sixteen. The man became frustrated, disappointed, and then left. Karen moved to get into the dresser drawer, and she heard him come back down the hallway.

The man in the hallway wrestled the door knob and said, "Hannah, I heard you. I know you are in there, you better open up now. We gotta date and time's a wasting. I'm in no mood to play games."

He banged on the door, then stopped, looked up and down the hallway to see if he had disturbed anyone. He bent down with hands and knees on the hallway floor and looked under the door. Seeing the light he walked away, but said, "I'll be waiting."

Karen did not know if he had left the hallway. Since the man called out for Hannah, Karen relaxed her breath. She figured if the person on the catwalk had been Hannah, then she did not want to see this man. Whatever their relationship, he wanted to see Hannah badly. Karen did not want to be a substitute. If she moved the dresser, he might hear her. She could probably get to her pistol in time, yet she did not really want a scene. She just wanted to get a good night's sleep and have her interview Monday. Besides, Karen thought, he just had the wrong door and would figure that out eventually.

Karen could see it now. The newspaper article would read, a woman in Rock Creek to interview for a job shot man in hallway outside her room. What with the apparent reputation of this hotel, she wondered what people would think. How would she have known, she wasn't from here, and besides, it's not like there are a lot of choices to pick from. Maybe she could have gone to the bed and breakfast, but who knows what is going on there too. She hadn't even known the Asherah House was there, until she saw the men walking the footpath to the back door. "What a great place to be on a Saturday night," Karen said sarcastically. "Won't this be an amusing story to share with Mom once I get home!"

Karen decided to tell the man he had the wrong room, if he were to return. He did not. She left the table lamp on and picked up the weekly newspaper purchased earlier. Reading the back, she read ads for automobiles to buy the desire of your heart, as one advertiser wrote. Then she read situations wanted, rental units with apartments, the Stage Stop Hotel, trailers, houses, and share a room. Discovering an intriguing ad, she noted it said: Opportunity to help restore a home, your part time labor for lodging. Send responses to the newspaper with the ad number listed or call the telephone number listed in the ad. Next, she was surprised to see a column titled Connections, with listing about women seeking men, men seeking women, men seeking men, women seeking women, and seeking other, a column listing adult services, escorts, private party dancers, sexy dateline, phone fantasy, hot teens over eighteen make your scene, massage outcalls, a series of 900 telephone numbers, dial a model, and other ads that play upon the lust of man.

"How sad," Karen reflected, "so many people want to feel good, have approval, to touch and be touched. I wonder what kind of people place those ads. Who responds?"

Karen had identified with the search for a genuine relationship with another person, female or male, yet without the attached secularity blatantly urged through the ads. She concluded that all people needed real friends, and then the song flooded into her thoughts, "What a Friend We Have in Jesus." She sang it softly no longer indulging the ads. She smiled with lowered head content with the truth. "I am satisfied with Jesus…but is he satisfied with me?" Karen mused. "And that folks is the approval we should be searching for!"

Continuing, Karen read employment ads: substitutes for teachers, bus drivers, cooks, secretaries, and custodians; high school science/social studies teacher and a

K-12 music teacher, both assigned to Jericho Springs High School. Part time work read: Help Staff, a temporary help agency with wages paid daily; drivers to deliver pizza; telephone solicitation; stuffing envelopes at home; ranch help at Claymore Flats. Not bad, Karen thought, if I get the high school job, I could get some work before reporting for school, which could fill in the rest of the summer. I wonder about exchanging labor for lodging, too? Possibilities! Even amongst the smut, there is hope if I remain rightly focused. I know to be myself and not conform to the society around me.

Learn about the community, Dad had advised, so let's see what else the paper offers. Karen reviewed block ads. All sorts of New Age posturing: hypnotherapy, harmony potions, meditation sessions, psychic healing and horoscopes, soul quests, shaman guides, School of Yoga, alternative health care, The Asherah House: Bed and Breakfast, call 633-3666. Nifty's Lingerie modeling, call 633-3667 for an in or out appointment. Those numbers stood out, she thought, then thumbed back through the ads to discover two other ads use similar phone numbers, teen escorts-633-3668 and massage outcall-633-3669. Could they be extensions of the same telephone? She concluded that people find a lot of ways to make a buck, then Karen remembered earlier, "And the waitress, Sarah, was suggesting I do it. I wonder where she rests her head. I wonder how she makes the most money."

Becoming bored, Karen thumbed through the rest of the newspaper noting some headlines; reading a half page of comics; checking community notices of upcoming events and meetings; liquor store ads; the editorial section. She recognized a picture with an article about a local rancher, Adam Claymore, but tired before reading it. Reclining on the bed, she reached to turn off the light and checked to make certain she had replaced the nails in the window. Earlier Karen had.

Karen heard laughter outside and engines starting, doors slamming, and groups entering the bar, bottles breaking, people swearing, but she slept. Tomorrow would take care of tomorrow. During the night, she missed the woman's return on the catwalk to room 216, and she did not see the man dressed in black, who roamed all of Rock Creek that night. Karen did not wake at the sound of a key turning the lock to her room. Unlocked, blocking the door, the dresser hadn't allowed the door to open. It proved to be an effective sentry.

Sheriff Bailey made his appointed rounds. He finished with his trip to the Asherah House. He had avoided the tobacco store. Leaving Rock Creek, Bailey drove a loop through Ridge View, stopped at his office, checked in with his deputies on night shift, sorted his mail, read some, tossed others, and then left saying good bye to Candy, who served as tonight's dispatcher. Candy was sweet all right, none sweeter or more deadly when double-crossed, Bailey had witnessed.

Candy no longer patrolled regularly. She had been covering dispatch for two months, as a punitive action for shooting rape suspects. When they tried to flee the scene of the crime, Candy disabled them by shooting each behind the knee. Community sentiment favored Candy, but deputies could not afford the appearance of having taken law into their own hands. Candy's case might have been just that. Deputy Cotton Candy wasn't a McNaughton. Candy had shot one. Some people would not forgive or forget what she had done. She protected a teeny-bopper trying to stop turning tricks. That's how Candy earned the scar on her face. Someone administered retribution, and Candy was reassigned to a desk job. The perpetrator was never identified, never found, but his face was imprinted in Candy's memory.

Sheriff Bailey drove past the transportation center in Ridge View and continued to the edge of town past the Cozy Corner Café and into the night. The sheriff halted before crossing the bridge on County Road 403 and eyed the Brownings' place. "Another newcomer," he snorted with disdain while spitting tobacco juice out the window of his cruiser. "It won't be long before I hear from you. We'll see how you like the valley then."

Bailey drove into Jericho Springs meandering up and down Main and side streets. Those not sleeping would know the sheriff's presence. He turned up hill, drove past the old three story house with the rotting clothes on front balconies, and paused. Understanding the issues, Bailey questioned aloud, "Really, who would want to live there?"

The sheriff resumed driving, made a u-turn at the south end of Main St., and then stopped his cruiser and turned off his headlights. Bailey watched a young woman through partially closed window blinds. She turned off her bedroom light, undressed, and retired to bed. "Not a smart move little girl," Bailey said sarcastically, "you never know who might be on the prowl. Careful or the same will happen to you that happened to your roommate."

The Rock Creek Convenience Store closed at midnight. Travelers would have to drive to Ridge View for gasoline until 6:00 a.m. The manager let her helper out the door. He tipped her fifty dollars. Locking the front and rear doors, she stashed cash register receipts in a floor vault, spent an hour preparing reports, and ate dinner at the owner's expense. The owner wouldn't mind. He had been indulging her and had written off the expense as shoplifting. Although she consumed expensive items, she rationalized that she deserved them. Calling the bar across the highway, she asked for her husband and told him she was ready to leave. As she waited, she prepared and snorted a line of coke from the glass top of her desk. She saved none and rationalized her husband had been doing who-knows-what across the way, while she worked. Of course, she had correctly assessed her husband's behavior.

Keeping late hours, the Rock Creek realtor locked his door, turned off the lights, dialed 633-3667, and waited. Minutes later a young woman left the Asherah House, walked to his back door, and knocked. She greeted him with laughter and said, "Well, Mr. King, you called for a model at this late hour?"

"Come in," he responded eagerly. She did.

Jerry, who delivered pizza and managed the store in Jericho Springs, drove to Rock Creek, crossed the bridge on County Road 403, and stopped in front of the first house on his right. Street lights glowed at each end of the bridge as had the one where the road intersected the highway. Leaving his car with pizza and flashlight, he looked around, flashed his light across the road, back at both sides of the bridge, and up both sides of the street. Relatively confident, he hurried to the house and flashed his light on the house and through closed curtains. He wished his customers would leave the porch light on for him. A dog barked. The pizza-man hesitated. The porch light snapped on, and the door opened. His customer met him with a friendly greeting in response to his, took the pizza, paid for the pizza and tipped him a dollar, closed the door, and turned off the porch light before the pizza-man left the porch. He hesitated and flashed his light toward the street, then up and down the county road before closing the gate behind him. Jerry opened his car door, entered quickly, closed the door, locked himself in, started his engine, turned on the dome and headlights, and recorded his tip.

A man can't be too careful, especially here where the dead body of Gloria Jones was found, Jerry thought, and then he made a u-turn and drove his old but reliable car back to Jericho Springs to pick up more deliveries. At 1:00 a.m. deliveries ended, and Jerry and another driver counted their tips, paid their bill, and helped the inside staff cleaned up before leaving at 2:00 a.m.

Somewhere in the night children cried themselves to sleep in response to the day. A battered woman soaked blackened eyes to reduce the swelling. A wife stole her husband's manhood with words. Child molested child. An adult fondled a young relative. A brother stole money from his sister's purse, while she slept. A sister mocked her sister. A brother lied to his father to avoid a spanking his brother received instead. A man drank his fill, vomited, and drank more. A mother harshly slapped her child for not finishing his chores. She didn't listen to his valid explanation. A roommate skipped town leaving the other to pay overdue rent. A boy stole a man's new car. A father defaulted on his child's support. Someone's mother squandered food money on drugs, and a woman stole her aged mother's silver and china. To spite her son-in-law, a mother refused to help her daughter buy some land. A father arranged for his son to spend time with a homosexual. One man beat another to gain a favored place to sleep in a shelter. A child gave birth to a child at the hospital, while a doctor performed an abortion on an unborn child at a clinic. A gang beat up a "wanna be." A pledge robbed a pizza delivery woman to fulfill his initiation, while a girl submitted to gang rape to fulfill her's. A grocery clerk left her thumb on the scales, weighed produce, and overcharged a customer. Several made copies of feature films they rented. A church treasurer altered her record books and pocketed the difference. A retail clerk shorted a coin from several roles she prepared. Inhumane acts multiplied exponentially. One person passed an offense onto another. Tainted memories escalated. Need for confession, repentance and forgiveness compounded daily. Guilt accelerated in some, while others seared their consciences senselessly.

Somewhere in the night west of Jericho Springs and into the mountain valley between the north and south peaks of Mt. Huajatolla, a scruffy old man slept in his truck. He mouthed a plea to his Lord: "Come tonight, Lord Jesus!"

Had the old oak tree on the mound behind the three story house any leaves or fruit, both would have withered tonight. As an ichabod, cloud cover blocked both moon and stars like a deceitful man without honor might hide the truth. Gentle wind enveloped the valley and brought with it a bone chilling mist. Only street lamps and late night places like the Stage Stop Hotel illuminated the darkness.

WORSHIP SUNDAY MORNING
CHAPTER 7

"My sacrifice, O God, is a broken spirit, a broken and contrite heart you, God, will not despise." Psalm 51:17

The cyclist, who lived down the street from where the man in the tan trench coat had been hiding in Jericho Springs, continued her morning routine. She unlocked the padlock and removed the chain attaching her hunter green mountain bike to her front porch railing. Taking her bike off the porch, she hesitated before mounting it. She looked toward the old mansion, then at the mammoth tree on the citadel behind it. Her gaze followed the southern rim of the mound where the rock slide had crashed against it. Forcefully, the slide removed top soil and tree roots, while exposing volcanic rock. No vegetation grew there. No nutrients fed plant life. Rugged rock created a barren surface on both the southern and western sides of the volcanic mound.

This Sunday morning the cyclist started her daily ritual earlier and rode out of instead of into town. Following a hunch, she peddled to the bridge over Rock Creek, across the west tributary of Rock Creek, and onto the dirt road leading upward toward the valley between the twin peaks of Mt. Huajatolla. She fixed her eyes on the northern peak as she peddled. Although her opinion varied depending on the vantage point, today she concluded the scar on the mountain clearly looked like a lamb and not a white buffalo or salamander.

The cyclist peddled to where the Live Oak stood on the citadel above the town. Laboring as she peddled, the cyclist reached the turnout where the road had a hairpin turn above the rock slide. She dismounted her bike and carried it over the guard rail and down the slope from the turnout where she hid it behind a boulder. From there she picked her way down the slide, west then north in hopes of not being seen. Without knowing whom, she felt as if someone were watching her. If her hunch were accurate, she did not want to expose the intruder below. Though warm vapors rose from cracks in the center of where a spring fed pond had been, she crossed the empty basin and laid down where she could peer over the edge of the dry pool at the mansion below. She waited thirty then forty-five minutes. As expected she saw someone moving around in the house in what she determined was the porch outside the kitchen. The cyclist watched and was not disappointed.

Below the intruder, the man in the tan trench coat, opened the porch door and peered outside. Walking only a few yards from the house, he carried what appeared to be a book under his arm. Carefully surveying the backyard, he stopped, stretched, and looked around. Listening, he looked some more. Admiring the sunlight upon the mountain, he then studied the mammoth oak through sad eyes. Though at a distance, he watched for signs of budding branches. He ventured next to the building toward where he could see the pools where the creek used to flow. Making certain to stay in the shadows, he stopped when the pools were in view. Sitting down, he unzipped what he had been carrying.

The cyclist watched him, as he sat cross-legged reading. He bowed his head, and she concluded that he had been reading his Bible and now prayed. Comforted, her curiosity increased. She was relieved believing that she watched a kindred spirit, and she was even more concerned about exposing his apparent need not to be discovered. The cyclist tingled with anticipation!

Aloud he said, "Man, tonight I've gotta bathe. It will be worth the risk to just sit in warm water and soak." He had slept through the night, no tossing and turning, yet in waking, he had become uneasy. Thinking to himself, he knew that he must remain hidden, undiscovered as long as possible and hopefully until Wednesday. After that, it would be hard to tell what might happen, once his presence was officially known. Following the wall back to the porch door, he closed it behind him and made his way back to the rear bedroom on the mansion's first and main floor. Having opened his suitcase and returning his Bible, he walked to the kitchen where he opened and ate a can of cold beef stew. He checked to see if the advertisement that brought him to Jericho Springs was still being published in last Wednesday's edition of the *Outcry*, the local newspaper. Locating the ad, he was pleased. He hoped many would respond before Thursday.

Above on the citadel, the cyclist remained at the side of the dry pond long after the intruder returned to the mansion. She wondered whether or not she knew him, then concluded she needed a closer look and would make contact with him but not where or when they would be seen. But, she decided, she must be careful for today safety was a relative term. She nearly jumped out of her skin, as three yearlings rustled debris as more deer crossed by the Live Oak on their way toward the small meadow by the ponds below.

The cyclist made her way back the route she had come not noticing budding branches on the north and east sides of the tree. She returned to the road and followed it speedily back to town where she continued her morning ride before church services along her usual route around Jericho Springs.

"Even Sunday morning on Claymore Flats, it is early to bed and early to rise makes a man healthy, wealthy, and wise," said Adam to Big Foot in response to Big Foot waking him. "Is that what you are telling me, Footers?"

Head now resting on the pillow next to Adam, Big Foot continued his affectionate display getting as close as he could to Adam. He didn't lick; he used his wet nose to touch Adam's, who reached across the big dog and pulled Big Foot, so his hind legs joined the rest of his body on the bed.

"You know, Big Foot, if I remarry, you won't be allowed on the bed, even in the morning to wake me up. A wife may not want you in the house. Now, what do you think of that?"

In response to Adam's sitting upright in bed, all seventy pounds of the fifteen year old, overgrown puppy climbed onto Adam's lap. Leaning his body fully against Adam with his head shyly tucked to the side away from Adam, Big Foot acted coyly. And the man gently held the beast and spoke softly to him.

"You're a good, ole puppy. If only Mary could see you now. She loved you as a little puppy, but now she would cherish you as much as I do. Good friend. You know how lonesome I am. Don't you?" Turning on the cassette tape on his night stand, Adam told his old friend, "Hear, listen to this as we start the day. It's from the play, *Man of La Mancha*." Adam began to sing along and Big Foot howled in unison, "To dream the impossible dream..."

With the singing, Adam shoved Big Foot away intending to signify it was time to get up, but the playful beast interpreted it was time to roughhouse. "No, no down boy, get down Big Foot! Away with you! Stay down! Enough!"

Big Foot both pranced and faced off in front of Adam, then faked one way and ran around the other end of the bed and out the door. Adam shut the door, so Big Foot couldn't get back in.

Adam showered, while Big Foot waited outside the bedroom door confused and watching for the door to open. Within minutes Big Foot lay against the door and napped, while Adam finished dressing for church services, while reviewing his sermon notes.

Below in the kitchen, Adam's cook, Rabbit Pinebow, prepared Sunday breakfast for the ranch hands, who had become accustomed to steak and eggs on Sunday morning. Only a few were required to work over the weekend. Most were permitted the time off but were always invited to attend church services in Rock Creek at the little church in the glen where Adam had prepared to preach this Sunday. Minimal chores had been required on Sunday, as their boss insisted on Sabbath rest. Tending milk cows was not an option, nor was feeding the rest of the livestock.

In response to Rabbit's call to come-and-get-it, five ranch hands occupied seats at the dining room table waiting for the boss to lead them in prayer. Big Foot waited beside Adam's chair, as he bounded down the stairs with Bible and sermon notes in hand. Adam announced to all, "Gentlemen, you are welcome to attend services with me. The Lord's given me a good message for all to hear."

In unison they responded, "And when doesn't God have a good message for you to give, Rev. Claymore?"

Kidding, Rabbit added, "Eat now. Preach later. Give thanks, white man. Hmm....me thinks... someone special in services this morning? I go with you. Watch over you and protect the interests of my kitchen on Claymore Flats. No want woman here! Job security!"

"I hope you're right. You know I saw a woman yesterday at the Stage Stop, who reminded me of Mary. Later I saw her sitting on the bench at dusk overlooking Rock Creek. She left her Bible on the bench, and I'm going to figure out how to get it back to her. Don't expect me to be home for dinner."

Then in fluid English, Rabbit sang, "Well, the boss might go sparkin' tonight!" and said to the wranglers, "Gentlemen, I will dutifully inspect the fair maiden if she attends services this morning. I am providing the special music today. I may have to change my selection to 'Love Song'."

Laughter filled the kitchen, the group prayed and feasted on Rabbit's offerings of charbroiled steak, eggs, and hash brown potatoes—all covered with his homemade green chili. More than once each hand echoed the other's compliment telling Rabbit someday he would make a good husband, if only he would do something about how he dressed and sang. Rabbit brought the kidding to a halt, as he gave them a sample of today's special music with his baritone voice singing, "How Great Thou Art."

Adam interrupted, "Hold on Rabbit. I'll save my preaching for later, if you'll save the singing for later!"

All finished except Big Foot, who feasted on rib bones outside on the porch. One by one wranglers excused themselves, while Adam left promptly so he could 'fire' the wood stove to 'take the chill off' the chapel before the congregation arrived for morning services.

Only Rabbit and Big Foot remained. Rabbit cleaned the counter, wiped the tables, put the jam and jelly in the refrigerator with the butter, and then started the dishwasher. Rabbit watched Big Foot munching on his bone collection and commented to the big dog, "Big Foot, let us hope romance enters into your master's life. For sure he has suffered enough with the loss of Mary and the battles he's taken on in town. Satan doesn't let up, when one of the saints is willing to take a stand for what is right. It sure would be good to have a woman in this house again to comfort that man."

Sitting on the bench on the mesa and overlooking the town of Rock Creek, Karen wondered what had happened to her Bible. She regretted her thoughtlessness in leaving her Bible on the bench the night before even though she had left in fright. The wet nose touching the back of her neck was just cause for Karen's abrupt departure, but as usual, she judged herself harshly by blaming herself mercilessly in the midst of understandable circumstances. Coupled with her unsettling situation at the hotel, she sat pensively. She had awakened early so as to leave without being seen in case the man at her door last night happened to still be around. After showering and dressing for church, she had left the hotel down the back stairwell with her newspaper in hand, and then had walked along the path to the mouth of the canyon where the roses climbed. Pausing to breathe in the fragrance, she had crossed the highway, had picked one crimson rose, and entered into the trees. Karen had walked through the cemetery, across the foot bridge, even had paused to pick some raspberries, and had climbed up the trail to the mesa, where she now sat on the park bench.

Although it was early August, last night's storm still chilled the morning air dropping the temperature to forty degrees in the valley yet even colder at the mouth of the canyon. The rain and cold night air had left a layer of frost on the wrought iron bench that had soon evaporated in dawn's early light. Now morning sunlight had already made its path down the slope of the mountain, and Karen sat basking in the sunlight, while the town below remained chilled in the shadows. Fog and chimney smoke clung to the trees and a haze blanketed the town. Without knowing, Karen sat where Mary Claymore used to sit praying on Sunday mornings prior to services, while her beloved husband chopped wood and stoked a fire in the small woodstove inside the little church below.

With eyes closed, Karen meditated on what had been happening, the fear she felt in response to the note left in her birdfeeder, and the man who had been at her door last night. Her purpose had been to come to the valley to interview for a teaching position Monday, but she wondered whether or not she would want to work let alone live here. She speculated that she needed to talk with Hannah, the desk clerk, and warn her about the man at the door to room 218, while she attempted to gain information from her about Rock Creek. Meanwhile, she read the newspaper and waited for someone to arrive at the church below. Karen hoped to talk with the pastor.

Karen opened the local newspaper she carried and read the school board agenda for a meeting Tuesday, August 5, about the school district's intent to hire a replacement for a missing teacher, about a revised transportation schedule, and a hearing for Adam Claymore, Chairman of the Rock Creek School District Accountability Committee. She read surrounding articles about fall football and volleyball seasons, an expected rout over neighboring Wolf City's football team as a young McNaughton was to come of age at quarterback, and an article featuring the McNaughton cousins who dominate the high school varsity volleyball team and junior high cheerleading corps. On the lighter side Karen read the comics featuring *Alley Oop, Hagar, Snuffy Smith, Beetle Bailey, Blondie, Wizard of Id, Garfield,* and her favorite, *Prince Valiant.* Next, she skipped to the ads for the Piggly Wiggly grocery store with triple coupons, the television schedule, the specials at the Cozy Corner Café in Ridge View, and the notice for pick-your-own peaches at the Wolf City Orchards. Later, she noted apartments for rent available under the management of the Rock Creek Realtors, an ad for home and auto insurance in Rock Creek, new and used cars in Ridge View, and even the grain and livestock report for the greater Rock Creek area. Karen studied the list of worship services and other church calendar and community events as well as the schedule for the county fair the week before Labor Day and the agenda for Tuesday night's city council meeting in Jericho Springs.

Then Karen read a small article titled, "This Week in History". After a week of severe rain and hail storms, fifteen years ago August 7, the Huajatolla Slide continued from the upper mountain valley between the twin peaks of Mt. Huajatolla down into the Rock Creek Valley. In its path the slide wiped out mountain roads, radically altered the bed of West Rock Creek, and deposited boulders filling the gap between Mt. Huajatolla and the volcanic mound at the west edge of town. In its wake pools from hot springs now occupied where the creek once flowed and the pond at the base of the mammoth Live Oak on the citadel west of town disappeared. Only vapors ascended from mud cracks in the hollow of the pond floor. What was once a bountiful landmark, the Live Oak no longer prospered on the citadel. With the devastation came a host of civil problems as new claims had been filed against property boundaries and mineral rights. When prospectors had found new traces of gold and an occasional nugget, trespassers had devastated the landscape. The article continued to report that the slide originated from another ancient slide that left the scar on the north peak of Mt. Huajatolla, which had been the cause for early prospecting in what is now known as the Rock Creek Valley. The article also mentioned the closure five years ago August 9 of the once popular Blair House, a boarding house located at the base of the citadel. Following the deaths of Peter and Lydia Blair, Blair House had closed pending litigation, since no heirs had been located and title to the property stipulated conditions preventing passage of the property to public domain. The article closed with reference to Thursday night's city council meeting and renewed discussion on condemning the Blair property and settlement of property boundaries and mineral rights.

Finally, Karen read an account of a confrontation between Adam Claymore, Chairman of the Rock Creek School District Accountability Committee and Dr. Maurice Wood, the Assistant Superintendent of Schools. It quoted a student representative to the committee who portrayed Claymore as a conservative malcontent and busybody lacking in progressive thinking and filled with old fashioned ideas that would keep the school district in the dark ages. The article also quoted another source, which refused to be identified, as saying that Claymore is the only voice bold enough to speak out against school programs that purpose at desensitizing students to traditional family values and sanctity of life issues. The article told of Claymore's confrontation with a group of youth after the meeting, where all concerned acted inappropriately. With raised eyebrows Karen reassessed her opinion of the man she had mildly discounted when retrieving her luggage Friday.

Karen failed to witness Adam's arrival, as he went about his chores undetected. He had parked his truck close to the front of the parking lot, unlocked the front door, and entered the church to prepare the sanctuary for service. He sprayed air freshener as he proceeded. Quickly, Adam checked the pews making certain hymnals were in place, and then picked up debris left from last Sunday's service. Adam opened the door to the wood stove to build a small fire to take the chill out of the air. Placing kindling on top of paper, he added three medium sized dried pine logs to the firebox, after stirring the ashes with an iron poker. Opening the flue, Adam struck the match igniting the paper, which was quickly consumed with the kindling. A small but efficient fire began as smoke billowed forth through the flue and out the chimney stack.

The addition of the haze amongst the trees surrounding the little church in the glen attracted Karen, who determined someone in authority had arrived at the church below. She climbed down from the mesa along the narrow path, crossed the foot bridge, and walked cautiously through the cemetery stopping at the white picket fence behind the chapel bordering the wood shed. Once there, she watched as Adam had begun to split wood unneeded until late fall. Resting against the fence with one foot on a rail and her right arm resting on the fence post, her chin upon the arm, she enjoyed watching him work. Minutes passed before Adam sensed her presence with a gasp, then with a quick glance and awestruck he stepped backward. Spellbound he rested the splitting ax on his shoulder unable and not wanting to speak. His eyes moistened.

Karen made the first move by walking through the gate to the stack of wood Adam had split. "Mr. Claymore, I've come to attend church services, but I wonder if I could speak to you privately, now or later."

"Where did you come from?"

"I'm in trouble, and I need your help."

"Were you sitting on the bench on the mesa yesterday?" asked Adam.

"Yes, yes I was, near dusk when the storm was rolling in."

"The foal frightened you....."

"And I scampered down the trail. Really, I'm in trouble." Closer she came to him. Their eyes met, and her fragrance dazed Adam.

"And you left something on the bench."

"You were there. Did you find my Bible?"

"Yes, we are all in trouble when we have lost the truth."

"Agreed, but that's not the trouble I've got. Will you meet with me later?"

"After church services, for dinner?" answered Adam.

"Oh, thank you. Thank you very much...... I'm sorry I was rude to you yesterday."

"Your Bible is on the pulpit inside. I was hoping to find you today. I was hoping you would attend services this morning."

"Then I am forgiven," questioned Karen.

"Miss Gustafson...I am very pleased to make your acquaintance."

"You're very kind."

"You'll have to excuse me. Well, you don't have to, but would you. I mean I'm not usually at a loss for words and right now I seem to be a little awkward."

"So, I gather."

"Huh?"

"I've been reading about you."

"Hmmm...."

"The newspaper."

"Don't believe everything you hear or read."

"I've read enough to know that you are a man I can ask for help. And I need help."

"Then it's dinner, after services. But now I need to gather myself for the services. Do...please come in and make yourself at home. Really, I'm delighted you have come to services this morning. Delighted!"

With introductions completed the couple entered the sanctuary together. They walked down the aisle side by side. Karen took a seat on the isle in the second pew on the left in front of the pastor's bench behind the pulpit, while Adam sorted his notes and checked the fire in the wood stove. He loosened his collar and tie but not in response to the fire. He murmured, "Help me Jesus."

Outside of Ridge View Ruth and Rob awakened early. Hurriedly, Mom and Dad dressed and went outside to finish the duck pen without waking Andy. They welcomed the opportunity for private discussion, especially to talk about what they heard at the Cozy Corner Café. As Rob hammered staples, Ruth held the chicken wire in place. Together they stretched the wire to fit and completed the two by four frames around the top and bottom of the wire pen.

"Rob, what were they saying about newcomers? Do they know we just moved here with you?"

"I've seen them around before. Some were in town at the café, others in Rock Creek at the Stage Stop Hotel and the tobacco shop behind the hotel on the highway. The heavy set man with the cowboy hat is the sheriff. Sheriff Bailey, I think. The fella sitting next to him has attended church in Rock Creek when I've been there. Other than that I don't know them. They sure made a point about wanting new people to leave. Question is how long does a person have to be here not to be new?"

"Probably long enough for people not to remember when you got here," offered Ruth.

"Long enough to marry into the McNaughton's clan is my guess. Anyway I don't think there is anything personal about their comments. I think, in general, they don't want new people moving in and especially now. There are some issues they are upset about."

"Really, such as?"

"Pull harder at the top and stretch out the wire more firmly," instructed Rob, as Ruth responded.

"Well," Rob continued, "it seems not too many years ago there was a gigantic rock and mud slide that brought some property boundaries into question. Mineral rights too. The last couple of weeks things came to a head. Seems one major piece of property on the west side has been in litigation for a lot of years and a time line was set on the settlement. The authorities were trying to locate the original owner, who deeded the property to a family if they would continue with the property and take care of the land. Adam said there was a child involved in it too. Adam said most of the old timers don't want the rightful owners to show up and claim the property. If they don't arrive to claim it, I guess everyone in the valley will have opportunity to get the property and some mineral rights too."

"Then that's why they are suspicious of newcomers. They don't know who might be relatives?" concluded Ruth.

"Think so, I mean, I wonder how I would feel if I lived here all my life, and had worked hard to get ahead. Even if I had a long history of family in the area, and then have the opportunity to get in on a windfall deal only to learn it would fall through if some outsider comes and rightfully claims the property."

"I guess I'd feel a little greedy and resentful. Bitter, too. On the other hand I could be glad for the people that it rightfully belongs to. After all, if such a fuss is being made, the property must be of considerable value, and sometime ago an old timer sold the land to a newcomer," Ruth surmised.

"Well, it seems these small towns have a general aversion to outsiders anyway. Kind of suspicious on one hand, and a desire to resist change on the other. Some people go to a small town so they can escape negative influences of city living; others want to gain some control of their lives and be influential in a small pond."

"And others move in to take over power or just be themselves, or just be left alone."

"Newcomers want to have a say and the old-timers want to hang on to what they have. If they lose the power, it would be more devastating for them than for a newcomer not to be able to get the power and prestige. If you have never had to move and if your family has lived in one place for generations, a lot more is at stake being pushed by new people coming in. Losing out means too much, it's almost life threatening," added Rob.

"Certainly, to a way of life."

"Kinda understandable either way you look at it."

"How do you mean? A little give and take could go a long way? Compromise and cooperation? Working together?" asked Ruth.

"I guess their answer is to put a wall around the valley and keep newcomers out, then control those who are already here. I don't think there's really too much Christian influence here. When you think about it, the area has a history of wild living."

"I think its money motivated, if they're worried about property and mineral rights."

"I think it's more insidious. Spiritual warfare," concluded Rob.

"How do you mean?"

"Well, when I stayed at the Stage Stop Hotel, I noticed a lot of wild stuff going on."

"Where you were staying?" asked Ruth, with raised eyebrows.

"There…at the hotel, the tobacco shop, the bed and breakfast, and well, the whole place seemed to be a hot bed for immoral activity."

"That's what they were talking about—what was going on in Rock Creek. Playing upon the lusts of man, snares."

"Prostitution, drugs, gambling…."

"Licentious behaviors appealing to addictive personalities, appealing to people who want to be somebody, who want to take short cuts to get what they want. I suppose the appeal is also for people who just want to be loved or accepted, even if it is at a price," speculated Ruth.

"And run by people who want to control others by knowing who has done what to or with whom. That's Adam's guess," informed Rob.

"Okay, I'll buy that but what about the other things they were talking about?"

"You mean the schools?" asked Rob.

"Yes, I really got disgusted with the foul language. I could have pasted that creep in the mouth and in front of Andy too. What was that he was saying about sex in the home economics class?" said Ruth.

"Adam spoke to me about the curriculum changes the schools are being confronted with. It's not just here; it's all over. So called progressive influences that seem to promote promiscuity on one hand, while also dumbing-down the standards. But it's not just home economics, it's other curriculum too."

"How about the quote, the joke the creep told, about how one of his dates had told him she had learned some new techniques in her class. She was using them at her job at the Asherah House?" asked Ruth.

"I don't think it was a joke," answered Rob.

"He didn't need to be so explicit either!"

"I don't get it. I'm certain school districts are not promoting illicit sex or training girls to be prostitutes," Rob asserted and said, "There, I'm almost done. Hold the wire tightly against the post and the building."

"Like this?"

"Just right. Adam says the values and philosophy controlling education are messed up. Liberalization has brought an abundance of rights without responsibilities, the religion of secular humanism he says. I don't know. But I do know I dislike the lack of respect and common decency those men demonstrated. If they are for it, I'm against it," declared Rob.

"They said some other things, I take it you were not happy with," commented Ruth.

"Including their comments about Adam Claymore?"

"Especially about Adam Claymore, and he's your friend isn't he?"

"He's more than that."

"They ridiculed him!" said Ruth.

"And slandered him."

"They made him sound self-righteous, even a joke."

"You noticed they didn't say it to his face. Adam Claymore is my friend, probably the best kind of a friend a fella could have," speculated Rob.

"How do you mean?"

"When I first came here, I repaired the lines in the canyon. I stayed at the Stage Stop Hotel, and I was intent on getting myself right with the Lord. I attended the church in Rock Creek where he is deacon. He befriended me and encouraged me to deal honestly with my issues. I opened up to him, and he said it sounded like I needed to forgive and be forgiven. He said I needed to forgive God."

"Forgive God? Isn't that being a little presumptuous?" asked Ruth.

"That's what I thought, but Adam said if we really can have a relationship with God the Father and Jesus the Son, then we need to relate to them openly and honestly. I mean if I'm angry with God, he already knows it, so what good does it do to cover it up."

"Good point," added Ruth.

"Adam said I needed a lot of healing too, but forgiveness is the first step to healing. Besides Christ calls us to a lifestyle of forgiveness

"What did you do?"

"I withdrew and isolated. I moved out of the hotel into a cottage on a back alley. You should have seen it. It was dark with a lot of shade trees. It was like…"

"A tomb?" asked Ruth.

"Yeah, it was dark, dirty, dingy, and like a tomb. Just what I needed. Instead of forgiving and mostly accepting forgiveness, I withdrew to my shame and blame to let old wounds continue to fester."

"And this was all before this summer?"

"Yup!"

"But you left there?"

"I did. One night the Lord woke me up. I dreamed he called me to come out. Three times he woke me and said Lazarus come out. I woke up and said come out from what and to what. He said come out from the dead and into the living," confessed Rob.

"He told me you would," Ruth said with a smile.

"What?"

"When we were separated, God gave me the scripture about Lazarus and told me it was for you."

"When was this?" asked Rob.

"During the worst of times, when I was frightened the most."

"That's when you said you could make it without me?" asked Rob.

"Exactly, I had his promise."

"Anyway, that's when I called you and came home."

"I'm glad you did!"

"There's more to the story. While I was here working the canyon and going to church, I applied for a transfer and I attended a men's Bible study at Adam's church. Adam and a traveling salesman named Kip Powell wouldn't leave me alone. The former pastor too," explained Rob.

"Former pastor?"

"Yes, at the church. He was a bi-vocational pastor, but he couldn't make it on the salary folks were willing to pay, so he accepted an associate pastorate in Jericho Springs at the Baptist Church, where they provided both housing and some salary."

"And, this was before you came home?"

"Yes, the three of them wouldn't leave me alone. Like true friends, they came after me. Ruth, they demonstrated Christ's love. They know you and I have had our difficulties. They said I was both bruised and flawed and then they encouraged me to let God heal me one file folder at a time. They got me into a Bible study on Ephesians and the Gospel of John."

"I read Ephesians recently."

"I even read some Christian novels including *Quo Vadis* and then I saw the movie, and Ruth, God isn't finished with me yet. I've asked God the Father to help me be the man he wants me to be and I know that includes marriage and family. I've also asked God to allow me to love his people the way he does. Then he did something very special."

"Whaaat?"

"He had me crawl up in his lap."

"You mean..."

"Right, like I never could with my father. Father God wants me to rest and return. To relax in him. Sit on his lap, lean back, and trust my daddy to do me no harm, no betrayal," Rob said as tears swelled into his eyes then cascaded down his cheeks.

"Like a child who can trust his daddy to do him no harm, no betrayal," Ruth said as she embraced her husband and laid her head upon Rob's chest.

"And that has been my issue."

"Betrayal?" asked Ruth.

"By those I should have been able to love and trust."

"Me?"

"Not you, far from it. You didn't betray me; I betrayed you. I projected, even expected you to betray me, then I worked things around in my head and got messed up presuming against you. But you remained loyal and proved yourself trustworthy," Rob explained.

"Like man's best friend?"

"Now don't turn this into something demeaning and slight yourself."

"Okay…I've got my own issues, you know," offered Ruth.

"I do. I mean trustworthy like a hero is trustworthy," added Rob.

"Hmmmm…wow," exclaimed Ruth enthusiastically.

"Then I came home and the transfer was approved and I moved here at the beginning of the summer."

"I understand why you have been so enthusiastic about coming here."

"There! I'm finished. Let the ducks out, and let's get Andy out of bed and go to church," proclaimed Rob.

"Yes…this truly is the day of the Lord, at least for us," Ruth said with outstretched arms.

Having finished breakfast and dressed for church, the Brownings headed toward Rock Creek, when they heard Honk! Honk!

"Who was that Daddy?" asked Andy.

"Don't you recognize the little green car?" asked Mom.

"Oh! Was that Krystal's car?" wondered Andy aloud.

"Yes, the Bond's must have finished their paper routes and are headed for church in Jericho Springs," Rob predicted.

"We must be midway between Ridge View and Rock Creek. The road they live on makes a T where the Rock Creek tributaries merge," offered Ruth, "I remember taking note of that road while riding the bus."

"Yes, and if we had turned left, we would have driven up to the ridge and onto the wide open plains. Actually, it becomes more like a desert after a few miles outside this river valley," Rob informed.

"Then the Bond's must live over there."

"Looks like it."

"Dad, how much further 'till church?" asked Andy.

"Rock Creek isn't too far, Son."

"Mom, isn't that where we were on Friday when we helped the lady with her suitcase, and she prayed with us and the bus driver?"

"Yes, her name is Karen Gustafson."

"If your driver prayed with you, he was Goodenough, I'll bet," said Rob.

"You mean, just right!"

"No, Mom, Dad's right. His last name was Goodenough."

"I'm just kidding, Andy. He was more than good enough. How many times have you had a bus driver pray with you?"

"That was really neat, Dad, and we made a new friend with Miss Karen. She's real pretty! I want to marry a girl as pretty as she is! She has dark blue eyes, bubblegum colored cheeks, and creamy white skin, and red nail polish," sighed Andy dreamily, "I bet Krystal will look like that when she grows up. Cept she has hazel eyes. Or were they brown, Mom? Or maybe that was Kristin. Gosh, I don't remember. I just remember…them! Can I marry both of 'em?"

"Andrew, never mind about girls. You've got plenty of time before they become an issue young man!" promised Ruth with an appreciative smile.

"I've met Morris. He has preached at church before, did a good job. He attends church in Rock Creek occasionally. I guess he got snowed in before and got acquainted with Adam," said Rob.

"We must get some pretty rough winter weather, Mr. Telephone Lineman. I don't think I like the sounds of that," said Ruth with a frown.

"How come, Mom?"

"Sorry, Rob," Ruth said apologetically.

"There's nothing to worry about, Son. No matter where you live in Colorado the weather can be severe at times. That's all part of it. You take the good with the bad."

"Are we there yet, Dad?"

"Just about, look there ahead of us."

"Where at Dad? I don't see anything but mountains. Kinda small ones though."

"Looks like a fort doesn't it? The mounds with sharp rock coming out of them look like a fort, and we can't see where the road and the creek actually go between two foothills. Anyway I guess that's what you call them," informed Rob.

"If this were an ocean, it would look like a giant wave about to break and the crest of the wave is the tall straight rock coming out of the center of the mounds," offered Ruth.

"You're right, Ruth, and if that's the case, then the waves look like fortress walls."

Andy nailed it when he said, "I think they look like hog legs, and the hogs are lying upside down on their backs."

"I wonder if we will see Karen?" said Ruth.

"Your new friend?"

"She was a godsend. The Lord provided me with a prayer warrior, a friend just when I needed one."

"You mean two, Mom."

"That's right, Karen, the passenger and Morris, the driver."

"Then I'll bet we will see her. We'll make a point of it. If she's not at church, then we will look her up. I would like to meet her," declared Rob.

"You'll like her, Rob."

"How could I not, since Andy wants to marry a girl as pretty as she is!"

The old blue Chevy decelerated between the two hogbacks into the strike valley, as Rob slowed down before entering Rock Creek. They passed between the sides of the emergency road closure fence, and then paralleled Rock Creek into town past the school offices, between the highway department building on one side of the road and the Stage Stop Hotel on the other, and through the intersection of the highway and County Road 403. Rob slowed the station wagon to a near stop, as he drove onto the driveway leading to the little church in the glen. The Brownings followed a pickup truck immediately to a parking space beside Adam Claymore's red truck.

"Rob, I totally missed seeing this church when we were here. I wouldn't have guessed there was a church over here. How quaint it is!" Ruth admitted appreciatively.

"Neat spot, huh?"

"I love it."

"Me too, Mom, I loooove it."

"Hush you silly. Don't make fun of your Mom."

"I looooove it. I looooove it," said Andy as he bounded out of the station wagon causing another incoming car to slide to a halt. Andy's little eyes were caught by the hostile stare of an angry driver he recognized from the group at the Cozy corner Café.

"Andy!" screamed Ruth, "Be careful!"

"I'm sorry, Mom, I guess I shouldn't have kidded you, huh?"

"Just use your head, Son. This may be a small town, but your mother and I want you to be alert to possible danger," Rob said with multiple meanings.

The man from the automobile passed by briskly without so much as a glance and entered the sanctuary.

"You mean like him, Dad? He was at the place where we ate yesterday. He's nasty, isn't he?" speculated Andy.

"Yes, his language yesterday was nasty. Not good, huh?" said Dad.

"Not good, Daddy, Jesus wouldn't be happy with what he said."

"You heard?" asked Mom.

"Yes, but I pretended not to. Is school really like that?" asked Andy with a worried look.

"I doubt it."

"I'm gonna ask Jesus today!" Andy proclaimed.

"Good idea, ask him to keep you safe, too," ordered Mom.

The driver of the other pickup truck approached Rob and Andy, "It's Rob Browning isn't it?"

"Yes, and Rabbit, I'd like you to meet my wife, Ruth, and son, Andrew."

Shaking hands Rob added as he introduced Rabbit Pinebow to Ruth and Andy, "Rabbit must be singing today. He works for Adam Claymore."

Though pleased to meet Rabbit, Ruth became nervous amongst people she did not know and started to fret immediately, "I'm pleased to meet you. Are you singing?"

"Yes, Mr. Claymore occasionally lets me out of the kitchen to sing in church."

"And you cook, too?" asked Ruth.

"Yes, Mum, I'm the cook at Claymore Flats, the largest ranch in the area! You will have to come visit my kitchen."

"Well, I think I'd like to," said Ruth, "and where is Claymore Flats?"

"Actually, if you walk around the back of the church, cross the footbridge you are on it, then go up the hill, you would be on it. But to get to the ranch house, you would have to take the road to Jericho Springs, take the first left, and follow that road toward Wolf City across the mesa. From your first turn off 403 to the limits of Wolf City is Claymore land. The homestead is about midway to Wolf City on the left. And from here to the mountain is Adam's land," explained Rabbit, chief cook and bottle washer on Claymore Flats.

Interrupting, Karen recognized Ruth and emerged from the chapel door, then shouted, "Ruth, Ruth Browning!"

And the two women closed the distance between them and hugged like long lost friends, while Rob, Andy, and Rabbit watched them. Adam came to the door to greet the arrivals and took note of Karen's exuberance with pleasure. He thought that not everything had been trouble for Karen.

Andy and Rob caught up with Karen and Ruth with Rabbit following behind. Rob and Andy were introduced to Karen, and then Rob introduced Ruth and Andy to Adam, while Adam and Karen stood side by side at the chapel door.

Rabbit observed the proximity of Karen to Adam then winked at Adam and commented as he passed into the sanctuary, "Well, this seems very natural."

Adam smiled and Karen flushed not knowing the meaning of his comment but knowing she had something to do with it. They all entered the church and seated themselves, while Adam assumed the pulpit. Ruth sat down beside Karen flanked by Rob and Andy, while Rabbit began to play the opening hymn on the piano. Seated in the back pew, the scowling driver of the pickup truck watched.

The congregation sang, "Morning Has Broken." As interim pastor Adam led the flock in prayer and shared the morning announcements. Explaining the article about himself in the newspaper last Wednesday, Adam offered an apology for his inappropriate behavior. A couple in front murmured but the small congregation voiced total support for him. Adam pledged to keep-on-keeping-on, which drew a chorus of amen's from all except the scowling man in the rear. Next, Adam introduced Karen Gustafson and shared that she was interviewing for a teaching position. He then asked Rob to introduce Ruth and Andy, which Rob did in glowing terms.

Those gathered together sang a few more worshipful songs and hymns, took a skimpy offering, while Rabbit sang "How Great Thou Art" inspirationally. Pastor Adam preached a message urging them to "Be Who You Is, You Can't Be Any Iser." Adam urged them to put on the full armor of God as children of the Lord, then to rejoice always, pray continuously, and give thanks in all circumstances. Adam reminded them it was not against flesh and blood the Christian fights, it was against the powers and principalities of darkness. Adam said Satan attacked using people to ridicule and slander, and persecute God's people, but Christians should consider ourselves fortunate when that happened, because that was a sign of whom we are as God's children. He reminded the congregation that God provided us with trials to test us and to make us more like Jesus, but Satan tried to tempt us in the midst of those trials. Adam closed with an encouraging word, praying for the church and their finances, a victory for family values in the schools, for a planning committee of churches in the valley that would be meeting next week, and for all to be who they are in Christ Jesus. He reminded them of the Wednesday night prayer meeting. The congregation rose to grasp hands in a benediction, as the scowling man in the back made his exit before Adam could greet him.

All left the sanctuary and chit-chatted, while Adam locked the door. Karen and Ruth talked, as Rob and Rabbit reviewed last night's ballgame of the Denver Bears team. Attendees from Rock Creek walked down the lane and emerged from the glen to the Valley Highway, while those who drove motored their way toward home. Andy found the alms box attached by the doorway and looked in. Andy removed two rocks and held them up for all to see.

"Hey, look at the neat rocks I found in this box. They were in this envelope."

"Rob, would you get your son and tell him what he has done," ordered Ruth.

Andy ducked his head sensing he had done something wrong and put his new found treasure in his pocket. Rob moved to grab him, while Adam lightened the tense moment with a comment that he should have checked the box but no one puts anything of value in there anymore. Jokingly, Adam asked Rob to let Andy check the box to see if any money had been put in there, which Andy did after checking with his father.

Ruth invited Karen to dinner, which Karen declined saying she had an appointment. Adam and Rob joined Karen and Ruth. Rob invited Adam to dinner, but Adam said he had a date. Karen flushed, and Adam changed his statement.

"I mean, Miss Gustafson has asked me to meet with her after services, and I suggested we meet over dinner."

Rob and Ruth traded glances.

"Yes, the Reverend.... Mr. Claymore, kindly said he would talk with me at dinner," Karen paused, looked at Adam, touched his arm, then continued, " and thank you, Reverend."

"Deacon, I'm not the real pastor here. I'm just filling in."

But Karen promptly responded, "You should be the pastor, your service touched me here and here," as she motioned to both her head and heart.

"Well, another time," said Ruth. "How long are you going to be here? Perhaps we can get together later this week."

"My interview is tomorrow, and the school board meets Tuesday night. The bus doesn't get here until Friday, so I'm here until Friday, at least."

"At least?" asked Adam.

"Yes, if I'm offered the job and decide to take it, I may stay over and make housing and other arrangements before going back home to get my things."

"If you take the job?" asked Rob.

"That's part of what I want to talk with Mr. Claymore about."

"Pastor...Mr...or Reverend...Deacon..."

"Adam, Mrs. Browning. Please call me Adam."

"Thank you, Adam, you've all confused me, and that's not difficult. You did say prayer meeting is on Wednesday?"

Adam nodded in affirmation.

"Karen!" Ruth interjected, "Why don't you come visit me on Wednesday morning. I'll come pick you up. Let's have lunch here or in Ridge View, you stay for dinner, and we all attend prayer meeting here Wednesday night. That way you can tell me all about your interview."

"And you can show me your house."

"That's a date!" Karen responded, glanced at Adam, and then smiled. And Adam realized she had purposely eased the earlier embarrassment he initiated with her comment.

"Perfect," said Adam with admiration.

Rapport and Strife
Chapter 8

*"...I fear that there may be discord, jealously, fits
of rage, selfish ambition, slander, gossip, arrogance
and disorder." 2 Corinthians 12:20b*

As the Browning's light-blue station wagon left the parking lot, Karen and Adam began to walk to the restaurant, when Adam stopped Karen and said, "Wait, I'd like for you to see something. Walk with me through the forest. It's at the mouth of the canyon."

"Okay," Karen replied, "I'm afraid I've been out discovering Rock Creek quite a bit. In fact I've got a couple of questions for you too."

"Then let's walk awhile."

They did walk through the woods along the path and to the guardrail at the mouth of the canyon where both Rock Creek and US 85/87 exit the valley.

"I like to come here and breathe in the moist air from the waterfall. It helps keep Rock Creek cool in the summer, but it also kind of creates heaviness in the air. Mixed with the chimney smoke and fog, it sometimes creates eeriness, a mystery of sorts."

Stopping at the barrier and gripping the top rail, Adam directed Karen's attention to an eagle's nest in the canyon wall. "See there on the side, about three fourths up the wall in a crag. An eagle has nested. I think several generations of birds have used that nest. See how they survive in the midst of people around them. Really, they prefer privacy."

"Are they like the Claymore's?"

"How do you mean?"

"They are rugged and individualistic, strong and yet vulnerable, picturesque and regal," Karen analyzed.

"Thank you!"

"Not at all, judging from the cemetery, I'd say the Claymore's have probably been in Rock Creek longer than anyone. Judging from the newspaper, it looks like you are individualistic and separated from the norm," continued Karen.

"Good assessment, there is a reason my people settled on the mesa instead of the valley. They wanted to be away from people but close enough to be with the people if they wanted to, or if they were needed. If that makes sense?" explained Adam.

"You mean you want to be close enough to be friendly and live amongst people but not to be like your neighbors, not to take on their habits," suggested Karen.

"You've got it. The Claymore's like most other clans in the valley are related to the other old families. We just didn't want to be gobbled up by them or become like them. We have a history of powerful influence with the valley, but we never wanted to rule or dominate like the McNaughton's do. Honestly, I think my people did not want to be caught up with what was happening in the valley."

"Yet you seem very much involved."

"I'm more of an advocate, a voice than a real participant. I want nothing to do with public office or private societies. But I do have a heart for the people, especially those in Rock Creek."

"More like a prophet than a king?"

"Yes, interesting way to put it. My wife taught me to care about the people, to be involved. She was a McNaughton. More often than not it seems I'm too involved. I get in trouble for what I say."

"Someone has to speak up when wrong is done. I heard that in what you said too. Your people have been ready to come to the aid of your neighbors."

"If the Lord tells them," Adam pointed, "Look over there. See her fly to the nest. In the crag her nest is sheltered. Like the psalm. The eagle and her offspring would be sheltered on the side of the cliff. It's like God has them in the palm of his hand. No, I take that back. It's like God's got his palm covering them."

"You mean like when the storms of life come, God covers us with the palm of his hand to shelter and protect us?" asked Karen.

"As opposed to when God is molding us in the palm of his hand to mold us as his own? Of course, he does that, too," Adam responded.

"You know when I first saw you...." began Karen.

"Friday morning when you got off the bus and Morris Goodenough, the driver, was helping with your two suitcases and two boxes," added Adam.

"Yes, and before I knew you were a pastor. You looked like the Marlboro Country Man in the cigarette commercial on television," Karen confessed.

"Really?"

"You have a mystique about you, but now I think you are more like the Lone Ranger," and then Karen added, "The sheriff parked his cruiser here last night. I think it's his routine."

"Then what did he do? Did he walk into town to the tobacco store?" Adam inquired.

"No, he went to the bed and breakfast across the way from the hotel."

"Interesting, but he didn't go into the tobacco store?"

"Like I said I didn't see him there, but I saw him walk the path to the big house on the end of the street. What is it, Indiana Avenue? I was watching but I did not see him go to the tobacco store. I did see a lot of other people go in there."

"You did? Where were you? Did anyone see you?" Adam responded with some concern.

"I was in my room, but no one saw me, except the cook or dishwasher."

"He's a McNaughton."

"Is that bad?"

"No McNaughton is just anyone."

"Oh, I'm sorry."

"No, no, don't get me wrong. Even though Harper is a cook and dishwasher, he is connected. He is related to the most powerful family in the valley. He gets jerked around; depending on how his boss feels, one day he is the cook, but the next he's a dishwasher. They play games with him. By and large they are good people. They are driven. It isn't wise to get in their way," explained Adam.

"Driven?"

"Like most people, they are driven. They pursue wealth. No, it's more than that. It's like a quest for power, prestige, position or wealth, land, gold, and water. Mostly they would like to continue to control what happens here."

"Sounds a little scary to me," concluded Karen.

"I'm sorry. I've made too much of that. It's really not that bad. I think. But you do need to be careful if you get the teaching position. We are small minded here, and you don't want to get caught up in the petty politics," Adam said apologetically.

"I'll remember that."

"You say the sheriff didn't go into the tobacco store?' asked Adam for confirmation.

"No, I don't think so."

"Good."

"What are you concerned about?"

"I don't know yet. It's too early to say. Let's just say I've got some concerns. Anyway, enough gossip, let's go to dinner. You said you were in trouble. I'm more interested in what you have to say than the doings of the sheriff in this small and sometimes hostile valley."

Karen and Adam quietly walked to the hotel. Each pondered their conversation and both tried to piece together what she had seen and the fact of the dishwasher seeing her watching both the tobacco store and the sheriff. Adam's comments added to her fear. She added to his growing awareness that things aren't right in Rock Creek. Wondering what he should do, he was reminded of the contents of the message God gave him for this morning's sermon. He mulled it over: have the full armor on; stand; defend what Christ has gained; be joyful always; pray continuously; and give thanks in all circumstances. Adam understood that was what God wanted him to do.

They entered the hotel and were seated at a window table by Sarah, the flashy waitress, whose warm 'hello' to Adam accompanied a jealous glance toward Karen.

"Brrrrr......." said Karen.

"Is it cold in here?"

"In a manner of speaking, I think the waitress has a case of the green eyed monster."

"That's something I'm not familiar with," Adam reflected.

"What do you recommend, Adam?"

Taking the menu in hand, Adam didn't hesitate to suggest Karen have the Sunday brunch buffet. It wasn't bad, he told her, and we won't have to wait to be served. They made their selection and began their first meal together.

"The Brownings should have a good afternoon?" said Adam.

"What's that you say?"

"Rob told me he was going to show Ruth and Andy the sights this afternoon. I encouraged him to take Ruth for a drive up Claymore Flats, but he said he thought Andy would be fascinated with the rockslide above Jericho Springs," Adam expanded.

"Is it the one in the newspaper article?"

"Yes, you read it, too. The old rockslide has created quite a commotion for the whole valley. It's like the gold rush all over. People seemed to have lost their senses hoping to have a chance to get something for near nothing or to gain a windfall. Fifteen years ago everywhere north of Palmer Lake was drenched. Flash floods erupted from all the canyons filling the South Platte River that flooded the Denver area in 1965. Flooding here caused the rockslide that altered the bed of Rock Creek and property lines changed within minutes. It nearly wiped out Jericho Springs except for an old volcano obstructing its path."

"How fascinating!" Karen responded.

"That's right! You are applying for the physical science position, aren't you?"

"Yes, one of the reasons I'm interested in the position is the topography of this region, like the canyon and the hills around Rock Creek. It's intriguing."

"Have you seen the slide?" asked Adam.

"Well, no, I've heard about it and, of course, read about it. In college, I missed a field trip exploring this area, so I've always wanted to come visit here," explained Karen.

"Hopefully, you will get the job and have plenty of opportunity to see the sights."

"I'd like that, I think. I'd really like to explore the volcano. It's peculiar that a volcano would be at the base of the mountains and that it would be able to withstand a rockslide of such volume. Let's see what happens. I must say I'm more than concerned about the climate here."

"Oh, really? Outside of Rock Creek, it is generally more pleasant. The canyon, mesa, and foothills around it make the weather kind of peculiar, as does the ridge. I'd think that would add to your attraction," Adam said with surprise.

"Oh, it does. That's not the climate I meant."

"Is that why you are in trouble?"

"Yes, there are some things that have happened that have me concerned. My father told me I should talk to the pastor at the local church when I told him what was going on. He suggested I call the sheriff, but frankly, the sheriff gives me the creeps," Karen explained.

"Bailey?"

Karen nodded.

"I've thought Bailey is on the level, but I'm afraid he may be choosing to ignore what's going on. I don't know what or why but there appears to be something going on, and whoever is gathering at the tobacco store has something to do with it. But, I'm probably just being suspicious," Adam admitted.

"Like I said, I saw him walk to the bed and breakfast after parking his cruiser at the mouth of the canyon. I saw people going over there from the hotel. And I saw people going in and out of the tobacco store. I heard the staff arguing when I was walking around back, and then someone knocked the dishwasher out the back door of the kitchen. He fell down and swore at this man. Two women were involved, too. One was the desk clerk, Hannah. She ran past me, up the stairs, and into her room," revealed Karen.

"Someone saw you observing what was happening. You were a witness to a McNaughton getting beat up? Interesting!" Adam said with surprise.

"That's right, and I noticed the newspaper want ads. An escort service, out-calls, and an assortment of other suggestive services—all with similar telephone numbers."

"Not exactly what you would expect is it?"

"Hardly, I haven't seen anything beyond Rock Creek, but someone just driving through here would never suspect what appears to be going on."

"Which is?"

"A real emphasis on the lust of man, or maybe just plain ordinary Hedonism. And that's not all, what happens when people stop here at the hotel, like on a Friday night?" Karen asserted.

"My guess it's not much different from other places on a Friday night."

"I wouldn't know that by comparison. What I do know is this is not where I would choose to be, under normal circumstances," admitted Karen.

"If you weren't here for an interview?"

"Right, I sat down here for a meal and our waitress tried to fix me up with some men at a table. I don't mean for a normal type date. I mean it was suggestive, like I had rented a room here to ...well to prostitute myself."

"You're kidding!" Adam replied with shock.

"I probably sound self righteous or something, but I've never been propositioned, at least in that way."

"As if someone presumed you were here for that purpose."

"Exactly, it gets worse."

"How?" asked Adam and Karen explained to Adam's dismay.

Adam retrieved a business card from his suit coat pocket and handed it to Karen and said, "Karen, I know you do not know me well, but call for me at my ranch. If I'm not there, my men will reach me. If you have anything peculiar happening, don't hesitate. I want you to locate the phone booth in the lobby so you know where it is, and there is a pay phone at the convenience store as well." Then Adam said with a smile, "In spite of what Rabbit might have told Mrs. Browning about his kitchen, you would be welcome at my house. If you have trouble you are welcome to be a guest at my ranch."

After church services Sunday afternoon, the Browning family traveled west on County Road 403. The family marveled at the beautiful and fragrant wild flowers as they crossed the plains to Jericho Springs. Stopping briefly at the lone convenience store in town, they met the Bond family, who had also just left church. Ken Bond introduced his wife, Katarina, to the Brownings and Mike Crowfoot, the clerk at the convenience store.

Andy talked his mom into buying him three pieces of bubblegum, which he took immediately and gave to Krystal and Kristin. Grinning from ear to ear, Andy handed one bubblegum to each girl and said, "This is for your ride home. It will help you later." Both girls had no idea that he meant for the gum to influence their beauty like Karen Gustafson's complexion, but they did giggle.

Ken recommended the Brownings follow a dirt road leading west of town into the mountains. If they would stop at the hairpin turn, Ken told them they would see the valley beyond a huge old tree. He went on to tell them about the rockslide and how the stream bed had been changed. He suggested they try to decide what the scar on the mountain looked like, to see if the Brownings could agree on their interpretation. If they could, Ken said, they would be one of few families to do so.

Adam left Karen at the hotel in Rock Creek and returned home on Claymore Flats, where he immediately instructed Rabbit to find him, wherever he may be if Karen Gustafson were to call him. Take a message, Adam instructed. He spent the afternoon at his computer updating his accounts, tending to Big Foot and other pets, and then called Whitney, Red McNaughton, his brother-in-law. Adam arranged an early Monday morning breakfast with Red at the Cozy Corner Café in Ridge View. Although Whitney wanted to know what's on the agenda for discussion, Adam only said he wanted Whitney to update him on his rental properties. Adam did not hint at his concern about the McNaughton clan's reaction to the injunction preventing condemnation of the Blair House. It had been well known they hoped to gain the land and, especially, the mineral and water rights. Adam hoped to learn what Red knew about the crowd at the tobacco store in Rock Creek. What were the "good ole' boys" up to?

Meanwhile, the intruder at the old mansion in Jericho Springs stayed inside and unnoticed because of an unusual amount of traffic on the street outside. He roamed the house carefully surveying contents and condition. Later he returned to his bedroom, located his copy of the *Outcry*, and caught up on more news. A featured story covered a special town council meeting called for Thursday. Originally, it had been called to conduct a public meeting to share the terms for condemning the Blair House and opening the land and mineral rights for public sale. A court injunction had halted those efforts. The original deed and title stipulated conditions for the property not to pass to public domain. Now the meeting promised to be more like a circus as most of the town was interested in learning how and who had managed to thwart the town council's efforts. Speculation was rampant the article said as rumors abounded that interest outside Rock Creek had a legal claim to the property. The author reported that many members of old families were incensed over the prospect of not being able to gain ownership of the property. Another article provided background on Peter and Lydia Blair, how they had operated the property as a boarding house for several years prior to both their deaths, how they had no relatives in the valley, and how relatives from Kansas sued unsuccessfully to claim the property. An editorial asserted the house belonged to the history of the area and since it was being considered as an historical building, it should revert to public domain and be managed by the city fathers. Letters to the editors took two sides to the issue. One, written by an Adam Claymore, advocated that the proper owner should be unobstructed in gaining what was his or hers legally. Another letter, written by a McNaughton, warned outsiders to keep out of Rock Creek and Rock Creek business. In fact, the author suggested the whole valley be fenced so outsiders could not take up residence near those who had worked to build what was here including the Blair House. The intruder read no more.

Back at the Stage Stop Hotel in Rock Creek, Karen relaxed for awhile in her room following lunch with Adam. Daydreaming about Claymore Flats, she wondered what it would be like to take advantage of Adam's hospitality. She had overheard Ruth's conversation with Rabbit Pinebow about his kitchen and wondered if there could be a place there where she could hang her log cabin birdfeeder. Sitting on the chair looking out of the window, Karen finally decided to prepare for her interview Monday.

Karen reviewed her credentials, letters of endorsement, transcripts, resume, and sample packets of lesson plans. Next, she planned her responses to anticipated questions about educational philosophy, classroom management strategies, instructional techniques, meeting student needs in a classroom of differentiated abilities. She developed her views on extra-curricular activities, the community as a classroom, and having the community in the classroom. Then, Karen made notes about both social studies and science curriculum and her thoughts on scope and sequence and interdisciplinary cooperation. Karen finally meditated on the key question certain to arise. Why did she leave her last position?

"How do I tell them I was asked to leave? ... It would be better for all concerned. We will make certain you get a good official recommendation. There will be no blemish on your record. ..... These things happen sometimes to the best of teachers. How do I tell them a student apparently killed herself after getting an abortion I advised her not to get? How do I tell them I went out of my way to prevent the abortion? The girl felt so guilty when she saw me she flipped out, and that was the last time I talked with her. At least I didn't tell her to get the abortion! I couldn't live with myself if I had," Karen said, then stopped her own examination and meditated on the school counselor and nurse who first advised the girl then had helped make the appointment for the teen. The nurse had driven the girl to the clinic.

Karen meditated awhile longer and prayed for the forgiveness and salvation of her former co-workers. Next, she finished her preparation. She reviewed her options and what was important to her. Again she spoke aloud to herself, "What do I do if they offer me the job? If they don't? From what I've seen and experienced, do I want to be here? How different is Rock Creek from other small towns? Good gosh! I haven't even been out of town yet, and I'm making radical judgments! Lighten up girl! What's important? Father, guide me."

With those thoughts, Karen returned to her dad's challenge. Her dad urged her to take with her the ten most valued things she cherished. Her selection would help her sort things out. Karen's dad had said to think about what each meant and why they were important to her.

"I need to finish that project!"

Karen gathered her ten items minus the birdhouse and the pistol and holster, which she had already focused on. She began with her photo album. Page by page she looked at her history in pictures, the good times, meaningful events growing up. Pictures of friends and family, of pets, and of places she had visited. Next, she reviewed the box with the letters she had received from Mom and Pop when she was attending college. Calvary Bible College had been difficult in many ways. This box of letters was a reminder that regardless of how she performed she was loved by those most important to her. Her credentials, she had already examined, and they contrasted the letters from her folks. The credentials testified to her job performance as well as to her character. The letters testified that she was accomplished as a professional regardless of her having been asked to leave her last position. Stationary? Why had she chosen to bring it of all things? Her need to communicate, to be responsive and a reminder that relationships carry a responsibility with them? Yes, she thought. I have a need to be in touch with others. I need to express my personal thoughts as well as professional thoughts in the classroom. Her diary, of course, was high on her list. Here she had recorded her prayer life as well as an occasional entry telling about people, places, and things. So likewise her camera, as she recorded with pictures. The jewelry box, a memento, a gift received, which left the crucifix hanging on the wall. It had belonged to her grandmother. A Catholic, Grandma was her role model, and Grandma had led her to the Lord. Karen's conversion had been a joy for the whole family, who were mostly Baptists.

"Okay, Karen, what is important to you?" "People, relationships, my Lord Jesus, parents, communicating, keeping record of my life. Like Adam's sermon, being who I is I can't be any 'Izzer'?"

"Next question, missy! How does that relate to a job?" "Answer, I need a teaching position where I can 'be who I is', where I can relate to both students and co-workers in a meaningful way. I think that means I would repeat what I did in my last position. I would really try to make a difference. I wouldn't let something critical happen from the sidelines." "Interview over. You've got the job!" "Yes, it's time to eat!" Having concluded her conversation with herself, she replaced her favorite items, dressed for dinner, and hurried down the hallway forgetting the trepidation she felt about the hotel. Buoyant and enthusiastic, Karen felt ready to take on the world, to interview, to wow 'em.

A different mood had overcome the Brownings. When the Brownings arrived home, they were not hungry like Karen. They were sickened. They had followed the dirt road outside of Jericho Springs and stopped before the hairpin turn above the huge tree that stands above the town below. They had marveled at the sight, the effect of the rockslide, the barren but massive tree, the parched pool before it, the broken down mansion, and the spacious valley beyond Jericho Springs. They had bantered back and forth arguing and interpreting the scar on the north peak of the mountain. Rob had driven their station wagon into the valley above where his family had seen a woodcutter loading his pickup truck with the fruit of his labor. The Brownings had played along the creek where it meandered through the meadow, then had returned at dusk through Jericho Springs toward Ridge View to their home off County Road 403. The first clue of trouble was the figure eights etched into the bed of their stone driveway. Rock had been scattered throughout the yard. Andy had noticed the dead animal on the doorstep immediately.

Ruth shrieked, then said, "Rob check on the ducks!"

"And Freda, too, Daddy!"

Rob bolted from the truck to the pens below. The fence was bowed where someone had climbed on it to get into the pen. No ducks appeared, but one frightened call came from under the coop. Andy and Ruth caught up with Rob after checking what was on the doorstep.

"Rob, someone killed a skunk and put it on our doorstep!" Ruth informed.

"Welcome to Ridge View, I guess," Rob said as he unlocked the garage door and lifted it upward. In moments he was out the side door and under the pen retrieving their pet.

"There's only one under here!" Rob shouted to Ruth and Andy.

"Who is it?" asked Andy.

"Surely the others are there!"

"Nope, and this one is terrified. Its heart is about to explode it's beating so hard," Rob said as the bird quacked in fear.

When Rob crawled out from under the coop, the duck tucked its beak in Rob's armpit attempting to hide. It stopped its wailing but continued to peep. Rob stroked its back and spoke gently to it.

"Daddy, it's Quackers. See the curly feathers on the top of its tail. Mom, it's Quackers!"

Ruth took Quackers from Rob and held and cooed gently to her. "What's happened to you, baby? Where are your brother and sister? Where are Donald and Daisy?"

"Peep, peep."

"Someone had the nerve to come onto our place, make a mess of our yard, and steal our ducks!" said an enraged Father.

"Freda! What about Freda, Rob!" said Ruth with tears flowing from her eyes.

"Oh, no, better check!"

"If they've got Freda, I'm gonna' kill 'em!" declared Andy.

"Andrew!"

"I mean it, Ma! If someone hurt Freda, I'm gonna' kill them real bad!"

"She's here," Rob called from the shed. "They scared the wits out of her too, but they couldn't get to her. Good thing I locked her in the shed. Somebody's gonna' hear about this!"

"What are you going to do, Rob?"

"I'm calling the sheriff's office first, and then I'm calling Adam. Remember Adam had said to let him know if anything peculiar happens."

"This is peculiar, Rob, two ducks stolen, the figure eight's in the driveway, and the skunk on the porch. It will take awhile for the odor to leave," said Ruth, whose fury mounted.

"Why would anyone want to steal our ducks?"

"Beats me, Rob, but they sure did? You call the police and you call Adam!"

Grabbing a shovel from the shed, Rob quickly buried the skunk, while Ruth opened a half gallon can of tomato juice and poured it slowly over the doorstep. Andy merely watched their quick action working together. Ruth ordered Andy to help her open the windows, while Rob replaced the shovel. Rob returned to the house and called the sheriff's office. Deputy Candy received the call from the switchboard.

"Deputy Candy, speaking, state your name please."

"Rob Browning."

"Address?"

"I don't know that I have a street address."

"You're outside of town?"

"Southwest of Ridge View on 403."

"Oh, the new lineman, you live south of the bridge. One of Claymore's places," pronounced the deputy.

"Yes."

"I know where you are. What's the problem?"

"Something peculiar happened today, while we were away from home."

"Peculiar?"

"Yes, I'm not sure if its vandalism or theft or just what."

"Tell me about it."

"When we got home, we drove into our driveway. Someone worked hard making figure eight's in the surface of the driveway. They put a dead skunk on our doorstep and broke into my chicken coop and stole two of our ducks."

"Made figure eight's, stole ducks from your chicken coop. I'm writing this down. Dead skunk, on your doorstep?"

"Yes, we poured tomato juice on the wood and concrete to get rid of the smell."

"Did it work?"

"Mostly."

"Interesting, I'll have to remember that one, that all?"

"I think so."

"Nothing else is missing? Did they break into the house?" asked Deputy Cotton Candy.

"There's no evidence of a break-in."

"No other livestock is missing?"

"No, they didn't get our dog and one duck?"

"Do you have any goats or sheep?" the deputy inquired.

"No, why do you ask?"

"Just curious, you say this happened before..."

"Before 5:00 p.m., we just got home."

"Okay, Mr. Browning, I'll have a deputy stop by. Anything else?"

"No, and thank you."

"Mr. Browning."

"Yes......."

"Call, if anything else happens. Turn on your yard lights," the deputy advised. Rob did.

Immediately, Deputy Candy fielded another call from Karen Gustafson at the Stage Stop Hotel in Rock Creek who reported a peculiar happening that took place

Friday night, unlawful entry and a menacing note. The woman said she thought the note was meant for a previous tenant. A deputy would be dispatched when available. The switchboard lit up again and again with calls from people experiencing peculiar harassing incidents. Deputy Candy added her notes to those received earlier on her shift. The deputy spread her notes before her on her government gray desk.

"Let's see, off road truck, figure eight's in driveway, pelted with beer cans by jerks in a truck, loud music from truck in her driveway. Dead skunk on doorstep, road kill in a plastic bag, fewmet placed before the entrance to a trailer, menacing note. And I don't know any of these people. All of them are new to the valley," observed the deputy.

Deputy Candy called to the only other deputy on duty Sunday afternoon, "Hey, Harley?"

"What have you got, Cotton?"

"An unusual number of pranks involving people I've never heard of?"

"From where?"

"Mostly outside of Ridge View, off 403, two in Jericho, the Stage Stop, one from one of the girls at the bed and breakfast in Rock Creek."

"Then, there's no concentration."

"No, but several involved an off road truck. All are from people I don't know."

"What do you make of it?"

"I may be off base, but it looks like the welcome wagon is working overtime harassing new people," concluded Deputy Cotton Candy.

"You mean the boys will be boys?"

"As the sheriff puts it, yes."

"Well, listen to my list."

"What've you got?"

"A brush fire east of the Valley Highway beyond the ridge, over by the guy who delivers papers. A peeping Tom. Firecrackers tossed from the ridge east of the highway at cars traveling in the canyon south of Rock Creek. Domestic violence in Jericho Springs. Would you say any of these are peculiar?"

"The firecrackers?"

"Okay, I'll give you that one but not the others. Seems like a typical but active summer day," concluded the other deputy.

"Maybe you're right, but let's watch what happens after the sun goes down." Candy asserted, and then she got a called from Paul Smith at the Stage Stop Hotel, who told her that he was calling at the request of John Law. Then Candy raised her eyebrows when Smith asked to meet her later in the week near the hotel in Rock Creek and when he said that she was the only one he was willing to talk with at the sheriff's department. He told her that she could call John to confirm the legitimacy of his contact.

HEROES EMERGE

CHAPTER 9

"...Take care of my sheep. John 21:16b

The late summer day ended like a door being closed gradually. Shades of night on this Sunday evening enveloped the valley. Neon signs pushed back the darkness. The pizza deliveryman began a long journey out of town, cross country beyond the East Ridge to make a delivery to a neighbor of the Bonds. Mike Crowfoot, the clerk at the convenience store in Jericho Springs, left the store for home but noticed the gang in a pickup truck talking with Sheriff Bailey. Mike recognized Deputy Butch amongst them. Mike waved at the old man in the gray pickup truck as it coughed by heading into the mountains. He walked Main Street, passed Bustos' restaurant, and nodded hello to Adam Claymore eating in a window booth.

In Ridge View most residents had settled in for the evening. Services ended at the Ridge View Community Church. Whitney McNaughton left the Cozy Corner Café with some cronies. The proprietor closed the door behind the friends and lowered the blinds. His cook finished dismantling the food prep station, changed clothes, and retrieved a box with two ducks in it from the storeroom out back. Two waitresses continued cleaning the kitchen, finished bussing the tables, and prepared to leave as well. One of the two entered the ladies' room and washed her face. She studied herself in the mirror frowning at what she saw.

In Rock Creek several trucks and automobiles pulled into the parking lot behind the Stage Stop Hotel. The drivers and a few passengers entered the tobacco store from the rear. A car pulled away from the Rock Creek Convenience Store but stopped abruptly at the mouth of the canyon. The bar at the Stage Stop Hotel nearly emptied, as men left and walked to the back door of the tobacco shop. Others from around town walked to the shop as well.

The old man stopped his pickup truck at the hairpin turn and looked out over the valley. In unison, the old man in the pickup truck, the waitress in the Cozy Corner Café ladies' room, the pizza delivery man at the crest of the ridge, and the driver of the car stopped at the mouth of the canyon bowed their heads in prayer.

North, south, east, and west- they prayed without knowing the exact needs but that the innocent be protected from the guilty, the good from the evil, and victims from harassers. They prayed that the walls of resistance fall down, which it would but not without a fight.

The first of the night's harassment began in the North, where the Brownings were targeted as newcomers. While the Brownings settled in for the evening, they remained watchful. Rob turned on the yard light at dusk. Both Quackers and Freda slept inside the house tonight, which delighted Andy as he had them to himself in his room for the night. Rob and Ruth sat shoulder to shoulder holding hands on the sofa.

"Rob, I wonder what's happened to Donald and Daisy."

"I doubt you would really want to know."

"Do you suppose someone wanted to make a meal of them?"

"Who knows for sure? I think it has more to do with what those guys were talking about at the café."

"Us being newcomers?"

"They said anybody who didn't belong was in for trouble. I don't know if they know me or not. I've met a lot of people, and I've had no trouble with customers or the guys I work with," Rob reminded Ruth.

"No enemies?"

"None."

"Nobody you got promoted over?"

"Not an issue."

"Then, just because we're new," Ruth said in disbelief.

"Like the guy said. They figure someone from the outside shouldn't be able to come in and get what should belong to the old families."

"The property in Jericho Springs?" Ruth asked.

"My guess is they think someone new in the valley has a rightful claim to the old boarding house and the mineral rights too."

"So they want to threaten anyone who's new."

"In hopes they can scare them off."

"Well, they're not going to do it. Not us. We're here to stay."

"Not a pleasant situation though."

"Let's take a look outside and see what we can."

"A walk in the moonlight?" Rob asked.

"With the yard light on?"

"Semi-romantic!"

Rob and Ruth walked arm in arm around the yard and to the driveway entrance, where they stopped and looked for traffic. There was none. They looked to the bridge where the pool was formed by the river. Ruth spotted activity on the other side before Rob.

"Rob, look there at the light across the river. Above the pond and right a couple hundred yards," Ruth pointed.

Rob walked to the edge of the light from their yard fixture and strained to see more clearly. The light grew and a bonfire became fully lit that illuminated the hill east of the river. Several figures could be seen running back and forth along the creek whooping and hollering. A pickup arrived, stopped on a highpoint, and glared its high beams in their direction.

"I'll bet that's who made tracks in the driveway!"

"What are they doin'?"

"Drinking and throwing more stuff on the fire. Come on let's call the sheriff's office."

"Ask for Deputy Candy," Ruth suggested.

The Brownings watched as the passenger from the pickup truck threw an object toward the fire. It sailed through the flames and ignited, while briefly rising above the flames only to drop to the ground beyond the blaze in a ball of fire. A second object was tossed with the same results.

The Brownings ran for the house and placed their call. The dispatcher answered and Rob asked for Deputy Candy, who was out of the office. The dispatcher told Rob, she would contact Candy and dispatch her. The valorous Candy would arrive shortly.

Meanwhile, harassment percolated in Rock Creek. Karen had returned to her room at the Stage Stop Hotel after finishing an uneventful dinner in the dining room. Sunday night activity in the bar paled compared to last night, she surmised. Until the shouting began, she had been oblivious of the traffic at the tobacco store. Turning off her light, she moved the dresser to the door and wedged it in place. Karen's curiosity drew her to the window. Below, a pickup truck repeatedly engraved circle spinouts in the parking lot. Men exited the tobacco store swearing at the driver, as he scattered rock and debris hitting parked cars. The driver shouted back at the others, while laughing and flipping-them-off. He stopped and shouted, "Mount up!"

Others came out, slapped each other on the back, and piled into cars. A few remained and went back inside the tobacco shop. Three men walked toward the Asherah House and two toward the hotel. Those leaving drove both west toward Jericho Springs and north on the Valley Highway. Karen continued watching from the relative safety of her room, and the man dressed in black watched from the roof of the hotel bar.

Someone opened the window to the room west of Karen. Unseen, Karen stepped to the left of her closed window. Karen listened, as Hannah, the desk clerk, crawled onto the catwalk and eased herself along it toward Karen's room. As Hannah began to pass by, Karen hastily opened her window and said, "Just a minute, you've got some answering to do!"

"Shhh! He might be in the hallway. Come out on the catwalk with me."

"So just scream. Here, I'll attract some attention," Karen said.

"Please don't!"

"That will just bring more guys from the tobacco store," Hannah responded.

"What about the people you work for?"

"They're at the tobacco store!"

Promptly, Karen complied, as Hannah continued, "Shut the window. If he still thinks I'm in your room, he may try to force the door open. He may even have a key from the front desk. He'll think he can let himself in. I don't know, but hurry won't ya."

"Who is he?" asked Karen.

"I don't know for sure! Just hurry!"

Standing up on the catwalk, Karen asked, "Why would he want to get in my room. Yours is next door?"

"Because before Friday morning, I was in your room. I'll tell you more in a minute. Come on and shut that window," urged Hannah.

The man in question knocked on the door and called for Hannah. When he got no response, he turned and ran down the hallway. He did not have the key but soon would.

"Do you recognize his voice?"

"I'm not sure, but he sounds like Butch," Hannah said with dismay, as she retreated to the catwalk. Karen hastily joined Hannah on the catwalk.

"Close the window," Hannah instructed, "if someone manages to get through the door or comes out on the ledge from another room and tries to get in, you want the window closed. They'll think no one's home. People don't generally think about climbing out on the catwalk, just you and me."

"Then you saw me earlier?" stated Karen.

"Yes, from the path in the woods."

"I thought so! It was you on the landing! But, you must think he might try the ledge," concluded Karen.

"You had your light on, right?"

Karen nodded.

Hannah continued, "If he checks the registration, he'll find out you're in 218, and I'm next door. If he doesn't, he's gonna' try to get into your room. He's gonna' wonder where I am and why he can't get in."

"He could get your key and mine?"

"He has before! Come on," Hannah said as she took Karen by the hand and pulled her along the ledge over the birdfeeder to the side above the stairwell.

"Wait a minute," Karen said, "I need to move the birdfeeder!"

"Yeah, that would clue him to come out on the ledge, if he sees it."

Karen hastily grabbed the heavy feeder and caught up with Hannah. They heard a man beating on Karen's door swearing. That man's companion shouted venomously. Butch unlocked the door and tried to force it open unsuccessfully. Butch called for Hannah and became infuriated when she did not respond. Lights appeared under doors in rooms 213 and 215, as hotel patrons responded to the disturbance. Butch and his friend ran downstairs to the hotel lobby.

On the ledge Hannah remembered, "The sheriff's car was at the mouth of the canyon earlier. Let's climb down the fire escape, not the stairwell, and use the footpath."

"Hannah, he's probably not there. I saw him park there the other night, then I saw him walk to the bed and breakfast."

Hannah snickered knowingly, and said, "You're right. He probably wouldn't be of much help anyway."

"Why the laugh?" asked Karen.

"It's more than a bed and breakfast. Besides, Butch is a deputy."

"Butch, who is after me or you, or both of us is a deputy sheriff?" Karen asked.

"He's after me, but he doesn't know you're not me. He is in a real foul mood, and you might not be too safe yourself. I bet he's been drinking. He does what he wants. Something is going on that has them all upset. Besides, Butch gets away with most anything. He's a McNaughton."

"You mean his drinking gets him in trouble?"

"I'm not sure what I mean, but I'm told Butch has done some bad things and gotten away with them and not because he is a deputy. That doesn't hurt for sure. He's a McNaughton and they pretty much rule the roost."

"Is there another officer we can call?"

"Candy. Come on now, I've done this before. Just over by the eaves behind the facade. The roof slopes down far enough near the frontage to create a real good shadow. We can hide there safely for now. We can wait to see what happens then climb down the fire escape and go inside. Once we're inside, I'll call the sheriff's office on the desk phone. I doubt Sheriff Bailey will tolerate Butch harassing another woman if he hears about it from Deputy Candy."

"If needed, I know where the pay phone is in the lobby, and I have a quarter."

"Great! You gotta' phone book?"

"No, but I know who else to call for help!"

"The man you had lunch with?" asked Hannah.

"Yes, Adam Claymore, and I have his phone number in my pocket."

"He could help!"

Swiftly, like prey, Hannah and Karen edged along the ledge to the eastside of the building. Once around the corner, they hesitated and listened on the stairwell landing before passing by the second floor exit door. Hearing no footsteps in the hallway, both continued but nearly tripped on the fire escape ladder. Around the corner to the front of the hotel, Karen placed the birdfeeder left-center on the ledge in the darkness. The women tiptoed down the front deck roof, where cloaked in the shadow of the facade, Karen and Hannah waited and listened.

"This has happened before?" Karen whispered.

"More than once."

"Why are you still here?"

"I guess I've liked the attention. It's not always like this. Butch can be real nice," confessed Hannah.

"Butch is your boyfriend?"

"Sort of."

"What does that mean?"

"I've got other friends, too."

"You mean other men come to your door?"

Hannah smiled shyly and nodded affirmatively.

"Ah, let me back up. I got here Friday. You gave me room 218, and now there is a man beating down the door trying to get in. You must be popular... Why did you switch rooms?" Karen asked.

"I was afraid."

"Why, if you are having such a good time?"

"Like I said, somethin's up. I'm not sure, but everybody's being weird lately."

"Listen, the lock is missing from the window. What gives? I left a note on the counter to have it fixed and no one took care of it. What happened?" Karen said sternly.

"They blew it off!"

"You mean they don't care that I can't safely lock my window."

"Usually, yes, now, no."

"Okay...I was in the dining room, and Sarah approached me and tried to fix me up with one of the customers."

Hannah grabbed Karen by the arm, "That's how I got here! Only I went out with the guy, then he came to my room the next night, and he forced me."

"You mean you were raped?"

"I guess so..."

"You guess so? You were either raped or not!"

"I gave in and I... the next morning there was a fifty dollar bill in an envelope left for me at the desk. There was also a thank you note," reported Hannah.

"Hannah, we need to have a talk..." Karen said, as she put her arm around Hannah.

Below, a man walked heavily on the wooden porch. Karen peered over the facade, "Someone is by the hitching post."

"It's Butch!" Hannah said, after moving forward to see, then ducked back under cover of the facade.

"Someone else was with him at my room."

Again, more carefully peering over the façade, Hannah whispered, "I don't see or hear anyone else, now!"

"That means they're inside, I guess."

"Karen, listen! I'm sorry I got you in this mess."

"Me, too, but here is another mystery. Someone must have been in my room. I found a note."

"You found it?"

"Did you leave it for me?"

Hannah paused, "After you left the other day, I went upstairs to my room. Since I saw you leave, I knew you weren't in your room. After a few minutes, I heard someone go into your room. I guess they had a key. I figured someone was looking for me, so I crawled out on the ledge to peek into the room."

"Did you see who it was?"

"No, when I got to the window and looked in, he was just going out of the door."

"It was a man."

"That much I know. But I didn't see enough of him to tell who he was, and then my boyfriend saw me."

"Your boyfriend saw you?"

"Yes, from the parking lot."

"You mean the guy who sort of raped you?"

"No, my real boy friend, Harper, he's the cook."

"The one, who was beaten and tossed out the back door? So, what did you do?"

"Yes, he is the one. I opened the window and climbed in your room."

"My room?"

"Hey, I didn't stay long. But I didn't want him to know I changed rooms. I checked the hallway and went back to my room."

"You didn't stay long, but you wrote me a note."

"It wasn't me, who left you the note. It was my boyfriend, I think."

"When was he in my room?"

"After I left, he climbed up the stairwell or fire escape by the kitchen, crawled along the ledge, and went in your room. He's afraid of heights. I think he wrote the note for me to leave while I still had a chance."

"Written on my stationary?"

"Yes, for real!"

"And he told you about the note?"

"He's been avoiding me since then. I haven't talked to him, privately," Hannah coyly stated.

"But, you knew what was in the note."

"Later he came by the front desk all worried like and told me he left me a note on my stationary and left it stuck in the chimney of the log cabin. I thought he was making a date. He said I better read it soon."

"It wasn't in the chimney."

"I know, I know, I got the key to your room, so I could go read the note. I went in your room and started reading it. Someone came to your door. I guess it was you. Since I didn't know if you had seen the note, I tried to put it back in the chimney. I pushed too hard. It went all the way in. I hurried to crawl out the window before you unlocked the door."

"So, that's why the note was inside the birdfeeder," concluded Karen.

Hannah nodded, "And that's how it was scooted up against the little table. That really is a big birdfeeder!"

"And you know the note is a warning to you."

"To get out of town while I still can," Hannah affirmed.

From behind, Karen and Hannah heard someone on the ledge. They watched a man stumble over the birdfeeder and struggle unsuccessfully to retain his balance. In his drunkenness he attempted to step forward and over what he stumbled on, but stepped directly onto the birdfeeder, which caused him to lose his balance completely. He fell onto the sloping roof, bounced on his shoulder, rose mid-air, and began to crash through the façade. Momentarily like a slow motion movie, he paused and pushed against the façade, turned to and recognized the women. "You," he yelled humorously, as he continued through the facade and crashed onto a wooden table below on the porch. Still drunk and conscious he moaned as he attempted to get up, and then collapsed while vomiting.

From the hotel lobby, Butch crossed the porch to help his friend. Karen and Hannah gave a high-five hand slap. Karen picked up the birdfeeder, as they ascended the porch roof to the catwalk ledge. "Which way do we go?" Karen asked as they reached the ledge.

Hannah grabbed her hand and replied, "Come on, we only have a second."

Hannah led Karen to the fire escape ladder on the east side of the building, looked over before descending, but realized Butch was already climbing up the ladder. Panicking, Karen threw the birdfeeder at Butch hitting him directly on the head. In an attempt to catch the heavy cabin of a birdfeeder, he released his grip on the fire escape ladder rail and fell backward tumbling to the ground below.

"Now we're in for it!" feared Hannah.

"Hannah, I just had to do it!"

"I know! Good shot. Let's go!"

Karen followed Hannah back around the ledge above the back parking lot. When they arrived at the window to Karen's room, they discovered it was still closed.

Karen opened the window saying, "Wait a minute. I can stop this right now."

"Are you crazy? One of them will be right behind us."

As Karen entered the room through the window, Hannah told her she heard Butch climbing the ladder swearing and threatening her. Karen crossed the room, pulled the dresser from where it was still blocking the door, reached in it, and pulled her holster from the drawer. It was empty. She jerked the drawer from the dresser and emptied the contents on the floor. Some bullets she found but no pistol. Then in a real panic, Karen didn't hesitate getting back on the ledge with Hannah, when from the hallway someone called for Hannah.

Karen caught up with Hannah who had already made her way to the west-side of the building. Together, they climbed down the fire escape ladder from the roof above the bar below, then down the ladder to the back parking lot. Butch spotted them from the ledge and watched as they ran into the cover of the trees. He waited to see where they went, but then made pursuit.

"Let's split up. Butch can't follow both of us. I'll go to Asherah House, then up to the water tower, if I can. You go for help. You can't go inside. Butch's friend is probably in there. Hide in the trees. See if the sheriff's at the bridge. If not, somehow call for help!" ordered Hannah.

"I'll hide, but it won't be in the trees," said Karen.

"Whatever!"

"Do you have my pistol?"

"No! I wish I did."

"Where will we meet?" asked Karen.

"You call Claymore. Have him honk his truck horn three times from the back parking lot. I'll know to meet you," said Hannah.

"It might take awhile," Karen replied.

"I know........."

The women fled in opposite directions. Hannah noisily dashed along the footpath to the back door of Asherah House. From the parking lot, Butch watched Hannah. She entered, dashed past a couple embracing in the hallway, and quickly exited the front door, crossed the street, ran the length of the sidewalk, passed a couple of houses, and disappeared. Under the cover of night, Hannah hurriedly crossed through someone's backyard. A dog barked a warning giving away her location, but Hannah made it to the hogback and climbed the hill. Butch didn't follow her, nor did the men entertained at the Asherah House. Butch decided to look and listen for the other woman.

Meanwhile, Karen followed the footpath to the highway where she crossed quickly unseen. The sheriff's cruiser was not there. She continued along the path to the church where she broke the window in the side door and entered Adam's office. She called Adam on the church telephone, told her story, and confessed to breaking the window. He laughed and complimented her quick thinking. Next, he told her to climb the path to the top of the mesa. He urged Karen to hurry. Adam promised to call Sheriff Bailey and have him meet us at the Stage Stop Hotel.

Karen sprinted past the cemetery, crossed the footbridge, and ascended the path to the mesa above safely. Knowing Adam would come to the rescue, she gathered stones and larger rocks for her defense. If Butch were to climb the path to the top of the mesa, he would soon realize there would be a fight waiting for him. She looked for where to run to if she did not discourage his ascent. Instead, she decided to make her defense from where she stood. For now Karen and Hannah waited to learn their fate. Karen prayed; Hannah did not know she should.

Meanwhile, Butch had entered the woods at the east end of the storage room and crept along the path to the canyon's mouth. Not wanting his prey to slip away, Butch paused to listen for footsteps and peered up one side of the street then down the other. He crossed the highway at the mouth of the canyon and entered the grove of birch trees along the mesa wall. Watching for clues, he continued along the trail where he arrived at the church parking lot. Approaching the front door of the church and he turned the door knob with hopes of being able to force his way in without damaging the doorway. Next, he peered through the window, and when he couldn't see anything, he remembered the shed and cemetery behind the church. When circling the building, he momentarily checked the side door and discovered the broken window. He was reluctant to enter the church, took note of the telephone, reached through the broken glass, turned on the light switch inside the office, unlocked the door, and entered. Since a row of light switches were just outside the office, he reached around the open office door and switched them on. In the light he quickly raced up and down the center aisle and entered the prayer room across the platform from the pastor's office where he also checked the baptistery. Switching off all the lights, Butch left the office, walked to the shed, and scanned the cemetery. He returned to the parking lot where he paused again only to return to the cemetery. Remembering the footbridge, he walked between the headstones shivering. Aloud Butch said to himself, "I must be nuts. How would a stranger know about this place?"

Outside of Ridge View, Rob and Ruth returned to their yard, but only after turning off the yard light. They walked to the edge of their yard and watched as the people on the other side of the river suddenly scrambled for their cars leaving the bonfire blazing. Minutes later, a patrol car stopped at the Rock Creek Bridge and the driver, Deputy Candy, illuminated the landscape with her spotlight. Candy radioed the Ridge View Volunteer Fire Department, called for assistance to extinguish the bonfire, as it would soon spread to the grass in the clearing and envelop the maple and elm forest near County Road 403.

"Ruth, I'm going over there. They might need another hand before this is over."

"Rob, I think you should stay here."

"We want to be accepted here. An outsider might not get involved, but someone who wants to belong should get involved," Rob asserted, like a knight errant on a mission to make right that which was wrong.

"And, it's the right thing to do," Ruth answered with resignation and with hopes of Rob's rescuing Donald and Daisy, if they were there.

Ruth turned on the yard light, as Rob exited their driveway in their Bronco and drove to help put out the fire. He reached a dirt road leading through the forest as the Ridge View Volunteer Fire Department began arriving. Deputy Cotton Candy led the fire truck and Rob along the forest road. Other vehicles filled with volunteers arrived including those responsible for the fire.

The volunteers acted with impressive efficiency. Men carrying shovels converged on the bonfire, as others operated the pumper. The firefighters quickly doused the blaze with water. Only steam and embers remained once the pumper finished its quick work. Men with shovels tossed mud and dirt on sparks smoldering in the grass. Water sprayed from the pump truck carried ash and cinder from the bonfire to the pristine pond. Debris would not easily pass downstream as it clung to the pond bank in the shallows of the pond.

"Isn't this peculiar!" commented one burley volunteer to the fire captain.

"What have you got there, Charley?" responded the captain.

"Looks light the remains of a duck! No feathers, but definitely a duck's beak and web feet."

"Let me see," asked Rob.

Several men gathered around. Those responsible snickered unnoticed.

"Here's another one. It's been toasted!"

A man, who had been there earlier, stepped forward to look at the specimens and said, "Looks like someone threw these pet birds on the fire," as he looked around then directly at Rob. With an attitude, he asked Rob, "Got any ideas?"

Rob realized the culprit confronted him. Looking the man square in his eyes, Rob retorted, "It's a small thing for a big man to steal a little boy's pets, and then kill them as if they were nothing. I'd say the people who did this are anything but real men."

Deputy Candy stepped between the men and asked, "Buddy Smith, what do you know about this?"

"Nothin,' Candy, I'm just guessing," Buddy answered, then turned away, and went to his truck to leave.

"Thanks guys! Keep an open ear. If you hear anything about this let me know. There's some goofy things happening tonight, and I'm going to find out what's going' on."

"Okay, Deputy, you be careful yourself."

Rob approached Candy and began to speak but she interrupted, "You must be Mr. Browning. You called for assistance about the fire and about someone stealing your ducks and such. My guess is you have your answers."

"About the ducks and who took them?"

"I believe so. It would be hard to prove, but my guess is these poor carcasses are your ducks and someone is dead set on harassing you. You are new to the area and the old-timers are pissed-off. Pardon my expression, but you get my drift. They want to keep things how they were, as if anyone here tonight didn't have relatives who moved here from somewhere else at one time or another," Candy advocated.

"It's all relative. They want something that rightfully belongs to someone else," Rob asserted.

"You got it! Now, do I need to come to your house tonight, or would it be okay if I checked on the other nutty calls I've gotten tonight?"

"Not a good night tonight?"

"It seems like all the weirdoes are out tonight wrecking havoc on newcomers."

"We're not the only ones?"

"Don't think you're so special. Sounds like a bizarre night. Mr. Browning, I'll get back to you."

"One question, Deputy, what is the name of the man I confronted?" Rob asked.

"Buddy Smith, Mr. Browning, and he is trouble."

The deputy left as did the others, and Rob realized he was alone. Rob looked across the river to his home and wondered how to explain what had happened to Ruth and Andy. Rob decided to take the carcasses with him and not shelter either his wife or son from the incident. Rob determined to demonstrate respect for the life of the birds by burying them with his family but not tonight. Tomorrow would be soon enough.

West of town at the Blair House, the bearded man in the tan trench coat left the confines of his shelter to bathe, finally. He undressed in the pale moonlight and laid his clothing on a jagged rock by the landslide at the base of the volcanic mound. At the water's edge, he brushed his teeth, then placed both brush and paste on the shore with his shaving gear in his toiletry kit and waded into the tepid water with soap in hand. Tepid water soothed as he soaped himself. Washing his hair with bar soap, he submerged himself holding the bar soap tightly. The soap slipped away and he playfully pursued it underwater.

While underwater, this gave his audience a chance to move closer. From the basin atop the mound, Janine Crowfoot, the cyclist and neighbor, hiked down the slope where she hid behind willows that blanketed the area adjacent the shoreline. Janine crouched and kept her eyes riveted. "Be careful little eyes what you see," Janine sang to herself. Janine gave in to her temptation, looked and lusted, when the intruder came to the brush and fetched his razor.

Still, Janine moved closer to where the bather's clothes remained, while he waded back into the water. Janine took a chance of exposing herself by walking into full view. Janine stole his trousers and retreated. In the shadows Janine searched his pockets for a wallet. The search produced the prize.

To herself Janine whispered, "Now Mr. Mystery Man, perhaps I'll find out who you are."

Boldly, Janine moved into the moonlight to inspect the wallet's contents. Some cash, the remains of his bus ticket, his driver's license and Social Security card. "Ezra Blair!" Janine read aloud softly with a flood of tears coming quickly from her eyes, "Oh, Izzy, you've come home." And Janine fell to her knees.

At the sound, the man in the water turned and looked toward shore thinking he heard something but not seeing his voyeur. Not confirming his suspicion, Ezra Blair, the once bearded man in the tan trench coat, continued removing his facial growth. Now with bold anticipation, Janine perched on the rock where Ezra placed his clothing. She waited on shore enjoying the spectacle, brushed her clothing, used her fingers to straighten her hair, and speculated about the immediate future. Janine daydreamed that Izzy would come out of the water, would seek his cloths, see her, would realize she was no longer a child, would call out her name in recognition, and then would embrace her passionately, as he helped her down from the rock.

Ezra did leave the pond, freshly bathed and clean-shaven, wearing only his jockey shorts. Ezra whistled softly, as he picked up his shaving kit. Alluringly, Janine crossed her legs and leaned back with both hands behind her. She grinned with admiration.

"Well, Izzy, it's been a long time!"

Startled, shaken, and embarrassed, Ezra looked for an exit while shielding himself with his two hands before him. "You recognized me, whoever you are. But, would you toss me my clothes?"

"Now, I had imagined you would have offered me your hand to help me off this rock. You used to be quite a gentleman, as I recall, and, often to my displeasure, somewhat of a prude."

"You have me at a disadvantage. I see you have my wallet, so you can tell who I am. You seem to know me as well. Who are you?"

Half-pouting Janine tossed him his towel then walked in a circle around him with her face turned away from his embarrassment "For years I have dreamed of this moment. Finally, to see you again. And here you are in the flesh!"

"My pants, if you please!" Izzy requested.

Janine handed them to him and continued, "You don't have a clue who I am?"

"Not the slightest. Please, my shirt, too."

"I think not. Not until I hear a pretty please."

Izzy took her hand and pulled her to himself and said, "Janine Crowfoot, can I please have my shirt." Then Izzy kissed her, and Janine wilted into his arms. Izzy held Janine gently and lingered in her touch. Ezra mused how she had taunted him and wondered how long she had watched him, as Janine wept with joy.

Finally after regaining her composure, Janine pulled back from Izzy and gently slapped him slowly. "Ezra Blair, where have you been? You stood me up the night you left town. I haven't heard from you for years."

"It's not like we were going steady. You were the girl down the street. Like my kid sister."

That sparked fire in her face, and Janine went for him now with a fist instead of a mild slap. Ezra blocked her blow and wrestled her to the ground, and kissed her again. With more passion, Janine returned Ezra's kiss. Lying on the ground arms in arms, Izzy said, "You're not a little kid now. Janine Crowfoot, you are drop-dead gorgeous." They kissed again but heard the sound of buckets breaking water. Both sat upright immediately. Ezra gathered and put on his shirt. They hid.

From the edge of the pond, Ezra and Janine watched an old man place the handles of two buckets on each end of a yoke. He lifted them to his shoulders, and proceeded to climb the slope to the Live Oak where he lowered the buckets and carefully emptied their contents at the base of the tree. Holding hands Janine and Izzy watched him repeat his effort seven times. Each time he either circled the tree dousing the bark of four connected tree trunks or poured the water on the roots down the north side of the slope.

"What's he doing?"

"Watering the tree," replied Janine.

"Oh, really!"

"Yes, but watch. After he's finished emptying the buckets, he embraces the tree. I think he is carving something."

"You've watched before?" Izzy asked.

"Most nights he's there. I've seen a truck stop at the curve above. Then one night I went riding my bike and watched him climb down the slope to the tree. He hid the buckets in the brush. I concluded he just spends some time with the tree. He talked to it."

"Does he talk to the tree? That's kind of nutty," said Izzy.

"Well, I've heard him, but I've never understood what he says," Janine informed.

"Then you weren't over here to spy on me?"

"No, you are a complete surprise," Janine said coyly, "You're hiding, aren't you?"

"Yes, I've got my reasons. I didn't intend to expose myself."

"And what an exposure!" giggled Janine.

"You're terrible, taking advantage of me."

"I was only living out my fantasy."

"Your fantasy?"

"Since the first time, we swam together in the basin."

Izzy looked at her, smiled, and asked, "I take it you're not married?"

"Never."

"Why not?"

"You have to ask?" Janine hesitated, "You promised to marry me." Janine rose to her feet pretending to watch the old man, as he left with his buckets.

"When you were ten? Tonight was our first real kiss!"

"Do you remember prom night?

"Often…"

"Then you remember this was not our first kiss and a promise is a promise. Come on let's follow him."

"I was a senior and you a freshman!"

"And I was more than just the girl next door."

"Yes, you were more than the girl next door, you were a best friend too," Ezra confessed as he put on his shoes and socks, and then joined Janine, and they watched the old man as he hid his buckets in the brush and climbed the rocky slope toward the road above them.

"Who is he?" Izzy asked, and then Izzy knew at the sound of "Cough, cough, sputter, cough, sputter, boom!"

"The woodcutter!" they echoed one another.

"Listen, Izzy, how about a late night snack? If you want, you could sleep on my couch."

"I could use something good to eat, but I think I had better spend the night over here."

"Always the gentleman," Janine responded with obvious disappointment.

"I just know some of my weaknesses… and your kisses!"

"I guess I should treat that as a compliment?"

"Absolutely!" Izzy confessed.

As they walk toward Janine's house, she said to him, "Izzy, I'm so glad you're back."

"Me too," Izzy responded, "and I'm glad you're still here."

Izzy and Janine strolled up the sidewalk arm in arm but stopped short of the house. Janine said, "Just like old times, only better." An occupied patrol car loomed down the street between them and Janine's house.

"Wait, stop, I don't want to be answering any questions," Izzy said.

They hesitated hoping they had not been seen when Janine asked, "Have you done something to worry about?"

"Nothing illegal, I just don't want the police to get nosey."

"You have a right to be at the old house. You are a Blair," stated Janine.

"Not really."

"What do you mean?"

"I thought I was a Blair, but I'm not."

"You're not?"

"I wasn't born a Blair, and they never adopted me. Not that they wouldn't have."

"When did you find this out?"

"The night I ran away!"

"I wondered why you left. Not much was said about that."

"What was said?"

"Just that the Blairs were heart broken when you left. Rumor had it they spent a lot of money looking for you," Janine reported.

Tears trickled down Izzy's checks unnoticed by Janine, "They would. They were kind and gentle people. Please, let's talk about the past later. Okay?" Izzy said as he wiped away his tears and put his arm around Janine's shoulder.

Suddenly, the sheriff started his cruiser, turned on his lights, and swiftly left.

"He must have gotten a call."

"I wonder what he was doing, what was he looking at?" Janine said quizzically.

They walked to where the sheriff was positioned. Ezra took note and gained perspective. "Isn't that your house?"

"It is."

"What room is the one with the light on?"

"My bedroom!"

"Well, I'm not certain what he was doing, but I do know he could see right into your room. The blinds are not pulled tightly down."

With that said Janine crossed her arms at her waist and stomped angrily across the street loudly saying, "The creep's been watching the window. I sensed it but didn't do anything about it. I've had a creepy feeling I was being watched. I've checked the blinds, but I've also had the window open." Janine paused, "Or more likely, he's looking for my roommate."

"Come on, serves you right for peeping at me tonight."

"That's different! I made myself known to you."

Laughing, "Sure, after I partially exposed myself. Anyway, I can't blame him."

"Ha!"

"You're a delight to my eyes, Janine, a sight for sore eyes."

"Well…okay! I guess you've redeemed yourself."

"Who's your roommate?"

"Come on, a car turned onto our street. We've both got a lot to explain."

Janine and Ezra entered her house. He asked if he could fix her blinds and gained permission. She promptly adjourned to the kitchen and prepared a plate of nachos. Entering her bedroom and immediately admiring her decorum, he noticed a picture of the two of them on her nightstand. They were posed before the old tree on top of the mound. His arm around her shoulder, as she was pictured gazing lovingly up at him. Closing her window, he locked it. Next, he forcefully tightened the blinds after directing them downward. "There!" Ezra exclaimed, as he walked back into the living room, where Janine had graced the coffee table with a plate of beef and bean nachos piled with sour cream, jack cheese, lettuce, onions, tomato, and guacamole.

"Izzy, you must be the one people are angry about?" Janine asserted.

"Who, what do you mean?"

"Well, the whole valley's upset!"

"About what?"

"About the Blair House not being condemned and someone has a rightful claim to it."

"You mean they want to get the mineral and water rights."

"Exactly!"

"And they think someone may be able to get the house and land."

"Isn't that why you are here?" asked Janine.

"I read about it in the newspaper."

"The *Outcry*?"

"A couple of years ago I had a friend order a subscription for me. I read about the controversy and decided to make a re-appearance. I even wrote to the lawyer handling the case for the claimant."

"Then you are the one!" Janine concluded.

"Not exactly."

"What do you mean?"

"The lawyer said I should come to Jericho Springs. He said if I did, I wouldn't be disappointed."

"And that's it."

"Except, he made me an offer."

"What kind?"

"He asked me to consider returning to Jericho Springs and help restore the Blair House."

"So, you dropped everything and came here."

"Not quite, I applied for a leave of absence at the University. They cancelled my classes for the semester and gave me some time to sort things out."

"You're an instructor or a student?'

"I'm an associate professor."

"Why have you been hiding?"

"That was the lawyer's idea. He insisted I come to town secretly and stay under cover until Thursday afternoon. He stressed it was for my own good. Something about the McNaughton's bothering all the new people," Izzy reported.

"I think it's a little more serious than that," Janine exclaimed.

"Now, you too have a mystery?"

"My roommate disappeared."

"That would be Jill Lowenstein, the high school teacher who may have been a witness to a murder. Apparently, she is a material witness who disappeared. The authorities suspect foul play," Izzy quickly summarized.

"You do read the papers."

"Who was murdered?"

"A girl from the Asherah House, the bed and breakfast on Indiana Avenue in Rock Creek, her body was found lodged in a crawlspace underneath the bridge where 403 enters Rock Creek from Jericho Springs. She was strangled after having been with someone. Her name was Gloria Jones," said Janine.

"Did you know Asherah was the Canaanite mother goddess and supposedly mother of Baal as in Baal worship?" Izzy inquired.

"Is the Asher pole related to Asherah?" asked Janine.

"Yes, have you seen any in the valley?"

"Not in Jericho Springs."

"Usually, they were erected at high points in tribute to Asherah," Izzy concluded, and then he asked, "Was the murderer caught?"

"Not yet, according to rumor Butch McNaughton is the primary suspect. My guess is that's why the sheriff is watching my place."

"Other than peeping in your window."

"Jill is supposed to report for school two weeks before Labor Day, but no one has heard from her. She has either been killed herself or is in hiding somewhere."

"What about her job at the school?"

"Oh, that's another problem. The school district is planning to hire someone to take her place."

"That's odd. What if she returns?"

"Izzy, that's just it. I think someone on the school board knows something."

"How so?"

"Well, they're planning to hire someone to take her place, but if Jill returns, the new hire will become a permanent substitute teacher."

"Any prospects?"

"Apparently, the superintendent is supposed to finish interviewing on Monday and have a recommendation for the board at their Tuesday night meeting."

"How come you know so much?"

"I teach English at the high school."

"At the high school?"

"Yes, at the high school."

"I'm impressed!" Izzy said with a smile, "And I teach literature."

They finished their snack, gazed dreamily into one another's eyes, and chatted for another hour. Embarrassing herself, Janine suggested they go to bed.

"I mean…"

"Say no more. Thank you for the snack and the offer to sleep on your couch. Fact is I could stand to take a real shower. As for anything else, I intend to function like the gentleman I always was with you."

"Thanks, I'm sorry I was such a tease at the pond. I was so shocked and excited about seeing you," confessed Janine.

"Then that's why you were at the pond? You did see me. I thought I had done a better job of hiding," replied Izzy with concern.

"I thought I saw you in the window earlier, but I wasn't sure. I wasn't there to spy on you. Like I said earlier, I was there to watch what the old man was doing. I've watched him a couple of nights, and I'm curious as to why he hauls the water up the hill."

"He wants the tree to live?" said Izzy.

"That's it, but, sometimes he whittles on the trunk and branches and a rather large root on the south."

"He whittles and he waters?"

"Yes, every night for the last two weeks."

"Okay, I know that's strange, but what do you make of it?" asked Izzy.

"I don't know. The tree's been dead for years. I can't remember when it had leaves…the landslide. It hasn't had leaves since the landslide years ago. The rocks crashed against the mound and removed all the top soil, including tree roots on the west side and all of the south side of the mound."

"It must have been in shock," Izzy speculated.

"Why?"

"The roots to the north are green and alive."

"The tree's alive?" Janine asked.

"And the old man is watering!"

"I hope it lives. It would be wonderful…" Janine mused.

"If it were restored?" asked Izzy.

Janine nodded. They kissed good night. Janine retired to her bedroom. Izzy wrapped himself in the clean blanket that she had given him, and then walked back to the Blair House under the cover of darkness. Each dreamed of yesteryear, each other, and the kisses they had just shared.

In Rock Creek, romance loomed far from the thoughts of Karen and Hannah. Karen perched on Adam's bench on the mesa above the town waiting for his arrival and unaware of the danger below on the footbridge. Across town, a vestibule for the Rock Creek floodplain, Hannah crouched near the water tower straining to see if anyone had followed her. She speculated only long time residents would know about the foot trail to the top of the mesa. Butch had left the bridge and gave up the search for Karen. Butch returned to the hotel by way of County Road 403 to check on his friend, who had fallen from the facade to the table on the front porch. Sipping a beer, Butch's friend sat on the hotel steps holding his head.

"Where ya been, Butch? I've had enough'a this. I wanna' go home. My back is killing me, and I feel like I got splinters everywhere. Next time you want a woman, go after one that's friendly!" said Butch's friend Roy.

"Okay! Okay! Let's call it a night. I got a headache too. Hannah went to the bed 'n breakfast. The other one's somewhere 'round here. She's out in the woods or down the canyon."

"Say, she really clobbered you, didn't she?" asked Roy, while noticing the large welt forming on Butch's head.

"Busted that darned thing on my head! Where is it anyway?"

"Still back there," said Roy, as he pointed toward the side entrance to the hotel. "I didn't pick it up. Fact is I had enougha that fool thing on the roof. What is it anyway?"

"Some kinda bird thing. I'm gonna keep it as a souvenir. Come on. Let's get it and leave. We'll finish this later," proclaimed Butch, promising revenge.

Moments later, Adam drove his red F250 truck between the mesa and the hogback on 403 where he was spotted by Karen from the mesa. He crossed the bridge and stopped at the intersection with the Valley Highway. Adam recognized Butch driving his truck, as it headed north on the Valley Highway. Adam surveyed the scene, drove across the highway, and circled the hotel to the back parking lot away from the tobacco store. As instructed, Adam honked three times.

Both Karen and Hannah descended from their respective perches and quickly attempted to join Adam by his truck. Someone yelled out a second floor window for them to be quiet. Sheriff Bailey arrived as requested.

"Adam, ladies, what's the problem?" greeted Sheriff Bailey.

"Sheriff, you may have met Hannah, but this is Miss Gustafson," Adam said as he made introductions.

Extending his hand, the sheriff continued, "Um, yes, please to meet you. You're staying at the hotel, and Hannah, I know you work here."

Acknowledging the sheriff, Karen went right to the point. "Sheriff, some men tried to and may well have broken into my room. They chased Hannah and me through the woods."

"Hold it, let me get my clipboard and make some notes. This has been a busy night," the Sheriff reported tiredly.

"You mean the boys are out tonight?" Adam questioned

"In spades, Adam. Miss Gustafson, what's your business here? Did you come to work at the hotel?" asked Bailey.

"She's not that kind of woman, Bailey!" protested Adam.

Angrily, "Then why is she here!" the Sheriff said.

"Sheriff, I'm a teacher. I'm here applying for a job!"

"That makes you new. And you are too, Hannah. How long have you been here now, a month?" Sheriff Bailey asked.

"I got here, yes, about a month ago," offered Hannah, "and I received a threat to get out of town."

"When?"

"Basically, in writing yesterday. Isn't that right, Karen?" Hannah asked.

Karen nodded and added, "It was put in the chimney of my birdfeeder."

"But I shoved it through. Oh, I didn't put it there, though. The dishwasher did."

"He did? He's a McNaughton," said the Sheriff.

"What's your point, Bailey?"

"Adam, my guess is the ladies, being new, are targets of the group that wants to get rid of anyone who might have a claim to the Blair House."

"What does that have to do with what just happened to us?"

"Miss Gustafson, you are new here. Folks figure someone, an outsider, may be able to come in here and rightfully get what people here figure belongs to them."

"The Blair House?" asked Adam.

"It must be some house. Have you seen it, Hannah?" asked Karen.

"It's not just the house, Karen," Adam informed.

"What do you mean?"

"Tell her Adam, tell her how you and I are just as interested as everyone else," said Bailey.

"Huh?" responded Karen with surprise.

"He's right Karen. All of us would like to have the Blair House and all that goes with it, gold, mineral rights, water rights to Rock Creek. Although a landslide altered the course of the creek, it belongs to the Blair House land. All the locals want it to become public. Naturally, ownership of Blair House means a lot financially. It's just that most people would try to get it legally," reported Adam.

"The others?" Karen asked.

"The others will try to get it anyway they can and that includes eliminating the opposition," responded Adam.

"Especially newcomers?" revealed Bailey.

"Come on, Bailey, you're going to scare her off before she's even interviewed for the job at the high school. There's a town council meeting on Thursday night. A lawyer obtained a court injunction that prevented the council from condemning the property, which would allow it to be sold. Apparently, someone has come here and apparently has a legitimate claim to the property. We think they will be at the council meeting," confessed Adam.

"Meanwhile, tonight we've had a fire at the paper carriers, you know the Bonds, and one on your house at the north end of 403, where the new lineman moved his family."

"Both are my properties. Do you see any connections?" asked Adam.

"I don't think so, just newcomers. We've had calls from all over town. My deputies must be crisscrossing the valley answering calls," Sheriff Bailey confessed.

"Are the Bonds okay?"

"I'm sure they could use your help, Adam," Bailey said, and then Bailey turned to Karen and asked, "What about you, Miss Gustafson?"

"Well, I assure you, I am not related to anyone in this area, nor do I have any kind of claim to any property. But, I really would like to get a job teaching."

"I hear you, Miss, but I think you can understand how people will be suspicious no matter what you have to say. Sorry," the sheriff concluded, "Hannah, do you know who it was chasing you?"

"It was Butch and his friend. I don't know his name, the dumb one."

"You mean Roy? And are they the ones who broke the façade around front?"

"Yes, and they were after us. I've dated them both…" admitted Hannah, which startled the other three.

Shamed, Hannah left their company and ran back into the hotel. The sheriff hollered for her to stop to no avail. Karen asked for the sheriff to explain how all of this excused what Butch and Roy did tonight.

"I'm not real certain what they have done, and I'll need for you to file a formal complaint tomorrow, if you will still want to," advised the Sheriff.

"Isn't that pretty obvious, Bailey?" said Adam.

"No, I don't think so. I'll need to piece things together. There's too much going on tonight. I'm not certain how serious things are going to get."

As an afterthought Karen added to the issue, "There's one other detail. My pistol was stolen from my room. I don't know if it was stolen earlier when Hannah was in my room, or the cook, or the person who scared off the cook, or just now when Butch and Roy were in there."

"You're here to apply for a job, and you brought a gun along with you?" said an amused Bailey, "You might do well here! This sometimes seems like the wild west."

"I like to target practice whenever I get the chance. It's a small caliber pistol, single action, frontier model colt," reported Karen.

"When did you discover it missing?" asked Adam.

"In the midst of the chase, I managed to get back to my room before they caught up with us. I had it in my holster, and it wasn't there when I went to get it."

"You think a woman with a little pistol would stop those two men?" asked Bailey.

"I don't miss."

"Not ever?"

"Not for the last five years. My father and I are rather accomplished. Tournament shooters," Karen proudly stated.

"Well, Adam, I don't know how you have managed to meet Miss Gustafson, but I think things are getting interesting. If you will forgive me, Miss, I have more to follow up. Please, do call tomorrow and come fill out a complaint. I'll be talking to Butch." Not waiting for a response the sheriff left Karen and Adam.

"Karen, I think you need to accept my offer, at least for tonight."

"Thanks, I was hoping you'd tender your offer again. I hate to admit it, but you're right. Let me get my suitcase. My other things should be all right for tonight."

Karen rushed to her room, gathered her credentials for tomorrow's interview, packed her suitcase, put the do-not-disturb sign outside on the door knob, nailed the window shut with her now souvenir rock, and met Adam at his truck. Smiling, Adam watched as she approached and admired her graceful steps. Adam stepped out from the truck cab, tipped his black Stetson, and escorted her to the passenger side, where Adam placed Karen's suitcase behind her in the truck bed. Adam assisted Karen as she climbed upward to the bench seat. Adam marveled to himself how Karen's touch sent a spark through him.

Karen asked, "Do you wear a mask? Do you have a horse named Silver or a dog named Bullet?"

"No, but my sidekick is a full blooded Ute, who claims he could make me silver bullets."

"You are my hero once more!"

"Well, my name is Claymore, like the actor," smiled Adam.

Their ride to Adam's ranch house on Claymore Flats transpired quietly, and Karen noticed and appreciated his glances of admiration. He drove remembering how it was when Mary rode beside him. He would drive through town where people would glance and wave as they passed. People had often shouted fond greetings primarily toward Mary, as her gaze upon everyone produced feelings of well being, genuine warmth, and neighborliness. He always felt proud to have her beside him, proud that she was his, and proud of whom she was. Among the church members, people said they could see Jesus in Mary. Adam thought as he drove and concluded that was what he saw in this young woman, and the fact that she was so appealing, so slender, yet so much a woman. For him the ride ended too soon, yet he had opened his home to her, introduced her to the help in the kitchen, and then escorted her to his unused master bedroom. She protested, yet his insistence prevailed. He told her the room was freshly kept but unused for years. Adam told her that he had his own room that he shared with his lap dog, whom she would meet again in the morning. Goodnight, Karen said to her champion.

Inquiry

CHAPTER 10

"For it is better, if it is God's will, to suffer for doing good than for doing evil." 1 Peter 3:17

Monday at daybreak Adam arrived with Big Foot at Mary's gravesite in the family cemetery on the east end of the mesa. His enthusiasm toward his guest turned to guilt, and he needed to make peace with himself and the memory of his beloved Mary. Unwanted loneliness persisted as a terrible companion, and his commitment to Mary still gnawed on his conscience when he noticed another woman. Adam sat briefly beside Mary's gravesite compared to other occasions, and he shifted his visit to the park bench where Mary had overlooked Rock Creek.

Adam studied the mountain peaks, as daybreak traversed Mt. Huajatolla like a downhill skier making rapid descent. Depending on the vantage point, each day the light and shadows revealed new features of the mountainside. He watched as light reduced shadow, which soon retreated downhill to the recent landslide and seemed to linger at the Live Oak above the Blair House. How sad Adam thought that such a magnificent tree had died and no longer dominated the landscape above the town.

Studying the town below, Adam's thoughts shifted to the present. He had left notice for his cook, Rabbit, to wake Karen at 6:30 a.m., well before her 9:00 a. m. interview at the school district offices. Adam had left her a separate note asking her to meet him for lunch at the Stage Stop. From the mesa he watched as the Rock Creek convenience store opened for business. As residents stoked their stoves and fireplaces, smoke billowed out of smokestacks and hovered in the treetops, yet Adam still caught a whiff of rose fragrance from below. A morning delivery truck left the canyon and entered what folks traditionally called the vestibule, the town of Rock Creek. Adam studied his church in the birch glen below and hoped his duties would soon revert back to being church deacon instead of interim pastor. Whistling for his horse, he removed the mare's tack, her bridle, saddle, and blanket, then slapped her backside and watched as she galloped away to fresh grass in the meadow and water in the stream behind him. Often Adam rode to this point and let his mount graze, while he worked in the cemetery or at the church below.

This morning, Adam carried the tack, climbed down the steep trail, picked and ate both wild strawberries and raspberries as he descended. He crossed the footbridge and walked through the church grounds to the parsonage, the third house from the church on Main Street. He had retained ownership of the house but donated its use to the church. After storing the tack in the garage, he showered and shaved, then departed in his two-door, gray '51 Chevy sedan that he kept in the dilapidated, wooden garage behind the parsonage. Adam rode out to meet with his cousin, who would be waiting for him at the Cozy Corner Café in Ridge View. Though related, Whitney McNaughton was a sometimes friend or sometimes foe.

Nicknamed Red because of his red hair and ruddy complexion, Whitney sipped his second cup of coffee as Adam arrived. Noting Adam parked the old Chevy in front of the cafe, Whitney guessed Adam had spent the night in Rock Creek. As Adam sat down at the table, Red greeted him, "You should let me rent that old place in Rock Creek."

"Red, I'll be staying there this week…I'm surprised anybody would want to rent the place. Besides, I need to repair the garage or tear it down and plant a garden. If we ever hire a pastor, the church will once again need a parsonage."

Red laughed and said, "There's a lot of places available."

"Seems most new people have left the valley or have been burned out," Adam reflected predicting Red had direct knowledge of the incident, "And more have a way of showing up."

"I hear you have a young friend staying at the Stage Stop. What do you know about her?" asked Red.

"She's nobody, has no relatives here. Name's Karen and she's from south of here," Adam said. "Don't worry about her. She's here to apply for Jill Lowenstein's job at the high school,"

"So, the board's going to replace her even though there's been no resignation?"

"Guess so, funny though, I'd thought she'd return, if she could," speculated Adam.

"Maybe just precautions in case Lowenstein doesn't come back, they'll have someone under contract who can teach her area," answered Whitney.

"And if she comes back?"

"Then they'll have a permanent substitute teacher."

"Why would anyone want that kind of a position?" reflected Adam.

"Someone who wants a job badly enough," Red speculated.

"Or someone who needs a quick change of scenery."

"Someone, who needs to be somewhere else."

"I'll bet you might think of another reason," Adam suggested.

"You think I would say that she is someone who's here for another reason and has come here under false pretenses. And we both know what Mary would say," proposed Red.

"'That God is at work and has brought Karen here for his purposes," said Adam, and he continued with, "If that's the case, what would you do differently? How would I react?"

They both paused in their speculation, until Whitney brought up the past. "Remember our last year at high school, about how we were in two-a-day practices. You were tailback, I was quarterback, and Bailey was fullback."

"How can I forget? You talk about it every time we are together," complained Adam.

"That was offense. I was safety. You were cornerback, and Bailey was on the inside on defense."

"Crowfoot was on the other corner, and Bustos was next to Bailey."

"No, Bustos moved with his uncle. We sure missed him," countered Red.

"He was real scholarship material."

"More so in baseball, that's why they moved him to Denver."

"And he signed with the Bears. He played a few seasons at Bears' Stadium after working his way up from the rookie leagues."

"Where Monkey Wards was."

"Didn't he play a couple of years with the Yankees?" asked Adam.

"I think so. I'm going to ask the next time I'm at their diner."

"In Jericho Springs?"

"We shouldn't have lost," said Red.

"But we did, Red," reminded Adam, "and that's life."

"We lost because Wolf Creek had all those move-ins."

"Old timers sold their land for a tidy profit. Besides, we still lost. Red, that was then and this is now. People move. The mines opened in Wolf Creek, and the newcomers had some tough kids. We lost legitimately. We played a great game."

"I should have called your number instead of my own," admitted Red.

"If I hadn't slipped on the turf, when their running back cut back inside," Adam countered, "they wouldn't have gotten past the line."

"And if I'd still been in the game instead of being benched."

"Red, the coach did the right thing. Your kneecap was dislocated."

"That new guy..."

Acting bored with the conversation, Adam slapped Red on the shoulder, "Come on Red! You still won the league MVP! You were great! You could have gone on and played at Western State, or Mesa, or most anywhere."

"Thanks, Adam, you've always been good for me, in spite of everything."

"Because I no longer let you call the plays?"

"Guess so, anyway this is your nickel. What's up?" asked Red.

"One thing I wanted to talk about is the bear up where our cattle have been spending the summer."

"What do you have in mind?"

"Two things," Adam said, "It's early, but I think we should start flooding our pasture east of Jericho Springs, and then bring down our herds before Labor Day."

"Instead of after Labor Day?"

"It's the bear. My wranglers say we have lost more calves than ever because of it. I'm going after him. I have a hundred head in the pasture now, but I'll move them to the mesa. Once we flood the pasture, I'll take some of my men with me, and we'll bring our cattle down the valley to the meadow above Blair House."

"Which means your herd won't be mixed with the cattle we own together. What about branding?" Red asked.

"Exactly, after a couple of weeks, the pasture will dry out and the grasses will have grown. We will brand down here instead of on the mountain or in the valley by the old woodcutter. Then I'll hunt the varmint."

"Well, Adam, your plan sounds good. I wish I could join you. You know the bear may follow you," said Red,

"He might. You are more than welcomed to come along, Red. I could use my buddy with me watching my back. It might be good to get away from all that's been going on. Consider this an invitation."

"I'll let you know, partner," said Red.

Deciding how to approach the rest of his agenda, Adam eased into the topic without revealing all his concern, "So, how are my rentals?"

"Well, the Bonds rented the place east outside the valley."

"And someone torched the trailer. It's a total loss! How are the Bonds?"

"I guess the Bonds are gone," Red said attempting to mask a smirk with his hand.

"Guess so, and they were newcomers," Adam said with a half smile.

"Then there's the new lineman, who just moved his family in on the Rock Creek property."

"And someone stole the little boy's ducks and killed them in a bonfire on my property."

"I wouldn't know about that, Adam, but the Brownings are newcomers. You know how a lot of folks feel about that," Red said.

"Yes, I do, and I know you and I would both like to have the Blair House and all that goes with it. Ours is a philosophic difference, Red, on how we treat people and whether the ends justify the means or the means justifies the ends. If there is a rightful heir to the Blair property, then it belongs to them. I'd be happy for them to have been blessed by God. If there isn't a rightful heir, then I think the move you made was fair and just."

"To have formed the corporation of all the McNaughtons and their kin?"

"Yes, that has been one of your best efforts, Red. You have included all of the family to have an equal share, if we end up with the property. Speaking of which, what about the rest of my rentals?"

Feeling better with Adam's endorsement, Red continued, "The four-plex is fully rented here in Ridge View. Janine Crowfoot still has the place by Blair House, and the woodcutter still lives in the cabin that the Blair's leased to you on their property in the canyon. He has barely made a dent in harvesting the pine killed by beetles. He does it the old and slow way. You know he uses teams of horses instead of trucks. The only vacant property is your Mary's old shack in Rock Creek as well as the Wolf Creek properties."

"How are your rentals doing'?"

"Filled with relatives, of course," Red confessed.

"What about the Blair House? What do you think is going to happen?" asked Adam.

"If I get my way…"

"And you usually do."

"Then I would get that all to myself."

"Unless I would," Adam laughed.

"You're not the competition I'd worry about. At least you're family," said Red as his faced flushed.

"By marriage."

"You know that still counts."

"Who are you worried about?"

"I'm pretty sure everyone will sign the incorporation papers, which will eliminate all family fighting, but Thursday night is going to be interesting. You know, Adam, you may have a lot of vacancies by then."

"I hope not!" Adam said emphatically, "So, you're the one creating all the excitement for the newcomers, aren't you?"

"I know what's going on, but who doesn't," replied Red angrily, "and you know how it feels to have newcomers move in and get what isn't theirs. The Blair House should belong to one of us or all of us… even if I don't get it."

"And it's okay for people to be tormented, harassed?"

"They need to go back where they came from."

"Everybody's got to be someplace…"

"But not here, not now, I don't care what it takes. I'm going to do all I can to get rid of outsiders who think they can come in here and get our water rights, the mineral rights, and the Blair House."

"Even if it's theirs?" Adam asked.

"How could that be Adam? The Blair's didn't have any kids. That kid Ezra ran off. He wasn't even theirs."

"I don't know. What I do know is that John Law was able to get the injunction and appears to represent someone with a legitimate claim."

"And you're content to let 'em have it. Have it all."

"Right is right. Means justify the ends, Red. Play the game by the rules. That is what has kept you and me where we are. You know we've benefited as family."

"You maybe, not me," said Red.

"And that's how you got injured in the game."

"Yeah, I tripped the guy and we got the penalty and they kept the ball."

"And you were out of the game."

"I would have done anything, Adam, to win that game, and I'll do anything to get the Blair House."

"Anything?"

The question remained unanswered, but Adam already knew the answer. Whitney, being true to his nickname, now flushed red with anger. He would do anything short of murder or so Adam thought, to make certain the Blair House, its mineral and water rights, would belong to the McNaughton clan. If Red wasn't directly responsible for the harassment of the new people, he was involved with those responsible. At least Red knew about it and must have given his approval by not saying anything against it."

"So, Adam, what's this argument you've got going with the assistant superintendent?"

"Does that have anything to do with my property being set on fire twice?"

"What do you mean?"

"I think I could correctly guess the names of some of the good ole boys, who burned my trailer on the ridge where the Bonds lived. They probably set the grass fire below the falls by Ridge View. That's where Rob Browning lives."

"I certainly wouldn't condone that. If I were in charge, I wouldn't want anyone using the effort by mixing in a personal vendetta."

"I wonder," said Adam pensively.

"What I heard is that you made an issue about Maurice Wood's plan to get condoms in the counselor's office?"

"That's part of it. Maurice just doesn't do things how they're supposed to be done. Red, he is not above board, and I get the feeling he is pulling a fast one, because if the truth is known, parents would probably be up in arms. Well, maybe some of them."

"And that bothers you to no end. They're probably saving lives and preventing a lot of mistakes. Kids need a choice like everyone else," admonished Red.

"The choice comes before the roll in the sack. The decision should be to save it till marriage. God's word is specific…"

"There you go Adam. You've got the right interpretation and everybody else is wrong," concluded Red.

"It's what the Bible says."

"That's not what I mean. You always did get into trouble by having to be right. It's like you can't stand to be wrong."

"And I always have to say something."

"My exact thought, Adam, you've heard this before, but I've seen you make more enemies because you won't let it go, perhaps even Maurice Wood," explained

Red with a smile. "You always stand up for what is right and you stand on the Word. You are the stand up guy I could always count on, if I was doing what was right."

Adam chuckled to himself then continued as they got up from their table and made their way to pay their bill at the counter, "Do you remember when I was courting Mary, and she called off the wedding?"

"How could I forget? You were a mess."

"She wasn't fond of my need to be correct. No, it was more than that. It was that I had to be correct and for everyone else involved to admit it."

"How did you two resolve it?" asked Red.

"Mary said she thought about it for a couple of days, and then she made her decision. Mary had me meet her on the mesa where the park bench is. She hiked there from her house, what you called my shack. Remember before Mary gave it to the church as a parsonage, she lived there. And I bought it back after Mary died, so the church would have money to continue paying the bi-vocational pastor. Anyway, this was before we used the trail to get to town. I rode out to meet her. We stood together overlooking the town, and after a few minutes, she made her statement."

"What did she say, Adam, this is a good story!"

"She said she would deal with me as necessary, if I made one promise."

"Conditional love?"

"Not really, she made me promise to keep doing what was right and saying what I believed as long as I kept my focus on the Lord."

"That's it?

"No, she said she was like me about the church in Rock Creek. That her passion for the church and the work there had potential of distracting and taking away from our relationship."

"I'd have thought her church work would be a positive?"

"Not if she obsessed about it to where the work damages the marriage relationship. To Mary, being in right relationship with your spouse was fundamental to doing church work."

"So that's it. Then Mary gave in and decided to get married?"

"I also promised her I would never give up on Rock Creek and the little church."

"And that's why you continued the work there after the pastor moved to Jericho Springs."

"She never complained again. I got better, of course, but every now and then I'd get on one of my toots and she'd call me on it."

"I can see her now getting' in your face about it."

"She did but not like you think," Adam said with tears swelling, "she'd take me in her arms and stand on her tip toes, then kiss me. That's all it would take for me to shut up. Then she would call me her perfect gift from God."

"God's perfect gift! That's too much," Red chuckled.

"She asked me to view her that way too. It's hard to get angry or find fault with someone who is God's perfect gift to you."

"You mean Mary really believed you were perfect?"

"No, she made a choice that if we were to marry, then God was giving me perfectly for her, so he could love her through me. She believed God is in the business of perfecting those that are his, and her job was to accept me as I am, despite knowing that I'm under construction yet perfect for her."

"She was very effective!"

"Very," finished Adam with tears in both their eyes.

Satisfied with the story, both men left the café, Whitney hurried to the lumberyard, but Adam sat in the old Chevy awhile reminiscing. "Yeah, I sure miss her,"

The woodcutter had been second to see Izzy at the Blair House Monday morning. First was Janine, now the woodcutter had spied him shortly after sunrise from the hairpin curve. Often in the early morning, the old woodcutter parked his truck above Jericho Springs to bask in the morning sunlight, while standing watch over the town. That morning the woodcutter had felt distressed. He had seen Izzy carelessly stroll through the backyard. He noted that Janine Crowfoot watched as well from her front porch, but that was not where the danger came from. A sheriff's cruiser approached from the north.

Quickly, the woodcutter returned to his pickup truck loaded with slab, depressed the clutch on entry to the cab, turned the key, and released the clutch. A loud boom pierced the morning air, as the engine caught hold following the fifth cylinder. Startled, Izzy quickly retreated to the shadows and safety, as the Gray Whiz continued toward town when the sheriff's cruiser passed by the front of the Blair House oblivious of the new resident. The Gray Whiz rounded the bend, crossed over the bridge, and continued down the road connecting with Main Street at the convenience store. There, the grisly driver turned north on Main and entered Janine's driveway.

Janine bounced down the stairs, light-on-her-feet, greeting the woodcutter with a wave. He stopped the truck at the rear of the driveway, waited for her to greet him, and then displayed a bouquet of mountain flowers from behind him. She took the floral treasure from him and gave him a hug at his descent from the Gray Whiz. Thank you, she said with delight, and then motioned to where she wanted the woodcutter to unload her wood. She handed him an envelope with $50.00 in it and a note telling him she was glad he was watering the old tree. Then Janine returned to the front yard in time to see the sheriff get out of his cruiser and approach the Blair House front porch.

"Sheriff," Janine called to distract Bailey yet thinking she did not want to encourage his interests in her.

Taking note of Janine's call to him, Sheriff Bailey hesitated momentarily, but then descended the stairs from the porch to the sidewalk below. Having jogged to the Blair House, she engaged him at the gate. Inside the Blair House, Izzy observed the scene from the piano room, then returned to the backyard and picked up his shaving gear and toothbrush he had left on the wash stand. Izzy could do nothing to cover the moist area where he had tossed the basin water.

"Miss Crowfoot, how nice, what can I do for you?" Sheriff Bailey said hoping for a favorable response.

"I saw you and wondered if you had any news about my roommate, Jill Lowenstein," said Janine.

"We work on that case each day, Miss Crowfoot. I'm sorry to say we have no new leads."

Janine glanced toward the Blair house, saw Izzy wave to her from the piano room, then heard the woodcutter start his truck.

"Excuse me, Sheriff, I just got a load of wood," Janine said turning toward her house.

"Just a minute, Janine!" insisted Bailey.

Startled, Janine stopped and turned, "Yes?"

"I'm here checking on a complaint that someone had been prowling around the neighborhood."

Janine's eyes narrowed as she looked directly into the sheriff's eyes. "And peeking in windows?" she questioned.

Realizing Janine knew of his own activity, Bailey answered, "The only complaint I've had, until now, is that there has been some late night activity around the Blair House. We're worried a prowler may be on the premises. Perhaps it's related to the Lowenstein case, I don't know."

"Sheriff, I do confess I have been over there in the pond pretty late. It's probably me someone's complaining about. Sorry!"

"You've been out skinny-dipping, have you?" Bailey surmised with delight.

"Oh, no, Sheriff, nothing that risqué! I just go over now and then to dangle my feet in the warm water. It's all very innocent and very appropriate. I assure you. I wouldn't want to attract unwanted attention."

"Well, Miss Crowfoot, perhaps I'll stop by and join you some time soon."

Walking away, Janine retorted, "Don't bother. I won't be doing it again." Certain Izzy was now careful not to be seen, Janine returned to her own porch but pretended to work on her bicycle, while she watched the sheriff wander about the grounds.

Sheriff Bailey inspected the front porch, peered into the windows of each first floor room, and caught a whiff of the odor of rotting clothes from the second floor balcony. He mused to himself wondering why anyone would want to fix up this old place. It would be better for all concerned when Blair House burned to the ground, he thought. Bailey returned to his patrol car and retrieved his flashlight. He followed the flagstone pathway around back, found the wash basin still dampened from Izzy's use, noticed where the used water had been tossed, and then detected the unsecured back porch door. Bailey peered through the screen door and saw that footprints disturbed the fine dust inside the doorway leading to the kitchen.

When Janine had delayed the sheriff at the gate, Izzy put his things in his suitcase from the bedroom to go to the basement. As Bailey opened the porch door, Izzy made his way to the basement down creaking stairs undetected. Before Izzy reached the bottom, Bailey entered the kitchen and began a room by room search of the house beginning with the first floor. Meanwhile Izzy noted that although some remodeling had been completed, nothing's changed below, nothing except the heating system. In the main bedroom, dust only partially covered where Izzy had slept. Bailey inspected dresser drawers finding nothing. Sensing he was not alone, Bailey moved quietly through the other rooms to the front of the house. Below in the basement, Izzy opened an exterior window on the north side of the house behind an over grown bush. With his loose clothing, Izzy disturbed the dust on the windowsill, table below, and other surrounding objects. Izzy propped the window open. Listening, he heard the sheriff descending the stairwell. Izzy quickly disappeared into the darkness of a storeroom and into a closet beneath the kitchen.

In moments the sheriff appeared, noticed the disturbed window, rushed to it, climbed onto the table, and then peered out of the opening. Speculating no one could have escaped the thicket of brush beyond the window easily, Bailey hastened to the kitchen and out the back door.

Leaving his suitcase behind him on a cluttered shelf in the darkened hideaway, Izzy followed from the closet and scurried through the house and up the second floor stairwell, while the sheriff wasted time venturing into the thicket of brush. Izzy continued to the third floor purposefully heading for one of two connecting bedrooms at the west-end of the house. Now enjoying this game of cat-'n-mouse, Izzy entered the bedroom, opened the window to the third floor porch, and again did not exit the room. Instead, Izzy entered the closet, which one time served as a servant's press room and servants' stairwell to the kitchen. Quick to elude detection, Izzy closed the door, and pressed against the west wall, which opened at his thrust reluctantly. Then quietly, Izzy waited behind the wall while listening for clues of Bailey's movements. If the electricity had not been disconnected, Izzy remembered that he could have descended the stairwell leading from the third floor press room down to the second then first floor and into a storeroom connected to the kitchen and drawing room. The elaborate system once allowed servants to begin their daily tasks by leaving their quarters in the early hours without disturbing the household.

Meanwhile, Bailey re-entered the back porch and predicted he had been duped. The sheriff carefully closed the door. Bailey waited and listened for any kind of movement. Upstairs Izzy speculated where Bailey stood and what Janine might be doing. Janine watched from her front yard and realized her neighbor, Rachel McNaughton, had come out from her house and was crossing the street to the patrol car.

Janine panicked and prayed out loud, "Lord, don't let anything happen to Izzy. I've waited too long for my love to return just to lose him. Father, I don't know what to do, but you do! Show me…please." Immediately, Janine got an idea. She approached Rachel and asked if the sheriff had found anyone.

"I just don't know," said Rachel, "Bailey's sly enough to catch a fox in a barnyard."

"Perhaps, we ought to help him," said Janine.

"Good idea!" responded old Mrs. McNaughton, as she crossed the street holding on to Janine's hand.

Reaching the back door and seeing the sheriff standing and listening in the kitchen, Rachel continued, "Bailey, you find anything?"

"Shhh!" Bailey responded too late, before a mouse scurried between them on the floor.

"Out of my way!" McNaughton shouted as she pushed past Bailey, "Varmint! I'll get you," Rachel said grabbing what weapon she could find from the closet and headed down the hallway.

"Mrs. McNaughton! You stop, now!" exclaimed the sheriff, catching up with the old woman. "You better tell me what you have seen over here that prompted you to call me," while coaxing her to the piano room, where he sat her on the dust laden sofa.

Listening, Janine heard Rachel tell Bailey, "I had a vision where I seen a man, maybe two or three over here late at night after 8:00 p.m. They had tools and were working. They prayed and they sang. They had paint brushes too! Sometimes they's walking upstairs or lookin' out the windows. Sometimes they's up by the tree watering it, hugging it. Last night, I heard them talking to my husband and Paul Blair. There was a woman too. I came over here to bring my husband home, but I couldn't find him here or at the convenience store…. either one."

"Her husband's been dead over three years, Sheriff," Janine explained.

"I know. Miss Crowfoot, that might explain everything," Bailey said to Janine, then to old Mrs. McNaughton, "Did you come into the house, Mrs. McNaughton?"

"Course I did, you silly, Lydia and I had tea. We always do…" Rachel added as the sheriff began to take her back home, then she added, "I think they were with the woodcutter. I don't remember his name. He gave me a ride home from the store, where Janine's brother works. He never says anything. Did you notice that? He went to Janine's house right now. I think he's delivering wood in that terrible old truck I don't like. I don't know why it still runs, but it does. Sometimes I thinks it's an alarm to alert folks there's evil in the town. Watch out!"

"That's right, Rachel, come on home now. We've found him. Let's get you home, dear," Bailey added tenderly as he glanced at Janine who was holding her hand over her mouth to keep from laughing.

Bailey whispered as he let go of the screen door, "Would you close the door behind you," then pausing he added, "Someone's been here. I'm certain. I closed a window downstairs that someone opened at one time or another. I think it's safe to say no one is here who doesn't belong to Mrs. McNaughton's memories of the past. I'll get her home, and then I'll check to see you are safely home."

"Don't bother, Sheriff Bailey, I'm right behind you."

Janine followed Bailey and Mrs. McNaughton to the street then hurried home before Bailey attempted to expand his contact with her. From a third floor window, Izzy observed Bailey and McNaughton, then longingly after Janine, as she pranced across the street, hair bouncing gracefully side to side almost in slow motion. He thought how he had wasted so many years. But no more, Izzy resolved and concluded that true love had waited for him even when begun at so early an age.

Under Izzy's surveillance, the sheriff left, then Izzy returned to his third floor hiding place to explore the servants' route to the kitchen area. Propping open the closet and stairwell doors, he discovered the trap he had been in. What he remembered as a narrow stairwell had been closed off in recent years where the stairs meet the floor. Instead what remained was an undiscovered storage room. Realizing his escape would have been blocked, he appreciated Janine's intervention even more. "Lord, she arrived in the nick-of-time!" Izzy said aloud to himself.

As promised, Rabbit woke Karen in time to have a leisurely breakfast and to prepare for her interview. Other than Adam and Robert Browning, Rabbit proved to be the most positive man that Karen had met in the Rock Creek valley. Both entertaining and informative, he was good company. He told her about Claymore Flats and how he had come to work there. He said he never really knew Mary Claymore other than by reputation. No one, he said, mentioned a negative thing about that kind and gentle woman. Mary had brought out the best in Adam and had inspired him to be the man he was today, a wealthy, community-minded, man of God. Without hesitation, Rabbit spoke endearingly about how Adam had been one of the best athletes of his time in the valley, how he had been outspoken on what Rabbit called civil rights issues, and how he had made a point of taking on morality issues in the schools and community. Rabbit also spoke of how Adam had a need to be right. Rabbit corrected himself and said it wasn't a need but more like a passion. Karen pondered Rabbit's characterization.

After breakfast with Karen, Rabbit started preparing a meal for the Bond family, which Mrs. Bond finished and served her family in the dining room. Meanwhile, Rabbit drove Karen to Rock Creek for her interview. He told Karen that Adam wanted to meet her for lunch at the Stage Stop at noon and that Adam had asked for her to call the ranch phone if that was not okay or if she had any kind of problem. As they entered County Road 403 from the mesa, Rabbit waved as the woodcutter passed them heading for the ranch house. Rabbit informed Karen the woodcutter delivered a full load of wood weekly both for immediate use and in preparation for winter. Karen asked why Adam's help didn't cut the wood. Rabbit said the hands stocked the line shacks as they repaired fence and tended to the stock around the line shacks, but Adam had made an arrangement with the old woodcutter to provide wood. In exchange for the wood, the woodcutter used Adam's cabin in the high mountain valley above the landslide. Then Rabbit corrected himself telling her it was actually arranged through Red McNaughton, who managed Adam's rental property. Rabbit chuckled and said no one had rented that place for years before Red had gotten the woodcutter to take the deal. Rabbit pointed toward the Twin Peaks of Mt. Huajatolla and told her the cabin was nestled in the trees at the base of the left one. Rabbit urged her to get Adam to take her for a drive to the end of the road into the valley explaining the view of the plains was exceptional, but the real thing to observe was the white buffalo on the northern peak. Rabbit told her how his people had used the valley as a refuge and how many of his ancestors had been buried there. Rabbit told her the area was sacred to his people, and then he became quiet until they arrived at the motel. Karen wondered about the beautiful woman who took over for him in the kitchen, but she didn't ask.

Karen thanked Rabbit and they exchanged goodbyes. She strode confidently into the hotel to her room, changed clothes for the interview, picked up her interview files, and walked downstairs into the lobby. At the desk she inquired about Hannah. A dowdy old woman told her that Hannah reported to work but had become suddenly ill and retired to her room. From the restaurant Karen heard laughter and recognized the voices. It was Deputy Butch and his friend, Roy, from last night talking with Sarah, the waitress.

Without hesitation Karen left the hotel and walked the short distance to the school administration offices in the old high school building. Pausing before the real estate offices, she crossed the highway, while being watched from the personnel office and from the insurance department of the real estate firm. Once inside she paused to read the building directory in the lobby noting the second floor location of the school district administrative offices. The historical society, library, and museum were on the third floor, while the warehouse and senior center were on the ground floor, rear entrance.

Karen entered the personnel office adjacent the Superintendent of Schools' office, where Beth Ellen McNaughton administrative secretary greeted her, after having watched Karen cross the highway.

"Miss Gustafson, I presume. Please have a seat. Dr. Maurice Wood, our assistant superintendent and personnel director will be with you momentarily."

Karen nodded affirmatively, took a seat, and opened the file she brought with her.

Beth Ellen returned from informing Dr.Wood of Karen's arrival and offered Karen a cup of coffee, which was declined. Beth shrugged off Karen's refusal and returned to her desk where she busied herself by preparing a flyer.

Dr. Wood emerged from a door leading to the superintendent's office, greeted Karen, and requested her to follow him. She briefly inspected him noting his short stature, bulging brown eyes, and black, dyed hair. He led her into the superintendent's office and invited her to take a seat next to him before the desk. Dr. Wood explained the superintendent would return momentarily. With that a side door leading to the hallway opened and a tall, athletic man entered closing the door behind him.

"Miss Gustafson, welcome to Rock Creek School District," he said crossing the office to his chair behind the oak desk with thick glass covering the desktop. "I'm glad you were able to interview today. I understand you arrived by bus Friday. Have you enjoyed your visit?"

"Yes, I did, Mr. Moss. I have had an interesting stay."

"I'll bet you have, Miss Gustafson," added Mr. Moss.

Sorting through a folder with Karen's name on it, Superintendent Moss commented, "Well, you come well recommended. Good grades in college, experienced, endorsed for secondary social studies and physical science, an unusual combination. Your references say you have commitment to the students' learning and welfare. Application is completed. And your former principal, Mr. Markley, said he would like for you to remain on his staff."

"I enjoyed my previous assignment."

"But you left for personal reasons?" quizzed Mr. Moss.

Karen turned to face him expecting to be bombarded with questions for her to explain what had happened. "Yes," Karen answered with a smile.

The two men glanced at each other. "I think her credentials are in order. Don't you Dr. Wood?

"I'd say anyone with training and experience in both science and social studies is a rare commodity."

"Fits our assignment perfectly."

"Miss Gustafson, let me get right to the point. Do you have any relatives in Rock Creek, the valley?" said Mr. Moss.

"None."

"Do you know anyone from here....other than those you may have meant since Friday?"

"As a matter of fact, I've never gotten off the Interstate to even visit here. I've met some interesting people at the Stage Stop."

"Oh, yes, we have a colorful group that tends to gather there."

Karen resisted telling them her story and did not, as she noticed the office door had been left open and Beth Ellen McNaughton stood just outside it. Mr.

Moss saw Karen's glance and followed with his own. "Miss McNaughton, did you need something."

"Oh, no sir, I'll just close this door," Beth Ellen said sheepishly.

"Miss Gustafson, Karen, the circumstances behind this assignment are, shall we say, delicate."

"I've been curious about that," said Karen.

"The assignment is to replace a very popular teacher, Jill Lowenstein, who has disappeared. The circumstances behind her disappearance are quite disturbing. You see there was a tragedy. A young woman recent to Rock Creek was missing. As it happens a pizza deliveryman discovered her body. Jill Lowenstein knew of this girl from Jill's church activities. She may have witnessed something."

"How dreadful," Karen replied, "Is there a suspect?"

"That we don't know for certain. Of course, there are rumors about a gentleman friend. The deceased worked at the bed and breakfast just down the street, behind the hotel. Frankly, Miss Gustafson, Miss Lowenstein may return before the school year starts, but she is considered a material witness, meaning the sheriff is looking for her. We just want to have the assignment covered, appropriately. And the school board has authorized me to do something rather unusual," reported the superintendent.

"How do you mean?"

"Explain Dr. Wood."

"Miss Gustafson, the board has created a position. If we are able to fill Miss Lowenstein's position and if she does return for this school year, then the person we hire will become a Permanent K-12 Substitute for the contract year on the regular salary schedule with all the regular teacher benefits-meaning health insurance and sick leave."

"And, after that year?"

"Yes, it would be a one-year contract as all our contracts are if or until one obtains tenure, but we would do everything possible to rehire the candidate for another position."

"Our high school social studies teacher, Rosa Jaramillo, has committed, in writing, to retire after this next school year after over forty years in the classroom."

"Are you offering that stipulation as part of the contract?"

"That's not possible. Based on successful experience, the school board minutes record that intent. Actually, being a permanent substitute would have some advantages. You would be assigned to the high school principal's office. You would primarily fill junior or senior high school assignments, and, of course, you would be assigned before any other substitute is used. If there is a long term assignment, you would be placed in that position."

"Unless it is long term, you wouldn't have papers to grade," said Superintendent Moss adding to Dr. Wood's explanation.

"Or lesson plans to create," added Dr. Wood.

"Or my own students," included Karen.

"Or required extra-curricular duties, but one," the superintendent slipped into the discussion.

"You would probably get to know more of the staff and students than most everyone in the school district," explained Dr. Wood.

"And Miss Gustafson, my guess is you would be well appreciated!" emphasized Mr. Moss.

"Well, that would be good. What is next?" asked Karen.

"You are still interested?"

"It sounds like a challenge. A little bit different. Yes, I'm interested."

"A formality, my assistant superintendent, our personnel director, has an interview process to complete with you, to get your perceptions. It isn't difficult and perhaps enjoyable though lengthy. Not to worry Miss Gustafson, you seem to be strong on empathy," said Mr. Moss.

"And an interview with the high school principal. No trouble there either. You both attended Western Bible College, but you graduated from Calvary Bridal College," Dr. Wood informed.

Karen smiled, then laughed, "I graduated from Calvary Bible College but never married. Thank you, Mr. Moss, Dr. Wood. I hope I am offered the position."

Both men chuckled, which startled her. "Oh, forgive us, Karen. No one else remained this interested after learning the circumstances. That certainly is in your favor. Besides your former superintendent and I were in the same fraternity. I had a lengthy conversation with him. If you want the position, I will submit your name to the school board tomorrow night."

Karen had finished the interview process. She followed Dr. Wood to his office and completed the sixty question interview administered by him. During the interview, he asked additional background questions double checking her knowledge of the curriculum areas. She commented about the uniqueness of the town of Rock Creek being surrounded by the mesa, the river canyon, the eastern ridge to the river valley, and especially the hogbacks and strike valley. He added that the unique physical makeup and history was matched by the personal, social history, which she would come to appreciate with her physical and social science background. Dr. Wood told Karen that she may want to spend some leisure time in the library's historical section on the third floor.

Next, Karen briefly toured the valley with Dr. Wood in a school district suburban and met with Mr. John Alden, the high school principal in Jericho Springs. Before returning to Rock Creek, she accompanied Dr. Wood on the road west of town, where they stopped at the hairpin turn above the Blair house. He invited her to join him in walking to the guardrail for a better look. "From here, Miss Gustafson, you can see the entire school district, except for the two rural sites further up the road."

"There are schools in the mountains?"

"Trailers, we have a school twenty-five miles due west on this road at Houston Creek and another twenty more miles south of there toward Wolf City. It's at Shirley Dam. There used to be a logging camp there, but now, two ranch families send their daughters to our school at the dam. Actually, the school is nothing more than a trailer with a small room added to it. I imagine neither school will be needed once the children get older, then the parents will get this suburban to use to bring the children into town. Of course, the McNaughtons will be hired as bus drivers to bring their children to town."

"Where do the teachers live?"

"That's what the rest of the trailer is for. It's hard to get a teacher to stay in those assignments more than two years. We rotate them back into town and send someone else out there."

"I'm surprised you have schools in such desolate areas."

"Well, you know how Colorado likes to keep its rural lifestyle. We receive $25,000 additional state aid annually just to maintain the rural schools."

"I thought only Wyoming did that!" said Karen.

"It's being phased out. In fact the state is encouraging home-schooling for those children. When distance learning becomes more advanced, I'm certain it would be less expensive to equip our rural families with satellite dishes and use television to provide educational services."

"That would appear to be less expensive than hiring a teacher to live in a trailer out in the middle of nowhere or hiring a parent as a bus driver to haul the children to town. What do the teachers do during the summer?" asked Karen.

"They either move back to town, visit relatives, or travel. Mostly, they get re-acquainted with people!" explained Dr. Wood.

They both laughed, and then turned their attention to the valley below.

"What a curious scene, Dr. Wood?"

"Interesting isn't it?"

"I haven't seen so many marvelous geologic sights. The contrasts are quite interesting. It appears a lot of water was one time held in the basin below by a natural dam that is now the mesa. At some time the dam broke and the rugged canyon was then carved. Over time the eastern ridge was formed as the river meandered back and forth establishing its boundaries."

"And what do you make of the scene below us, Miss Gustafson?" asked Dr. Wood.

"It looks as though," Karen turned around looking west toward the twin peaks and noticed the scar on the north peak, "as though there has been a series of mud or rock slides, probably originating from that scar area that looks like a lamb on..."

"On the north peak of Mt. Huajatolla?" finished Dr. Wood.

"Yes, what does that mean?"

"Breast of the Earth, it was sacred to the Indians and still is to the old Indian families whose roots date back before early settlement days. It is interesting, Karen, you see the scar as a lamb. Many see it as a white buffalo or a salamander."

"Really, anyway it appears some kind of slides have created the scene below us. Curious."

"How so?"

"Well, I would say the slide has altered the course of the creek and damaged that mound below. It looks like steam is coming from the two ponds on the right, which suggests some geo-thermal activity. I would need to do more investigation, but my guess is that mound with the crater in the center is or was volcanic. Was the crater once a pond?"

"Very astute, Miss Gustafson, you are absolutely correct. As a boy I would occasionally swim in the warm waters of that pond. At one time a pipe ran from the pond to the house providing heat for the occupants. I'm not sure it did much good. Mr. Blair was a man of ideas, very brilliant in sort of an off-beat way."

"Was he the builder of the house?" asked Karen.

"I was about to say the owner, but that isn't true. Mr. Blair ran a boarding house down there in his latter years. He and his wife died penniless several years ago."

"They didn't sell the house?"

"They couldn't. The story is that a man just gifted use of the house to them until he requested it back. Apparently he joined the special forces during the Vietnam War and never returned. Word has it they couldn't sell the house and the house cannot go to public domain. That has created quite a controversy."

"Really, say, what altitude are we?"

"7,800 feet."

"Close to the precious metals zone," surmised Karen.

"Again Miss Gustafson, you have a sharp eye."

"I can see why this is valued land."

"Valued and valuable, it holds the water and mineral rights to the valley below, and it is significant to the Indian's beliefs," Dr. Wood clarified.

"Is that what I will find in the historical museum?"

"At least part of the answer."

"The tree below is not native to this area," Karen stated.

"The dead one on the mound?"

"Yes, I have no idea what it is or was. If it had leaves, I could probably tell."

"It was a Live Oak. Apparently it was planted by either Freemont's party or by earlier European explorers, perhaps by Indians. It hasn't had leaves on it for years. Local lore says it used to shade the whole town at the right time of day. I guess it covered and protected the town from the hot searing sun," explained Dr. Wood. One tale is that the health of the tree reflects how people in the valley treat one another. Someone once wrote a poem to that effect. I think it may still be featured at the museum."

From the valley above came sounds startling both of them. Cough, cough, sputter, cough, sputter, boom. Cough, cough, sputter, cough, sputter, boom.

Catching his breath Dr. Wood laughed at himself, "Miss Gustafson, here comes more lore of the area. But, you won't discover anything about this old timer at the library. In a moment the woodcutter will come by. Anyway our tour is over. I'm sorry to tell you I have a luncheon appointment. I must say this has been a delightful morning."

"Thank you very much. I appreciate your hospitality. Perhaps I will be able to read the poem at the museum," responded Karen, as the coughing truck wheezed by them, the driver waving.

"There he goes the latest addition to Rock Creek lore. Miss Gustafson, perhaps you will be the next one."

The ride back to the school district offices was uneventfully filled with empty yet pleasant chatter. Karen had won over Dr. Wood, a skeptic, one Adam Claymore considered an enemy. Accurately, she had perceived Dr. Wood to be a competent educator with sincere intent to help provide a quality education for the valley's children, which, of course, meant doing things his way. Dr. Wood offered to return her to her lodging and dropped her off at the Stage Stop. Adam was already inside waiting at a table for Karen.

PLANS

CHAPTER 11

"May he give you the desire of your heart and
make all your plans succeed." Psalm 20:4

Unassumingly, Karen ascended the front steps, crossed the porch, and entered the Stage Stop Hotel lobby. She checked at the desk for messages, brushed back her hair, and then turned to enter the dining room. Standing beside his table dressed in a western-cut, three-piece suit with light and dark gray pinstripes, Adam removed his gray, broad brimmed Stetson when he saw that he had caught her eye. With his Stetson in hand, Adam motioned for Karen to sit beside him.

Before advancing Karen studied this tall rugged figure clothed in gray finery. "Hmm," she said under her breath, "he does clean up well. Mr. Claymore either has an important meeting, or he is certainly working hard to impress me."

"Karen," Adam said as he pulled the chair out from the table to assist seating her, "I hope your interview went well."

Seated Karen replied, "It did and I guess I will be offered the position."

"And?"

"And I will consider whether or not I want it. It's not exactly the best of situations."

"No, but the kids need a person like you to teach them. You would be such an asset to the community. We all need you here!"

"Mr. Claymore, if the people here are at all like you and not what I've experienced at the Stage Stop, then I'd be a fool not to take the offer," Karen asserted surprising herself.

Beaming, Adam found he was again at a loss, not for words but because the emotion swelled his chest and tears glistened in his eyes. The waitress took their order interjecting a brief respite. "Excuse me. I've missed the compliments from a woman I care for." Then Adam stammered, "I mean I'm glad....you..."

"Value your friendship," Karen offered emphasizing the word friendship.

Relieved Adam added, "Really, you're the kind of person we need in Rock Creek. I'm certain you will be a fine school teacher."

"Thank you. I'd like to think I'd be able to make a difference. You certainly look nice today, especially after such an early departure this morning."

"Oh, I've been very busy this morning. I keep clothes in my vacant rental across the street. It comes in handy. So, what are you going to do the next few days?"

"The school board meeting is Tuesday night. I think I'll attend."

"You want to hear you got the job first hand?"

"That and I want to watch the dynamics of the district leadership."

"Oh, you'll find it interesting, I'm certain."

"Also, I'd like to explore the library… and there is an ad in the newspaper I'm going to check out."

"Oh, what kind of ad?" asked Adam.

"Well, if I get and take the job, I want to find a good place to live, and there's an ad that interests me. Someone is looking for help in restoring a house in exchange for room and board. I figure I could help and earn my lodging."

"Interesting, I'm not aware of anyone restoring a house that way. Who is it?"

"No name was given, only the ad number and a telephone number. I don't remember what it is, but it is listed in the newspaper ad."

"You may want to consider my rental here in Rock Creek. It's just across the street," offered Adam.

"Thanks, but I'm curious about this offer, and it is in Jericho Springs, which would be close to work at the junior and senior high schools."

"Any other plans?"

"I'd like to get to know the area more, meet some people."

"I could…."

"I thought about delivering pizza. I could lose some weight and get some exercise…" continued Karen.

"If you don't eat a lot of pizza," interrupted Adam.

"That's a fact. Seriously, that would be a way to make a little extra money, meet some people, and learn the area. I think I would enjoy delivering something people like."

"I'll have to order a lot of pizza. I can see you now running to the door."

"If Big Foot didn't take the pizza from me! I know, I'll meet you at the door and say, 'Cold pop and hot pizza, sir," said Karen.

And I'll say, "Miss, your company promises prompt delivery. Within one half hour."

Then I'll say, "Sir, I made this specially myself to insure fine quality. Quality takes more time to make, and then you'll tip me $5.00." Their eye contact lingered, and they both laughed. She knew he would tip well. Karen paused, and then reflected, "I'm concerned about my pistol, the deputy, and Hannah. I doubt he meant any harm, but I don't like what appears to be going on here. Plus I'm missing two of the ten things I value most, my birdfeeder and my pistol."

"Then you need to follow through. File a complaint, but wait until after tomorrow night. If you think you want the job, I wouldn't raise any controversy just yet," Adam advised.

"Other than you being my friend!" asserted Karen.

"Then that's a fact!"

"I do have another favor to ask."

"Name it."

"I'd like to borrow your car for this afternoon," asked Karen.

"You got it, but there is a condition."

"Hmmm...?"

"Return it tonight by dusk and have dinner at my place," offered Adam.

"You are very generous, Mr. Claymore."

"Adam," asked Adam.

"Pastor Adam?"

"I think you had better just call me Adam," he laughed in response. "You do keep me in check, Miss Gustafson."

"As I should, Adam," Karen responded both smiling and gazing into his eyes. "Well, defined boundaries are important when beginning a relationship."

"I think I like that. It's old fashioned like I am," Adam added, "and quite respectable. Is there anything else?"

"If I have any problems, I'd like to be able to contact you."

"You do that, Karen, you do that. Is there anything else?" Adam said as he once again wrote his telephone number on a paper napkin and handed it to her. "I check in at my ranch several times a day. Just call me."

"Well, yes, would you let me rent the house across the street through Thursday?"

"You can stay there at no cost, my friend," Adam offered.

"Boundaries, business is business, and I don't want to be the cause of unfounded rumors," Karen asserted.

"Okay, dare I ask if there is anything else?"

"No, you have supplied all my needs. Mr. Claymore, Adam, I do believe you are a godsend!"

Adam took Karen's hands in his and replied, "And you a blessing!"

Lunch finished, Adam helped Karen collect her things from the hotel. She paid her hotel bill, asked about Hannah, and learned she was scheduled to work that evening. Adam and Karen stored her things in his Rock Creek rental, and then she drove him back to his ranch house on Claymore Flats. Their small talk continued as both shared more about themselves. Arriving at the house, Adam confirmed their arrangements, leaned over, and gently kissed Karen on the cheek.

Karen flushed and gently said with a smile, "Watch that, Sir," then she drove off broadening her smile. Now she thought let's take care of some business: first call the number in the advertisement, then stop at the pizza parlor, and later file the complaint against Deputy Butch and report my missing pistol.

Stopping at the convenience store in Jericho Springs, Karen dialed the telephone number from the ad she had copied down and put in her purse.

"Hello, Offices of John Law, Attorney. This is Amanda speaking. How may I direct your call?"

"I'm not certain I have the correct telephone number," Karen responded.

"Who were you trying to contact?"

"I'm calling in response to an ad in the newspaper."

"The *Outcry*?" Amanda questioned.

"Yes, that's right."

"Are you calling in regards to the advertisement offering lodging in exchange for help in rebuilding a house?"

"Yes, I hope I'm not too late."

"Not at all, your name and number please."

"My name is Karen Gustafson, and I'm calling from the pay phone at the Jericho Springs convenience store."

"Mr. Law is in a meeting right now. It may be over soon. Do you have a number where I can call you later today in case it is a long meeting?"

"Yes, I have a friend that would take messages for me at 634-0007."

"Interesting, you said 0007?"

"Yes?"

"Is your friend Adam Claymore?"

"I just arrived in town last Friday, and I've applied for a teaching position with the local school district. Meanwhile, Mr. Claymore has befriended me," Karen explained.

"Well, lucky you! I'll have Mr. Law return your call."

"Can't you tell me anything about the situation?"

"Yes, but Mr. Law wants to handle this personally. You see, a client of his is trying to gain assistance from reputable people who would be interested is doing him a great service. The fact you are a friend of Adam Claymore will certainly help your cause."

"Really?" Karen replied with mild surprise.

"For this purpose, you couldn't have a better endorsement. You did say you are new to the area?" Amanda asked.

"Yes, I just met Mr. Claymore. I've never been here before; I don't have any relatives or friends here."

"Wait a minute, Mr. Law's door just opened. I'll see if he can take your call."

In the background Karen heard a man tell the secretary, Amanda, to ask Karen to make an appointment with him for tomorrow in his office before noon.

Amanda returned to the telephone and asked, "Could you meet with Mr. Law tomorrow just before noon?"

"Yes, where?"

"At Mr. Law's office, First Avenue and Main Street, second floor above Bustos' Mexican Restaurant," explained Amanda, "and you will need to use the side entrance off First Avenue."

"Thank you, tomorrow just before noon on First and Main Streets, on the second floor," restated Karen, "And I thank you!"

Karen decided to ask for directions to the pizza parlor. Karen approached the cashier behind the counter, a young man of Native American heritage, "Excuse me, sir, could you tell me where the pizza parlor is located?"

"The one that delivers, or the sit down restaurant?"

"The delivery one?"

"Go north to the end of Main Street. It's on the right. You can't miss it."

Offering her hand, Karen stated, "Thank you, are you Mr. Crowfoot, Mike Crowfoot?"

"Why, yes..."

"You must be related to Rabbit?"

"He's my half brother. How do you know him?"

"I had an early breakfast with him this morning, and he spoke well of you."

"Then you must be Karen Gustafson and you are a teacher here to apply for the high school position," inferred Mike Crowfoot.

Not to be out done, Karen noticed Mike wore the sign of the fish, "And you must be a Christian."

Mike responded with a grin, "Are you one too?"

"Yes, I am for some time now."

"I accepted Christ as my Lord and Savior earlier this summer. I'm going to be baptized Sunday at the Baptist Church. Won't you come and celebrate that with me?"

"I really would, but I won't be here. I leave Friday."

Saddened, Mike shrugged his shoulders.

"But, I'll probably be moving here shortly."

"Then I'll see you again."

"If I get the job."

"Well, until then!"

Karen turned to leave the store not noticing that Deputy Butch had entered the store and stood behind her. She bumped directly into him, and he grasped her arms just below the shoulders to avoid a complete collision. Butch sized her up lustily.

"Say, don't I know you?" Butch said.

Looking directly into his eyes angrily then to his hands on her shoulders, Karen forcefully said, "No, I am quite certain we have never met and let's keep it that way." At Butch's prompt release, she eagerly moved to leave the store but shortly turned around noting his back was to her. She placed her finger over her mouth to caution Mike's saying anything, while in an overhead security mirror, Butch detected her gesture.

Butch watched Karen drive off in Adam's car and said to Mike, "I don't know who she is, but I see she does know Adam Claymore or else she wouldn't be driving his old car from Rock Creek. What were you two talking about, Mike?"

"Oh, nothing you'd be interested in Deputy?"

"I'll bet, give me a tin of dip," Butch ordered.

"Copenhagen?"

"That'll do?"

"And do I put it on your account?"

"Right, smart guy, here take it outta this," sneered Butch as he handed Mike a five dollar bill.

With haste Karen drove the old Chevrolet down Main Street to the pizza parlor. She parked behind the building in hope that Deputy Butch wouldn't see the old Chevy, if he followed her. He had. He did not see where she had turned and continued out of town driving toward Ridge View. She shivered, called him a creep, and then made her way to the Main Street entrance. Once inside Karen approached the counter and briefly watched a young woman making a pepperoni pizza.

"Can I help you?" the pizza maker said, while finishing her creation by placing it on a conveyer belt to take the pizza into an oven and out within seven minutes.

"Yes, thank you, I saw the ad in the newspaper, and I'd like to apply for a job?" Karen explained.

"Inside help or driver?"

"Probably inside help, for now anyway. Are you the manager?"

"No, I'm just curious. I'd like a couple of weeks off before school starts. Making pizzas every night has been a drag! Just a moment, Jerry, there's an applicant here to see you! Come here and hire her will ya," she said smiling at Karen. "It's really not so bad. I make decent money and they're good to work for. What's your name?" the pizza maker asked.

Reaching over the counter they shook hands, "Karen, Karen Gustafson, I am pleased to meet you."

"I'm pleased to meet you, I'm Dorothy King. Here comes the manager now. Smile at him and you'll get the job."

A slender man came out from behind the office window wiping his hands, then his face with the corner of his apron. "Welcome, Miss, did Dorothy say you wanted to apply for the job?" Jerry Sunday asked invitingly.

"Yes, I do, but it depends on some other circumstances."

"How's that?" Jerry asked.

"Well, to be honest with you I'd like to work full time until school starts then I'd like to work evenings, Friday and Saturday nights."

"Come on back to my office. Tell me more as you fill out the application."

Karen followed the pizza manager into his office. Surprisingly, it appeared spotless. Papers cluttered the metal desk, but everything else appeared exceptionally clean. Jerry invited Karen to sit down, which she did, while he sat in a comfortable and sturdy black office chair on wheels. Behind his back loomed the store safe, while aprons, bags, office supplies, and odds and ends surrounded him on shelves. From a file in his desk drawer, Jerry selected an application, handed it with an ink pen, and asked Karen to complete the form.

"Now, tell me why you want to work such a specific schedule."

"If I get the teaching position with the school district I've applied for, I will want to move here immediately, so I can get settled and learn about the area," answered Karen.

"You're a teacher and you want to work here?" Jerry inquired.

"Why not?"

"Nothing, it's not often the teachers have second jobs," Jerry explained.

"Depending on my assignment, I might have some extra time. I like to keep busy."

"Well, I could sure use you between now and when school starts. Dorothy has wanted some time off, and then I could use you weekends during school. Did I hear you say you would be interested in working Friday and Saturday nights but not on Sunday?"

"Exactly, I need to be able to attend church on Wednesday evenings and Sunday."

"I usually don't allow my employees to dictate the schedule, but you would be good to have around here. It would help clean up the language with you being a Christian and a teacher. You'll get to know some of the students for sure. What position are you applying for?" asked Jerry.

"What are the options?"

"Well, if you could work inside making pizzas and taking orders, I could let Dorothy have the time off. Do you have a car with you?"

"I borrowed a car from a friend, but I will drive my car when I move. It's in the garage back home."

"Really, it would be good if you could drive for us too! When can you start?"

"If I get hired by the school district, this Tuesday night, I take the bus back home in Quail Point Friday, and then I would need the weekend to pack, pick up my car, and get back in town," Karen paused, and then concluded, "Realistically, it would take a full week, because I would need to get some things out of storage in Colorado Springs where my parents live."

"Well, Karen, I hope everything works out. I think you would do well here. I don't work on Sunday or Wednesday evenings either, so I might see you in church,"

"Thanks! I will call you daytime Wednesday."

"I'll probably know before you do. Dorothy's dad is on the school board."

"Small world, isn't it?"

"You'll learn soon enough!" Jerry chuckled.

Karen left the pizzeria and proceeded north to Ridge View along County Road 403. After traveling several minutes, she drove past a house by Rock Creek and noticed Andrew Browning playing in the yard. She stopped the Chevy, backed up, and entered the driveway. Andy ran to greet her, and Ruth Browning emerged from the garage with the chicken coop attached to it. With delight, Ruth hurried to greet Karen.

"What a joy! How have you been, Karen? Where did you get the car?"

"Can she stay for lunch, Mom? I'm starving. Let's have 'Mickey Mouse' specials. You remember those don't ya, Miss Karen? Come on!" Andy said as he grasped Karen by the hand and began to drag her to the garages. "You need to meet the Princess Freda Louise. She's not a real princess, at least I don't think so. Is she Mom? Hey, Mom! Hurry up! And we've got ducks, too. Well, we had ducks, but now we just have one. Somebody, bad and terrible, stole two of our ducks. I'm gonna' kill 'em real bad. Dad buried them for me. Someone roasted them in a fire, Dad said so!"

"Whoa! Andy," said Ruth catching up to them, "he's right though. We've had some strange things happen since we saw you last?"

"Me, too!" Karen reported.

"Look, here's where they climbed over the fence, then they stole my ducks. Dad saw a man in the creek just walking around. He didn't kill the ducks though. He was just acting weird," Andy said rapidly.

"Did you say you've had some weird things happen to you too?" asked Ruth.

"Yes, in fact I'm on my way to the sheriff's office to complete a report on a theft. Adam told me to wait, but someone stole a pistol from my room," Karen explained.

"A pistol! What on God's good earth are you doing with a gun?" asked Ruth.

"That's a long story, and the short version is that a sheriff's deputy and his friend were chasing me and another woman on the roof of the Stage Stop Hotel."

"Karen, that sounds peculiar! What's come over you since we last met? You seemed so refined," added Ruth laughing.

"Seriously, that is exactly what happened. I'm not certain what would have happened to me if it wasn't for Adam Claymore. He loaned me his car and let me stay at his ranch last night."

"My lans Karen, you should see your expression when you mentioned his name. Dear me! Is there something else you need to tell me about Pastor Claymore," inquired Ruth.

"I know. I'm surprised too, and thanks for reminding me he is a preacher.

Interim that is. Really, I can't stay long now. It looks like I'll be offered the job at the high school," Karen added. "Are we still having lunch Wednesday?"

"Yes, and let's plan to go to the prayer meeting at the church. It sounds like we have a lot to pray about. Our paper deliverer has had some trouble too! A fire!"

"Really," Karen responded, "is he all right?"

"Ken Bond and his family are at the Claymore ranch. I'm surprised you didn't know."

"Hmm…that might explain the woman in the kitchen," Karen said.

Heading back towards the '51 Chevy, Karen added, "Andrew, I like the Princess. She is lovely. I'll see you Wednesday. Oh, Ruth, give me your phone number again. There is a telephone at Adam's house in Rock Creek, and I have his phone number in case I have any more trouble. Hopefully, I'll be able to show you my pistol and explain how and why I had it with me."

Ruth gave Karen the telephone number, and they made plans to talk later. The idea of lunch was forgotten in the excitement, except for Andrew, who couldn't seem to get a word in edgewise. Karen hurried to the borrowed car, when Ruth called to her, "Karen, what has the Lord told you to do?"

"What?"

"I just got one of those gentle nudges. You know, I'm sure you've had more experience than I with when the Lord wants you to do or say something?"

"What is it?"

"I said, 'What does the Lord want you to do?'"

"You're right, Ruth, I haven't prayed about any of this, recently anyway. I've just been so excited, and I just started doing things I knew should be done to make things happen the way I want them to," Karen replied.

"Sounds to me like you're headed for trouble. Sometimes I rush into things, and I end up settling for what isn't good for me or even settling for what is good and missing what is best for me."

"You are correct! Often I think I ought to be able to handle anything that comes my way. I need to listen to wise counsel. Pray with me now, then Ruth."

"Me too, Mama! God answers my prayers! Look at Daddy!"

"For sure, let's pray."

"Father, your word says to seek you and your kingdom first and all else will be added unto us, to put your will before our own, and to go the pathway you point out. Father, I confess I have not considered and I have not followed your lead. Without consideration, I have made plans and already carried out much of them, but I am willing to be redirected. But Father, you need to point me in the right direction," Karen prayed.

"Karen, I think you already have been pointed in the right direction. Didn't Adam tell you to wait until after the school board meeting before going to file a report? Was his counsel wise?" Ruth asserted.

"Yes, and the sheriff already knows about the incident and the theft. Also, I just saw one of the men who chased us. He is a deputy, Butch McNaughton. I was asking for directions at the convenience store in Jericho Springs. When I turned around, I bumped directly into him. He took hold of my shoulders. He has a powerful grip," Karen reported.

"How long had he been there?"

"Not long. I think the cashier would have said something, if he was."

"Could you be running ahead of the Lord on anything else?" asked Ruth.

"Well, I've rented a house from Adam for a few days, and I applied for a second job at the pizzeria. Also I responded to an ad in the newspaper about a situation to exchange work for lodging."

"And what time does that allow you to have a life?" asked Ruth.

"I need to keep busy. I get a lot out of working, helping kids."

"No, you didn't hear me. That's helping the lives of others, which is good, in balance. It looks to me like you have someone who is interested in you and you in him."

"Yes, but…"

"And it sounds like you are building a fence around yourself, so you won't have time for him to court you," said Ruth.

"I'm just establishing boundaries! I think?"

"Well, slow down and have some lunch with us," offered Ruth.

"Thanks, I've already eaten, but I will have a glass of water."

The ladies walked into the house. Ruth prepared lunch for Andrew and tea for Karen and herself. Andrew watched a man in a pickup truck toss something onto their driveway. Andy ran to where it landed and picked up a model of a log cabin. He thought it was a large toy playhouse and carried it to the house where he took it inside and left it before the open door. It was an effective doorstop. Although he tried to get his mother's attention to tell her about it, Andy gave up quickly. He couldn't break into their lengthy conversation.

Finishing her tea, Karen excused herself and started to leave the Browning's new home, when she discovered her birdfeeder before the doorway. "Ruth, how did you end up with my treasure?" Karen said as she pointed at what had been a cabin shaped birdfeeder.

Picking up the broken and unrecognizable object, Ruth responded with "I've never seen this before, and we just came inside for tea through this door. How did it suddenly appear?"

"Mom, Mom, are you listening to me?" asked Andy.

"What, Son? I'm all ears!"

"I found it in the driveway. Some man in a truck tossed it into our yard."

"Butch McNaughton, I'll bet. I hit him in the head with it. Check to see what's on the bottom,"

Turning the cabin upside down, Ruth looked at the bottom side, "Sure enough, Karen Gustafson is written here. I can't wait for Wednesday. Good thing you are not going to the sheriff's office. You have a gun and assaulted a deputy in the head with a broken down birdfeeder that no respectable bird would eat from."

"Sounds like clues to the game," Karen replied, while they all laughed.

"Mom, Mom, let's play Clue! Clue for two, me and you! If Miss Karen will stay to play, we'll make it three!"

Karen backed out the door, as Andy raced to get the game. She waved goodbye, as Ruth hopelessly raised her hands, then sat down, and said, "What if I have more boys?"

NIGHT RIDERS

CHAPTER 12

"All these evils come from inside and defile a person." Mark 7:23

Monday at dusk the summer sun lingered between mountain peaks above Jericho Springs. Storm clouds gathered and darkened the valley from Ridge View along the eastern ridge where the Bonds had lived on highway 96 and then on toward the town of Rock Creek. Automobile lights provided evidence of travelers leaving north on the Valley Highway, like centipedes falling in a video game. Vehicles penetrated fog entering from Rock Creek Canyon and along the tributaries of the creek north to Ridge View and west to Jericho Springs. Ominously, with sunlight's passing only a remnant of light persisted as fog and darkness pushed back the dusk to make the invasion complete.

From all directions, many watched and responded as the valley changed. To the east a former neighbor friend of Katarina Bond peered wistfully out the window above her kitchen sink at the changing sky. She, a McNaughton wife, peeled an onion, a few potatoes, and some carrots, while wondering who had set fire to her friend's home. To the west the woodcutter, the grisly old man who did not speak, paused to watch daylight's retreat at the hairpin turn above the Blair House. Tonight, he had sensed, was not a good night to be out alone in the valley. To the north, a passenger exited the bus at the station in Ridge View to stretch her legs. Her long ride would continue in minutes, but first she had moments to look around and stretch. To the south Rabbit Pinebow hauled a bucket of vegetable peelings to the chicken pen and tossed the feed to those that had not already retreated to their night's perch. All felt chilled at the same time, as these prayer warriors were prompted to pray for the safety of those in the Rock Creek Valley. Their prayers were extended more like the flight of a spear from a knight in full armor than that of an archer sending forth a quickly shot arrow.

A survey of the valley Monday night would have revealed residents in more than half the homes with televisions tuned to watch "Monday Night Football". Others viewed "Monday Night at the Movies." Still others perched on bar stools like those at the Stage Stop Hotel. Supposedly, many had gathered for a cigar at the tobacco store in Rock Creek. The parking lot overflowed with trucks and automobiles, forcing others to be parked in front of shops along the highway. From behind lace curtains in Karen's new but temporary residence, she scanned the highway, the parking lot across the road, and the gas bays at the convenience store up the street. She felt the same chill others had experienced. "Lord," Karen softly prayed as had others, "I feel terribly uneasy tonight. I ask you to calm my spirit and give me your assurance. Gather your angels around me, Father, and cover me with your feathers. Hide me in the cleft of your hand while the storm passes by me."

Karen decided not to go out for dinner. She pulled down all the window shades and turned on one small light in the kitchen to avoid being noticed by anyone who might wonder if Adam were at his Rock Creek house for the evening. Searching for food, she found a note in the refrigerator from Rabbit, which told her that Adam had instructed Rabbit to stock both the cupboards and refrigerator with provisions. Rabbit added that he hoped her interview went well, and then he invited her to attend the prayer meeting at the church on Wednesday evening. Rabbit closed his message writing that he thought Karen would be especially interested in learning how the locals were planning to take the area for the Lord! Warmed, Karen relaxed and smiled, while fixing a broiled pork chop, a can of kidney beans, some cottage cheese, and two slices of cracked wheat bread. "What a thoughtful man!" Karen stated aloud, smiling about Adam's tenderness. "Prayer meeting on Wednesday. Now, I am curious."

Across the street in the cigar store, members of the McNaughton clan gathered with others. Many glared at one another. Although most were relatives, they bore malice toward at least one other person in the room. Bitterness and resentment permeated the air as most lit stogies. None of the negative feelings were as strong or intense as the feelings they bore toward outsiders who might have a rightful claim to the Blair House and the water and mineral rights that went with it. Although most sign the name McNaughton, the clan included those married into the McNaughton family, thereby earning at least marginal acceptance. Family was family, and tonight family met to finalize plans for the balance of the week.

Red McNaughton entered through the back door and the crowd quieted. "Let's waste no time," Red said, "Thursday night is council meeting, so we have tonight, Tuesday, and Wednesday to get rid of the problem."

"Red, clarify what you mean!" shouted Butch from the back of the room.

"No one is advocating we break the law. Let's be certain of that. There's plenty we can do within the law to make it uncomfortable for whoever is here to get what should be ours."

"Yeah, right!" someone shouted.

"We don't want to do anything that could land any of us in jail," warned Beth Ellen, the secretary to the assistant superintendent. "We are here to get what should be ours."

"Settle down! All of you! We need to plan for the next few nights to take care of the outsiders. Let's get to work," growled Red.

"Yeah, then we can fight amongst ourselves after that!" joked one of the men from the Cozy Corner Café crowd. The crowd roared admitting the truth of the matter.

Red looked around the smoked filled room noting who was there and who was not, then he began outlining the valley with chalk on the board. Let's map out our time line. "Tonight is Monday. On Thursday night the town council meets in Jericho Springs to make a decision on condemning the Blair House. If it is condemned then the property becomes public domain and will be disposed of. If John Law proves the person he represents has a legitimate claim to the property, then our effort is finished. If Law doesn't, then we all have a chance to get the house, the land, the mineral and the water rights. You all know what that means. The last time we met we agreed to file incorporation papers. You elected me as President of the Rock Creek Land and Cattle Company, Inc. That's accomplished. All of you need to register as members of the corporation. We need to act together. When we get the property, we will all share equally from its benefits. We must do this together. Everyone will have jobs to do. All of you need to sign this paper, and you need to sign it now." Red handed Butch a clipboard for all to sign.

"On Thursday night I will speak for us…"

"Yeah, as long as things go our way…"

"Shut up, Roy! You've got a big mouth I'm going to shut if you talk like that!" warned Butch.

"Or what, Butch, you gonna' do me like…" said Roy until he saw the menacing glare from Butch. Roy took that to mean his thought was bound to be exactly what would happen to him, if he didn't shut up right now. Roy didn't finish his statement and others noted the possibility of what would happen if Butch or Red were crossed.

Red continued, "We have a right to the property. Our family settled this area. Our kin cleared the forest, built homes, farmed the land, and gave their blood, sweat, and tears to build this valley. Justice is on our side. We have a right to the Blair House. It's our responsibility to make certain we get it for our family and those who follow after us." As Butch circulated through the crowd getting signatures, Red continued, "You need to sign the incorporation papers, and then relax. I've ordered food for all of you. The pizzeria will deliver shortly. Sarah will bring pitchers of beer and pop for all. I want to meet with Butch, Beth Ellen from the school district offices, Ralph from Wolf City, Seamus from Jericho Springs, Van Alan from Ridge View, and Sam Gelding from here in Rock Creek. We're going to meet up the street at Gelding's insurance agency. Be here tomorrow night!"

The crowd applauded Red's speech and followed his orders by signing the document. As Red left the tobacco store with the others, Jerry Sunday, the pizza delivery man, greeted them at the doorway. As Red took two pizzas, he laughed and said to those in the crowd, "Give him a good tip. Since we're all here, he might not have much business elsewhere tonight!"

"Thanks a lot Mr. McNaughton, thanks a lot," Jerry beamed.

"Hey, Red!" greeted Sarah as she crossed the parking lot from the hotel followed by Hannah, with both leading a procession of the cook, the dishwasher, and bartender. Each carried four pitchers of beer, while Harper, the sometimes cook and full time dishwasher, balanced a tray of glasses above his head. "Hi, honey, long time, no see," Sarah flirted, "take one of my pitchers, will ya?"

Butch interjected, "Have Hannah bring the pitcher and come with us. I need to talk to her!"

"No, you go with them, Sarah. I'll deliver these inside. You go," urged Hannah.

"No way, sweetheart, if Butch wants you, he gets what he wants. If you know what's good for you, you do your job, and do it now," instructed Sarah. "You'll be all right as long as the others are with him."

Reluctantly, Hannah followed Butch, Red, and the others to the insurance agency, which shared half of the real estate building. The others walked ahead while Butch stayed back to talk with Hannah. "Where have you been, girlfriend? What's going on? And what's the deal you running away from me with that school teacher the other night? You really disappointed me," Butch said while grasping Hannah's arm firmly and bruising her with his grip, "I really miss you, ya know!"

"Sure Butch, you just scared me, that's all. And that creep you had with you. I don't like him."

"So you run from me and that ditz hits me on the head with some stupid birdfeeder."

"How is Roy? He was pretty funny going over the facade," laughed Hannah.

"Roy's okay, but a little stiff from the fall. If he'd been sober, he probably would have been hurt, but you know how drunks are."

"Actually, I don't. Butch, I've been thinking. You've got me all wrong. I didn't come here to work at the hotel," Hannah asserted.

Butch stopped dead in his tracks. He stared menacingly at Hannah and said, "I forgot you've only been here a couple of months. Why did you come to Rock Creek?"

Sensing the danger, Hannah continued, hurrying to catch up with the others. "I just stopped here on my way to nowhere, Butch. At first, I liked how you made me feel welcomed."

"What's wrong, Hannah? You know I like you. I want to be with you. You're my girl."

"You scare me, Butch, and the talk around town about you and that dead girl scares me."

"I swear to you, I didn't do it. Yeah, I spent some time with her. A lot of men in this town did. That's the kinda girl she was."

"What about the school teacher?" Hannah asked.

"Jill Lowenstein? I never met her. I don't even know what she looks like. I mean I guess I could have run in to her at school, investigating something, but I don't know her," Butch paused. "So that's it. You think I killed Gloria Jones," Butch concluded, while shaking his head.

Arriving at the insurance agency front door, "I didn't say that, Butch, but if you're honest, you would wonder too," Hannah added, nearly panicking. "Here, you take the beer. I've done my job."

"Not quite," Butch responded taking her in his arms and kissing her forcibly. "I'll see you later tonight. You be in your room." With his demand stated, Butch went inside, while Hannah was half way dazed by his kiss and the rest of the way with fear of his intent

"Not if I can get away you won't," Hannah whispered, while running back toward the hotel. Hannah brushed past Sarah and the others as they left the cigar store.

"Hey wait Hannah, honey. Tell me about it. Is Butch gonna' stop by tonight?" Sarah laughed knowingly.

Hannah entered from the front parking lot entrance and nearly ran past the desk clerk, who had been covering the bar. "Hannah, you have a telephone message. The number belongs to Adam Claymore, but it's from a woman," the clerk said.

Hannah grabbed the message, garbled a thank you, and went directly to the telephone booth. Hannah took a quarter from her tip money in her front pocket and dialed the number.

"Hello," answered Karen.

"It is you. Am I glad or what? Karen, I need your help. I've got to get out of here. It may be a matter of life or death."

"If you are serious, you better do something right now," encouraged Karen.

"Where can I meet you?"

"If you need to leave, get what you have to have and meet me at the bridge on 403 in ten minutes."

"I'll be there…thank you."

Without a word Hannah bounded up the stairs to her room and threw her things into her one suitcase. Hannah paused and looked around, "I don't know where I'm headed or what I'm going to do, but good riddance!"

Karen left Adam's house in Rock Creek immediately through the rear door and walked promptly to the church parking lot, through the cemetery, across the footbridge, then down to the bridge covering Rock Creek on County Road 403. Hannah waited for Karen under a street light, until she heard Karen call out to her from the brush. Hannah crossed over the bridge, left the road, and walked down the path through the brush to Karen.

"Thanks, you may be saving my life, Karen."

"Come on and follow me," Karen urged Hannah, and then paused shivering, "Adam told me this is where they found the dead girl, right there!" Karen pointed to the crawl space under the bridge. "Come on. Let's get out of here."

Like frightened rabbits they scampered along the path to the bridge. At the footbridge Karen paused to look back. With her finger to her mouth, Karen told Hannah, "Shush!" Karen demanded, "Listen."

Entering the light from the street light, Hannah's boy friend, Harper McNaughton, the dishwasher and relief cook, had followed Hannah. "Slouch down. Let's see if he follows," Hannah insisted. Harper had not seen them leave the road, and instead, he looked in every direction before running down 403 toward Jericho Springs.

"Let's get something straight right now. As long as you are with me, no men! You don't tell anyone where you are staying or so help me," Karen stammered with fist within inches of Hannah's nose.

"All right, all right, Karen. I understand, I understand. It's just I've never been as popular as now," Hannah mocked, smiling with interest that Harper had run after her.

"Come on," Karen said, "and be quiet." They crossed the footbridge, hurried through the fog-covered cemetery, and on to the back of Adam's house.

"Whose house is this?" asked Hannah.

"Not a word until we are safe," Karen insisted, guiding Hannah into the yard and through the back door. "Do not turn on any lights. Let's wait to see what happens."

At the insurance agency Red, Butch, Ralph, Seamus, Van Alan, and Beth Ellen joined Sam Gelding at his conference table to discuss what newcomer might have a rightful claim to Blair House, the gold, and the water rights.

Red addressed Beth Ellen, "We need to know what's happening at the district offices, Beth. Who are the applicants for Lowenstein's job? Do they really think she is not going to return for the school year?"

Butch added, "Did she see who killed Gloria Jones?"

Several laughed at Butch's self-serving question. "Hey you guys, I didn't do it. I didn't do it."

"Sure, Son, don't worry, you are family. We understand your concern," Red laughed. "You just want to know if she is going to clear you!"

They laughed loudly, and then Beth Ellen responded, "Today, we interviewed Karen Gustafson for the job. If Jill doesn't come back, then she has the job. Either way Gustafson will be hired. Miss Gustafson will be a permanent substitute if Jill returns, so I don't know if Jill is expected to return."

"Come on, Beth Ellen, any correspondence, telephone calls, meetings?" asked Seamus.

"None, but we have two outsiders staying at the hotel. Hannah could be the one," answered Beth Ellen.

"Gustafson could just be a teacher applying for a job," Ralph corrected.

"When are they going to hire her?"

"Tomorrow night, Red, at the school board meeting at the school district offices," Beth Ellen retorted, then getting up to leave, "I'll let you know if anything comes up. I've got to get home. Henry is watching the kids."

"I'll see ya later, and Beth, keep a good lookout."

Butch added, "Hannah's not the one, she's dumber than a box of rocks!"

Beth left. A man appeared out of the darkness from the back office. He had a banker's look. He wore a three piece, black pin stripped suit with a watch and gold chain hanging from vest pockets. With cuff links accenting his freshly starched white linen shirt, Chauncey Brown joined them.

"Councilman," the group said as they rose to greet him, "welcome!"

Chauncey joined them at the table and asked, "Well, after hearing Beth Ellen's report, I need not guess why you've called me here, and it's not for me to arrange a loan for you."

Red spoke up, "I knew you would want to be a part of this. You've helped before."

"Excuse me, but right now I don't know a thing about what you just said and if you know…"

"Keep a lid on it, Chance. I'm not referring to anything," Red said as he glanced around the table. "I'm sorry, okay."

"What do you want?"

"Just like Beth Ellen with the school board meeting on Tuesday. We want to know what you know about the city council meeting on Thursday. Who is John Law representing? How is the council going to vote? What's the mayor up to?"

"You know I'm married to a McNaughton, so you know I have as much interest in this as you do. John's not talking. He's tight lipped. I know he isn't saying anything to anybody until the meeting. Adam Claymore tried to get some information out of him at the Rotary meeting last week."

"If John didn't tell Adam, he won't tell anyone."

"They're two peas in a pod. I was surprised, but Law didn't even give a hint other than saying we would not be surprised."

"That's it?" asked Butch.

"That's all, but did you notice the ad in the newspaper?"

"What ad?" Red questioned.

"The ad inviting people to help restore a home in exchange for lodging. My guess is that whoever has a claim to the Blair House intends to restore it. They plan to exchange lodging for labor. At least Red would get some business," said Chauncey smirking.

"Who is the contact person for the ad?" asked Ralph.

"I recognized John Law's phone number. Have you talked to Amanda, his secretary?" added Seamus.

"Amanda is as tight lipped as the zipper on my father-in-law's wallet. You can't get anything out of Amanda or about her. Amanda goes to church, and she's a 'for real' Christian lady," said Van Alan with admiration. "As much as I'd like to find out, it's a good bet we won't get anything out of Law or his secretary."

Rising to leave, Chauncey offered some advice, "Gentlemen, don't play all of your cards just yet. If John Law's client does win and I'm afraid he will, knowing John, someone is planning to restore the Blair House. That doesn't mean he plans to be here or to be directly involved in the restoration. If he does plan to be here, he may want to sell the property. Perhaps he won't understand the implication of what he owns."

"You mean there's a chance we would be able to buy the property?" asked Ralph.

"I'm sure you would be involved to make certain a fair price was paid. Right, Mr. Banker?"

"Business is business, Red," Chance responded. "If I can't make the money through the corporation, I'll likely be involved some other way."

"You always are!" the others chimed in.

"Good night, Chance. Thanks for coming," offered Red.

"I'll leave you gentlemen to your scheming," Chauncey Brown said while leaving through the back entrance.

"I don't care if he is family; I don't like him," snapped Butch.

"He's not so bad. Like us, he's a man trying to build a fortune. Some men work hard all their lives to earn it; others like us believe we won't get enough of it unless we help ourselves to somebody else's good fortune," eulogized Seamus.

"And your point is?" Ralph added, while they laughed in unison.

Ending the frivolity, Red focused, "Let's check our status. Chauncey knows nothing, nor does Beth Ellen. John Law and his secretary are not talking. John Law knows the value of the property. There is an ad in the paper inviting inquiries to restore the Blair House. Who are the new people in town? Why are they here?"

"Karen Gustafson, the teacher applicant…"

"Hannah, the desk clerk…"

"The Brownings, near Ridge View…"

"The Bonds, just east of the valley…"

"Who are they?"

"Ken Bond, he delivers the newspaper. They're taken care of. A fire completely destroyed the trailer they lived in."

"Seems fire is going around. The grassland by the Bonds, the two ducks… somebody enjoyed playing with matches."

"I bet Maurice is happy about that!"

They laughed as Red told them to write the names down of new people in town. Even Ralph from Wolf City added a name to a short list.

Next, Red asked a question. "Who do we need to...um...discourage? Raise your hand!"

"The Brownings on 403 by Ridge View," included Van, "we killed..."

"Don't say any more of what you did or plan to do. We don't want to know the particulars. Share the names, and then make a list of who is in your area." Then looking directly into Butch's eyes, Red challenged, "What about Sheriff Bailey? Can we count on him to look the other way?"

"You know him better than I do, Red. You know I'm on administrative leave while the Gloria Jones investigation is going on. He did question me about my reckless driving and about the dead ducks, but he hasn't made any accusations. He's been real fair with me, while everyone else has been saying things and pointing fingers about the death of Gloria Jones and why Lowenstein is missing," answered Butch.

"Could be Bailey's giving you enough rope to hang yourself," Red responded.

"Don't under estimate him, ever," said Seamus.

"I don't know about that. You fellas need to know that the fire at the Bond's destroyed the trailer they rented from Adam Claymore. Nobody was hurt, but I suggest nobody say anything about that. Arson means possible jail time. And no one wants to mess with Adam, not even Red," said Sam Gelding.

Sobering, Van Alan returned the focus, "Let's finish up so we can make an appearance at the family gathering. Besides I want to hear the end of the Broncos game. I've got ten dollars on the Denver team."

"Yes, the game's still on and the night isn't over yet. It may be preseason, but there is still time for a lot of excitement."

Red took charge, "Van you've got Ridge View, Ralph—Wolf City, Seamus—Jericho Springs, Sam—Rock Creek, Butch—the hotel. You've got two to deal with."

"Hannah and the school teacher," Butch responded, "but I'll help out in Jericho Springs until later."

"Don't forget the guy on the third floor," offered Van. "Sarah passed me this note when she delivered some beer earlier. Seems we over looked someone."

"Add him to my list," said Butch. "What's his name?"

"He registered as Paul Smith, but I have a hunch that's not his real name! Sarah says the guy is black. I wonder if he is related to Gloria Jones?"

"That could be a coincidence. Gloria didn't have any family," Butch responded visibly shaken.

"Or at least that was her story," added Seamus. "Gloria had a way about her.... made you feel sorry for her...kinda needy."

"And vulnerable," concluded Ralph.

"Well, gentlemen, the plot thickens. Although Gloria was a part-timer, it appears we all knew her," concluded Red, "and I thought only Butch was the suspect."

"Butch was just the one she had her hooks into. The rest of us didn't fall for her story."

"At least, not as hard or far."

"Interesting! And you guys are letting me take all the heat. The accusations and innuendos," Butch responded venomously. Seething Butch rose from the table, "Come on, we need to make an appearance at the cigar store, and then get about our business."

"Is Adam going to stop by?"

"No, I had him sign the incorporation papers at breakfast. He's in," informed Red.

"What about the pizza man? Hasn't he only been here a year or so?" asked Ralph.

"He's mine," Seamus answered.

"One last thing, I want you to tell your men that this is not a time to mix side issues into our effort. I hope burning out the Bonds wasn't a way to get at Adam for somebody else. The last thing we need is for the general public to side with newcomers. That could really bite us. Do you get my drift?"

The group understood and committed to do their part, and then they returned to family members and mutual hostility at the cigar store. Meanwhile, Karen and Hannah hid behind lace curtains and window shades covering the windows of Adam's rental. They observed the men leaving the insurance office then enter the cigar store. More cars and trucks arrived including the Gray Whiz, but that driver went into the restaurant. Butch and Roy exited the back door with a group of men Karen did not recognize. They talked and laughed, then parted company. Butch and Roy came around the front of the Stage Stop and entered the hotel. Hannah identified Van Allen and Seamus but had not recognized Ralph from Wolf City. The three men separated. Red McNaughton emerged from the insurance company office with Sam Gelding, who did not join the others at the cigar store. Ralph and Seamus traveled County Road 403 toward the mountains but parted company at the turn off to Claymore Flats. Ralph followed the road to Wolf City. Van Alan waited for Red McNaughton. When Red arrived to pick up Van, Red asked if Van had seen Adam. Van had not. The two sped off to join thugs waiting for them in Ridge View. A few others left, but the majority of the McNaughton clan stayed to watch the Denver Broncos' game in the back of the cigar store. None of them even suspected that anyone had been watching them, but the man dressed in black from room 319 not only observed what had transpired at the insurance agency and tobacco store but also had recorded license plate numbers and physical descriptions of all who had been involved.

From across the street, Karen asked, "Hannah, did you recognize any of those people?"

"All, except for a man in a black Chevy pickup, and his license plate isn't from here. I think it's a Wolf City tag or there about."

"Then we've seen people take off in all directions."

"Except south into the canyon."

"Does anyone live there?"

"In the canyon?" questioned Hannah. "It's several miles of rock wall before there's a wide spot in the road. No one lives in there. Look, more are leaving."

"Do we stay put or check things out?"

"Karen, I'm afraid to be seen tonight. I've got bad vibes, and I overheard the talk from the kitchen about tonight being a rough time to be out and about."

"Don't forget the warning you got from your boyfriend."

"That you found in your birdfeeder? What happened to that anyway?"

Karen walked into the single bedroom and emerged carrying her once sturdy log cabin feeder. "Let's have some tea. Maybe you can help me restore this."

"My lans, what has happened to that? You must have really nailed Butch with it," laughed Hannah.

Butch and Roy wasted no time, nor did they wait for the desk clerk before checking the hotel registry. "Well, I'll be, Hannah did switch rooms," said Roy.

"Look there! Karen Gustafson, room 218, and Hannah moved next door," laughed Butch, "that little vixen."

"Check for Smith. The others are overnighters according to Sarah," urged Roy.

"Check anyway, in case Sarah missed anyone."

"There, room 319! That's the last one on our right, two floors above the kitchen opposite Beatrice Jaramillo."

Lila, the night desk clerk, arrived to protest their examination of the registry, and Butch shoved her aside. "Sorry, police business."

"Sure Deputy, but if you're looking for Hannah, you missed her. Hannah left here about a half hour ago. Hannah quit her job and told me she was getting out of here and going back home," the older woman mocked Butch with a sneer. "I guess that's one got away from you!"

As Butch moved toward her with fist clenched, Roy interceded, "Come on Butch, we still have Gustafson and Jones to deal with."

"She left too. Long time ago this afternoon."

"What's that you said? Hannah and Gustafson are both gone?"

"That's right, Butch, they are both gone. I don't know where they went. I just know Hannah was really frightened and in a hurry," Lila explained.

"That leaves Smith."

"Hannah was on foot and it was after dark. Last I saw of Hannah, she went out the door and headed in the direction of the convenience store."

"What about Smith? Have you seen him?"

"He ate in the dining room about 7:00 p.m. and went upstairs. I ….."

"Thanks, Lila, you've been a big help. I'm sorry I was disrespectful."

"It's all right, Butch, you can buy me a beer later," Lila offered as she returned to her work.

"What do ya think, Butch? Do we go upstairs or look for Hannah?"

"Where could Hannah go?"

"Hannah could be walking around outside. She could be at the convenience store. Maybe she hitched a ride."

"Which way?"

"Who knows? She could be walking to Jericho Springs?"

"What about the bed and breakfast?"

"Could Hannah have gone to any of the houses across the street?"

"Who would she know?"

"What night is this?"

"Monday."

"So no one is at the church."

"Come on, I'll check the store and you go to the bed and breakfast," ordered Butch, "and Roy, come right back. Meet me at the kitchen back door in fifteen minutes."

"Gotcha'."

Roy hustled the back way to the bed and breakfast relishing the thought of seeing who was spending their evening with the women there. He knocked on the door and quickly gained admittance. Butch didn't leave the hotel porch and remembered the last time he chased after Hannah. The knot on his head remained a reminder. Instead, he considered the possibilities. People at the convenience store may have seen Hannah. The houses too! Hannah could be in the trees before the mesa or across the street. Butch considered asking at the cigar store, but he determined that would produce more jeers and laughter. He walked toward the convenience store, lit a cigarette, and listened for an unusual sound. He looked, listened, and sensed he too was being watched. Crossing the highway, Butch peered back toward the hotel porch and recognized someone quite large sat on the porch out of the direct light.

Butch entered the convenience store and sauntered to the magazine rack while backing up to the store window. Too big to be Hannah he thought, then more brooding. Maybe eerie he judged. Butch looked over the rest of the store and meandered toward the checkout, recognized Mike, nodded hello, and then punched the clerk on the shoulder as he passed by to restock the milk case. "How's business, Mikey?"

In an attempt to avoid the deputy's attention, Mike failed to respond. Certainly, Mike avoided all contact with law enforcement, especially any contact with the bully Butch McNaughton. Mike had no way of confirming whether or not Butch was part of the group that controlled most of the crime in the valley. Mike attempted to continue toward the refrigeration unit but didn't make it. Butch grabbed his arm and accosted him. "Look you piece of trash. I know who you are and what you do. I'm not here to bust you. I'm looking for a woman."

"Come on, Butch, you know they're across the street. How can I help you with that?"

"That's not what I mean. I'm looking for a woman maybe carrying a suitcase, came out of the hotel about forty minutes ago."

The boy looked at the store clock then back at Butch. "You mean Hannah, the desk clerk from the Stage Stop?"

"Right, did you see her?"

"When I was emptying the trash out back, I saw her walking by. She stopped at the bridge just like Gloria Jones…" instantly fear struck the boy as he realized what he had said and that he had said it to the number one suspect in the murder of Gloria Jones, part time prostitute, barmaid, bed and breakfast escort, and someone's daughter and sister. Mikey recoiled from Butch, as terror gripped him, and his face turned white. Mike wetted himself and finished his statement, "Gloria walked by here on the last night anyone saw her. She was carrying a suitcase, too, and went down 403, Deputy. Now if it's okay, can I go fill the milk case?"

Disgusted, Butch let the drug dealing store clerk out of his grasp. Butch thought better about following after Hannah. Since he enjoyed making the boy uncomfortable, Butch bought another pack of cigarettes from the store manager at the counter. Out of the manager's sight, Butch tapped the pack in his hand and pulled out a smoke, lit it with a match he then flicked toward the drug dealing clerk, who recoiled with fear of the deputy.

Leaving the store, Butch noticed the hotel porch had been vacated. He checked his watch noting he had eight minutes before meeting Roy behind the hotel. Butch listened for footsteps and any other human sound. Nothing but crickets echoed in the night, crickets and familiar sounds from the bar. The soles of his shoes scrapped against the gravel with each step he made down County Road 403. Nothing, no one, he thought, I'm all alone. The lights in each house had been darkened. Only the street light at the bridge illuminated the night. Clouds blocked the moon. Fog and smoke from wood burning stoves and fire places mixed together and gathered in the trees creating a wide variety of optical illusions. Near the bridge Butch smelled a whiff of fresh mown grass, then the fragrance of rose bushes planted beside the chain link fence.

Butch paused at the bridge where he studied each side of the creek waters. Tears came to his eyes thinking about Gloria's body being stuffed in a crawl space under the bridge. Butch had liked Gloria, had enjoyed her, and had told her he loved her. Was it just the moment when they were intimate or was it real Butch wondered. Butch had found it difficult that people thought he killed her. Was his reputation that bad? Sure he played the role of an uncaring tough guy, but killing Gloria? Still Butch thought again, Gloria was an outsider and right now everyone who was not from the Rock Creek Valley was not wanted, was an enemy. Could he kill? Butch chuckled at his answer. Of course, he could.

Butch walked further, searching for a sign, any kind of clue. Instinct kicked in as he passed the narrow pathway west of the creek. Funny, he thought, I haven't walked this path since I was a boy attending church here. Butch thought of Adam Claymore and his wife, Mary, and how she had counseled him when he accepted Jesus Christ as his Savior. Had he meant it? Did it matter to him now? Irrelevant, he thought. How in my job, my life, here—how was Christ relevant today? No, he thought, I guess not. I wonder if Gloria Jones accepted Jesus as her Savior. What had she said or thought when dying? He turned around and went back to the path leading from the bridge, and he quickened his pace down the path shivering as boyhood memories of the creek and the church came to mind. Can someone who has killed go to heaven? Committed adultery? Was it real, Butch wondered?

At the footbridge Butch paused again looking at the water and visualizing how it looked when he was baptized in the creek below. Twelve years was a long time to have not gone to church, but that's how long it had been. Again, he chuckled, and then he laughed. Finally, outloud Butch said, "No one would let me darken their door. My sin is too great. The pastor would collapse at the altar if I walked down the aisle. Yes, even Adam Claymore!"

Walking through the cemetery presented a bit of a problem for Butch. The tough guy remembered the graveyard stories and how his older brothers had tormented him there and told him the bogyman would rise up out of the grave and snatch young boys walking by. Man, he thought, I'm getting out of here. Breathlessly, he ran past the grave markers along the path to the white picket fence. He looked into the shed, then the windows of the chapel and around the front door. Spooked, he hustled into the stand of trees beside the highway and looked up and down the highway before continuing. To the left the several old buildings revealed nothing, until the deputy illuminated complete darkness with his cigarette lighter. Remembering Adam's house, he crept stealthily toward the broken-down garage behind the old wooden house. Since that Gustafson woman had been seen having lunch with Adam, Butch figured it worth checking both the house and the garage for Adam's old car.

Watching the highway from the small kitchen table, Karen and Hannah extinguished their lone candle before Butch saw them. The reflection of his cigarette lighter glistened through the widow in time for them to seek cover. "It's Butch!" Hannah whispered, "He's looking for me!"

"Is the door locked?"

"Would that stop him?"

"No!"

"Then shut up and come over here," ordered Karen from the shadows in the living room.

Hannah responded immediately. In unison the women cupped their mouths in fear as Butch pressed his face against the dirty outside of the windows. Attempting to peer inside as much as he could, window shades blocked his view of details in the dark. He could not see the cups and saucers on the table nor Hannah's suitcase just inside the backdoor. With his pocket knife, he slid the blade between the upper and lower frame in an attempt to move the window lock, so he could open the locked window. Butch abandoned the effort, crept away from the house, and stumbled in the driveway, as he made his way back to the church parking lot.

Inside the women listened for Butch's movement away from Adam's house. Karen and Hannah hastened to the front window and watched as Butch crossed the highway at the street light before the mouth of the canyon. They watched him follow the pathway through the stand of trees growing before the canyon in front of the mesa. Sporadically, they observed the flicker of his cigarette lighter that he used to light his way as he moved through the thicket and disappeared behind the back of the hotel. Having lost visual clues, Karen and Hannah feared not knowing where he was as much as seeing him nearby. Butch might return, they thought.

"No luck, huh?" Butch asked Roy.

"No, what's next, Butch?" said his sidekick, Roy.

"I gotta' hunch Hannah is still around here. I just don't know where for certain."

"What did you learn, anything?"

"Just that everyone thinks I killed Gloria Jones."

"And?"

"And if Hannah left walking on 403, she is either headed for Jericho Springs or is hiding somewhere else."

"Where could she be hiding?"

"I didn't see anything, but I've got a hunch she and Karen Gustafson are both still in town."

Roy paused then asked, "So, you didn't do it?"

"What?"

"Kill Gloria Jones."

"Now what do you think? Most the time I'm working or with you."

"Except when you're with Gloria or Hannah or Sarah or ..."

"Shut up! You're no help at all. Now listen. Someone was on the porch when I went to the convenience store just now."

"Who was it?"

"I don't know, but he was a big guy. About my size, and he was sitting in the shadows watching me from the porch."

"So are we going to check him out?"

"Here's what I want you to do."

Following Butch's instruction, Roy left the front parking lot and retraced Butch's walk through the trees to the mouth of the canyon. Systematically, Roy examined potential hiding places by checking the grounds from the hotel to the canyon. Confidently, Butch ascended the hotel's back stairwell to the third floor landing, entered the hallway, and knocked on the first door to the left.

"What do you want?" said a voice from the inside.

"Open the door! It's the deputy sheriff. I want to ask you some questions."

Opening the door, a tall man, Butch's size yet stately, greeted Butch with penetrating eyes, "Which deputy are you?" he inquired.

"Butch McNaughton."

"Come in, Deputy, I've been watching you."

"You have huh. Listen, I've come to warn you."

Not intimidated, the man responded, "You warn me. Interesting."

"It's time you moved on. People don't want you here. You're an..."

"Outsider?"

"That's right. I don't know who you are or why you are here, but you've been here long enough, Paul Smith."

"Paul Smith is my alias. I'm here on family business, Butch McNaughton, Jones family business."

Defensively, Butch instantly threw a punch Jones blocked. "Gloria Jones was my sister, and you are the prime suspect, McNaughton. Not only that, I know you are on administrative leave, while you are under investigation in the murder of my sister," said Jones.

Butch backed up and postured a judo move. Jones reached for the table lamp and pivoted, while Butch swung into the air and around with a back leg kick. Jones did his own swinging with the edge of the table lamp hitting the outside of Butch's leg at the kneecap, bruising tendons and ligaments. The force of the kick and the lamp had collided before Butch's kick affected any damage.

Not stunned by Butch's kick, Jones retaliated with unexpected quickness, his forearms smashed against Butch's chest and neck pushing Butch against then through the door into the hallway wall. Another rush from Jones slammed Butch to the wall, Butch's head snapped backward. Butch started to run, but Jones tackled him. Butch's temple and scalp caught the door knob to the room across the hall from Jones as Butch thundered to the floor. Blood gushed from the scalp wound.

Jones gathered himself, rushed to McNaughton, and then ran to the forward stairwell, while calling for help. As Jones bounded down the stairs toward the hotel lobby, two shots were fired into Butch's back. Hallway doors opened too late to view the shooter, who eluded discovery by descending the fire escape ladder instead of the stairwell. The shooter threw the pistol into the grove of trees toward the ridge before climbing on the roof over the porch behind the façade, where he entered the second floor window to his own room. Closing the window he crossed his room, took off his apron, and entered the hallway. In the hallway several hotel patrons witnessed him exit his room and leave through the exit door on the second floor. He hastened to the fire escape ladder and quickly descended to the front porch entrance of the hotel below. The shooter promptly disappeared inside the hotel.

Emerging from the front stairwell, Jones balked at the scene. Mrs. Jaramillo, a permanent resident of the third floor in room 320, now stood over Butch with others joining her, saw Jones, and scampered back into her room. Butch stirred and sat up holding his head. One hotel patron examined Butch's scalp wound, while two others examined where two bullets had entered Butch's back.

"You've been shot. Looks like flesh wounds, one on each side of your back below the shoulder in muscle," said a balding gentleman.

Looking at Jones but unable to lift his arm to point, Butch exclaimed, "He did it!"

"Couldn't have…."

"He just came up the stairs."

Mrs. Jaramillo, peered out her door shaking, pointed toward the fire exit, and said meekly, "It was the fella who went that'a way."

"Check that door! Just see if it is ajar. Don't look outside," commanded Jones.

"Are you a cop?"

"Detective, Denver P.D."

"It's been opened…" replied the balding man.

"I was nearly downstairs when I heard the shot. I was going to call for medical help, an ambulance, but came back here when I heard the shots," added Detective Jones. "Someone, please, go call for help."

"I will," said a rotund woman.

Kneeling beside Butch, Jones examined Butch's back where the bullets had entered through his shirt then lodged in the muscle on the outside of each shoulder blade. Jones proclaimed, "Small caliber, probably a twenty-two short. Bullets entered and didn't come out. Don't hurt much now, but they will. Right?"

"My knee hurts like heck….and my head…..but not my back. If you didn't shoot me, who did?"

Now emerging from her room, Mrs. Beatrice Jaramillo added, "Butch, you nearly broke off my door knob," then pointing toward Jones while shaking terribly, "Like to scared me to death, you two wrestling on the hallway floor, then this here huge black man rushed away down the hall calling for help. My lans, I didn't know what to think."

"What happened next?" inquired the balding man.

"Well, I had closed my door most the way like I did just now. And I could barely see, but I saw the other man come up behind Deputy Butch. He gloated and he was shaking violently. And I seen him pull the hammer back on his pistol…like a cowboy gun. He shot and pulled the hammer back… and he shot again! Boy, did his hand shake. I'm surprised he hit you, Butch."

"Who was it?" said Roy, who had climbed the exterior stairwell.

"Was it him?" asked Detective Jones pointing toward Roy.

"No, he's with me," said Butch.

"Don't know...but I seen him some place...let me think..."chirped Mrs. Jaramillo.

"What was he wearing?

"A wet, dirty apron," added Mrs. Jaramillo.

"I know..." concluded Butch.

"Why...he's a McNaughton, too," ended Mrs. Jaramillo as she re-entered her room and closed her door.

The ambulance arrived and delivered Butch to the clinic in Ridge View. Roy followed in Butch's truck. Deputy Cotton Candy arrived at the crime scene and began the investigation by interrogating both Detective Jones and Mrs. Jaramillo, which led her to search for Harper McNaughton, dishwasher and relief cook at the Stage Stop Restaurant. Learning Harper had fled the scene, Candy called for an all points bulletin to arrest Harper, who was probably armed. Neither the bar patrons nor the crowd at the tobacco store paid attention to what had happened at the Stage Stop Hotel. Only two pairs of eyes peered out windows to look at events across the street.

Meanwhile, the plans of conspirators who had gathered at the insurance office were enacted and a chorus of other maliciousness ensued. One perpetrator stealthily hanged a headless coyote in a tree bordering the Browning's driveway. The skinless body dripped fresh blood like a pagan ritual. One group inspected remains of the trailer the Bond's had rented from Adam Claymore through Red McNaughton. Harper, the dishwasher and part time cook fled to Wolf City. In each city thugs committed random mayhem upon innocents like a pack of ravenous dogs with blood lust. Two slugs were removed from Butch's back at the clinic, and Roy picked up a six pack of beer to share with Butch on the ride home from the clinic.

Adam and outsiders rallied to support the innocent. Having received a distress call from his friend, Kip Powell, the book salesman, had left home in Denver earlier than planned to return and help the Bond family in Jericho Springs. Kip had read the newspaper advertisement about free rent for help in restoring a house. He concluded he could be of assistance to the Bonds immediately, while waiting for his appointment with John Law, Attorney for the Blair Estate. Also, Morris Goodenough had stirred from napping and called Adam Claymore to tell Adam that he would be attending the Wednesday prayer meeting. Morris shared that he had been awakened and knew he was to call Adam and that he was to respond to an ad he had read in the *Outcry*. Adam Claymore, who had collected the Bond family and had brought them to his home, called Karen Gustafson at his house in Rock Creek. Adam told Karen about the fire and how the Bonds were now at Claymore Flats, then he asked if she had met them. Karen sighed and told Adam that she had heard and that he was wonderful, and then she told him of the events of Hannah and her hiding from Butch. Next, Izzy left the safety of the Blair House to make certain Janine was safe. Finally, a lonely figure crept down from the road above the tree, gathered yoke and watering buckets, and refreshed the ground surrounding the tree with pond water. Finished, the grisly old man, a woodcutter, a woodcarver, hugged the tree and prayed for Christ's return. Almost in an instant, the dark cover concealing mischief disappeared as evening clouds opened and moonlight illuminated the Rock Creek Valley.

LOVE PREVAILS

CHAPTER 13

"If you love me, keep my commands." John 14:15

Early Tuesday morning Andy Browning hopped down the stairs from his bedroom singing "I got Mohawk in the morning, I got Mohawk in the morning, I got Mohawk in the morning, this fine day," to the tune of "Peace like a River." Next, Andy said to his mother, "Look ma! I woke up and look at my hair. I gotta Mohawk," and then Andy sat down, and continued, "Mom, we need some chickens and one rooster! And do you know why? I had a dream last night and I was the rooster and I woke up and looked out the chicken coop door and saw the hawk in the sky. And do you know what I crowed, Ma? I crowed I got Mohawk in the morning, I got Mohawk in the morning!"

"Rob, come in here. We have to return to the city. Your son is loony."

Rob return inside from where he had been on the porch with a long and sad look on his face. Sitting down between Ruth and Andrew, Rob took both their hands and led them in prayer and thanksgiving for their food. He gave thanks for the food, their new home, and for how God had preserved their marriage and family. Then, Rob prayed for physical safety and for knowledge to deal with the witchcraft that had plagued them the last two nights.

Ruth responded, "Rob, what is it? What has shaken you so?"

"First, it was the animal sacrifice with the ducks, and now outside in the trees alongside the driveway. A dead animal, it's headless. It's been skinned and hung in the tree."

"I wanna see this," shouted Andy as he bounded from his chair to the screen door.

"Stop!" ordered Ruth.

"Come back here, Son," said his father, "I don't want you to see this. It is a crime scene."

"Rob, call Deputy Candy."

"Okay, but if she comes here don't tell her my song. I want to sing it to her," added Andy, "This is weird, Dad. I don't think people like me bein' here."

Ruth embraced Andy, as sadness took over his countenance. Ruth proclaimed, "Andy it's not about you. Rob, I want you to get to the bottom of this. I'll not have our son thinking like this!"

"Yes, Ma'am, I'll call but I'm only talking with Deputy Candy. Ruth, I need to report at work. I'll dispose of the carcass, after I take a picture of it. I'm going to the feed store, too. I'm going to get some buckshot and maybe another rifle for distance. It would be good for hunting deer anyway."

Ruth knew not to be disagreeable at this point, and somehow she felt safer knowing Rob was prepared to protect their home. She urged Andrew to finish his breakfast, and then to go upstairs and make his bed, which he did directly. Andy had a clear view of the driveway and trees beyond from his bedroom window where he watched his father back up his truck with the bed positioned under the skinned coyote dangling from the tree. Andy watched his dad take pictures of the headless animal then swiftly cut the rope with his hunting knife letting the cadaver fall into the truck bed. Andy wondered what his father was going to do with the body.

Rob drove to Ridge View, punched the time clock at the utility company garage, picked up his assignment schedule in the office, and gained authorization to make a stop at the feed store and the sheriff's Office during his lunch hour. When Rob shared about last night's events, all the linemen, mechanics, and office help at the utility department came out to see the dead animal. Some joked about the incident having been part of one of the welcome wagons perpetrating the devilment the previous night. Others wondered whom Rob had offended, some pitied the dead animal, and one reminded the others about a coyote being like a varmint—a good one is a dead one. Roy, friend of Deputy Butch, asked what Rob was going to do about it.

Rob asserted, "First, someone takes my son's ducks and tosses them live on a bonfire, and then there's a headless coyote hung in my tree." Then Rob paused, "A man's home is his castle, a man has to protect what is his, and that's what I'm going to do."

"What does that mean?" asked Roy.

"I'm going to the feed store and get some shotgun shells and a new rifle."

"Well, city boy, do you even know how to tend to a rifle? Ever shoot one? Have you killed anything?" continued Roy.

With that said, Rob, looked squarely into Roy's eyes, rolled up his short shirt sleeve revealing his tattoo, "I've served my country. I did what I had to do."

"Special forces and a sniper," a journeyman worker said, "I guess he'll handle what comes his way."

Another added, "Good for you, Rob, I wouldn't blame you a bit if you defend what's yours."

Still another veteran advised, "Be careful, Rob, there is a narrow line between protecting oneself and becoming a perpetrator."

Roy backed up, no longer mocking Rob and concluded, "Guess whoever messes with you had better think twice about it."

Rob left and the others continued chatting. The oldest among them commented, "Desperate people do desperate things."

"You mean what Rob's doing?" asked Roy.

The old man replied with anger, "No! I'm fed up with you McNaughtons and the others who are dead set about getting the Blair House, the mineral rights, and the water rights. Messing with a man like Rob, you may end up dead. I suspect there are others, too. That nice young family east of town, the paper guy—the Bonds. Someone lit a fire and they lost all they had. That's just not right!"

"At least they're gone."

"Or, so you think!"

At the feed store, Rob showed the carcass to Irv Moss and told him what had happened to two of the ducks. Irv told Rob that everything should calm down within a few days. Irv shared with Rob about the concerns the old families had about not being able to get the mineral and water rights and that a new person was coming into town and was supposed to have a claim to the Blair House.

"Try not to take it personal, Rob, surely you realize what's at stake."

"I sure do! My home is my castle. That's why I want to buy some shotgun shells and that 30-30 rifle with a scope behind your counter."

"You're serious?"

"Irv, I get it that people here are envious about how an outsider like me could be the rightful owner of the mineral and water rights. I get it how they think I wouldn't deserve them. I don't get how you folks believe you are entitled to something that is not yours just because you had the good fortune to live here a long time. I'm appalled at the extent your people are willing to go to get what really doesn't belong to them."

"Rob, you don't understand what people went through to settle here and preserve life here."

"Like the current generation really suffered and did a lot of hard work, what, to tame the West? I've got news for you. I have no claim on the Blair House or anything related to it. I'm an outsider and I'm happy that someone has the good fortune to gain a real windfall. I choose to be happy for them whoever they may be! You know why?"

"Tell me."

"They are blessed. God is in control of circumstances, and whoever is going to get the Blair House and all that is included doesn't deserve the riches that follow. Irv, that's like salvation. We don't deserve it, but Christ died for us so we can have eternal life. It is a free gift and we don't deserve it. Think about that one."

"I...I don't know what to say."

"Don't say anything. Just sell me the thirty-thirty and the shells, and maybe, just maybe, I'll only be shooting game to put food on my table."

"I'm sorry about the ducks. That was a mean thing to do to a kid," Irv concluded.

Rob's next stop was the Rock Creek Valley Sheriff's Office in Ridge View. Upon entering, Rob asked if Deputy Candy was in, to which the desk clerk stated that she had her on the phone right then. He asked if he could talk with her. The clerk asked Deputy Candy if she could give Rob the number she was calling from, and Cotton Candy asked the clerk to put Rob on the telephone. Candy explained that she was calling from Jericho Springs, and asked Rob to go ahead and make a report to the clerk, and then meet her in Rock Creek. Candy promised that she would follow up with the report, which Rob completed. The desk clerk told Rob that if Candy said she would get back to him then he could count on her word, good as gold.

Deputy Cotton Candy had a reputation for being a hardnosed, tough as nails cop. No one messed with Candy including the other deputies. It wasn't that she was hard to get along with. The deputy firmly and fairly enforced the law no matter whom you were related to or what position you occupied. If you drove over the speed limit, she would ticket you. If you dealt drugs, she made no exception whether you were a youngster or an adult. She had no regard with how a drug conviction affected a teenager's future life. And if you battered your wife, girl friend, mother, sister, prostitute, or escort, she turned very sour toward you and your situation before, during, and after being booked, and yet Candy often revealed a very soft side.

As a result when the deputy arrived in the Stage Stop Hotel parking lot, the manager at the convenience store shouted a warning that Deputy Candy was across the highway. While Candy had a lengthy discussion with someone who had been attempting to hitchhike going north, the manager rearranged the magazine rack by covering unsavory nudie magazines with magazines about the latest news and features. Mikey, the bottle boy, who stocked the coolers and sold dope, came out from the coolers and peered out the windows. One marijuana customer promptly left the convenience store to drive to Jericho Springs to buy his weed. No one in the convenience store suspected that Candy and the hitchhiker were discussing what had been happening in and around the store. Jones revealed his arrangement with John Law and that Law urged that Candy be included in their effort to sort out what had been transpiring not only at the tobacco store, hotel, and bed and breakfast, but also to gather data on who came and went from those establishments. Jones was convinced that there were more issues than the human trafficking his sister had been involved in, which probably led to her death.

Seeing Deputy Cotton Candy from behind the curtain at Adam's house in Rock Creek, Hannah told Karen that the deputy had helped Paul Smith, who was really Gloria Jones' brother. Candy helped Detective Caleb Jones catch a ride heading north on the Valley Highway with a utility company lineman named Rob Browning. Although it was against the utility company policy, Candy told Rob to tell his boss that he had been commandeered by her and that Jones was working with her on a case. Rob promised to drop Jones off near the Chevy dealership in Ridge View where Jones would rent an automobile.

Hannah alerted Karen that Deputy Candy was now walking around the parking lot and grounds across the street. Karen hurried out the back door of the house and around the south side stopping just short of the front of the house. She remained in the morning shadows until Candy had walked across the parking lot parallel to the south end of the house, which was toward the end of the parking lot. Coming out of the shadows, Karen exposed her location by doing jumping jacks waving her hands back and forth over her head to get Candy's attention. Candy paused when seeing her, and Karen motioned for Candy to stop and not come across the road. Karen then motioned for Candy to go to the hotel and then through the trees to the mouth of the canyon. Karen pointed to herself and pointed toward where the church was located to indicate that she would meet Candy there.

Immediately, Candy returned to her squad car, radioed dispatch, and informed them she would not be close by for awhile. From there she walked back to the hotel porch where she scanned the area for the weapon used to shoot Deputy McNaughton. Candy climbed down the three-story, fire escape ladder from the porch to the ground, headed due east into the trees before the cliff, and then followed the well trodden game trail used by all sorts of people heading south to the mouth of the canyon. The deputy also noticed that the trail led north beside the ridge to area she had not yet discovered. She resolved that she would follow the trail north before leaving today. With expert eyes looking for what did not belong along the trail, she soon discovered the frontier model, single action, twenty-two caliber pistol at the base of the ridge. Picking up the pistol by the nose of the barrel, she smelled the end of the barrel and placed the weapon in an evidence bag retrieved from her back pocket. Deputy Candy concluded she had found the probable weapon and determined now to discover the motive behind the shooting of Butch McNaughton, deputy on administrative leave and chief suspect in the murder of Gloria Jones, part time prostitute and someone's daughter and sister.

Briskly, Cotton Candy covered the ground to the mouth of the canyon, where, after looking both ways, she crossed the highway and entered the woods on the west side of the Valley Highway. Exiting the woods Candy visually sized up Karen who was sitting on the front steps of the church in the glen. While approaching Karen, Candy wondered about her: Back shooter? Pale blue eyes, short blond hair, ample yet modestly dressed. Prostitute? No make-up. Not a harlot. Five foot five inches, she's not over one hundred and twenty pounds. Piano hands, big teeth, full lips, and works inside. Tick, Candy noticed, Karen brushes back hair that isn't there. What's with that, Candy thought.

"I saw you motioning for me to meet you here. Looked like you didn't want to be seen," said Candy. "How can I help you?"

"For one, I see you found my pistol," started Karen.

"Turn around. Now! Put your hands on the church wall," commanded Deputy Candy.

Complying Karen begged, "Please, you've got me wrong. Why are you doing this?"

"For the attempted murder of Butch McNaughton last night on the third floor of the Stage Stop Hotel," responded Candy, "and you already told me this is your gun."

Arriving from the cemetery behind the church and in full view, Hannah covered for Karen, "Couldn't have, she was with me all evening until just now. We spent the night hiding from Butch in Adam Claymore's house. Adam told us to hide there. Butch roamed this area last night looking for us and even came up to the window and peeked in."

"He didn't see us!" added Karen.

"Quiet blondie, let her do the talking for now. What happened from there?"

"Butch..."

"You know Butch? You have a history with him?" Deputy Candy interrupted.

"Yes, Deputy, I know Butch all too well. Enough to have suffered bruises at his hands," offered Hannah.

"That's enough reason to be hiding from him, but to shoot him in the back?"

"Would you take these cuffs off me? I was trying to flag you down to tell you my pistol had been stolen out of my room. Yes, I did not want to be seen, because Butch and his friend Roy have been harassing us and Butch is a cop. We were told by Adam Claymore that we could trust you but not others at the sheriff's office. Adam told me to make the stolen gun report directly to you!" spouted Karen, unintentionally spitting with anger.

"I apologize, Karen Gustafson, applicant for the science/social studies position currently vacated by Jill Lowenstein. Guess you know what it's like being falsely accused and presumed against. Somewhat like how many students feel during their school career."

"No need to demonstrate that Deputy, been there, done that," summarized Karen.

"Butch could make the sanest person, even a nice school teacher like you, he could make them go crazy enough to do something desperate," responded Candy, "that doesn't mean you didn't shoot him."

Hannah continued, "Karen was with me. We saw Butch cross the highway and go around the west side of the hotel. From there my guess is he went up the stairs, had a confrontation with someone and was shot. I'm surprised Butch was shot in the back. How is he?"

"This puny gun only shot a twenty-two short. One entered his back but didn't go in very far. The other hit the muscle above his other shoulder and was easily extracted. Neither hit anything vital. He's all right. Once the shock to the area wore off, Butch felt plenty of pain especially from the swab the surgeon forced through the bullet hole and my guess he and Roy self medicated afterwards. He's probably still asleep," explained Candy as she removed the handcuffs.

Rubbing her wrists Karen added, "The night before, Roy and Butch came to my room and banged on the door looking for Hannah. She had changed her room to elude Butch. When I didn't open the door for Butch, he went downstairs and got a key to the room. Meanwhile, Hannah and I climbed out on the ledge and hid around the front of the hotel where Roy, in a drunken stupor, stumbled over my birdfeeder and crashed to the porch below. Roy landed on one of the tables on the porch and broke it."

"Okay, this is getting too goofy not to be true. Who stole your gun?"

"I think it was my boyfriend, Harper," Hannah admitted, "I know he was in Karen's room looking for me after I moved to room 216. He left me a note telling me to get out of town as soon as possible. That I wasn't safe here."

"You think he went through Karen's things and took her pistol?" asked Candy, then addressing Karen, "Why do you have a gun?"

"With all that's going on here, you have to ask?" replied Karen.

"You're an outsider. Most wouldn't be carrying a pistol to an interview."

"I'm a tournament shooter. Champion with a pistol, small caliber, and rifle, moving target or not. I wouldn't have shot him in the back or from a distance. I would have come right up to him and either shoot him in the eye or temple, if I wanted to kill him. But that's not what I do. I don't shoot people," finished Karen.

"Right, and Hannah, what's your boyfriend's name?" asked Candy.

"He's a McNaughton, cooks and washes dishes at the hotel. He was jealous of me and Butch, mostly he was angry that Butch would come to my room and just take me. Butch knew his cousin Harper was my boyfriend."

"And Butch came and raped you anyway," clarified Deputy Candy.

"Not at first. I let him. I liked him, but when I started dating Harper, I didn't want Butch's attention. But Butch just kept coming around like he was entitled to have me whenever he wanted," said Hannah as she began weeping.

Embracing Hannah, Candy comforted her, "We've got the weapon, probable motive, and probable suspect who fled last night and hasn't been found. Karen, I need to keep your pistol for awhile as evidence. I'm sorry. And I'm sorry I cuffed you, but it was reasonable to suspect you."

"It looks like I'll be back here. I've accepted the teaching position and I'll be appointed tonight unless the board is scared off by this situation," asserted Karen.

"Don't fret, not a negative word will be said, besides, Mrs. Jaramillo room 330 confirmed your story. She saw a smaller man in a dirty wet apron shoot Butch. I knew that meant Harper," explained the deputy.

"When I come and get my pistol, perhaps we can go to the range...and compete."

Looking at each other, Deputy Cotton Candy, a smirk on her face, concluded with, "I look forward to some real completion, moving target or not."

At sunrise the old woodcutter had finished hauling water from the warm pond to the north side of the tall oak tree. He paused before the scene he had been carving earlier. He listened to a babbling brook formed from a culvert that drained excess water from the creek that flowed by the road above. Next, he flooded the north side of the mound with water he carried by repeatedly filling his buckets. Eventually, he tired from hauling and emptying the precious liquid that gave life to what roots remained active just barely under the soil. He touched the roots and prayed that God would restore and heal them from the trauma the rock slide had caused. He prayed the tree would heal from what was happening in the valley below. The old man prayed for his own healing from damage caused by memories of years spent in a cage in the jungle and from his nightmares of what happened to him and his friends as well as what he did to men, women, and children in the name of war. His prayer shifted to whom he knew would soon arrive and her friend hiding in the Blair House below. A smile crossed his face and he began to radiate, tears glistened in his bright blue eyes, and his gnarled hands picked up the water buckets one more time. This time his two buckets would be used on that portion of the tree trunk where he had been carving a story, an inscription no one had yet seen but soon would find inspirational. Eventually, he hoped the whole town would pass by the tree trunk out of respect.

Janine had risen early; a smile crossed her lovely face. Her brown eyes glistened. With a new song in her heart, she hummed the tune while she dressed and prepared breakfast for her beloved friend Izzy. He had been the boy next door. For the last fifteen years, he had been the object of her dreams. She had been Izzy's ninth grade date to his senior prom. Often Janine had prepared breakfast to eat at the pond before taking a dip. Today the tray felt heavier and her steps quicker than ever before. Janine's raven hair flowed behind, as she pranced up the sidewalk where she crossed the street before the Blair house and hurried around to the back door where she entered in with breakfast for two. Janine burst joyously into song, "This is the day, this the day, that the Lord hath made. I will rejoice, I will rejoice, and be glad in it."

Izzy had slept on the third floor but had descended the servants' stairwell to the kitchen. Suddenly, he appeared having reopened the door to an old press room that had been used to store cleaning supplies and tools. He proclaimed, "You are here! Your perfume carried to me on the third floor."

"Hmmm, that part of my plan worked...and are you hungry?" Janine said as she loosened her robe revealing her yellow bikini.

With that Izzy waited no longer to hold her in his arms kissing her good morning and kissing her again, then again..., "You need to excuse me I shouldn't have done that...I...need to talk with you...," Izzy proclaimed.

Janine did not let go and held Izzy, standing on tiptoes she sought his lips and melted into his arms...and then said, "Oh, Izzy, I've waited so long for you to return. Now you are here...it is my dream come true. I loved going to prom with you, then you left after graduation. I know about you getting angry and running from the house with the Blair's chest that was hidden behind the stairwell cupboard."

"That's one reason why I am here. Janine, that night I flipped out. I lost the chest and the gold inside. I don't remember where I was or what I was doing. I drank and must have been stupefied. The other day when the bus stopped in Rock Creek, I waded into the creek and the ponds in it where the water backs up, hoping to find the chest..."

"I..." Janine tried to say.

"Then in Ridge View, I waded through the pond at Little Eden, you know the pond by the bridge," Izzy had continued.

Janine nodded.

"When I got here, I bathed in the pond and walked as much of it as I dared..."

Janine grabbed Izzy again kissing him to silence him by fully embracing him, and stirring his passion even more.

"You said finding the chest was one of the reasons you came back. Is there another reason?" asked Janine as she stared into Izzy's eyes.

"Three more..."

"And..."

"I need to make right that which is wrong."

With growing excitement, Janine grabbed both of his shoulders, while she bounced up and down, "What else, Izzy, what else!"

"Another reason is that I have a meeting with the lawyer, John Law. He was able to track me down. He wants to talk with me about the Blair House and the Blair Estate if there is any."

"When?"

"Thursday."

"Same as me, I answered the ad."

"And that is another reason. I'm to lead in the restoration of the Blair House, to restore it to its former stature and beauty. And you...my lovely Janine...Janine Crowfoot not even knowing I was coming here to do what I must, had already decided to join me in what I must do. That is so much of how I remembered you."

"One more Izzy, tell me Izzy, say it."

Without hesitation, Izzy held Janine closely to himself and whispered, "I promised you I would return and marry you!"

"Hallelujah! Praise the Lord! I knew it," Janine said as she pushed him aside, danced before him, both bouncing and swaying while giving thanks, then pouncing upon him with legs wrapped around his waist as she hugged his neck. Crying now, Janine continued, "Izzy, I prayed for your return and that you would be pleased with me. God said for me to pray for you and to keep myself unto you for our wedding night. Lord knows I am so stirred for you. Please don't make me wait too long!"

"Janine, I was captivated when I saw you at the pond. Your kisses drive me insane and you are drop dead gorgeous. I love you…I always have and always will." They kissed again more tenderly, more peaceably. "And I want to spend more time talking with you, so you will know what you are getting into."

"Then is this official?"

On his knees before her, holding an old jewelry box, Izzy opened it for her to see, "Janine Crowfoot, love of my life, my north star, will you marry me?"

Shaking and weeping now, Janine said, "I do, I will…"

"When?"

"Now!"

"Where?"

"They stumble that run too fast," Janine stated, remembering Friar Lawrence's advice to Romeo and Juliet.

"I'd rather deal with the consequences of hurrying than of defiling the commitment you made and what the Lord told you to do. I will not be able to contain myself much longer. My resolve to wait grows weaker with every kiss," urged Izzy.

"Then you are not only saved, but also seek to walk in his lordship?" Janine said as she grinned enthusiastically.

"Indubitably, yes, without a doubt!"

"We have to get a license," Janine said as they kissed again but longer.

"A justice of the peace won't do," said Izzy, as they kissed again, "but we could have a civil ceremony, then arrange a proper wedding at your church."

"We could wait. If we had gone through premarital counseling with him, Adam Claymore would marry us. I have spoken of this many times to him. It would be best for you, for us, to have as little contact with the world until after Thursday and even then there is going to be trouble," stated Janine.

"As I recall the courthouse is just two blocks away…"

"We can go there. Your name will be recognized, as will my car. We can walk to the convenience store down the street on the corner. My brother Mike will loan us his car, and we can drive to Adam's ranch on the mesa by noon. Once there surely, we will be married, and I'll bet Adam will insist we honeymoon on his ranch."

"At least for the afternoon."

"Shouldn't we pray about this?"

"I did most the night!"

"Me too, in between planning your breakfast, what I would wear, and how I would seduce you if you didn't find me pleasing to your eye. Shall we wait?"

"No, I think we better hurry, at least we would be married in the eyes of the state, then we can deal with a proper church wedding soon after," Izzy said as they both stumbled toward the courthouse.

From the hill above the scene, one solitary figure witnessed the proceedings and with tears in his eyes, the old woodcutter closed the knife he had been carving with and walked to the road above where he sat in the cab of The Gray Whiz where he prayed for the children down below.

Cough, cough, sputter, cough, sputter, boom! The Gray Whiz announced with a roar as it slowly ascended the mountain and into the forest beyond.

ESTEEMED

CHAPTER 14

"A good name is more desirable than great riches; to be esteemed is better than silver or gold." Proverbs 22:1

In the 1950's a movement to merge Colorado school districts had prevailed. Most rural schools had been only one or two room buildings on the plains or near mining camps in the mountains. Most had outdoor privies and lacked running water. Often male students left school after the eighth grade to farm the land. Many towns lost their kindergarten through twelfth grade schools in favor of having more resources and alternatives when combined with a neighboring town usually of greater population. County superintendents were eliminated. Staff was brought together, and the teacher who taught and managed a first grade through high school classroom became a specialist teaching only one grade level. Students remained in school longer, and graduation from high school was no longer the exception. What was lost was the benefit of older students helping the younger ones, small class sizes, and a lot of individualized instruction. When a small town lost its elementary school, it lost a source of community pride and belonging. Often towns withered and died, but not always due to the school reorganization.

Rock Creek Valley communities changed for two reasons—school reorganization and highway construction. Three smaller school districts merged as one. Jericho Springs had prospered with an elementary school and the valley's only high school, which prompted more housing. Rock Creek had withered as a community by losing its K-12 school despite becoming the site for the school administration offices. Ridge View had flourished, gained a new K-8 school building, and had become more than a truck stop. When the interstate highway had been completed, the Valley Highway, formerly a major business loop of US 85/87, became a minor route. Now only area residents traveled the route regularly. Other travelers came by accident, while some came expecting to be able to hunt on private land and in the national forests that lie beyond the front range of the Rockies. Most hunters had learned to find an easier, more accessible, and more accommodating route to fabled hunting grounds. Only Ridge View merchants welcomed tourists and their spending.

Built on the west side of the Valley Highway on the north end of Rock Creek where Indiana Avenue made a T with the highway, the Rock Creek School had become the school administration site for the valley by default. Rock Creek no longer boasted a population comparable to Jericho Springs and certainly paled substantially compared to what had been projected for Ridge View. Though empty, Rock Creek had an available building. The red brick Rock Creek School was solid and well built but lacked students. A few families still had school aged children in Rock Creek and brought their children to wait for the school bus at the bus barn to go to Jericho Springs for high school and Ridge View for elementary school. In a word, it was convenient, still home spun, and supposedly safe. The children remained inside the bus barn and out of foul weather. During good weather children played outside where they were enclosed by chain link fencing, while briefly waiting for their departure. Parents believed their children were protected.

Across the street, employees, who arrived early at the insurance and real estate offices, watched over children waiting for school buses to arrive. Tuesday evening one lone figure stayed late at work and stood behind tinted windows waiting for the sun to disappear from view and for the superintendent and school board to arrive for the night's meeting. Mr. Samuel Gelding wrote insurance for the municipality and school district in all three towns in the valley. Additionally, Gelding extended his business to other towns along the Valley Highway business loop and into the mountains. Gelding traveled to Wolf City south and west of Claymore Flats and to Quail Point, south through the canyon and beyond. Gelding thrived in the valley because he was married to a McNaughton. Tonight, Gelding had been scheduled to conclude a policy update for the school district as a board agenda item, and he was curious as to how the school board and administration would handle the contract of the missing school teacher, Jill Lowenstein. Technically, Lowenstein's contract was secure not only because she was a quality tenured teacher, but also because teachers were not yet required to report to school. However, it was community or valley knowledge that Jill Lowenstein was both a missing person and a possible witness to the murder of Gloria Jones. Several had monitored the home of her roommate, Janine Crowfoot, who lived across the street from the Blair House and the hot springs south of it. Further, it had been public knowledge that Deputy Sheriff Butch McNaughton was thought to be a suspect and had been placed on paid administrative leave until the murder had been solved.

Tradition dictated the arrival of the officials for the school board meeting. First to arrive would be the superintendent and his assistant, then the board secretary, followed by the elementary and high school principals, who were responsible for serving peanuts and cold soda pop to the school board members and central office staff. This time honored practice kept the principals humbled regardless of their responsibilities of supervising their teachers, secretarial staff, custodians, volunteers, food service workers, and bus drivers plus watching over all their students and interacting with a relative multitude of parents and other residents both during school hours and at all home athletic events. Last to arrive would be anyone scheduled on the agenda. Rarely, did the public attend school board meetings like they should.

Tonight would be different. Butch McNaughton and his friend Roy Sentry arrived and parked on Indiana Avenue several houses from the main intersection. Before entering the school administration building, Butch and Roy waited for the school board to arrive. Though having counseled with Adam much of the afternoon and against his protestations, Janine believed she needed to be at the meeting in case Jill made an appearance. Izzy and Janine returned her brother's car to him at the convenience store in Jericho Springs. Hoping to maintain some semblance of anonymity, Adam met the newlyweds there, drove them to Rock Creek, and dropped them off at the intersection of County Road 403 and the Valley Highway, one of US 85/87 business loops. From the intersection Izzy and Janine walked across the front of the volunteer fire station along the highway to the school district administration building. Next, Adam drove to the church parking lot before the mouth of the canyon where Karen and Hannah waited for him. A casual observer would think nothing of his effort to hide where the women were staying. Adam then drove the women to the administration building, and he parked in the insurance company's parking lot. The three crossed the highway together and entered the school building. Next, Amanda Sentry, secretary to Attorney John Law, arrived with a radiant Janine Crowfoot, roommate of Jill Lowenstein, and a clean shaven and recently cropped Izzy Blair. Both followed closely behind Amanda. Izzy was noticed for the grin on his face but not recognized by anyone. A few other residents filed in followed by additional school personnel. The last to arrive were Deputy Sheriff Cotton Candy and the old woodcutter, whose presence had been first announced by the cough, cough, sputter, cough, sputter, boom from the engine of The Gray Whiz.

Only then had Samuel Gelding crossed the street. He climbed the stairs from the lobby to the school board chambers and took a seat at the long table on the north side of the room reserved for school officials, the lawyer for the school district, and those providing contracted services. Once all officials were seated, the school principals distributed soda pop and peanuts to the school board members. No one failed to understand this humbling gesture.

A slight commotion ensued as Hannah noticed Janine's ring, and Janine introduced Ezra her husband. Janine failed to mention Ezra's last name. Some people responded that they had not known Janine dated, Janine replied that their courtship and engagement were brief. Karen leaned around Adam, who sat next to her, and recognized Ezra as the man in the tan trench coat from the bus ride to Rock Creek. Karen and Ezra's eyes locked and Izzy nodded in recognition, as he brought his finger to his mouth to ask her to say nothing. Karen nodded in turn, and Adam leaned toward her and whispered that he would tell her of the day's events later. None of this was missed by the assistant superintendent Dr. Maurice Wood, insurance representative Sam Gelding, Deputy Sheriff Cotton Candy, and Deputy Sheriff Butch McNaughton. All of them looked around to see if Jill Lowenstein happened to be attending the meeting.

Only Adam wondered why the old woodcutter always attended both the school board and city council meetings. In fact the old woodcutter also attended the chamber of commerce meetings and rotated his attendance at Sunday morning and evening services plus mid-week services at churches throughout the valley. People speculated he was trying to find something that was missing in his life, which was true for the most part. Many had tried to and actually did share the gospel with him, and all he would do in response was to point at his heart. Finally, people gave up trying to get him to say something, and they just nodded hello not saying anything to the old woodcutter. He had just wanted to bless and be blessed.

The meeting progressed swiftly and uneventfully until an executive session was called for a personnel matter. All the audience was asked to leave the board room with the exception of Karen Gustafson, Adam Claymore, and Deputy Sheriff Cotton Candy, which took Karen by surprise. Superintendent Clarence Moss introduced Karen to the school board and reviewed her credentials, which were superlative. Board member McNaughton asked two questions with the first being why Karen had left her last position, to which Karen told the truth that one of her students had died, and as a result, Karen wanted a change of scenery to heal from that loss. The other question had to do with whether or not Karen was related to anyone in the valley, which, of course, was not the case.

The board secretary then noted that two persons were present to speak to the matter of Karen Gustafson's application. First was former school board chairman, Adam Claymore, who gave at first a reserved recommendation that evolved into an enthusiastic one, which slightly embarrassed both Karen and Adam. Several, who had served on the board under Adam's leadership, showed their amusement at Adam's obvious infatuation with the young woman to which Adam could only reply that we could all benefit from the wholesome influence of Miss Gustafson. He stated that Karen had sterling endorsements from her previous employers in Quail Point.

Next was an unexpected endorsement from Deputy Sheriff Cotton Candy. "At the request of board member McNaughton, I completed a background check on Miss Gustafson beyond the traditional one conducted for the city and the school district due to our current political situation and the matter to which most of the valley is concerned. Namely, the murder investigation of one Gloria Jones and the pending condemnation of the Blair House property on the west side of Jericho Springs. In both matters, I found no connection to either item. I did find one matter of note. Miss Gustafson is a marksman and not an ordinary one. She has won female and coed competitions using both a handgun and rifle at all levels including national competition."

"What does that have to do with anything?" asked Superintendent Moss.

"Nothing, except that it was Miss Gustafson's gun, stolen from her room at the Stage Stop Hotel, that was used to shoot Deputy Sheriff McNaughton," Candy replied.

"Again, how does that matter?"

"Miss Gustafson's talents match our culture. I look forward to competing against her. It will be fun to have another woman around who can match or beat most men using weapons of choice. Besides think of what she brings to our situation. We have gun safety classes and we talk about offering self protection programs for women."

"Then I take it you are endorsing Miss Gustafson as a full time substitute teacher."

"Yes, even more so than her having a regular classroom position. By having her subbing throughout the district, her renown with a gun will have even greater influence."

"What say you to that, Miss Gustafson? You have the endorsement of two of the valley's most beloved citizens," asked Superintendent Moss.

"I do! I will...take the position," said a blushing Miss Karen Gustafson, looking first at the board, then to Deputy Cotton Candy, and resting on the joyous Adam Claymore, who sat grinning next to her.

"One thing, Miss Gustafson, I know our situation has been discussed with you about Miss Lowenstein. Jill is an excellent teacher. We hope she will return for this school year. We have not heard otherwise; however, and as Deputy Candy can attest to, she may be the key witness in a murder case. If Miss Lowenstein does not return for this school year, we will place you in that position contractually. If Jill does return, she may miss a lot of school due to the pending trial. With your qualifications, we would want you to substitute for her whenever she is absent. If she does return, you will continue the school year as a full time substitute and would receive, of course, preferential assignments especially in your curriculum endorsements. Assuming you do well in either assignment, we will be having both science and social studies vacancies next school year. They will be filled first by interested staff persons, and you would be considered as full time staff as opposed to our regular substitute teachers," restated Superintendent Moss.

"There may be another project we would want you to do, which the school board will be discussing shortly. It's called the Community Leadership Identification Process," informed Mr. Arthur King, elementary school principal.

"With the advent of state required testing, we are required to have citizen accountability committees for each of our schools," added Willa Sentry, School Board President.

"Basically, it's a process where formal and obvious community leaders are identified, then interviewed to identify other less obvious community leaders. By having the leadership respond to five questions, we gain information on how our community's leadership perceives our community's problems and resources that can be used to solve our problems," concluded Principal Alden, junior/senior high school principal.

"I take it we have reached consensus to hire Miss Gustafson," stated Superintendent Moss, which all board members affirmed.

"Now if Karen, Adam, and Deputy Candy will excuse us, we have additional staff issues. Thank you," finished the board president, Willa Sentry, watchdog for quality education.

Outside at 9:00 p.m., a drama unfolded. Janine and Izzy had caught a ride with the old woodcutter back to Jericho Springs. Although curious about the man with Janine Crowfoot, Butch McNaughton and his friend Roy had made no effort to find out more information about him and instead they had cornered Hannah once she left the board room. At first Butch was friendly and apologetic, but after the others had gone to their vehicles and were leaving the area, Butch became amorous and both he and Roy attempted to take Hannah across the street to the hotel where Butch would get a room for them to use. For the first time, Hannah slapped Butch. Angered, Butch slapped her in return knocking Hannah to the ground. Roy egged Butch on, and Hannah knew that this time would be dangerous for her. Hannah screamed and slapped at Butch again, while struggling to free herself from his grasp.

Hearing Hannah's scream as Deputy Candy descended the steps from the board room, Candy burst through the building's front doors drawing her night stick from her side. One look from Candy had Roy backing up as he warned Butch of her arrival. Before Butch released Hannah, Candy gave Butch a manly thrust with her baton to his injured shoulder, then another to the back of his knee. Collapsing, Butch rolled on the ground to his right but regained his footing. While Candy tended to Hannah, Roy nodded as Butch motioned for Roy to grasp Candy from behind. Hannah warned Candy of Roy's movement, and as Candy moved to defend herself, Butch attacked her slamming her head first to the ground and knocking her unconscious.

Realizing what he had done, Butch knelt over Candy and called her name. Karen quietly emerged from the front door and saw Roy picking up Candy's baton. Roy moved toward Hannah shouting, "See what you made us do!"

On the ground before Karen was her own pistol that Candy had been holding as evidence. Reaching the pistol and cocking it before Roy reached Hannah, Karen fired one round that whizzed by Roy's head as he had raised the baton to strike Hannah. Cocking the single action colt revolver a second time, Karen ordered Roy to stop by yelling "Drop to your knees, buster. You are messing with the wrong woman!"

In response, Roy dropped the baton and turned his back to Karen, as if he were hiding, while claiming, "I wasn't gonna' do anything to her. I just wanted to scare her."

Meanwhile, Hannah rose from the ground and picked up Candy's baton, first knocking out Roy with a whack to his face, which both broke his nose and temporarily knocked him senseless. Next, Hannah ran to Butch as he leaned over Candy weeping with remorse after he realized the gravity of what he had done. Hannah first whacked Butch on the shoulder to get him to turn around, and once he had, Hannah plummeted Butch repeatedly on the head, face, and shoulders, which knocked him to the ground.

"Hannah! Stop! No more!" shouted Karen, as she ran to Hannah and disarmed her.

From inside the building, the school board members responded quickly to the sound of gunfire outside. They arrived in time to see Karen shout at Roy as he fled, "Stop or I will stop you!"

Roy paused and shouted, "She broke my nose! She broke my nose." Then he turned to flee and dropped right in the middle of the highway, when Karen shot him in his right heel.

Karen turned toward Adam and shouted, "Adam, please get him off the highway."

Adam shouted to the board secretary, "Call Sheriff Bailey. Don't call the switchboard. Call Bailey at home. He needs to handle this himself. Tell him Butch has met his match and will be on his way to the emergency room."

"I'll call for the ambulance. At least two of these people will need one. All four need medical attention," said Dr. Maurice Wood.

"What on earth prompted this?" shouted board president, Willa Sentry.

"A genuine hero has arrived in town, and it looks like 'The Lone Ranger' has made a friend," said Superintendent Clarence Moss, as he watched Adam Claymore comforting Karen Gustafson, heroic marksman confirmed.

"I'm certain when the truth is known we will learn that Butch McNaughton was justified in what he did!" exhorted Mrs. Beth Ellen McNaughton. She promptly returned to the board room and called her brother, Whitney, the father of Butch McNaughton. Beth Ellen told Whitney that he had better get to the hospital and he had better get the lawyer.

"Frankly, Scarlet, I don't give a darn who he is. What he did to Deputy Candy cannot be justified, especially when he is on administrative leave and a suspect in the murder of Gloria Jones. We've had enough of the privileged treatment Butch has had because of family ties. Enough is enough! Butch is out of control and should be locked up. That goes for Roy too. I'll see to it," finished Aquila Parson, school board member, Judge Parson's wife, and friend of Roy's mother, Willa Sentry, the school board president. Willa had not comforted her wayward son.

Adam whispered to Karen that she and Hannah would be taken in to the sheriff's office for questioning. Adam told Karen not to be concerned that she needed to be careful not to say anything to the local media, and she should let what would be favorable town gossip get word out about what happened. Otherwise, Adam said, the incident might come back to haunt her. If cornered, she could say that the incident was tragic for all concerned. Let the lawyers draw out your comments in what was certain to be a criminal court case. The next thing Adam said totally surprised Karen.

"The hospital and jail are in Ridge View. So is Bailey's office. I hope to catch up with you and Hannah. You need to stay at the ranch, instead of in town. You won't want to be anywhere else tonight. But for now, I have to get to the hospital. If I don't meet you, have Bailey take you to the Rock Creek house."

"For heaven's sake, why?" replied Karen.

"Exactly, for heaven's sake, I'm Butch's uncle. I baptized him and I obviously didn't do a good job making a disciple of him."

To Adam's surprise, Karen rose upward on her toes, put her arms around Adam's neck, hugged him and said, "Thank you! Not just for the ride but for the endorsement as well."

Adam wanted to kiss Karen, but all he could do was to hold on to her, smile, linger in her embrace, and tell her, "You are welcome."

As predicted, Sheriff Bailey arrived after the second ambulance departed with Candy and Roy, who was terrified to ride to the hospital with her. Bailey asked Hannah and Karen to ride with him to his office after he secured Karen's weapon. Bailey ordered his deputies to gather statements from the other witnesses, which ended up being a significant number. Not only had townspeople observed what happened from across the street, but also had clients and tarts from the brothel on Indiana Avenue. Even old Beatrice Jaramillo, still dressed in what most people recognized as her uniform, came to watch the shellacking from her third floor hotel room, as did the men from the tobacco store. Most of the conversation centered on how Deputy Butch had first abused two women, and then was beaten up by Hannah, who had not been reporting to work as desk clerk at the Stage Stop Hotel. Everyone saw Karen shoot Roy in the heel after warning him to stop running away. The story would grow to where Karen pistol whipped and shot both Roy and Butch. All agreed that the new school teacher was no one to mess with. No one would remember Izzy until Thursday night or that he and his bride had left the scene before the crime with the old woodcutter in the Gray Whiz. All heard the truck's departure as night air resounded with cough, cough, sputter, cough, sputter, boom! Only two would remember seeing Sam Gelding, the insurance agent, as he drove away south on the Valley Highway. One was Hannah's boyfriend, Harper, who though nearly undetected had watched everything from the bus barn roof. The other was Detective Caleb Jones, who saw Gelding leave town and also saw Harper watching from the rooftop.

When what many found to be entertainment was concluded, spectators went back to where they came from with four exceptions. Sam Gelding, insurance salesman, had already driven south through the canyon, while Harper, Hannah's boyfriend and part time cook at the Stage Stop Hotel, leaped off the building he had hidden on, then ran to the bridge over 403 where he headed for the trail to the mesa. Harper had concluded the only safe place for him was to go to Adam's where he would tell the truth and ask for help. Uncharacteristically, Beatrice Jaramillo, the third spectator did not go back to where she came from, but walked along the highway to the canyon's mouth, found a bench in the church yard thicket, and prayed. It was then Beatrice felt compelled to end her seclusion at the Stage Stop Hotel and to attend Wednesday's prayer meeting, not only because of what her grandson Butch had done, but because she had a growing sense of what was to come.

Although they had left before the crime occurred, the old woodcutter turned around at the sound of gunshots in time to see Hannah pummel Butch and Karen shoot Roy in the heel. Once the crowd cleared, the old woodcutter drove Izzy and Janine to Jericho Springs, past the Blair House, and up the road to the curve above the old tree. With tears in his eyes, the sad old man reached across the Whiz's cab and opened the door. He grabbed a bucket from behind his seat, handed it to Izzy, and pointed toward the tree.

Izzy knew what to do. Before crawling out of the cab, Izzy prayed aloud for all three. Saddened, they departed, shoulders sloping and spirits dampened at what played out tonight. The newlyweds filled the bucket with warm water from the pond and poured it on the roots at the base of the old oak tree.

Adam raced his truck to catch up with the ambulances, while praying for God's mercy and intervention in the ordeal. He thought of Karen, Hannah, Cotton, Roy, and Butch. Adam wondered where the pistol came from and how Karen managed to use it. He knew what would happen tonight as Butch's friends, led by Buddy Smith, would learn what had just taken place. Adam asked God to give him the words to say to Butch that would make an eternal difference. Speaking to Butch's father, Whitney "Red" McNaughton, would be more difficult. Adam knew Red would say the entire incident was the result of newcomers coming to the valley.

In the east three travelers stopped at different intervals along the roadway. Not knowing why, they each felt compelled to pray for the valley that lay before them. One drove on to Ridge View, another to Jericho Springs, and the third into Rock Creek. Once on location each prayed for a hedge of protection to be around believers in their respective town as each drove side streets in their settlement. Once around the towns, each left their assignment only to meet at the north end of Ridge View, where they unknowingly formed a caravan of prayer warriors heading north. Behind them storm clouds gathered.

Buddy Smith in the lead, night riders began to drive through all three towns looking for and finding trouble in the wake of the shootings of Butch and Roy. A newcomer shot them both, though they deserved their beatings for having attacked both Hannah and Deputy Cotton Candy. Another stranger, had arrived, who might have claim to the Blair House, the water, and what might lay underground in the wake of the slide. Liquored up, they raced up and down County Road 403 and the Valley High Way throwing empty beer bottles at whatever and whomever they could find.

Dressed in black, slight Beatrice Jaramillo was startled when she attempted to cross the highway from the thicket at the church to the grove of trees on the other side, as a rental car raced past her and into the canyon. Watching it, Beatrice stepped onto the pavement but turned to see a yellow pickup truck bearing down on her. Riding shotgun, Buddy Smith tossed a beer bottle in Beatrice's direction and struck her head. Beatrice rolled off the highway and into the thicket and out of sight where she lay unconscious. This would bring more trouble for Butch and his friends, as night riders raced south through the canyon like confused warriors pursuing their prey in the wrong direction. One spectator hadn't made it home safely.

Make Me an Instrument

CHAPTER 15

*"Those who cleanse themselves from the latter will be
instruments for special purposes, made holy, useful to the
Master and prepared to do any good work." 2 Timothy 2:21*

While the newlyweds lingered in bed at Janine's house, Hannah and Karen rose early Wednesday morning, as did Adam and Harper, who had survived well after spilling his tale truthfully to Adam. Adam told Harper he could borrow a horse and ride across the mesa to where the park bench overlooked Rock Creek. Once there, Harper was to leave the horse and go the back way to Adam's house where Harper could borrow Adam's '51 Chevy from the garage. Adam advised Harper to turn himself in to Sheriff Bailey in Ridge View for shooting Harper's cousin, Deputy Butch McNaughton, in the back with the pistol he had stolen from room 218 at the Stage Stop Hotel. Adam told Harper that if he chose not to, then he should not leave Hannah in town.

Fidgeting with the steering wheel, Adam eagerly drove to Rock Creek anxious to meet Hannah and Karen at the rear door of his house on the Valley Highway. They had declined going to Claymore Flats as he had urged. Adam replayed yesterday's events in his mind. Feeling like Friar Lawrence in Shakespeare's play Romeo and Juliet but unlike the Friar, Adam decided not to perform a quick wedding ceremony for the Blairs. After learning they had already settled for less than best by having a civil ceremony at the courthouse, Adam honored their civil ceremony but secured their promise to submit to pastoral counseling and a church ceremony in God's house. He warned them that he stumbles who runs too fast, especially in matters of the heart, and he cautioned them further learning that John Law had urged Ezra to keep a low profile. Going to the courthouse had been foolish. Adam had sworn not to expose Ezra Blair, apparent rightful heir to the water rights, gold, land, and least important, the Blair House. Next, Adam thought about Harper, who had confessed to shooting Butch in the back with Karen's pistol, and they had hatched a plan with two choices. Harper would have to make his choice, but Adam was certain to be declared an accomplice in Harper's flight. Also, Adam realized that testifying for Karen at the board meeting with his obvious enthusiasm would cost him no small amount of kidding in town and at the ranch. And then Adam surmised that although Butch seemed convincingly remorseful about his attack on Hannah and Cotton, he knew to say what people wanted to hear. Hannah had plummeted Butch. Adam had watched Karen shoot Roy in the heel. And a beautiful woman had pressed herself against him and had hugged him gently. Sigh, Adam whimpered and concluded he too could commit the same mistake as Janine and Izzy.

When both women began to exit the doorway, Adam told Hannah to stay at the house and gather her things. Surprised, both women looked at each other to which he said, "Trust me." In quick response, Hannah rushed to pack, while Karen joined Adam by mounting the truck through the cab door.

Karen looked at Adam and said, "Wherever, I'm with you."

"Then don't look back. Didn't you say you were going to visit Ruth Browning this morning?"

Karen nodded.

"We were going to have breakfast this morning in the dining room at the Stage Stop, but I think it best we get you out of town quickly," predicted Adam.

"Too much notoriety?"

"Yes, and the stories will grow."

"Will the school board change their minds?" Karen blurted.

"No, you are solid with them. Pretty much everyone is sick and tired of Butch and his nonsense," Adam said, then pausing, "You know, I was quite impressed with how you handled yourself, first at the school board meeting, and then in the school yard when you caught that young rooster right by his heel. That was fine shooting."

"I don't miss."

"Where did you get the pistol?"

"It's mine, but it appeared on the ground in front of me. Deputy Candy told me she had found it in the woods at the hotel after someone shot Butch in the back outside my room. Later she confirmed it was mine but kept it as evidence. Candy made me feel like I was a suspect. After the school board meeting, I guess I wasn't. I would have thought she would have stored it at the sheriff's office. Would that be in an evidence room?"

Adam shook his head, "My guess is she carried it in her boot, which was risky. It's single action?"

Karen nodded, "Cotton either didn't have opportunity to store it or didn't think it would be safe in the evidence room."

"The latter…but Karen, people are really impressed with you, including me. You are a woman of excellence with good references and you answered well the question about why you left your previous position."

"Was it obvious that I was affected by what happened?" asked Karen.

"Yes, and I'd say your student, knew you cared for her. I'd say you are bruised," replied Adam.

"Can one care too much?" Karen asked hypothetically.

Both sat in silence, as Adam continued the drive. At the bridge before the Brownings' new Eden, Adam pulled over and pointed to the scene below.

"Lovely, isn't it?" Adam stated.

"Yes, but it looks like there has been a fire over there," Karen said as she pointed toward the east bank of Rock Creek, "Recent remains!"

"I'll bet there's a story to that. Bet you'll learn about it today," predicted Adam.

"What about you, Adam, What's your day look like?"

"I'm back to the jail. Karen, I've made some good progress with Butch. You know I'm his uncle. For awhile, I was a mentor to him, but there wasn't lasting fruit. I know he's done a lot of wrong for quite awhile. Privilege hasn't been good for him, but if ever he needed the Lord, it's now."

"And you need to follow through," Karen concluded.

"If I can, I want to help make right what's wrong. Butch was very close to my Mary and her death was hard on him too."

"You put a lot on yourself, don't you?" asked Karen.

"Yes. I do …but it must be done."

"You are like me. We are both bruised."

"And flawed. Is there hope for us?"

"I think you are wonderfully amazing," Karen softly said as she dared to move closer to Adam on the truck's bench seat where she clasped his free hand. "Doing what is both good and right; being a respecter of women like Boaz, the kinsman redeemer."

"You can glean in my field anytime," Adam smiled, as he thought of marrying a younger woman who was a crack shot.

Stopping again before entering the Brownings' driveway, Adam switched off his truck ignition switch, and said, "I'm sorry I missed you last night. I was afraid for you. I'm not sure how long I'll be. I have our Wednesday prayer meeting. I know you are an independent woman, but would you call me at the ranch when you are ready to go."

"I have your telephone number," said Karen, thoughtfully, "I have some things to take care of. I have to buy a bus ticket for Friday and I'd like to see Miss Lowenstein's classroom again in case she doesn't show up."

"Then you will be here for the city council meeting?"

"I'm sure that'll be interesting."

"Gold, water rights, and the Blair House, we are all interested in seeing if the city council condemns it, but Izzy being here makes a complete difference," clarified Adam.

"Maybe that's where the ad's about?"

"The one about lodging?"

"Yes, in the *Outcry*…about trading labor for free lodging…helping to restore an old building. I have an appointment Thursday at John Law's office in Jericho Springs," Karen replied enthusiastically.

"Then it must be true! The McNaughtons….and others…have feared someone would show up and have rightful claim to it all! Money has already been spent and partnerships organized. A lot of hopes have been raised," Adam retorted immediately, started his truck, and drove into Brownings' driveway stopping short of their front porch.

"That's not all. I plan to work at the pizzeria doing inside work. I have an appointment there this afternoon to tell them it is definite I will soon be moving here," added Karen.

"Then you are going to teach and work after school making pizzas?" Adam said with obvious disappointment.

"At least for the rest of the summer," Karen said as she opened the truck door and stepped to the ground.

"Then you are going to leave Friday and come back soon?"

Peering in the window, Karen replied to a smiling Adam, "As soon as my parents are able to help me move here," and then she skipped away and added coquettishly, "I'll ask to be off Sunday's and Wednesday nights."

Pleased, Adam drove off before both Ruth and Andrew appeared from the back porch. Andy shouted, "Member me! Member me? Who was that? S' he your husband? Your daddy?" then he turned and ran back inside.

Smiling, Ruth added to Andy's inquisition, "Gentleman friend?"

To which, Karen replied, "Yes, I think so. Definitely, a friend and gentle man, a true help. Someone I can count on…there's just one thing…"

"Oh, this is interesting," Ruth responded, "Come in, and tell me more."

Andy reappeared bearing gifts, "We wuz makin' Mickey Mouse specials. Do ya 'member?" Andy nearly exploded, while handing a peanut butter and jelly sandwich to Karen, "Mom, tell her about the coyote. Tell her 'bout goin' to town and those scary men. I still have Quackers! Can ya' stay for lunch? Will he be back soon? Wanna see the Princess Freda Louise? She's been naughty again. Mom put her in the shed cuz she's been naughty! And Quackers, too!"

Karen replied, "Yes, no, yes!"

Puzzled, Andy looked at Karen, threw up his arms, and said, "I forgot what I asked ya!"

"Let her see Freda and Quackers, but then you run go play inside, and let us have some girl talk, mister," insisted Ruth.

Down at the shed, when Freda saw Karen, it was love at first sight. Freda jumped up and down and immediately became a nuisance, until Karen soothingly spoke to the puppy. Karen sat on the ground and Freda climbed onto her lap. Karen said, "I love her, she's delightful. If there are any others like her, I want one."

Ruth responded, "Look at you. You have a way with animals. I'll show you

Quackers. She's been hiding. Some strange things have been happening around here."

"You, too?" Karen questioned.

"Someone hung the carcass of a headless coyote in the tree in front of our house. And…what happened to the ducks."

"What's with that?" retorted Karen.

"Just as weird was seeing that man from the bus wading in our pond," Ruth added.

"Who do you mean?"

"The bearded man in the tan trench coat walked all around the pond holding his coat over his head. He was looking for something, but I don't think he found it," finished Ruth.

"I saw him last night with the roommate of the teacher I'm replacing this coming school year," Karen added, "he looks pretty good. He shaved off his beard."

"Then you got the job!" Ruth said while clapping her hands, "Yeah! I have a friend in town. This is really good news. When are you moving here?"

"I need some help," offered Karen.

"Name it…how can I help?" inquired Ruth.

"Well, tonight I need to meet Adam at the prayer meeting in Rock Creek…"

"Adam, do you mean Adam Claymore?" asked Ruth.

"Yes…"

"Rob says he is not only the best of the eligible men in town, but he's a man of God. Someone whose yes is yes and no is no. Why, he is one of the reasons Rob and I are back together," Ruth explained, as tears sprang forth.

"He's older and kinder and generous and thoughtful," confessed Karen.

"And wealthy!" mused Ruth, "And you've just been here a few days!"

"And he is lonely. You know Adam is a widower. His wife Mary must have been a wonderful woman, and she loved Rock Creek. The whole valley," concluded Karen.

Karen and Ruth became silent as they sauntered toward the house, then Karen said, "There's plenty of time for romance, but not until I resolve some things… besides I've got two new jobs, and that's where I need your help."

"Two jobs! You are one proactive gal! Explain," asked Ruth with surprise.

"Instead of eating here, how about driving me to Jericho Springs? I read an ad in the *Outcry*, the weekly newspaper, about Bustos' Mexican Restaurant. I'll buy lunch if you'll take me to Jericho. I need to stop at the pizzeria and let them know my situation, and then I need to go to the high school to see again what might be my classroom. Oh, if it's okay I need to find out where John Law's office is located. I have an appointment with him Thursday. Could I impose on you for that?" asked Karen.

Hurrying to the house to get Andy and her car keys, Ruth responded, "Impose? I'm glad to help you, friend. Besides, we can plan some strategies for you to snag one Adam Claymore. Rob calls him the Lone Ranger. You know like the old TV program. He fought for truth and justice. We are going to Adam's prayer meeting tonight at the church in Rock Creek."

"They stumble that run too fast," murmured Karen.

"Who?"

"What Friar Lawrence said in *Romeo and Juliet*. I don't want to get ahead of God, especially in matters of the heart. I already have a lot on my plate. The school district also wants me to help with a community study that sounds real interesting," shared Karen.

"Tell me more on our way. Karen, this is exciting. Thanks for coming to see me."

"Me too, Miss Karen," chirped Andy.

Ruth thought pensively and said, "I was trying to remember the actor's name. Didn't the Lone Ranger have an Indian side-kick that stood shoulder to shoulder with the Lone Ranger in the midst of trouble?"

"Tonto, I liked the story. It's connected to the Arthurian Legend and the principles of the Code of Chivalry. A hero with humble beginnings comes out of nowhere and leads people with truth and justice instead of revenge as the motivator. Let's see. Might for right, right for right, equal justice for all, making right that which is wrong, and proper treatment of women. Let's see, I think there's one more."

"We need all that. Do they teach the legend at school?" asked Ruth.

"I hope so; I'll find out," promised Karen, and then she added, "Yes is yes and no is no!"

Ruth drove, while Andy played with match box cars in the back seat, which allowed Karen to further update Ruth about the week's events to date. Karen told Ruth about using her top ten treasures in her decision making process, about Hannah and their adventure culminating in Roy's landing on the table on the hotel porch, and sitting on top of the mesa praying at dusk. Also, Karen told Ruth about someone stealing her pistol from her room and using it to shoot Deputy Butch in the back, and then how Deputy Cotton Candy retrieved it from the woods. Next, Karen told Ruth about her interviews with the school district officials and at the pizzeria, hiding out at Adam's house in Rock Creek, the school board meeting, and how she came to shoot Roy Sentry in the heel. Finally, Karen told Ruth she had seen the bearded man in the tan trench coat at the school board meeting with his new wife, that he didn't want to be recognized, and then Karen smiled and told Ruth about Adam.

Before driving into Jericho Springs from Ridge View, Karen asked Ruth to stop when Karen saw how the tree, which Dr. Wood had shown her on her tour, dominated the landscape in the distance. With a hogback ridge before them, they looked where the man made road parted the uplifted earth. Ridge to the right and to the left, narrow passage allowed only for the two lane highway and barrow pits leading from its shoulders for drainage. Not much of the city was visible except the magnificent tree. From the distance, the tree appeared lifeless to the naked eye, yet in recent days tiny buds had begun showing, especially when warm water from the heated pond had been gently poured upon its roots.

"Could we...," began Karen.

But completed by Ruth, "Investigate the tree after you do your errands? I'm with you."

"Looks like a rock slide behind it," commented Karen.

"Mom! Mom! Zat a sample of the story you told me 'bout faith moving mountains?" interjected Andy surprisingly. Drawn to the scene and the vision of the tree, Andy moved forward on the rear seat to peer over the front bench seat.

"Way to go, Son! We don't know, but maybe we can find out."

On a mission, these three aliens hurriedly accomplished Karen's tasks only to slow down to savor their enchilada entrees smothered with pork green chili, onions, and cheese at Bustos' Mexican Restaurant. They had devoured an order of hot sopapillas covered with powdered sugar and cinnamon and served with butter and honey. Karen had bitten off a small end of her sopapilla and demonstrated how to put butter and honey in the center. Since John Law's offices on Main Street were directly above Bustos', Karen located a side entrance leading to the second floor offices. Next, Karen went in the pizzeria, greeted Dorothy King, who was busily tossing a pie, and reported to the office of Jerry Sunday, the pizza store manager. Jerry and Dorothy were glad Karen got the teaching position and welcomed her full time help even if only for a few weeks. Karen committed to start working after she found a place and moved in. From the pizzeria, Karen visited the high school east of town and at first received a chilly reception from Mrs. Gelding, principal Alden's secretary. Karen asked to see the room she may be using and was directed down the main hallway. Since all doors were opened and cleaning crews hardly had taken notice, Karen was in and out without making any contact and without returning to the front office.

Since Ruth and Andy had been exploring the grounds, Karen reached in the driver side window and honked the horn. Getting their attention, Karen called out, "Mission accomplished!"

The two Brownings raced back to the car where Karen declared a tie with their arrival. Karen said, "Are you ready for the main event?"

Ruth responded with "Yes, but we better hurry in order for me to drop you off and get home before Rob shows up for dinner."

With the tree sighted, Karen and Ruth calculated the route and drove south on Main Street but slowed to observe Blair House and the vapors from the ponds. They continued to the end of Jericho Springs' city limits where Main Street becomes County Road 403. Ruth turned off the pavement and followed a dirt road, which headed up the canyon along the side of town next to the creek. At the crest of a hill before the road began a hairpin turn, Ruth stopped her Bronco west of town above the pond and mound where the tree stood. While climbing down slope, the trio heard cough, cough, sputter, cough, sputter, boom announcing the arrival of the old woodcutter in his gray pickup truck. All three turned and waved as the woodcutter drove by with a load of wood, and then the trio proceeded to climb to the top of the mound where Karen made her first discovery.

"This is an oddity! The assistant superintendent brought me here when he took me on a tour of the area. I became enthralled with this scene and just had to come back here. There has been some geothermal activity here," Karen said as Andy jumped into the center of a dry pool formed within the crater.

"Do you mean volcanic activity? Are we standing on an active volcano?" asked Ruth.

"Well, not much happened here, but based on how this pipe is positioned, my guess is it carried hot water from near the center of this dry pool to the house below. The water may have been hot enough for bathing or for kitchen use or maybe even to heat the house," Karen surmised, then she grasped the pipe and told Ruth and Andy, "Look at the vapor rising from the pond. The two are connected. The boulder behind us and off to the side might have something to do with what's happened here. The boulder must have hit this mound during a rock slide that happened not too many years ago. It probably cracked the inner core of the mound and caused water to drain out through a crack somewhere instead of rising to the top of the mound where it filled this dry pond. It probably joins with what flows through the culvert that provides drainage from somewhere above here. Look," Karen pointed, "where bubbles appear in the stream from the culvert. That must be where the hot water joins with the cold. Anyway that's my guess."

"What about the tree?" Andy asked.

"How do you think it got here?" wondered Ruth aloud.

"It's not native. I don't know how it managed to grow so large here of all places. Someone planted it long ago. My guess it's a Live Oak or related species that came west with original settlers," explained Karen, as the three investigators walked to the tree.

As they began to circle the tree counter clockwise, Ruth took notice and said, "Karen, at first it looked dead, but look here..." as she grasped a branch and examined how buds were beginning to appear on the east side of the tall oak tree.

Andy kicked one of many exposed roots and blurted, "Miss Karen, the root is wet and it's cool under the dirt. And look, look, the ground is wet."

Karen added, "We haven't had but a little rain, but look where water has pooled by the roots. I wonder if someone has been watering the tree."

"Wow, that's nice. It looks dead, but comin' back to life," Andy noted.

Ruth stood before the tree on the north side, mouth opened, and amazed, "Check this out you two! See the wood chips on the ground and the fresh carving in the bark. What do you suppose?"

"I'm not certain what I see," Karen said at first, then she sat on a large protruding root joint, "and I'm not the first to sit right here and look at the carving. Look how the ground has been scuffed, as if someone sat here digging the sides of their shoes into what soil is here. Perhaps whoever carved this sits right here and plans the picture and meditates on the design."

"It's beautiful, isn't it," marveled Ruth.

"It's a message," in an epiphany Karen replied, "I want to think on this and memorize what I see."

"I wanna see it, I wanna see it," said Andy, then he boldly said, "Mommy, I see it. It's a picture of a man. He's naked. He's at an altar. Something's on the altar. There's black things around the altar. The altar's before a tree, and the man's gonna' pick that apple off the tree. But what's that above the tree like a flower...?"

"A sunflower with its stalk or trunk descending to the ground and deeper, rooted deep down," added Karen, then concluding, "It's not finished!" Karen fell to her knees and prayed, and then reported, "I know what I must do."

Ruth and her son had followed suit and Ruth said, "Me too...." and after a little while Ruth reported, "Karen, we probably shouldn't be here," then she rose to look around, "There's an old lady by the house below us. Let's go. And a man and a woman have come out of a house down the street."

"Okay, Ruth, but let's ask about this tree tonight at the prayer meeting. Adam might know something about this. We had better hurry..."

"So, I can drop you off in Rock Creek and make it home in time to feed Rob and get to the prayer meeting," concluded Ruth.

"Mom, can we come back. I feel warm here like I just sat in the lap of somebody big and warm."

"Me, too, like I was being held in God's lap," answered his mother.

"Like you were resting your head against him and God had his arm around you," added Karen.

"Yes, Karen, you felt it too!" Ruth replied, and then asked, "Is it the tree or the mound that made us feel so warm?"

"No, it wasn't because of the tree, although it is certainly special or better yet unusual. It may have had something to do with the carving or the heart of the person who carved it. I think God chose to meet us there. Maybe to honor the artist who carved the message on the tree. But clearly, God spoke to me, not audibly but inside my head and we both felt God's presence."

"It was wonderful!" Ruth added and then softly sang, "Be still... and know... that I... am God...be still..."

Karen reminded all, "Remember, they stumble that run too fast. Let us seek wise counsel and biblical confirmation."

On the ride to Rock Creek, all three remained silent thinking about the tree and what they had seen. Karen didn't know the details, but knew it was tied to her coming to this place and her teaching assignment.

As Karen opened the door to Ruth's car in front of Adam's Rock Creek house, Ruth said, "God's got a plan…and you and I are involved in it together."

"That's what I received as well. See you later tonight," promised Karen.

Ruth and Andy waved enthusiastically when starting to head north for home. Karen watched as they left processing all that happened so far today. She looked around behind her at trees before the rim, the mouth of the canyon where mist from the stream that drained runoff from the mesa began enveloping the thicket of birch trees west of the highway. Looking affectionately at the driveway entrance to the church in the glen and north at the row of houses including Adam's, Karen paused when looking at the convenience store, and noted 4:30 p.m. on her watch.

Bold and courageous, Karen crossed the highway, decided to see if she had any messages at the hotel, and then rested in the lobby before eating at the restaurant. Quietly sitting in the red overstuffed chair, she watched the arrivals and departures at the convenience store. Thinking back to her encounter with God under the Live Oak Tree, she began to understand how important the community leadership study could be in helping the valley's leadership. The study would help community leaders to not only identify what the leadership perceived as problems, but it would also identify those leaders who would be interested in mobilizing resources to find solutions to those identified problems. After one week in Rock Creek, Karen identified five crime related problems including drug trafficking at the convenience store as well as pornography, prostitution at the hotel and the Asherah House, and gambling at the tobacco store. She also listed the night riders as gang related activity and wondered about under age drinking. Becoming contemplative, Karen realized the real problem was a spiritual one. Who profits from the situation? Who has the power to control what's going on? Who would resist change? She leaned back in the chair and slept until awakened just before six o'clock by cough, cough, sputter, cough, sputter, boom.

HEALING BEGINS

CHAPTER 16

"If my people, who are called by my name, will humble
themselves and pray and seek my face and turn from their
wicked ways, then I will hear from heaven, and I will forgive
their sin and will heal their land." 2 Chronicles 7:14

Awakened in more than one sense, Karen bounded from her rest, down the
porch steps, and trotted across the parking lot, but was reminded again
about stumbling for running too fast. Heeding the warning, Karen paused at the
highway before crossing over and was spared the sudden arrival of automobiles
carrying the Bond family, Izzy and Janine, the Brownings, and one more auto each
from Jericho Springs and Ridge View. A few folks walked to church from houses
neighboring Adam's Rock Creek home, the one time home of Mary McNaughton
Claymore. The recent arrivals joined Adam and ranch hands Rabbit, Barney, and
a wrangler named Pilgrim plus the old woodcutter.

Presiding, Adam opened with prayer and led the flock in singing "Amazing
Grace" acappella. Adam began introductions of newcomers beginning with Karen
and asked each of them to tell about themselves and share a prayer request.

Adam introduced his friend Karen who said, "Hello, I'm Karen Gustafson,
and I've just been hired as a new secondary school teacher. I've been here almost
a week and have explored much of the valley. I've already made several friends
and an enemy or two. I believe God brought me here. I didn't know why until this
afternoon. I'm no one special but God has a plan for me to help build his kingdom
here. I'm far from perfect, and I confess things have not always gone well for me
at church. I didn't know about his plan until this afternoon when I stood at the
base of that Live Oak on top that volcanic mound with a dried up pool on top."

"Huerfano!"

"It's a little orphan."

"Let her finish."

Karen continued, "God chose to meet me there. Father God held me on his
lap as I bowed on my knees to him and prayed. He told me I would be healed here

and that I am to share his gospel in what I say and do. God told me that he is at work here and the walls of resistance will be falling down. Soon I will be moving here and will be working the rest of the summer at the pizzeria in Jericho Springs. I need prayer to find housing, prayer for my parents I will be leaving behind, and also for a meeting I have tomorrow at noon. I need prayer for wisdom to understand God's message this afternoon."

The people rejoiced and prayed for Karen!

Next Adam asked Rob Browning to come forth and introduce his family, and then said, "You remember Rob. He has met with us for several months."

Rob began, "Thank you for the warm reception you gave me when I arrived and have continued. Adam has led me in a discipleship group for weeks on end with Rabbit, Barnabas, and Pilgrim. Thank you, Gentlemen, for your friendship. I'd like to introduce my lovely wife Ruth, who usually doesn't want to speak before a crowd…"

"Tonight I do! I have something I have to say," said Ruth rising from the pew, "My son Andrew and I arrived here on the same bus as did Karen Gustafson. Andy and I saw Jesus in Karen. It was her eyes, and we made friends with her in the parking lot outside the Stage Stop Hotel. Something wonderful happened today. Karen came for a visit. Rev. Claymore dropped her off this morning, and we spent the day together, my boy and I. It's as Karen said. We drove to Jericho Springs from Ridge View. We stopped before entering town when we saw the tree through a gap in the ridge. Karen had some errands to do, and she did 'em. What we wanted to do was go see the tree. And we did. We parked on the road above that big old house, and we walked down to the tree. I knelt before the tree and saw this carving in the bark. You've got to see it. I closed my eyes and prayed, and then it happened. I felt like a little girl and Jesus cupped each side of my face with his hands. It was wonderful. In my head I heard him. Not with my ears. But it was like he spoke to me. 'Rest in me, build my kingdom.' I know God has a plan for me, and it involves Karen and what is happening here at this little church."

"Hallelujah!" the people said.

"I, too, need prayer. Please pray that God prepare me to be the wife my husband needs and the woman God wants me to be. Give me the strength to be consistent with my prayer life, in reading the Bible, and in sharing the Gospel. Oh, I forgot, see that's how I am. God told me I was like a cracked pot and the beauty of Jesus was going to shine through the cracks. I'm not sure what that means, but God will show me."

Andy jumped up and said, "I wuz there. I saw a man in the tree. He spoke to me too, but in pictures. I'm s'posed to be put under water, all the way, and be raised up by my father." Andrew looked at his father and asked, "Can I Daddy? Can I?"

Rob looked at Adam, who nodded, then answered, "Yes, my son, Pastor will talk with us first."

Adam added, "We have a baptismal service in two Sundays."

Those gathered sang the chorus "Jesus is Lord," then prayed for the Brownings.

Next, Adam asked for the Bonds to come forward, and then said, "You're at least aware of the Bonds if you have home delivery of the Denver Post and/or the *Outcry* weekly. Recently, the Bonds met with tragedy."

Ken Bond introduced his wife Katarina Rose and daughters Kristin and Krystal, and said, "Recently, we moved here and have been delivering the newspapers ever since. We moved into a trailer on the ridge east of the Valley Highway on Colorado 96. Fortunately, we survived a fire that completely destroyed the trailer. We lost everything." The four Bonds put their arms around each other. "Before coming here I had a massive heart attack. Although I have a bachelor's degree in Christian ministry and a master's in educational administration, I was attending seminary at the Conservative Baptist Seminary in Denver to become a pastor. When the heart attack happened, I survived, but I couldn't continue my studies. The Hebrew letters danced all over the pages. It was all Greek to me."

All shared in his laughter. The Bond women both laughed and wept.

Ken continued, "It's not by chance we have come here. God directed our footsteps. We read in his word to rest and return. We had been directed to come home to Colorado from New Jersey where we had been living, then I entered seminary. More specifically, God brought us here. Recently, we read an ad in the newspaper about exchanging labor for lodging and we have a meeting tomorrow in Jericho Springs. If we are accepted, well, that would be answered prayer."

"Where are you staying?" asked one of the prayer warriors.

"Thankfully, Adam took us in. We are staying at his ranch on the mesa and we are enjoying Rabbit's cooking."

"Ah, don't tell him that! Barney and I have to live with him!" To which Rabbit playfully punched Pilgrim's shoulder, and more laughter ensued.

"One thing you ought to know. The fire was arson. Someone, maybe several, were involved, according to the sheriff. I think they didn't like us being here."

"That's because you're a newcomer. There's a sickness here."

"A lot of people don't want newcomers to move here, especially now."

"It's all about money, greed, entitlement. People think they deserve what's not theirs."

Adam added, "All of that and more. Including most of my relatives! Isn't it sad that people seem unable to be glad for others who become fortunate and receive unmerited blessing. They covet the good fortune of their neighbors?"

The congregation murmured, and someone said, "Times are tough for a lot of us."

"You're right and I hope you never lose everything you have. I hope you never have a heart attack," Bond concluded.

Adam said, "Let us pray for the Bonds that God will use them mightily and that they receive his blessing along the way."

All prayed earnestly for the Bonds.

Finally, Adam called Janine forward and told her to bring her gentleman. While Janine and Izzy came forward Adam explained, "You all know about Janine. She's no newcomer. Janine teaches English at the high school, and she's going to be married here."

"I didn't know you were dating," someone blurted out.

"I confess we made a mistake. I was in a hurry. We went to the court house and got a marriage license. We had a civil ceremony, but then we went to Adam's ranch and asked Pastor to perform a proper Christian ceremony," explained Janine.

Adam interrupted and said, "I convinced them to favor us with my performing a wedding ceremony in two Sunday's, after they go through pre-marital counseling with me."

Andrew shouted, "When I get baptized?"

"Yes, Andrew! The Lord's day will be full of blessings."

Janine continued, "I want you all to meet the love of my life, who like the prodigal has returned home," and then Janine wept, but added, "He promised he would marry me when we were kids!"

"Ahhhhhhhh!" said the crowd.

Karen leaned over to Ruth sitting next to her and quietly said, "They stumble..." to which Ruth finished, "Who run too fast."

Izzy took it all in, wrung his hands, and confessed to all those gathered, "Years ago, I lived here. In a fit of anger, I sinned greatly against God and my parents. I took a box of gold nuggets and ran away. I made certain no one would find me. God worked in my life and required me to return here and make right the wrong I had done. I also left behind my sweetheart, whom I love dearly. My name is Ezra Blair."

Silence came over the flock, as they processed what that meant.

An old woman said, "You're little Izzy Blair. I knew your mother and your father. Honey, Peter and Lydia loved you, dearly, and forgive me for saying this but you broke their hearts when you ran away. I didn't say that to hurt you. You were hurt enough already. What you need to know is that they forgave you. I know. I was Lydia's best friend. I live across the street from the Blair House."

"Why, you're Rachael McNaughton! You were my babysitter. I remember you and your chocolate chip cookies," Izzy reminisced.

"Bless you boy, you remember me," answered Rachael.

"Indubitably! It is inconceivable I would forget," smiled Izzy in response. "Also, Miss Rachel, you are my piano teacher, who worked with me for years. I plan to play for you regularly, and you will be able to teach me more!"

"Pastor, there are several reasons we need to pray for this couple. I'm very happy for their wedding, but they need to be kept safe, especially until tomorrow's city council meeting," said Pilgrim.

One of the flock slipped out the back door to go tell others, as another newcomer entered and took a seat at the back of the chapel.

"I reckon we will need to get them to a safe place tonight and keep them there until tomorrow night," said Adam, "and I'm not real certain where that will be."

"Then we need to pray about that and ask God to provide safe shelter. But don't tell anyone where it is, not even us," said a prayer warrior.

The congregation prayed for Janine and Izzy, their wedding and marriage, Izzy's healing, and their safety.

Adam noted the new arrival as much as he saw the Judas who left to tell others and perhaps to summon them that a rightful heir to the Blair House, the gold, and water rights had truly entered the town. The truth was that the prayer meeting may soon be invaded. The old woodcutter disappeared for a few minutes and returned with a long barrel shotgun, a very imposing weapon, which no one in the church had seen him carry inside. Adam was not finished, "We have another visitor who arrived just minutes before. Won't you participate? If you are uncomfortable or not a believer, we understand."

"No, but thanks for your consideration. In fact, I need your prayers and help," said the man who came forward to introduce himself, "I'm a detective from Denver. My name is Caleb Jones. I've been staying this last week at the Stage Stop Hotel, where I registered under an alias. My sister was Gloria Jones, whose body was found under the bridge near here on County Road 403. Last night another woman was murdered south of here in Quail Point. The details match what happened here."

"But, Butch is in jail," stated another prayer warrior.

"Was it Buddy Smith?" spoke a voice from outside the doorway, and then she continued, "Help me, help me please!"

"It's one of the McNaughton grandmothers."

"Beatrice, what has happened to you," said Janine as many gathered around Beatrice and brought her forward where she could be heard.

Blood covered Beatrice's face and she was deeply chilled. Adam grabbed a blanket from the pastor's office at the front of the chapel where the side door led to the outside. Returning he also grabbed a towel and dipped it in the drinking water on his desk. Carefully, he covered her with the blanket and he wiped the blood from her face and brow.

"Last night after school board meeting and the shootout where my great grandson was rightfully taken to jail, I walked along the road toward the chapel. I planned to sit and meditate on the bench outside, but changed my mind when I heard the hellions raising a ruckus. I decided to go the back way to my room at the hotel. You know... I wanted to walk where I used to play. That's where I got my first kiss. I should have married that boy, but no, the McNaughtons didn't like him even though he was related, and I listened."

"Beatrice, you need to stick to the story," instructed Adam.

"Yes, dear, you look just like him, Adam. He too was a Claymore and your granddaddy. Anyway, I was crossing the highway when Buddy Smith hot-rodded right by me. He threw a beer bottle and hit me right here in the head...," Beatrice paused as she touched her scalp wound, "He did it on purpose. He meant to kill me! And I lost my balance and rolled into the birch thicket. I crawled to here, but I wrenched my shoulder and did something to my hip," as Beatrice took hold of her soiled dress and continued, "I'm so cold. The mist blanketed me and the night was dreadful. Please take me to my daughter's house. I really hurt and I've got a bad cold coming on, I know it, but I need to speak tomorrow night at city council," Beatrice explained.

"If you are able to, dear, if not we will have you write a letter one of us will read in your place. We will call your daughter, but Gramma Bee, you need to go to the hospital or to your daughter's," insisted Adam, to which Beatrice nodded agreement.

Rabbit volunteered to take Beatrice to the hospital, while Barney used the telephone in the pastor's office to call her daughter, Rosa Jaramillo, to meet her mother at the hospital in Ridge View. Barney then called the emergency room to get a wheelchair and room ready. The rest of the flock knew what to do. They held hands and formed a circle around Bee and prayed both for Gramma Beatrice and Caleb Jones. The flock prayed for God to reveal the truth and to provide justice.

Adam closed the meeting by requesting everyone that can to be here tomorrow night at 5 p.m. for a meeting and then prayer walks beginning no later than six o'clock Adam said, "Part of you need to cover Rock Creek, while the rest of you need to walk in Jericho Springs starting at the court house where city council meets at seven o'clock. At least one of my men will be at each location..." Adam paused, "It's time the body of Christ go on the offensive."

"We need to invade this town for the Lord and claim it for God's kingdom... like what Mary Claymore urged us to do," said prayer warrior Priscilla King, wife of Arthur King, the elementary school principal, and mother-in-law of Dorothy, the pizza maker and sister of Aquila Parson.

"My sister is right. We need to walk each street and stop before every house and building to pray for the people and their safety," added Aquila Parson, school board member and Judge Parson's wife. "My Randolph must take notice of all this disgraceful business. And I'll speak to Rosa, Beatrice's daughter. She used to be president of the PTA. And I'll talk to Willa Sentry, our current school board president."

"Please call Red McNaughton and let him know about his aunt," asked Adam, and then he closed in prayer.

"I'll bring pop and pizzas at 5 p.m., so nobody needs to eat before coming," offered Jerry Sunday, manager of the pizzeria.

"How much do we need to contribute?"

"It's my contribution to the effort. I have to work tomorrow, so just let me provide the food and drink. I'll bring plastic-ware, plates, cups, and napkins," concluded Jerry.

"Daddy, this'll be great! Can I eat and drink all I want? Will it be okay if I belch and...you know the manly thing to do!" asked Andy looking sheepishly.

"Absolutely not, young man, you'll be on your best manners," said Ruth, now embarrassed as she gave Rob a scolding look.

It was then that Andy returned the two rocks he had taken from the alms box on Sunday. As Adam talked with various people, Andy passed by the Pastor and tried to talk with Adam, who was eager to catch up with Janine and Izzy Blair. Not being able to get Adam's attention, Andy slipped the two stones into Adam's suit coat pocket.

Adam took charge. Holding back Janine and Izzy, who at first protested but then listened, Adam told them to go through his office and out the side door, and then to go home with the Brownings. Next, he had Rob and Ruth move their car around the side to take Izzy and Janine home with them. Also, Adam reminded them to be careful when they got home as people would soon be on the prowl. Additionally, Adam told the Bond family he knew Ken had to get up early to meet the Denver Post truck, but that they should follow Rabbit to the ranch and stay there until permanent lodging could be arranged. Asking Karen to walk with the others heading for the north end of town, he told her to break off from them at his Rock Creek house. In a little while, he would be back to meet her for dinner at the hotel. Adam reminded Karen there was a Winchester in the coat closet. He told Barney to make all accommodations at the ranch house and to encourage them to be wise in what they say and do. Demanding silence and waiting until all were listening, he gave one more order for all to hear. Adam beseeched all to pray for God to speak to each one, so everyone would know what to do individually and as a church. Next, Adam quoted *2 Chronicles 7:14* and then said now is the time for all of us to get right with God, so God will heal our land. All nodded in agreement.

As the crowd filed out, Adam asked both Detective Jones and the grizzly old woodcutter to insure safe passage for everyone to which Jones nodded and the woodcutter gave a thumbs-up. Adam asked Jones to meet with him later to let him know what was going on. Jones informed Adam that he was not at liberty to go into details, as it was an open case. Jones told Adam that he needed to talk with Adam's good friend, John Law, who Jones would be meeting with later tonight in Jericho Springs. All carried out Adam's orders.

Ken Bond, his wife Katarina Rose, and their daughters Kristin and Krystal drove County Road 403 on the road to Jericho Springs. Ken passed the turnoff to the ranch house on the flat, and instead, he followed the road west and stopped above the tall oak tree. Ken said, "Girls, we need to pray for the valley. I hope justice and truth prevail. I pray our offensive will be successful in advancing God's kingdom here on earth."

Robert Browning drove north on the Valley Highway with his wife and son plus Janine and Izzy as passengers, but turned east and up to the top of the ridge where the remains of the burned out trailer stood proclaiming the injustice of what happened to the Bond family. Ruth, Rob, and Andrew joined Janine and Ezra in prayer for peace in the valley, provision for the Bonds, and safety for all the prayer warriors. They sought law and order, not revenge.

Since Aquila and Priscilla shared a ride together, Priscilla drove her sister toward their homes in Ridge View. Priscilla asked her sister to pray for travel mercies on the way home. Priscilla entered town and stopped her automobile outside the Cozy Corner Café. With her sister beside her, Priscilla said, "I think we are fortunate to have all those new people here. Change is coming, and it's about time. Us old timers need to help."

Aquila added, "We need to share the power."

"It won't be easy, but it's time folks like us cooperate with what God's doing instead of being stumbling blocks."

"Yes, Priscilla, I can't help the past, God love us, but I'm going to find out where he's working and I am going to join him."

"We got a good start tonight! Aquila, look, the opposition!" Priscilla said pointing at the Cozy Corner Café.

Priscilla and Aquila watched a dozen of the valley's finest exit the café and pile into their cars and trucks. They recognized Red, Irv, and Ellis plus Buddy, Roy, and Maurice Wood. Priscilla noted physical descriptions, while Aquila wrote down license plate numbers. Next, the sisters prayed for victory. East, west, and north were now covered.

Throughout the valley telephone lines were buzzing, as word about Ezra Blair relayed from telephone to telephone and back again. Judas had done his work, as residents gossiped about Ezra, the rightful heir to the Blair fortune. Some speculated whether or not he would see tomorrow's sunlight or make it to city council's meeting Thursday night. Cooler heads proclaimed caution that there had been discussion about his not really being a child of the Blair's and may not rightfully receive the property. When Amanda Sentry heard, she called John Law, who swore when he heard his advice had not been followed by Izzy. The marriage bureau clerk spread word about the Blair marriage license and civil wedding at the courthouse performed by Judge Randolph Parson. More speculated about where the couple was staying. Another round of arguing ensued between spouses, as their despair heightened the tension of marital discord prompted by lost opportunity for gold and water rights. Night riders roared up and down roadways looking for victims to terrorize. Sheriff Bailey ordered his deputies to cover all three cities, but he decided to stake out the Blair House and the home of Janine Crowfoot himself to see if the young couple would spend the night at her house.

Instead of waiting for Adam to pick her up at the Rock Creek house, Karen met him at the Stage Stop Restaurant after carefully crossing the highway wary of the increased traffic. Patrons in the bar commented that there goes Annie Oakley as Karen passed by, and she heard another ask if anyone had seen Hannah, the desk clerk. Adam interrupted his conversation with a Ridge View pastor, excused himself, and rose from his seat, as Karen entered the dining hall. Conversation stopped and all eyes turned to her as if she owned the place. It was as if her presence commanded an audience, which it did. Some knew about the incident on the roof top resulting in Roy's plunge to tables below. Others wondered how her pistol appeared to be used in the shooting of Butch McNaughton. Another questioned how she shot Roy in the heel while protecting Hannah and Deputy Cotton Candy. A cluster knew Karen had been appointed to a teaching position the night before at the school board meeting in spite of being a newcomer. Still others wondered how she knew Adam Claymore, or more precisely, what the two of them were doing together. One said he heard Karen was a special agent here on an assignment from the Denver Police Department.

Unaccustomed to the attention, Karen promptly sat down, flipped her hair that was no longer there, and looked at her menu. Immediately, she realized Adam was looking at her the same way as the others. "What are you doing?" Karen asked.

"Admiring a remarkable woman," answered Adam, "you have totally impressed everyone, including me. I hope you will keep in contact with me when you move here. I'd be disappointed if you didn't."

"I wouldn't have it otherwise. I look forward to your preaching and teaching. Tonight's prayer meeting was miraculous. All the newcomers testifying to how God is at work in their lives, and how you took charge at the end. You barked out orders like in *2 Thessalonians 5*, as an officer telling the troops how to enter battle," marveled Karen, "and I'm proud to call you friend."

Taking Karen's hand in his own, Adam softly said, "Then, you really are coming back?"

"Absolutely," Karen replied, "I want to be a part of what is happening here. God is at work. You know that when I rode the bus to Rock Creek, I was finishing a crossword puzzle that included clues about Canaanite cities and Jericho. One of the words was vestibule, and driving north in the canyon then coming upon the entrance to Rock Creek...well, it looked like a walled fortress and the town of Rock Creek is the vestibule where the defenders of the city engaged the enemy. In this case, we are the enemies, the newcomers. Trouble is we didn't have a clue. And then there's Jericho. I think the walls are tumbling down. Tomorrow night will tell."

"Good analogy. It is good to have reinforcements. You know the opposition includes a lot of my family and friends. They are mostly good people who think they are entitled to the Blair wealth. Not only are they covetous and jealous, they are fearful of losing control. It's greed or lust, like the scripture says: *For the love of money is a root of all kinds of evil...1 Timothy 6:10a,* " acknowledged Adam.

With that said, Sarah arrived at their table to take their order and said, "Well, if it isn't his lordship and Miss Annie Oakley. What'll it be?"

"Be nice, Sarah," chided Adam, and then he order Morris Goodenough's favorite, the Rocky Mountain Cheeseburger Deluxe with fries and a cola.

"I'll have the same. Sarah, in a minute we will be giving thanks for our food, and I'd like to pray for you. How can we pray for you?" Karen asked genuinely.

Stunned, Sarah replied, "I'm good, I'm good," and she scurried away to submit the order only to promptly return where she sat down next to Karen.

Quietly Sarah said, "Karen, you need to be careful the next couple of days," then Sarah paused and said with tears in her eyes, "Karen, I'm pregnant. The father could be any number of guys, except Adam. Pray for me. I don't know what to do."

Karen asserted, "Don't abort it. Take care of yourself. I'm going away but I will be back within two weeks. Let's talk when I return. Okay?"

"Yes, yes, don't forget me," implored Sarah.

"I promise…."

Karen and Adam sat silently for a couple of minutes, and then he gave thanks for the food and prayed for a waitress named Sarah. After dinner Adam reluctantly consented to Karen's request to stay the night at his Rock Creek home. He advised her not to go outside and to keep his Winchester handy, as there would be trouble tonight. Adam revealed that after the prayer meeting he had called Sheriff Bailey from the hotel and asked for a deputy to watch over Janine's home and the Blair estate. Bailey promised to cover the surveillance himself unless there was an emergency somewhere in the night.

Adam walked Karen to his home and predicted, "Storm clouds are gathering and the moon likely will be hidden behind the clouds. It will be dark and stormy tonight. Call if you need me," and then he gently kissed her cheek for the first time. In response, Karen embraced Adam and gave him a first kiss he would never forget. All he could do was say thank you and leave.

Before dressing for bed, Karen decided to take a walk through the church yard and over the bridge to the trail leading to the mesa where she had sat previously over-looking the town of Rock Creek. She wanted to pray to have evil unmasked. Wondering if she would meet Adam's colt or dog on top the mesa or even a black bear, Karen felt inspired by both the prayer meeting and her time with Ruth at the tree in Jericho Springs above the Blair house. She relished the idea of sitting where Adam's wife had sat years ago and in having taken up Mary Claymore's pastime of praying for the town below and all of Rock Creek Valley. Arriving at the top of the mesa, Karen found the bench just before heavy laden storm clouds blackened the sky and blocked the light of the moon. Residential lights had already been switched off and only two street lights at the old school building and east of the bridge on County Road 403 illuminated the out-of-doors, while dim lights from the Stage Stop Hotel barely revealed stairs leading from the porch.

Two figures, each a hunter, one evil and one good, caught glimpse of Karen, one from the hotel porch and one from below the bridge. The one below the bridge watched the one on the porch, since he had exited the hotel and sat on the porch. The one on the porch lost sight of Karen as she left the road and entered the church parking lot, while the other by the county road noticed her only after she left the footbridge and began to climb the path to the mesa. Neither to startle her ascent nor to forewarn the hunter on the porch, the latter sprinted to the footbridge stealthily. Both awaited her return to the footbridge, the hunter from the hotel porch hid in the dogwood bushes just east of the bridge, unaware the latter hid in the cottonwood tree above the bridge.

After Karen descended the trail, she hesitated before crossing the footbridge. She listened to the waters below and peered into the darkness, which revealed nothing. Hesitantly, she advanced onto the footbridge wishing she had brought a flashlight from Adam's house as well as the Winchester. Fear enveloped her and now she wished she had listened to Adam's wisdom to stay inside tonight. She had prayed on the mesa completing prayer coverage over the valley from all four directions. Grasping the handrail, she inched her way to the other side. From behind the bushes the hunter from the hotel porch rushed Karen. Clouds separated and she saw her attacker. When she recognized his face, she turned and fled but stumbled. Karen struck her head on a side rail as she tumbled head first into dirt beside the bridge post. Blood gushed forth from a scalp wound, stained the rail, and formed a puddle on both the bridge flooring and on the moist ground.

When the hunter from the hotel porch stopped pursuit of his quarry, he became the hunted when from above he heard a mournful cry. From the tree canopy another hunter skillfully ran the length of the bridge top rail and expertly scissor-necked the first hunter with his legs. As the second hunter spun himself over the bridge rail, he pulled the first hunter with him. The second hunter grabbed the bridge floor with both hands, but the body of the first plunged into rushing waters below. His head cracked against jagged boulders, and then he was sucked unseen into a swirling pool that dragged his body to the depths below. The first hunter, now victim, would not now resurface.

Unconscious, Karen lay at the mercy of the assailant of the first hunter. The assailant looked for but could not see the first hunter in the rushing water. Gently, Karen's protector lifted her to himself and carried her to his truck. Had anyone been on the porch at the Stage Stop Hotel, he or she would have seen her protector put Karen in the cab of his truck and would have heard the acclamation as the Gray Whiz slowly eased its way out of town with a cough, cough, sputter, cough, sputter, boom.

Picking up speed as he rounded the curve to ascend the road above the Live Oak below, the old woodcutter sped past mine tailings and rock slide, through a sparse forest and into the clearing above with his engine announcing his approach. He turned off county maintained road and onto his rutted path to the old cabin in the forest where he worked his saw mill to provide firewood and sawdust for the people in the valley below, leftovers from the milling of planed board. Safely tucked beyond sight, the grisly old woodcutter parked near his cabin's doorway where his lovely, blonde friend opened the door and waved at him. This was twice he had rescued women in distress from evil that hunted and killed women, some virtuous and some not. The old woodcutter had fulfilled Adam's charge to make certain all got home safely.

Once Karen had been tended to by capable hands, the old woodcutter waved goodnight and climbed the ladder to the loft above. Karen wakened to view beautiful blue eyes and long blonde tresses that flowed nearly to the young woman's waist.

Holding a wet compress on Karen's forehead, the blue eyed blonde with rosy cheeks assured Karen that she was safe. She asked Karen who she was and how she happened to get there in such condition. She told Karen she had been at the cabin herself for months and had seen no one and no one had explored the area looking for her to her surprise. Karen told her story about how and why she had come to the valley.

"Last night I was hired by the school board to replace Jill Lowenstein, a social studies and physical science teacher at the high school," said Karen with a knowing smile, "I heard she was quite lovely, a blue eyed blonde. Perhaps you know her?"

"Indeed I do! I had an accident and for several months I knew nothing. That old man nursed me back to health, and only recently my memory returned."

Karen replied, "I was introduced to him at tonight's prayer meeting at the church in the glen in Rock Creek. He was at the school board meeting on Tuesday night, but he just grunted."

"I don't think he can talk. I'm not sure he has a tongue. I've never seen one when we eat. He is unusually kind and gentle, yet gruff at times and occasionally scary. I don't even know his name, but he spends a lot of time reading his Bible in quiet meditation. Sometimes it sounds like he is weeping, then he rigorously exercises inside and outside. He practices swinging from a rope to the loft and down to the front door. Outside he runs along logs and vaults to high points on rock outcroppings, as if he had his own obstacle course. And...I really feel safe here in the woods with him, even when he is gone," said Jill.

"How does he live here, alone in the woods with no electricity?" inquired Karen.

"I believe he receives a pension. I don't know if it's from the government or not. He has a battery operated cassette player. When I can I'm going to buy him the Bible on cassette, " replied Jill. "Look around. He makes beautiful wood carvings of the animals and mountain scenes he sees in the back country. A mountain with a slide area with a scar that looks like a buffalo or a lamb, twin peaks that resemble breasts, a large mesa with a stream that flows from it, the little volcano by the Blair house with the huge tree, but with leaves all over, not how it looks today. And there are more that he has sold."

"Wow!" Karen exclaimed as she examined some of the work and added, "I think I've seen some of his work on the tree behind the Blair house."

Jill clarified, "That's across the street from where I live."

"Then you are Jill Lowenstein and you room with Janine Crowfoot," said Karen. "I bet you don't know that Janine got married!"

"No way, she never dated. She's waiting for some guy to come back to town. He ran off when he found out that the people who raised him weren't his parents. She said he felt both abandoned and betrayed. He figured his father didn't want him and that the Blairs deceived him. He didn't know who he was and flipped out. I told her she was crazy to wait for him. She could have dated some really nice guys."

"That's him! They got married at the courthouse and they were at the school board meeting Tuesday night. I guess the pastor of the church refused to perform a marriage ceremony until they completed a six session marriage counseling program with him," explained Karen.

"Izzy Blair has returned as Janine said he would. It is her dream come true and he is the groom and the pastor would be Adam Claymore!" continued Jill, "Adam deserves his reputation as a stickler!"

Karen's face flushed, "I know, I've had the pleasure of spending some time with him. He is quite proper, and really, he is a champion for many people in the valley."

"Mine wasn't meant to be a negative comment. He is very dependable. You can count on Adam to do what is right and good," Jill concluded, then added, "you have a crush on him, don't you...?"

Smiling, Karen could not deny her feelings, "I haven't been here long enough to have one, I mean, I don't want to rush into something. I haven't even moved here. Tomorrow, I have a noon time meeting at the offices of a local attorney, John Law."

"You're responding to the ad in the paper about helping to restore a house in exchange for lodging." When Karen nodded, Jill continued, "I am too. I'm not certain how that will work out. I room with Janine at her house, and since she's married, she won't want another woman in the kitchen with her husband."

"They will both be at the meeting tomorrow, Izzy and Janine. You know most people think you are dead. The school board just hired me to take your place, if you don't show up. How are you going to handle that?" asked Karen.

"Good question. Here's the deal. The old man is going to take me, us, to the meeting. He will be on guard, and if there is trouble, he is quite capable of taking care of us. Whatever his story is, he can be a real bad dude. I watched him slit the neck of a mountain lion without being scathed. He was quicker than the cat, then he gutted the animal as it was bleeding out," Jill revealed, "I know it's hard to believe. I didn't and I saw it. He must have been in a special forces unit in the war. Anyway, after the meeting, I'm to meet with John Law. He will tell me what to do."

"I could use some sleep. Where can I lie down?" Karen asked.

"We have the couch and the bed. Take your pick."

"Couch, if there's a blanket."

"One question for you, Karen, what happens to you when I show up?"

"I signed a contract to fill your position, but if you show up, I become a permanent substitute teacher and project manager to do a community leadership identification process for the superintendent and the two school principals. It's intended to help them include community leadership on advisory committees and special task forces. They want to build a community based communications system, all of that to help solve community and school problems. Oh, the school leadership will also work with the city administration to start a community foundation."

Jill then made this suggestion, "I would go easy explaining all that. A lot of people may feel threatened by and mistrust both the school board and city council. It sounds like a good thing, but politicians have a way of perverting things for personal benefit."

"I think that's why they have me conducting the interviews. I'm an outsider and I'm new."

"You will have to be careful about having a relationship with Adam," Jill asserted. "You'll find out what I mean. Anyway, let's hit the sack."

"Okay, Jill Lowenstein, mystery woman who returns tomorrow to the Rock Creek Valley. Let's pray for your safety," yawned Karen, as she reclined on the couch and went right to sleep.

"You too, Karen, you may be in for quite a surprise when you learn what's going on here. May God protect your naivety," Jill said as she turned down the lantern wicks and went to bed knowing reinforcements had arrived to aide her hero, Adam Claymore.

Sheriff Bailey had followed the Gray Whiz out of town to where the old woodcutter turned onto the rutted road. Many times before, Bailey had watched the truck climb through the woods up the side of the mountain, then suddenly stop and disappear. Bailey never followed him, but stayed below. Bailey had investigated the saw mill and surrounding sheds by the county road finding nothing to be suspicious. Bailey didn't know the old woodcutter's history, but reckoned he was a positive force in the community. The sheriff returned to town at the sound of ruckus and a shotgun firing.

At the Blair house, Buddy Smith had led the night riders in a spree of smashing windows. The night riders had prepared torches to ignite Blair House, when from across the street, neighbor Rachael McNaughton hurt herself by discharging her deceased husband's shotgun in their direction. Before coming outside the old lady had called the sheriff's office and talked with Deputy Candy who told her the sheriff should be in the area. Candy described Buddy Smith's car and Rachael confirmed it was parked on the street. Immediately, Candy thought the little old lady might end up in trouble, so Candy answered the call herself.

Other neighbors suddenly appeared outside their homes to help Rachael when sirens announced approaching law enforcement. The neighbors were not ready to shoot at anyone. As the hoodlums sped away, neighbors rushed to extinguish a grass fire begun by a torch dropped by one of the vandals. Some cars escaped Sheriff Bailey by turning east on 403 then right on the road to Wolf City through Claymore Flats. Others headed north on Main Street and out of Jericho Springs, but turned around when Deputy Candy turned her cruiser sideways in the road at the gap in the hogback. Siren blaring, Candy stood, leaning over the hood of her police cruiser, with shotgun aimed toward the approaching traffic. Candy caught occupants of two cars as they crashed together when attempting to turn around. Two other cars hid in the darkness behind the high school, while the last three sped east on 403 to Rock Creek. At the Stage Stop Hotel bar only one of the night riders stopped, while the other two vandals sped north on the Valley Highway to escape detection.

Leaving his car in the hotel parking lot, Buddy Smith fled his hotrod and ran to the church across the parking lot in a vain attempt to avoid the arrival of more deputies. Buddy's effort proved futile. Recognizing Buddy's hotrod, the deputies called Buddy by name and pursued him. Buddy sprinted through the cemetery but tripped and fell where Karen had fallen earlier against the bridge side rail and into the moist dirt on the west bank of the creek. Coincidently, Karen's blood, mixed into soil kept moist by mist from the waterfall, now mingled with Buddy Smith's blood and stained his clothing. This would make him a suspect in the assault on Karen and later a suspect in the death of Sam Gelding, local insurance representative to both the school board and city council. Desperately, Buddy would plead innocent to both charges.

In his stupidity, Buddy swore at the deputies and resisted arrest. Deputies enjoyed administering paybacks for what he had done to Beatrice and other innocent residents. They laughed heartily and charged Buddy with every citation they could think of in hopes something would stick.

Unfortunately, the real perpetrators escaped unscathed, as Whitney "Red" McNaughton, Irv and Ellis Moss made it home without detection. The Moss' stepfather Maurice Wood had instigated the plan, but had not taken part in any of the actual vandalism. After all, Wood was the Assistant Superintendent of Schools and too old to engage in such activities.

Sheriff Bailey booked all those captured, impounded vehicles, and called influential parents. Bailey knew he would have quite a report to present Thursday night to city council.

TRUTH REVEALED

CHAPTER 17

*"Then you will know the truth, and the
truth will set you free." John 8:32*

Dressed in a brown pinstriped, three-piece suit with a Jones of New York store label, John Law was the epitome of a refined western lawman. His long sleeved brown shirt and tie complimented the suit, as did a yellow gold pocket watch that connected both vest side pockets, a wide brown leather belt with rodeo buckle that held his trousers at his waist, while brown leather boots with squared toes covered his feet. Law's straight brimmed brown Stetson, shoulder length gray hair, bushy eyebrows and full mustache nearly topped off his picturesque image. Even John's brushed leather briefcase matched his pinstriped suit and leather boots. Although red, the small feather in his hat band was a stark anomaly given him by his very proper secretary, Amanda. What topped off his image was the pair of diamond studded cufflinks John Law wore at his wrists.

John Law and Adam Claymore were kindred spirits and business partners. They made considered decisions and proceeded with caution when taking risks, yet both were known as men of action. Their yes meant yes, and their no meant no. Often John and Adam purchased land, water and mineral rights together. Often they served together on organizational boards and committees and contributed to the same causes. Adam was more out front and the spokesman, while John would work for consensus behind the scenes. One thing John didn't share with Adam was the confidentiality of his clients' cases, and John was a stickler about that. In a word, John Law and Adam Claymore were good friends and a handshake was still binding between them. Both once pursued the same woman, but Adam, the younger man, had won the heart of Mary McNaughton. John never married, and both grieved Mary's passing.

John looked forward to his Thursday noon meeting to fulfill conditions of a trust involving the Blair House. After finally locating Ezra "Izzy" Blair and convincing Ezra to return home to lead the rebuilding of his childhood home, John told Ezra he had some papers for him that would not only reveal how Ezra came to live with the Blair's but would also reveal his true identity. John had said this would be important to the project and the future of the Blair House estate. John told Ezra that if he did not return, the house might be condemned and the water and mineral rights had a chance of becoming public domain. What John didn't reveal to Ezra would prove to be of even more importance.

Having walked to his office above Bustos' Mexican Restaurant from his home two blocks north, John stopped at the intersection and admired the building he had purchased with Adam. It had a classic small town appearance for a brick building situated on a main street corner. Although an entrance to the second floor was accessible from a side street, the main entrance formed the long side of a triangle. A square of bricks formed a pillar as the axis of the other two imaginary sides. Visitors could enter from both the main and side streets. Large plate glass windows flanked the entrance on both streets, which made people watching easy for those inside. An old fashioned, hand crank awning could be lowered to protect those nearest Main Street. What really made this building distinctive was the brick. While most small towns with such classic buildings situated on primary street corners featured red or brown brick, the one in Jericho Springs had been built with golden brick.

John Law had walked east along the street side of the restaurant and climbed the steps to his law offices. He remembered to leave the original glass door unlocked, so that his neighbor and secretary, Amanda Sentry, and his guests would be able to climb the stairs for their meeting in his conference room upstairs. His office featured a large lobby with leather couches and chairs, a magazine rack, large potted palms, and Amada's elegant natural walnut desk and chair complimented by her own grace and charm, which like the Cheshire cat, he had watched developing over the years. A walnut armoire flanked Amanda's desk and served to hold her personal property only. A separate file room led from the east side of the lobby with ornate restroom doors on each side. A large conference room faced west with a walnut table, which seated twelve without adding additional leaves. Remarkably, a Live Oak seedling stood in a large earthen pot before a window in the file room, where it captured morning sunlight.

Since Amada had prepared the conference room the night before, John Law was instantly prepared for the meeting. In his office he awaited the arrival of people who were coming in response to his newspaper advertisement about exchanging lodging for labor to restore a house. He had received a phone call from Adam Claymore, who was wondering if one Karen Gustafson had arrived for the interview. John asked if she was the woman recently hired to fill Jill Lowenstein's position at the high school and wasn't she the young woman who manhandled Butch and shot Roy in the heel. Of course, Adam responded affirmatively. Adam asked John to have Karen call him after the meeting and for John to call if Karen did not arrive soon. John told Adam that he had Bailey on call in Jericho Springs, if he was needed.

Amanda had pre-screened telephone inquiries. When applicants heard John Law was interviewing and that this was an offer of free lodging for labor in rebuilding the Blair House, most lost interest. John instructed Amanda to usher Jill into his office when she arrived. One of the night riders from the night before arrived first. Amanda called the sheriff.

Although Irv Moss worked full time at the feed store in Ridge View, Irv had been sent by his stepfather Maurice Wood to apply for the position. Maurice wanted Irv to be a mole bent on derailing the effort to rebuild Blair House. Irv welcomed an opportunity to locate gold on the land for himself. Irv would also benefit in having lodging even if it meant doing some hard labor.

Next to arrive, Kip Powell, the traveling Christian bookseller, also had additional purposes in applying for the position. One purpose was out of genuine interest in the project and gaining lodging for work, and another was to establish a Christian book store in Jericho Springs where he could also conduct in-home parties like those selling Tupperware. Also, he planned to serve local pastors and churches with educational materials, pastoral resources, Bibles, and music. Actually, he was thrilled with an idea to help establish a movement to bring Christian radio to Rock Creek Valley residents, who were largely ignorant about the abundance of Christian music. Kip believed people in the valley were going to be blessed.

Ken and Katarina Bond arrived with their children, who would wait with Amanda in the lobby. The Bonds would benefit the most compared with the other applicants. The trailer Ken had rented from Adam Claymore through Adam's rental agent Whitney McNaughton had been destroyed by night riders when arsonists burned it to the ground. While Ken delivered both the daily Denver Post and the weekly *Outcry*, he needed more income to support his family of four. Daughters, Kristin and Krystal, would have a short walk to school; however, the housing still could be an issue for them.

Unexpectedly, Jerry Sunday, the pizza store manager and deliveryman, arrived as well. Currently, Jerry roomed with a local family for just short of a year but believed he was supposed to help rebuild the Blair House. He had been drawn to the idea of rebuilding something and restoring it to its former greatness. When Jerry saw Blair House, he recognized what could be not what was. Jerry hoped that was how God viewed him.

Newlyweds, Izzy and Janine, arrived promptly at noon. John Law introduced Izzy as the project manager and the couple as Mr. and Mrs. Ezra Blair. All made the connection and presumed Ezra was the Blair estate heir. They had heard and experienced enough from night riders to cheer for Izzy.

Conversation between the applicants stopped when they heard the cough, cough, sputter, cough, sputter, boom of the Gray Whiz. Each looked at the others and laughed, while below on the side street the truck stopped by the curbing and idled. Each dressed in blue jeans and a hooded parka, Karen and Jill exited the old woodcutter's truck cab and promptly ascended the stairs to Law's office. Amanda quickly ushered Jill into John Law's office and escorted Karen into the conference room, and then Amanda called Adam as ordered.

John Law asked, "You must be Karen Gustafson?" To which Karen nodded affirmatively. John continued, "What happened to your forehead?"

Karen replied with "Foolishly, after prayer meeting and dinner at the Stage Stop in Rock Creek, I walked to the top of the mesa behind the church in the glen to pray and watch the storm clouds gather," Karen paused, looked at each face, and then continued, "I had a great time with the Lord, but when I walked down from the mesa, someone waited for me at the footbridge and ran toward me. I got a glimpse of him, but when I turned to escape, I fell and hit my head. From there, I don't really know what happened."

Sheepishly, Irv Moss commented, "What I heard is that a lot was going on last night."

Amanda entered the room and announced, "All have arrived."

John Law eyed Irv, "Irv, I know you. I know your truck. Last night, I saw your truck near the Blair House when all the raucous behavior was going on. I saw you holding the torch, and Bailey knows. He's coming right now to arrest you. Adam Claymore may stop by, and he wants to talk to you about a couple of fires too. Are you sure you want to be here?"

Moss bolted for the door from his seat by the window, while Amanda opened the door for Irv to leave. When Amanda heard the glass door to the outside slam shut, she followed down the stairs and bolted it. She grinned as the old woodcutter clocked Irv and knocked him out with one blow to Irv's chin. Then, Amanda returned to John's office to bring Jill Lowenstein to the meeting. The grizzly old woodcutter safely tucked Irv in the bed of the Gray Whiz, and then waited for Bailey to arrive. Bailey arrived minutes later and took Irv Moss into custody for attempted arson. Irv joined the crowd already residing in the cells.

When Jill entered Janine rushed to embrace her saying, "Oh Jill, I thought I'd never see you again." They wept and were hugged by Izzy.

Jerry asked John Law, "Is she the missing school teacher?"

Jill introduced herself, "Yes, I'm Jill Lowenstein. I teach English at the high school. I came out of hiding, because I want to be a part of restoring the Blair House."

"Tonight's city council meeting will be the next step," informed John Law, "although the council and most citizens want to have the Blair House condemned and become public domain, I'm going to be able to block that."

"Because Izzy came home?" Janine added.

Jerry questioned, "What difference has that made?"

"Izzy is related to the Blair's. He's their adopted son," explained Janine.

John Law surprised them all with, "Or so everyone thinks!"

Jerry responded, "Hey, whatever. All I know is that I'm here and God wants me here to help rebuild the Blair House. I was just hanging out in Denver, not doing much, living with my parents, when I attended a Youth for Christ Rally at the auditorium next to the Denver Zoo. I went forward when they gave the invitation. I accepted Christ as my Lord and Savior. On the stage, God told me in my head. He called me by name. He said Jerry Sunday, go to Jericho Springs and wait. The next day I came to the valley, or maybe God brought me here on the south bound bus. A guy named Adam happened to be at the bus terminal. He walked up to me and asked if I needed help. I said yes that I am supposed to be here and I need to go to Jericho Springs. He said I can help you, and he gave me a ride here and dropped me off at the pizza parlor where I got a job."

"To work for him!" said Ken Bond pointing skyward.

"To evangelize the valley!" said Kip Powell.

"To make right, that which is wrong!" said Izzy Blair.

"To use our might, for what is right," said Janine, the teacher who taught the Arthurian Legend.

"To bring healing to God's people," said Katarina.

"To have women treated properly," said Jill.

"Equal justice for all," said John Law, barrister.

"That truth would prevail. Yes will be yes and no will mean no," finished Karen.

"Do you realize there are eight of you?" asked John.

"Is that significant?" probed Jerry.

"It is. In the Bible seven is the perfect number. Six is the number for man, but eight is the number for new beginnings. From what you have shared, this is a new beginning for many of you," clarified John Law, "And I'm glad to be a part of this too. There is another who has agreed to help. In fact he has been milling boards for your use, and he has been making saw dust pellets for the fire places and wood stoves."

"That would be the old woodcutter. I got to help when he thought it safe for me to do so," concluded Jill.

Law added, "My good friend Adam Claymore said he would help."

Karen smiled, and Jill and Janine noticed, and then shot a look at each other. Silence enveloped them all momentarily, as they contemplated all they had heard.

"John, what did you mean when you said 'or so everyone thinks' about Izzy being the Blair's adopted son," inquired Janine.

"I wondered too," Izzy added.

John Law revealed, "We have had a mystery that will be solved tomorrow noon. Let me share just a little, the short version. Hold your questions and comments and let me tell you the story. Izzy, this may be hard for you. You will all be influenced by this, as we get into the project."

Those so assembled murmured and in unison said, "Tell us more!"

John continued, "Years ago, in the midst of the war in Vietnam, the Blair's were asked to raise Izzy as their own child by Izzy's father, a widower, who was called to war. Izzy's mother had recently died in childbirth. The Blair's were happy to do it, because they were given the use of what has been called the Blair House for so many years. The deal included the water and mineral rights that extend from the property down the street and up both sides of the canyon above it. This included water rights to the West Fork of Rock Creek and whatever lies beneath the surface…gold. It included the forests covering the foothills to Claymore Flats through the canyon to the next mountain range, 3,000 acres. Izzy, you were never adopted. The Blair's were your guardians and guardians of the property for as long as they functioned as your parents or if and when your father returned. Izzy's father didn't return from the war in Vietnam. He was a prisoner of war in Cambodia for years. With the deaths of Peter and Lydia Blair and with no known heir, the city had sought to condemn the property and have it become public domain. People knew Izzy as an adopted son, but Izzy had disappeared and didn't let himself be found. As a result most of the community now wants all or part of the property, especially the old timers. They want the water and mineral rights, especially after the rock slide revealed a significant vein of gold.

"This is too much! First, I learned I had been adopted, and I flipped out. I didn't know any of this and I ran away," said Izzy.

"You didn't think your parents wanted you and gave you away?" interpreted Janine.

"But I have always been grateful the Blair's did want me…I just had a hard time with it all."

"And now?" asked Jill.

"I don't know who I am. I mean what's my name?"

"Apparently, it's not Blair," commented Karen, "who is he?"

"What's my name?" asked Janine Crowfoot Blair.

John Law interjected, "Janine, you know you are tied to the original people that called the valley home. You, dear, are an original," John paused and looked intently in Izzy's direction. "Izzy, your father wants to meet you tomorrow."

"My real father, he's alive and he is here? He will be here…tomorrow? Where?" Izzy asked.

"Noon at the old tree behind the Blair House," John asserted.

"Well, I'll be. Then I'm not the heir to the Blair House and all that goes with it, but my father wants me to lead in restoring the house."

"You are named in the Blair will, but not for the Blair House. Your father is alive and he never relinquished ownership of the property. You, Izzy, would be his heir. It is his house, and your father asks you to lead in restoring the Blair House," proclaimed John Law happily

"Then the city council has no basis for declaring the property public domain," said Kip.

"The Blair House must not remain vacated," declared Ken.

Katarina concluded, "The rightful owner is here and father and son will be reunited. Praise the Lord!"

"Izzy, your father wants you to know your name tomorrow and not before, and then together you will proclaim it to all who care to hear," insisted John Law.

Izzy's response was to the point, "Then we need to be at city council tonight."

"I'll handle the council, I'm prepared to deflate their balloon as city attorney," John Law stated.

"Does Adam know about this?" asked Karen.

"Adam doesn't know the details. It is imperative he not know. He just knows I'm working to defuse the public uproar, besides Adam has enough on his plate with Butch's mess. Can you, Karen, and the rest of you keep the secret?"

All said yes, and John continued, "Then you are a team."

"We do have some details. We need to occupy and protect the house. All of you who can move in now should do so as soon as possible. Can anyone move in today?" asked Izzy.

They bombarded Izzy with responses. Kip Powell said he had most of what he owns with him, except for his bookstore inventory in a storage locker from which he operated his business. He needed to service some accounts, change his delivery locations with suppliers, and he could pick-up his inventory with a small rental trailer. Izzy told Kip he had an idea about using one room in the front of the house as a Christian bookstore, so Kip could store his inventory there as soon as the house was secured. Kip said that was answered prayer. Jerry said he just needed to let his boarding house know he was leaving. He had already talked with them about the possibility. Jerry also said he needed to develop a work schedule that allowed him to manage the store and deliver pizza. Karen said she was taking the bus home tomorrow to get her things in Quail Point and that her parents would bring the rest of her things from Colorado Springs. Karen emphasized that she would be back in time for the wedding, which was in two weeks. Ken and Katarina said they were ready to work, but wondered how it would work with their children. Janine suggested that since Jill was already planning to move into the house and if Izzy agreed, she and Izzy could move everything they have to the Blair House and have the Bonds live in her house she rented from Adam Claymore.

"That works!" said Izzy, "And I will help work out the rental with Adam Claymore. All four of you can help with the project, if you want."

Kat responded, voice shaking, "We would have a house at least as long as it takes to rebuild the Blair house. That would be good for Kristin and Krystal."

"We will figure something out. Once the house is completed there will be more work to do with the grounds and in the mountains. For now, let's think of it as a permanent arrangement, unless my father says differently, besides I believe we are going to be more than physically restoring Blair House."

Ken responded, "We're good with that. God truly blesses us all!"

"I think God has more in mind. What if the house is a base from which we, as a team, work to build his kingdom here in Rock Creek Valley? Tonight and the last few nights we've experienced major battles. I think it's because walls of resistance are falling down. We need to persevere," said Jerry.

"John, what about Karen and me? I saw who killed Gloria Jones, and it wasn't Butch McNaughton, but I'll need to go back into hiding," said Jill.

"And I saw who attacked me," stated Karen.

Law thought a moment, and then answered, "Jill, you gave away your connection to the woodcutter. No doubt someone saw you come to town. If you drove down Main Street, former neighbors may have recognized you. You work at a high school. You know how quickly a rumor mill gets started… What about hiding in plain sight?"

"You mean hiding at the Blair House," Jill asked.

"I do, and there is one thing more. Last night I talked with Detective Caleb Jones, Gloria's brother. There was another woman murdered last night in Quail Point. She was a prostitute. Someone stuffed her body under a bridge. The police think the two murders are connected. Detective Jones followed a car from Rock Creek to Quail Point, and then tailed it back here. He was to check with motor vehicles this morning. The case may soon be solved," explained John Law. "Jones has gathered data that will have far reaching implications for our local law enforcement as well as ministry opportunities for yourselves."

"Jill, you are right. Butch McNaughton has been in jail since Tuesday night. He couldn't have done it," informed Karen, "but again, what about me?"

John Law replied thinking the case was a cinch, "Well, Buddy Smith is in jail."

"Who is Buddy Smith?" asked Karen.

"He's the one who hit Beatrice Jaramillo with a beer bottle Tuesday night and attacked you last night?" answered John.

"I wouldn't know Buddy, if I saw him," said Karen.

"Do you know who you saw?" asked John Law.

"Absolutely!" Karen replied.

"Are you one hundred percent certain? Sheriff's deputies caught Buddy on the bridge behind the church in Rock Creek. They caught up with him when he fell on the bridge. Your blood was on him," said John in disbelief.

"Indubitably?" asked Janine.

"Yes, without a doubt, his face is stuck in my mind. Now I remember where I saw him. The man who attacked me was at the school board meeting. He made the insurance presentation to the school board. I don't know his name, but his offices are across the street from the school administration offices. One night, when I was staying at the hotel, I saw a woman walk from the Asherah House to the back door of his offices and he let her in," Karen elaborated.

"Sam Gelding? He is Mara Gelding's husband," added Janine.

"Who is she?" asked Izzy.

"She's the high school secretary," answered Jerry, "She's a frequent customer. I delivered pizza to her house Tuesday night."

"Was Sam Gelding at home?" asked Izzy.

"No, Mrs. Gelding never orders when her husband is at home, and she always seems so sad," answered Jerry.

"Karen, I hate to say this, but I hope you are wrong. Mara Gelding is a nice person, at least once you get to know her," retorted Janine.

"Assume Karen is right. How soon could Mr. Gelding be arrested?" asked Jill.

John Law replied, "If we assume Karen is correct and if Detective Jones confirms the license plate of the car he tailed belongs to Gelding, my guess is he would be arrested this afternoon."

"Then as soon as Gelding is picked up, I can move into the Blair House," said Jill emphatically.

"Why is that?" asked John Law.

"Because I saw Sam Gelding kill Gloria Jones," explained Jill.

"Why didn't you come forward earlier?" asked John.

"For one thing, I was injured. The woodcutter nursed me back to health, and I didn't know where I was. He is hard to communicate with. His cabin is way back in the woods. Only recently did I realize I had been staying near County Road 403. Recently, I helped him some at the saw mill making wood pellets out of sawdust. I couldn't keep up with it, so he bagged much of it. I guess he sold it somewhere. He also has huge piles of slab, you know, what's trimmed off the log when he square cuts a tree. Anyway, I saw the highway signs. Besides, Gelding is a good 'ole boy, and I know how cronyism works in this town. They take care of one another," answered Jill.

"You never tried to escape?" asked Kat.

"Why would I? I wasn't a prisoner. The old man made me feel like an honored guest. He had me read his Bible to him every morning, and he loved hearing me offering prayers at meal time, saying grace. In the evenings, he would bring me a hymnal to sing from," explained Jill.

"Didn't he sing with you or pray aloud," asked Izzy.

"No, he didn't, and I don't think he can speak. His eyes brightened and glistened when I sang, especially 'Amazing Grace'!" concluded Jill.

"Interesting, Sam is on the agenda tonight. Let's see if he shows up. I'll call the sheriff and let him know what both of you have reported to me. Sheriff Bailey will be glad to hear both of you are safe and accounted for. I'm certain he will want to talk with each of you. It would be better if you don't go to the sheriff's office for the reason you already stated."

Izzy spoke up, "After hearing all this, is everyone still in? Karen, Kip, Kat, Ken, Jill, Jerry? Janine, honey?"

They looked at one another and said in unison, "We're a team!"

"It's a good thing, because as executor of the trust, I had Amanda call to have everything turned on this afternoon, electricity, water, sewage, and mail service. The woodcutter has been asked to deliver the first of two loads of wood too! I also had Amanda open an account in my name at the lumber yard in Ridge View. Hopefully, it's already filled. Irv Moss would usually fill the orders, but as you know, he just left. Izzy, I only ordered enough materials to secure the place— plywood for the downstairs windows, deadbolt locks for all outside doors and windows, brooms, mop buckets, and a lot of tools. You will have to order window glass. Later, your name will be added to the account."

"Wow! God is at work!" concluded Jerry, who led a group hug.

John spoke again, "Jill and Karen, maybe you should go back to the cabin with the old woodcutter and stay there for a couple more days to make certain Gelding is locked up and for the Blair House to be secured. Jill, I can make an announcement that you are alive and well and will report for work at the school. Karen, please call Adam and tell him you are alright. Apparently, he called you last night at the Rock Creek house, and when you didn't answer he drove there to find you. He said you have his phone number."

Jill nodded accepting his instruction, and then looked at Karen and gave her a thumbs up!

"I do have Adam's number. I leave tomorrow on the morning bus headed south. Couldn't I just stay at Adam's house in Rock Creek?" asked Karen, "Besides, we have a prayer walk."

"Lady, what does it take for you to understand the danger you have been in?"

"Mr. Law, Karen can stay with us. We will be with her all day, and we'll make certain she's on the bus," said Izzy.

"I'm sure Adam will make certain Karen is okay during the prayer walks," offered Jill with a smile.

"Then I'm staying at the Blair House with the rest of the team. I think it is important we make an appearance at council meeting," said Jill with conviction.

"Okay, but I don't think it's a good idea," said John.

"Thanks for all you are doing," smiled Jill.

It was Janine, who spoke up as the team began to leave, "Remember, we have a prayer walk tonight. Please, meet at the church in Rock Creek at 5 p.m."

John added, "Folks! Some of you need to come to the city council meeting at seven o'clock here in Jericho Springs."

Karen said, "Thanks for mentioning that. I thought the meeting was at the school building in Rock Creek tonight. Where does the council meet?"

John clarified, "Three blocks north of here. You can't miss it. That is where the city square is. The grounds are one square block. Go in the main entrance, which faces west."

"Before you go, let's gather around," said Izzy, "it may be hokey but..."Izzy stretched out his hand toward the others, who gathered around and grasped his hand. Laughing, the team said, "One for all and all for one!"

Though she watched the team while standing beside John, Amanda said, "I don't think that is hokey at all. You have inspired me. I am in the grandstand cheering already for what you are going to be doing to restore Blair House, and I believe restoration will have to do with much more than the building. If your mission includes returning Blair House to its full glory, you can count on my help. God has a plan and I'll want to be a part of it."

As the new team left the offices of John Law, Karen walked with Amanda to her desk and asked to use her telephone. Amanda smiled and said, "Yes, you need to call Adam and tell him you are safe and sound."

"Thank you," Karen said as she placed her call, which was answered by Rabbit. After exchanging pleasantries, Rabbit informed Karen that Adam had left for an appointment. Disappointed, Karen said, "Please tell Adam not to be concerned. I am safe and sound and that I will see him tonight at church."

VICTORY BEGINS
CHAPTER 18

"With God we will gain the victory, and he will
trample down our enemies." Psalm 60:12

Thursday afternoon the occupation of the Blair House began as six team members gathered their belongings and moved into the house in Jericho Springs. Kip Powell deposited his suitcase in the southeast corner bedroom on the second floor over the proposed bookstore. Immediately, he left to drive home to Denver on South Ogden Street in the middle of the Dutch neighborhood. He visited the Pearl Street Creamery and had a malted milkshake at the old fashioned soda fountain, where he said good-bye to childhood friends. Renting a one way trailer, he loaded his clothes from home and his business inventory from his storage unit. Another trip would be needed to finish moving. Jerry Sunday drove his '53 Chevy to the boarding house on the north end of Jericho Springs and settled accounts with the owner. After promising he would continue leading their Bible study, Jerry shared prayer and a fond farewell with many borders. His belongings fit in only four grocery bags, the sum total of his possessions. The Bonds returned to Claymore Flats where they said their good-byes and loaded what had survived the fire in their station wagon. Rabbit loaned them four bed rolls and told the Bonds, "God be with you!"

Once water, electricity, and waste water had been connected and lumber and tools had been delivered by the lumber yard in Ridge View, Karen and Jill came out of hiding. Soon the full crew arrived minus Kip Powell and began cleaning and securing the lower level. Izzy assigned people to jobs and warned of the need to keep an eye open in case of trouble. He asked Jerry Sunday to lead the group in prayer, which included hurling the spears of lengthy prayer against the opposition. All rejoiced! Since they had so little time before going to their church in Rock Creek for the prayer walks, the women opened the water line in the basement. They checked for leaks in the pipe leading to the kitchen and one bathroom on the first floor, so running water flowed within the house. The men began nailing plywood over all broken, first floor windows and installed dead bolts on doors. Soon the women joined the men to help secure the house. The grizzly old woodcutter delivered two loads of firewood, and then prepared the wood stove in the kitchen for use. All sang as they worked!

Neighbors came out from their houses and looked in wonder at what was happening to the Blair House. Telephone lines buzzed throughout the valley. More and more people drove by slowly with passengers craning their necks to get a better view of those working on Blair House. Buds became leaves on the Live Oak.

Still in light of the summer day, Thursday evening promised excitement for the congregation of the little church in the glen, the only church in Rock Creek. Church members and attendees began arriving at 4:45 p.m. Priscilla and Aquila arrived earlier than the others to set up for the pizza dinner Jerry Sunday had promised to deliver. The ladies transformed a small, narrow lobby where flyers and church bulletins could be placed on a long, narrow table. Only the table adorned the left side of the lobby, but it was functional and allowed adequate room for members to come and go without being impeded. It served well for a buffet line. The back of the sanctuary featured wooden strips with coat hooks on each side of the back wall. Before the coat hooks, the ladies set up what tables and chairs they could find where people would sit to eat the meal and fellowship.

Like the helm of a ship, the pastor's ornate pulpit stood before the pews and next to a small pipe organ on the left side and an upright piano on the right. Both in good repair, the ladies' weekly duties included waxing organ and piano to a luxurious sheen as well as sweeping and mopping the hardwood floor. Priscilla and Aquila filled each book holder attached to the back of each pew with sharpened pencils, Bibles, and hymnals. At least once a year, they oiled each wooden pew with Old English polish, while men of the church waxed and buffed the floor to a lustrous sheen. As they worked these faithful ladies prayed for their pastor and for the message he would present from behind the pulpit.

Two small cubicles flanked the pulpit. In the left cubicle, a large walnut desk and chair dominated the pastor's study. Six folding chairs stood against the west wall where towering bookcases spanned floor to ceiling. A small group could meet there with or without the pastor. Both for ventilation and escape if need be, a door to the outside often proved functional as had been the situation the night before. In the right cubicle, the prayer room provided access to the baptistery, a large tub where hundreds had been baptized over the history of the building. Also, cleaning supplies for church maintenance neatly filled one corner of the room, while ancient red choir robes gathered dust where they hung on wall mounted hooks. Beside the robes, one of the pastors had hung his wading boots and robe used when performing baptisms. In a word the congregation and its pastor kept a functional ship that handled both smooth-sailing and rocky storms, revivals, and church splits. Tonight's gathering foreshadowed another major event.

Having blessed the church body with pizza and soda pop, Jerry Sunday had long departed to make deliveries in his '53 Chevrolet with pizza sign held on his rooftop by a magnet and suction cups. As the congregation arrived, chatter and laughter began to fill the sanctuary. Newcomers and old timers made introductions and exchanged pleasantries, which evolved into genuine conversation. Old ladies fussed over the men and served them food and beverage, while the men folk helped seat the ladies and gathered used plates and cups, then emptied the initial trash and returned chairs and tables to where they had been stored. Aquila and Priscilla policed the area and ordered Rabbit to empty the remaining trash they had collected. Adam asked his flock to be seated as the ladies blessed the congregants by leading the group in singing "Onward Christian Soldiers" and "Pass It On."

"This afternoon and tonight we march to carry-out what we prayed about last night. I don't remember the last time we have gone into the community and prayed for the people. We want God to heal our land, and we believe the promise of what *2Chronicles 7:14* states," said Adam, and then he quoted the scripture. Next he said, "We will march forth preparing the way of the Lord. We have asked God to soften their hearts toward him that they might be saved."

"Amen," said many.

Adam continued, "There are seventeen of us gathered here, eight are old timers and eight are newcomers, and Ezra Blair is a long time son who has returned home. Others are not here, but they are with us in spirit. Tonight, we march beyond our walls taking our offense into the valley. One team will start here in Rock Creek and the others go on to Jericho Springs where the city council meets. One agenda item is to consider the condemnation of the Blair House. Greed and covetousness motivate many attending the meeting to want what is not theirs. They have a sense of entitlement for water rights and gold and land rightfully owned by another who has been absent, but already soldiers of the Lord are repairing the walls like in the book of Ezra. People of the Lord are occupying the Blair House. I believe it will be a home base, operating to advance God's kingdom, an oasis with cool refreshing water inside and warm mineral baths outside," Adam paused, "for healing. But...I spend too much time talking..."

"Preach it, Brother..."

"Our team in Rock Creek is to be led by my wrangler, Pilgrim. Karen Gustafson, the Brownings with Rob, Ruth, and Andrew, and also Rachael McNaughton are to go walk the streets praying for each household, each business. You don't have too many streets to cover and be certain to include the fire station, Stage Stop Hotel, tobacco store, convenience store, and the Asherah House. Each of you need be certain to carry a few Bibles and give them away! When you finish, come join us at the courthouse in Jericho Springs if you can," directed Adam.

"One Jericho team has to be at city council for the meeting. We will pray about the meeting by asking for truth and justice to prevail. I'll intercede for the council members to be blessed with wisdom, knowledge, and understanding. Before the meeting, we will cover what streets we can and we will pick up Jill Lowenstein at Blair House and we'll take her to the meeting," announced Adam.

"She's alive! Praise the Lord!"

Adam continued, "The old woodcutter will be on guard at the Blair House, while some of us are occupied at the meeting. I will go to the meeting as will Izzy and Janine, and Detective Caleb Jones. Beatrice Jaramillo will join us there and will probably speak during public comment."

"What about the rest of us?"

"As a team Rabbit will escort the Bond family south on Main Street past the Blair House and will then cover streets east of Main to the high school and back to the courthouse. So that's Rabbit, Ken Bond, Katarina, Kristin, and Krystal. Barney will lead the last team with Aquila and Priscilla. If John Law doesn't need his secretary Amanda Sentry at the council meeting, she will join you," instructed Adam.

"I'm sure my granddaughter will join with us," proclaimed Aquila Parson.

"Oh, yes! She will and maybe her other grandmother, Willa Sentry, will join us." added Priscilla King.

"Barnabas, lead your team north on Main Street to the end of town. Next, work the streets east of Main, and then come back south to the courthouse. When the team arrives from Rock Creek, we will have them work the few streets west of Main Street. Remember to share the Gospel if you have the chance. Let's load up!"

All departed singing "Victory in Jesus!"

When the Jericho Springs teams left to fulfill their missions, Pilgrim led the Rock Creek team on its charge to walk each street and pray at each household and business. They walked north on the US 85/87 business loop past the houses leading to County Road 403 including Adam's house and the convenience store, where they lingered as they prayed against evil represented within. Next, they walked to the bridge and prayed that the murderer of Gloria Jones be revealed. Then they crossed the road and walked past the former grocery and three houses, praying as they walked. The group turned left and prayed for those who serve as volunteers at the fire station and walked north past the highway department, post office, and bus barn. Quickened, the team paused and prayed for the safety of the children who waited for school buses there behind the chain link fence. Next, they paused at the old school building where Butch McNaughton had assaulted both Hannah and Cotton Candy. They prayed for the school board and administration plus the museum and senior center. The Rock Creek team crossed the highway at the base of the hogback, a significant uplift of sedimentary rock and stopped. There they prayed for travelers going north and south on the highway. The group knew they were likely to confront evil on Indiana Avenue.

Fog gathered and clouds drew near overhead. Andrew noticed first, "Mama, it just got real cold." And Rachel looked upward then bent down and rubbed her right knee, as cold damp air impacted her arthritis.

"Hold my hand, Son," Rob said, as they kept walking first along the north side of the street to the end, and then the team stopped before crossing over Indiana Avenue.

Pilgrim gathered them together and formed a circle where they put their arms around one another. "A lot happens across the street," Pilgrim said, "I've never been inside, but what I hear is that young and older women spend much of their lives there. Working there cost Gloria Jones her life."

"Did she die inside there?" asked Ruth, as she covered Andy's ears.

"I heard her body was found under the bridge on south County Road 403," offered Karen, as she was not to tell what she knew.

"Her body was actually stuffed in the bridge structure just under the roadway in what amounts to a crawl space," explained Pilgrim.

"I thought she was found in the water," said Rob, "the killer had to be pretty strong."

"This Asherah House represents evil," declared Rachael, "and somewhere around here is an Asher pole. I seen it long ago."

"Why hasn't the house been shut down?" asked Karen.

"I can't answer that," responded Pilgrim, "but I know they need Jesus just like everyone else."

"Then let's pray for that, and for justice for Gloria Jones," declared Karen.

"And for God to remove this place from our valley," added Rob.

With grace and mercy, Andy added, "And the women. Don't they need Jesus?"

"That's right, Son, God's grace and mercy. Jesus died that all may live," said Andy's father.

From a second floor balcony, a woman stood up from a rocking chair and opened a French door and shouted to those inside, "Hey, everybody! Some people outside are talkin' about how we need some guy named Jesus! Anybody know who he is?"

Someone answered, "Go find out, if they will talk to you."

The team continued west on Indiana Avenue and turned south on the highway. Someone left the Asherah House and walked the path toward the hotel. The team paused before the insurance and real-estate offices and prayed, which made Karen anxious as she realized that was where Sam Gelding conducted business.

Next, Pilgrim led the team to the tobacco store, where he stopped just before the doorway. "Here is another place of real and present evil," Pilgrim revealed. "Numbers, gambling, and I'm not sure what else happens here."

"And yet it is allowed to continue?" commented Karen.

"Yes, let's pray it be removed?" asserted Rob.

"We need to pray for the hotel, too?" said Pilgrim, "We have made good progress, but let's get out of here before people inside take notice of us."

"Good," said Rachael, "I'm getting tired. Tonight stirred some memories I need to think about and remember some history of this town. This was a good start. Will you take me home, Pilgrim?"

"We won't be going to Jericho Springs," Rob said, "We need to get Andy home."

"Okay," said Pilgrim, "I'll take Rachael home and we can touch base with the old woodcutter who is on guard at the Blair House. Karen, are you with me?"

Karen said, "Absolutely!"

Ruth said, "We'll see you when you get back from Quail Point, Karen. When you arrive, call me?"

"Yes, and thank you all. I've never done this before. It has been a revelation and I believe God is at work," declared Karen.

Only Andy had seen the woman who had followed them from the Asherah House. She had crossed through the parking lot behind the hotel and between the hotel and tobacco shop and then, at great risk, she had crossed the Valley Highway and stood in the shadows near the volunteer fire station.

Briefly, the woman stepped out of the shadows and fog when the Brownings passed by and waved at the occupants of the station wagon. She waved and Andy waved in return. The scantily dressed woman emotionally said, "I want to hear about Jesus."

"Dad, Dad, did you see that beautiful woman wave at us by the road?"

"No, Andy," Rob said then he looked in his rear view mirror and caught what he thought was a fleeting glimpse of something running across the road in the fog.

Ruth turned around in her front seat as their automobile passed by Indiana Avenue and prophetically said, "Maybe our prayers are already being answered, if it really was someone and not just your imagination."

"Shouldn't we turn around?" Andrew asked.

When well travelled Pilgrim, Karen, and Rachael arrived at Rachael's home across from the Blair House in Jericho Springs, they came upon some of the boys from Ridge View corralled in a standoff with the old woodcutter. The boys intended to inflict mischief. When the boys had parked on the street just north of the house, they discovered the woodcutter rocking in a chair on the second floor porch with his shotgun pointed in their direction. Without Butch or Buddy Smith to lead them, their courage waned, and they neither drove off nor got out of the car. Their anxiety increased when they recognized Pilgrim, a bull and bronco rider of renown. Some claimed he was comparable to Casey Tibbs, All American Cowboy of yesteryear.

Rachel asked Karen, "Miss Gustafson, after you move in across the street, will you accompany me to the museum and library at the school building in Rock Creek? There's some things I need to remember and you need to know as a newcomer. Things this handsome young man beside me doesn't even know about."

"Thank you," said Karen, "I want to learn more about this valley."

Taking his Winchester from the gun rack on the back of the crew cab, Pilgrim walked Rachael to her porch before she shouted to the boys, "I'm goin' inside to get my shotgun. I saw you boys last night. I got your license plate numbers. If you are still here when I get back, I just might spray you with salt pellets or something more exciting."

The boys left immediately, and Pilgrim waved to the woodcutter as he and Karen left to find the other teams. On the way Pilgrim told Karen he thought he ought to drop her off at the courthouse, while he would return to the Blair House to back up the old woodcutter. Pilgrim thought he should cover the west side of the house in case someone attempted a rear assault on the house. When they found Barney and team had been joined by Willa Sentry and Amanda Sentry, Karen conceded and had Pilgrim drop her off at the courthouse, where she could observe the proceedings.

Karen stood at the door to the council's chambers and noticed Izzy and Janine were seated close to the front while Jill sat just before Karen. She was greeted by Jill Lowenstein, who had saved an empty seat next to her on the back row left side. Immediately, Jill told Karen that insurance representative Sam Gelding had not shown for his portion of the agenda to which both raised their eyebrows and nodded. Jill continued to tell Karen that John Law had told her to wait in the bathroom until seven o'clock sharp, so she could be seated without fanfare. Law had draped his top coat over two chairs to reserve the seats. Law had told Jill not to attract attention. Jill snickered and said she obeyed his lead and occupied one of two stalls in the lady's room, which had not been well received by many in need. Also, Jill revealed that Karen had not missed much of the agenda except that several citizens had addressed council on issues not on the agenda, and that the city owned utility department had presented background on a proposed electric rate increase, and that council had some discussion regarding Gelding missing his special presentation. Finally, council had just passed all items on the consent agenda, which meant the main attraction followed on the agenda.

Beside Jill sat Beatrice Jaramillo, the frail old lady who had crawled into the sanctuary at the little church in the glen during last night's prayer meeting. Karen noticed the public packed seats on both sides of a single isle by which public waiting to speak would approach the podium when invited by the mayor. Behind the public seating, space had been cleared on all sides to allow passage. A small group of spectators sat against the rear wall behind Jill and Karen on both sides of the isle. Against the back wall to Karen's right, stood a small rectangular table where the city clerk had stacked copies of the council meeting agenda, a sign in sheet, and a small stack of cards for public comment. If anyone wanted to speak during the public comment portion of the night's agenda, he or she had to submit a completed card before the meeting began. In addition to name, address, and phone number, he or she had to list the topic of concern. Members of the public could each speak for only a maximum of three minutes on a topic not on the agenda. A red light on the podium flashed on and off if a speaker exceeded the three minutes.

Against the east wall a newspaper reporter from the *Outcry* perched attentively behind the press desk. Before her two rows of large rectangular tables with microphones had been positioned for city employees to sit and make comment, if called upon during the meeting. Karen noted that City Attorney, John Law, sat at one front table, and on his right were both the city manager and his assistant, while on Law's left sat Sheriff Bailey, who enforced the law for all three towns in the valley. At the other row of tables behind the first sat the fire chief, director of public works, and the director of the city's utilities. Except for Sheriff Bailey, all sat attentively and ready to contribute. Bailey sat scanning the audience.

In front of Karen, the Jericho Springs city logo had been mounted on the north wall. The logo faintly looked like the Live Oak behind the Blair House. Flanking the logo the American flag stood prominently to the left and the Colorado flag to the right. To the right of the Colorado flag, an electronic device, fixed to the wall, displayed results of how council members voted. Members of the city council sat before the wall with the city logo, and the mayor sat center and flanked by three council members on each side. Each council member had a microphone and buttons at each station used to place a vote or to signal the mayor that any one of them wanted to make comment. Although each had a golden name plate, Karen could not distinguish any of their names.

West of the council members sat the city clerk, who had prepared packets for the mayor and council. She recorded notes throughout the meeting. Seated behind her desk, she had begun the meeting by taking a roll call vote, after a council member had led the audience in the pledge of allegiance. Next to the city clerk sat a man who taped what was said from any microphone. Beside him a screen hung from the ceiling to be used by city staff or members of the public to make audio-visual presentations.

In the center of the room stood the podium where speakers would come forward to make comment with the permission of the mayor. Residents had to state their names and addresses before speaking, while employees stated their names and titles. All meetings were taped both by audio and visual means. In the public seating area front right of the isle sat Adam Claymore and Detective Caleb Jones in the front row. Before and after meetings both employees and council members interacted well with the public readily, but if someone wanted to raise an issue with an employee, they were ushered to the lobby where interaction became private. Often the employee made an appointment with the person for later in the week. Once the meeting began, all were expected to sit at attention.

"John Law, please come forward to address our first old business item," said the mayor, as Law approached the podium. "Old business item one, proposed is a resolution to condemn the property on the south end of Main Street, also known as the Blair House, and to revert to public domain all land, water and mineral rights as well as forest extending from the house south to Claymore Flats, west to the Wet Mountain Range including the West Rock Creek Valley, and bordered by the national forest north of the valley totaling 3,000 plus acres. This includes water rights and mineral rights on the Blair House property and all other parts of the property, which includes what we have affectionately called Little Huerfano and the Live Oak that once stood as a monument for Jericho Springs before it died," said the Mayor, as he pointed toward the Jericho Springs logo mounted on the wall behind him.

"It's beginning to leaf out," said Izzy loudly from his seat.

The mayor responded by calling Izzy forward, while John Law hung his head and looked at the surface of the podium. Shaking his head, Law moved to the side, so Izzy could speak. Beth Ellen McNaughton was heard to say from the audience that this is preposterous. The crowd murmured. Tradition had been violated.

"Young man, who are you? You must state your name and address if you want to say something here," said the mayor.

"Yeah, probably some newcomer," someone said. Most of the crowd nodded in agreement.

Reaching the podium and adjusting the microphone's position, Izzy introduced himself, "My name is Ezra Blair. I was raised in Jericho Springs by Peter and Lydia Blair. Last Friday I began to live... again... at the Blair House on Main Street. The Live Oak lives. It is producing leaves again. Today, I had a team working to restore my home. All city services have been turned on. There are no back taxes. In a word, we have occupied the Blair House!"

Some in the crowd cheered, while others clapped their hands forgetting how Izzy's statement impacted them and their interests. Many realized what Ezra's statement meant and became sullen. Red McNaughton and others stood up and shook their fists at the council saying that doesn't change a thing. John Law stepped back to the podium, as all could hear cough, cough, sputter, cough, sputter, boom!

"Mayor, if I may."

"Yes, John, please explain, and the rest of you need to listen," shouted the mayor. The crowd grew silent so as to hear.

"Izzy, please stand by. I think everyone here needs to remember that we are talking about the estate of John and Lydia Blair. We have had no finer people living amongst us," Law paused then continued, "Mayor, as a private attorney, I met with a group of young people, who responded to an advertisement I placed in the paper for the rightful owner of what we have called the Blair House. The ad offered free lodging in exchange for labor to restore the Blair House to its previous glory. Ezra Blair was one of those who responded to the ad, as did Jill Lowenstein."

Sitting next to Beth Ellen McNaughton, secretary to the school superintendent, Dr. Maurice Wood said that he wondered if Jill would show up. Beth Ellen grumbled that it was too bad that Jill hadn't made her appearance before Tuesday night. Other malcontents chimed in. Tradition unraveled.

"Jill Lowenstein? Isn't she the missing teacher?" responded the Mayor.

"Yes, Mayor, Jill Lowenstein is the teacher who allegedly witnessed the murder of one Gloria Jones, whose brother happens to be here. Please stand, Detective Caleb Jones of the Denver Police Department," said John Law.

"I suppose he is here to help solve the murder case?" asked the Mayor.

"Yes!" said the detective in a booming voice.

Again, the crowd murmured. Gossipers snarled with malevolent intent, and many speculated as to who was the murderer. Butch McNaughton's name surfaced as the likely candidate, while throughout the crowd McNaughtons agitated spectators in an attempt to gain more supporters for their cause.

"Will Jill be back at school?" asked a councilwoman.

"I am happy to say I will be back at school," answered Jill from the back of the room to which the crowd cheered and clapped loudly.

"John, I suppose this means there may no longer be any basis for condemning the Blair property, especially since a team is already occupying the house and has started repairing it. Am I right?" asked the Mayor.

"Correct!"

"Are the taxes up to date, as Ezra Blair has said?"

"All property tax have been paid in full each year. That was part of my function as executor of the Blair estate," John Law clarified.

"One other thing, John, you said the rightful owner had you put the ad in the newspaper and that Ezra Blair responded to the advertisement. That sounds like Ezra isn't the heir to the house," stated the Mayor. Pockets of the crowd found encouragement with those words, which were quickly dashed.

"Ezra is heir to the Blair estate, but the Blair's did not own the property. They lived there by an agreement made with the rightful owner that as long as they functioned as parents for Ezra Blair, they were to be managers of the estate."

Red complained that Blair is going to have to prove his identity. Dr. Wood babbled something about a court injunction. Others rose from their seats shouting with fists in the air, while the mayor hammered his gavel and ordered the crowd to sit down. Some of the crowd complied immediately, while others continued their rant. Some of the public told the agitators to sit down that they wanted to hear more from John Law. Sheriff Bailey rose from his seat and stared down Red McNaughton, and the remaining agitators sat down.

"Who is the rightful owner?" asked the Mayor.

"I am not at liberty to tell you until he is properly introduced to his son," answered John. "I can tell you he is not a newcomer." Ellis and his group of what night riders remained out of jail stormed out of the meeting.

"Not a newcomer," said a man in the crowd as the crowd looked at one another searchingly. "Who could it be?" asked someone from the crowd.

"I got something to say," said a frail old lady from the back of the room, as she made her way forward, and said to John Law, "step aside, Sonny, I got something to say."

Smiling, John Law stepped aside while saying, "Yes, Ma'am."

"You people. You grumblers, you complainers and malcontents! I've been praying for you for years that God would change your hearts and save you. I separated from my kinfolk because of this very issue--land, gold, and water. I am Beatrice Jaramillo, almost full blooded Uncompaghre Ute. Right now I live at the Stage Stop Hotel and you do not need to know my room number! I'm a McNaughton grandma, and if you don't know what that means, I ain't telling ya. See here, I've been watchin' and listening to all you speak'in about how you're entitled to the Blair House, mineral rights, and gold. I've news for ya. You don't have the salt in ya to match what my people did to have the land and all that goes with it. It was passed down from generation to generation, which included my people, including me, marry'in some of your people. My people planted the tree that stands on top of Huerfano. Shame on you for wanting what ya didn't work for. You're not entitled to anything, especially any part of the land in question. I can't wait to meet the rightful owner. If he's not married, I'm putting on my courtin' dress even if he's old," exclaimed Beatrice, to which the crowd howled.

"Mr. Mayor, I recommend we take a break; this item should be a closed issue," said John Law.

"If all things are as you say, then the council needs not follow through with the proposed resolution. This item is tabled until next council meeting in two weeks. Let's take a five minute break," said the Mayor.

Red McNaughton threatened, "This isn't over! We'll be back with a court injunction!"

"Red, you don't even live in Jericho Springs, but I'm sure you and your group of naysayers will cause us all a lot of heartburn. You know when we next meet. At least for now, this matter is closed!" the mayor said, while slamming his gavel once more.

Both well-wishers and naysayers from the audience gathered around both Jill Lowenstein and Ezra Blair, while Karen and Janine withdrew and attempted to become wallflowers. The crowd introduced themselves and welcomed Ezra and Jill back to the community. Others left the council chambers in disappointment, because the property appeared to be a closed issue. Hopes dashed, greed dissuaded, most McNaughtons accepted what seemed to be just. Gramma Jaramillo sought Janine and hugged her, then said she expected a dinner invitation once the house was settled and Ezra's father was identified.

High school secretary to the principal, Mara Gelding, the wife of Sam Gelding the insurance representative, went from person to person stopping to ask if they had seen or heard from her husband. Mara approached Karen and Janine and told them she was worried sick that something terrible had happened to her husband Sam. Both immediately embraced and prayed for Mara Gelding.

Before the prayer ended, Mara found herself cornered by both Sheriff Bailey and Detective Caleb Jones. While Karen and Janine left, Bailey and Jones escorted Mrs. Gelding to a conference room and began to reveal their suspicions. Detective Jones told Mara that he had tailed her husband's automobile to Quail Point where he lost him. Jones explained that when he talked with authorities there, they shared evidence they had from another case that matched the description of her husband's automobile. Although the Quail Point police did not have a complete license plate number at the time of their discussion, Jones confirmed that the partial license plate number matched the one for the car he had been tailing. He reported that he managed to come upon the same automobile during his return drive through the Rock Creek Canyon. Unfortunately, he was not able to keep up with the automobile, while navigating the sharp curves and occasional falling rock. Although he lost the car when he returned to Rock Creek, he did get the full license plate number. Detective Jones told Mrs. Gelding that he had contacted the license plate division of motor vehicles and confirmed the number belonged to Sam's car.

Next, Sheriff Bailey shared the results of his investigation, which included testimony from Jill Lowenstein about the murder of Gloria Jones as well as the attack on Karen Gustafson. Both confirmed all evidence pointed to Mara's husband. Bailey reluctantly informed Mrs. Gelding that her husband Sam would be arrested as soon as he was located. Mara confessed that life with her husband had become very ugly and she was not surprised, but still collapsed after promising to contact the sheriff if Sam returned home or contacted her. Sheriff Bailey told Mara that he would be informing the mayor and council about the situation tonight during executive session. Bailey arranged for Deputy Cotton Candy to take her home. In private, Mara sobbed.

Meanwhile, Adam had already rescued and escorted Jill and Karen out of the council chambers and transported them to their new home, the Blair House. Adam invited Karen to spend her last night in the valley at his ranch house on Claymore Flats, which she declined. She hoped he would understand her desire to spend the night with members of the team and to get her belongings situated. All team members and Adam's wranglers that were present stood nearby watching Adam and Karen.

Karen whispered to Adam to join her on the front porch. The team and wranglers moved to the windows and continued their harassment. Taking hold of Adam's hands, Karen asked him if he would pick her up in the morning in time to catch the south bound bus at nine o'clock at the bus stop in front of the Stage Stop Hotel. He told her that he would if she would have breakfast with him there. She told him that she made a mistake by not listening to his wise counsel last night. Without much elaboration, she told him what happened. Confessing she had been foolish by going for a walk to the top of the mesa by herself to pray and without taking a weapon, she explained she had been attacked when she attempted to cross over the footbridge. Next, she told Adam that she was not certain what happened. Someone rescued her, but how she did not know nor did she know what happened to her assailant. Assuming the woodcutter had rescued her, she told Adam that she had blacked out and awakened at the woodcutter's cabin in the woods where she met Jill Lowenstein. Remembering they were being watched, both looked to the windows at the smiling team members and wranglers. Adam said I believe we have their approval, while Karen smiled and waited for his kiss that was not delivered in front of the audience.

At the Blair House Karen selected a second floor corner room for herself with a window on the west side and one on the south side. From there, she had a clear view of the pools of lukewarm water to the south, while to the west, she could clearly see little Huerfano and the Live Oak. After wiping clean her closet shelf, she placed one suitcase and two boxes on the shelf in her one closet on the east side of her room. The other suitcase she placed by the doorway on the north side of her room. All Karen's treasures she had used to analyze her situation were safely stored but two. Her pistol was back in Deputy Candy's custody and presumably placed in the sheriff's evidence room. Karen held the other treasure in her hand by a rope. The rope had been laced through the roof and knotted once through the floor boards of her cabin shaped birdfeeder. She carried the heavy birdfeeder outside the second floor exit door to where Izzy had already prepared a heavy duty hook in a main beam of the porch ceiling near her southern bedroom window. Ken Bond had set up a step ladder to climb and hang this treasure Karen's mother had given her. The gentle men both offered to pour the sunflower seeds through the chimney to fill the cabin's insides and then hang her birdfeeder. Treasuring the event for herself, she had declined further help. Karen had found her home. No need to look elsewhere.

Returning to her room, Karen left the ladder in the second floor hallway and stood in the doorway of her room. She was grateful for the electric pump she used to fill the air mattress she could sleep on in her bedroll. She visualized where to place her furniture from her apartment in Quail Point and the items she had stored at her parent's home in Colorado Springs. Karen devised a design for her belongings, turned out her lights, and went right to sleep.

August 8, 1980

CHAPTER 19

"The LORD has done it this very day; let us
rejoice today and be glad." Psalm 118:24

Adam arrived Friday morning promptly at 7:30 a.m., met Karen at the front door of the Blair House, and carried her one suitcase to his truck. He opened the door for her and placed her suitcase behind her seat in the cab. Inside the cab, she noticed a Winchester rifle in his gun rack. When he entered from the driver's side, she slid across the bench seat and sat next to him while resting her head against his arm. Pleased, he looked down at her, and she looked him square in the face and told him thank you. Adam beamed.

During the short drive to Rock Creek from the Blair House in Jericho Springs, Adam told Karen that an arrest was soon to be made regarding the murder of Gloria Jones and that it would not be his nephew Butch McNaughton. To his surprise, Karen told Adam that Sam Gelding was who would be arrested. She explained that both she and Jill Lowenstein identified Gelding as her assailant and the murderer of Gloria Jones. Adam added that Sam would be accused of at least two other deaths in Quail Point, one was a high school girl and the other a recent victim murdered earlier this week.

Immediately Karen said, "Oh, no, not another death of a high school girl! I probably know her. Was she identified?'

"No, I'm not certain that information has been released."

Both agreed they were sad for Gelding's wife, but hoped that the truth would be revealed and justice would be served. Karen asked Adam about the rifle he was carrying in the gun rack of the truck. His response was that he carried it for varmints and the valley was still much like the wild west. Just having it there may be a deterrent to mischief.

In Rock Creek, Adam escorted Karen to breakfast at the Stage Stop Restaurant. They lingered as long as they could. She had sat next to him, not across from him at the table. Finally, Adam and Karen stood together outside on the hotel porch waiting for the nine o'clock bus to arrive, he with his arm around her and she with her head resting again on his shoulder. Sarah, the waitress, who had served them, watched from the dining room window not with jealously but as one encouraged by what she saw. Sarah and others enjoyed witnessing the proper treatment of women.

The couple just stood before the scene in front of them. They smelled the roses and marveled about what had happened over the last week right where they stood and in the small town around them. It was as if Karen and other newcomers had arrived on the bus and had been encountered by evil from the beginning. Karen's encounters began at the hotel, continued after the school board meeting Tuesday night, and then ended with being attacked on the bridge Wednesday night. The Brownings, as well, had the dead skunk on their porch, the coyote hanged in their tree, and their ducks stolen and killed in the fire along the creek. Hannah had been terrorized in her hotel room then assaulted in front of the school building. Butch had been shot in the back, and Karen had shot Roy in the heel. Next, Adam and Karen counted how many perpetrators were now in jail and concluded by discussing how newcomers helped solve a murder mystery and had been instigators in discovering the identity of a serial killer.

"The good, the bad, and the ugly," said Adam, "some of God's people arrived including bus driver Morris Goodenough, Christian book dealer Kip Powell, the Bonds, and you. And look what has happened, basically in one week!"

"Don't forget the man in the brown trench coat, Izzy. He had to enter into town in disguise and hide in his own home, but there he found his beloved and married her within days. Now, he is going to meet his father today. So, don't be discouraged, Adam, we have all survived, even prevailed despite our bruises and flaws and our secrets," answered Karen.

"Thank you, I know you are right. There is more. By God's grace, look at all the old timers including members of my congregation that came to help and are going to continue the effort. Truly, our merciful God is at work using old timers and newcomers. I never thought I would see the day when my flock would go again into the community and that's the truth!"

"It is wonderful what God is doing, and we get to be a part of it," added Karen, and then she asked, "What happened with your conversations at the jail with Butch?"

"Well, it looks like justice is being served, because Bailey finally fired Butch after he charged him with assaulting Deputy Candy, attempted murder, attempted rape of Hannah, vandalism, conspiring to commit arson, and resisting arrest. I think there were more charges. Butch has certainly hit bottom, but listening to me about Christ? I don't know…" answered Adam.

"Here's another. Any idea where the money came from for all the supplies to rebuild the Blair House?" asked Adam after pausing.

"John Law?"

"No, Wednesday night someone put two gold nuggets in the pocket of my suit coat. I have no idea who did it. I figured one would go for direct ministry of the church to prepare the Rock Creek House for a pastor with a family and the other for the Blair House restoration and community outreach," Adam said and paused. "Karen, it more than paid for the materials that were delivered. It was worth several thousands of dollars. I don't even know how much John was able to get for the one nugget. I meet with him next week to do some planning, and John's secretary is making calls for me to set up another meeting with as many pastors from the valley that will come. I think God wants a united effort where every church will have a part in reaching every home in the valley for Christ. As for my church, I visualize us working with the restoration of Blair House as a base in Jericho Springs. We are the only church in Rock Creek, so, of course, we need to target this town, but each of the three towns impacts the others."

Together, Karen and Adam enjoyed the moment. Mist from the stream, falling from the grand mesa of Claymore Flats, enveloped them like it had enveloped the glen of birch trees in front of their church. A breeze blowing through the canyon carried more moisture that covered all of the hotel and the thicket before the earthen rim east of the kitchen. Karen commented that the moisture seemed like it was coming from a hose with a misty spray setting. Adam said that it cleanses and brings life anew.

Adam interrupted the moment with some news. "Karen, there is a problem I have to tend to, which could mean I might be gone for awhile."

"After all that has happened that sounds ominous, Adam. What would cause you such concern?"

"Shortly, Red McNaughton and I will open flood gates from the creek near Jericho Springs, so we can flood our pasture land before bringing our herds down from the mountains before winter. We do it every year."

"How is that a problem?" Karen inquired.

"I may have to bring the herd down sooner than usual. At least one old bear has been very successful bringing down calves. It is peculiar how crafty he is. Hopefully, he won't follow the herd to the flatlands. I'm going to hunt and kill him, if I can."

"Please be careful. You are a good friend to me and a godsend to so many people in this valley. I'll be praying for your safety and success."

"I'll depend on that," Adam confessed, then continued his confession. "Karen, last night you made a confession and, well, here is mine. I was relieved you called my ranch and left a message for me with Rabbit. I was disappointed I didn't get to talk with you. Actually, I'm hesitant to tell you how badly I felt with the prospect of something terrible happening to you. It forced old hurts to the surface. Wednesday night when I called the Rock Creek house and you were not there, I drove to Rock Creek looking for you. Truly, with all that is going on, I feared for your safety, but the thought struck me that maybe you wanted to spend time with someone else. I felt foolish. Karen, minimally, I want to be your friend on a long term basis."

Pulling into the parking lot and swinging the front end of the bus to a halt, Morris Goodenough, the south bound driver, brought the Bronco orange and blue bus to a quick stop. Morris welcomed Adam and Karen who were holding hands as they walked to the bus.

"Well, Miss Karen Gustafson, it looks like you won more than the teaching position," said Morris.

To which, Karen smiled and said, "Yes, I think I did."

Adam just grinned and said, "Indubitably!" and then Adam kissed Karen goodbye.

Thinking of a movie phrase Karen had heard, she directed a finger at Adam and said with a baritone voice, "I'll be back! I'll be looking for you!"

Both grinned fully and eyes twinkled in anticipation of what was to come.

"I trust you had an exciting time, while visiting Rock Creek?" asked Morris as he directed the bus toward Rock Creek canyon and hummed the theme song from the Bonanza western television series.

Karen sat behind Morris for the ride home, and said, "Morris, there is a lot you can pray about in the Rock Creek Valley. Do you read the *Outcry*?"

"Oh, yes, Miss Karen! I purchase it at the convenience store every trip through the area. I bought a copy in Ridge View this morning, when we all had breakfast at the Cozy Corner Café. I always learn a lot of news when I eat there just by listening and keeping to myself. Yes, Miss Karen, you have had an exciting time," concluded Morris with a knowing grin on his face.

Morris continued, "If you don't mind me saying, Miss Karen, you did not look like you wanted to leave Adam and Rock Creek. You arrived with two suitcases and a couple of boxes and now you carry just one suitcase. You bought a one way ticket, which is what you had when you arrived."

"You know, Morris," Karen explained, "coming here I wanted to leave what was behind me, and now, well, I'll be moving everything here, and you wouldn't be able to load it on this bus!"

"Miss Karen, I may be moving to Jericho Springs. I wrote a letter in response to an ad about helping to rebuild a house. There was a meeting I missed because I was driving yesterday. The ad said free lodging would be provided in exchange for labor. I called yesterday afternoon, August 7, and had a telephone interview with Mr. John Law. Have you heard of him?"

"Morris, that's where I'm moving. It's the Blair House on the west side of Jericho Springs. All the people moving there are Christians like us. It's like God is bringing some of his people to the valley," said Karen with a wide grin.

"Praise the Lord! You know it's about more than rebuilding that house," Morris continued, "and all the circumstances are working out. I'll be able to continue driving my bus. My boss said I'll be able to connect with my scheduled runs through the bus terminal in Ridge View."

Karen thought I wonder what else God has planned for us.

Friday noon John Law arrived early at the Blair House to meet with Izzy before they climbed Huerfano to the tree. John said he had waited a long time for this to happen and that Janine should accompany Izzy to meet Izzy's father now that they were married. The three exited the rear door of the Blair House and began to make their way up the mound to the tree, while from below they witnessed evidence of green overtaking ends of branches as leaves budded forth with new life.

Although no one had seen or heard his arrival, the old man had whittled on the tree since dawn. He had cut into bark and trunk forming a picture he meant for all to see. Purposefully, some would come see it and others would happen upon it accidently. When they reached the top, the old man rose from the stump to greet the trio.

Izzy's father was as picturesque as a western dandy. He sported a white derby hat with a red feather in its brim like that of old time lawman, Bat Masterson, one-time marshal in Trinidad, Colorado and Dodge City, Kansas. Ezra Sr. appeared clean shaven with only a thick gray mustache left as a reminder of the grisly beard that graced his face until last night. Ezra Sr.' black, three pieced suit needed some ironing, yet he still looked dashing. With a twinkle in his dark blue eyes and ear to ear grin, he waited to greet them where he stood. While his weathered hands betrayed his dandy appearance, he was strikingly handsome. Although he worked hard cutting timber and wrestling logs, those same hands had artfully crafted the magnificent carving on the tree.

Janine was not fooled by Ezra's garb and rushed to him and embraced her father-in-law, and said, "My friend…"

John Law stood before the three, and said, "Izzy, meet your father, Ezra Freedom Senior, who, like you, has come home."

At first they just shook hands, until Izzy's faced filled with emotion, a mirror of his father's, and then father and son embraced as tears flowed down their faces.

Izzy said the one word he had not been able to say when he called his father, "My daddy, it's so good to meet you. I look forward to learning about our last name."

Ezra Sr. just nodded affirmatively.

"Izzy, your father can't speak. He has no tongue," reported Janine.

"He was a prisoner of war. Captured in Vietnam and imprisoned in Cambodia," explained John Law.

Izzy said, "And you have been watching over us since I got here."

Ezra Sr. nodded and motioned with his hands first to his eyes then pointing his fingers to Izzy and Janine.

Izzy continued, "You watched and rescued me more than once when the sheriff was tailing me and you drove by and picked me up before he was able to reach me."

Again Ezra nodded and pointed to Janine, who said, "And you have watched over me for years, and you have brought new life to this old tree with your daily watering."

Ezra smiled and put his right hand on his chest over his heart, then pointed at Janine.

"I love you, too!" she said and placed her hand over her heart and pointed at Ezra in return.

John Law had a question as well, "Are you the one who put the two gold nuggets in the alms box of the church in the glen where Mary McNaughton used to attend?" Ezra Sr. nodded affirmatively.

John was quick to correct himself, "Mary McNaughton was Adam Claymore's wife. Unfortunately for me, she chose him over me, but I have loved them both. I'll bet you are the one who has been putting gold nuggets in collection plates all over town. I hope you haven't given all of them away!"

Ezra smiled but didn't give away his secret.

Janine said, "I have a hunch you were the one who rescued Karen Gustafson on the footbridge at church. Thank you for keeping her safe."

Again Ezra nodded, and then with both hands, he pointed at the carving on the Live Oak, grinned, and pointed to himself and his son. His countenance radically changed and he mouthed, "I'm sorry."

"Me too, Dad," said Izzy as he walked to the carving and put his hand on it. He turned and said to his father, "This is my story. This is Freedom's tree."

Ezra Sr. wept.

And Izzy moved to embrace his father, "Bruised and flawed, we are both home," said Ezra Freedom, Junior.

Once back in the Blair House, John Law told Ezra Sr. that he had enough money to buy a new truck, but Ezra declined shaking his head violently. Ezra stretched out his arms sideways like a figure on a cross then laid on the ground with his arms folded across his chest, then got up smiling. Just because the Gray Whiz died on his rutted road leading to County Road 403 from the cabin, he wanted it resurrected. It would never again announce his arrival with its cough, cough, sputter, cough, sputter, boom. John would call the dealership in Rock Creek to send a tow truck before Friday evening and would authorize a full restoration of the Gray Whiz.

Below at Blair House restoration already had begun. On homemade sawhorses, Ken Bond and his daughters, Kristin and Krystal, fashioned a table, as Ken nailed a four by eight foot sheet of plywood to the horses. From across the street Ken Bond's girls carried chairs that had been donated by Rachael McNaughton. John Law insisted Rachael join them for lunch and used her telephone to call the auto dealership in Ridge View to arrange restoration of the Gray Whiz and then ordered pizzas that Jerry Sunday delivered to the Blair House. Rachael joined the team for lunch, while John Law left to take care of business for the Freedoms. Lunch preceded an afternoon of basic household cleaning.

For now, Izzy and Janine had selected the northwest room on the third floor, which had the closet with the hidden door leading to the kitchen and furnace room below. They could peer out the window and see the old tree standing on the little orphan mound. Still only one knew of the gold that resided below the Live Oak, captured in the earth where tree roots enveloped nuggets galore, and he, Ezra Sr., spent this night in the master suite sleeping in his bed roll on the floor. His three piece suit hung neatly in the closet. Ezra dreamed of when he had slept there before the war, before his beautiful wife died in childbirth. He wept but cherished his memories and was ready to reveal himself to those beyond Blair House, in due time and according to his plan. For now Ezra Sr. wanted to make memories with the child, now a man, he had left behind to go to war. Janine and Izzy slept dreamily in each other's arms in a double bedroll placed on an air mattress on the hard wood floor.

Seven nights of prayer from the north, east, west, and south had caused the walls of resistance to come tumbling down in Jericho Springs, and at least for tonight the opposition remained silent.

Come Saturday Morning

CHAPTER 20

"Sing to the LORD a new song, for he has done
marvelous things..." Psalm 98:1a

A gentle morning breeze rolled down the mountain valley. Part of the breeze made a chilly entrance into the newlywed's bedroom. Izzy awakened with a start. He shivered and then shook Janine gently until she too was wide awake.

"We must go look at the carving," Izzy said, "I think my father left more of a message there for me, and God wants me to see it now. I'm sure of it."

"Oh, Izzy," Janine said coyly, "stay here with me in this warm bed."

Getting up, Izzy went to the closet door, and pleaded, "No, no, put on your robe and slippers and come on. I must see it as dawn is breaking. I need for you to go with me."

Izzy beckoned Janine to follow him down the stairwell to the kitchen below. Izzy switched on the light bulb in the closet he had replaced the night before, and together they descended the stairs noiselessly. They paused and kissed in the kitchen, then left the confines of the back porch to ascend the hill.

"I think you're right," Janine said, as she began to sing "Morning Has Broken."

Izzy told Janine to climb on his back like the old days when he gave her piggyback rides, so the rock would not hurt her feet, while Izzy carefully climbed. Promptly, she embraced the idea and him. Reaching the top of Huerfano, he squatted on the large knuckled root where his father had sat and had created the images he had carved in the Live Oak. Somewhat giddy and not immediately interested, Janine sat on Izzy's right knee and embraced him. Morning sunlight had crept down the mountain to the valley below to the top of the Live Oak, and then upon Izzy and Janine. The sunlight warmed the couple and illuminated the message the old woodcutter had carved into the tree. Both shaded their eyes as the light became brighter. Izzy led Janine in prayer that God would reveal to them what he wanted them to know from his father's art work.

In the carving before them, Janine and Izzy saw a man, naked, standing before an altar with a globe set on it. Behind the altar stood four hooded figures dressed

266

in black. Above the altar was a large tree in full summertime display. Pictured in the tree trunk was a sizable cross with spikes in the cross piece and one in the long piece. The man before the altar appeared to be reaching for a singular apple on a tree branch. Above the tree was a giant sunflower that appeared in place of the sun with a stalk that extended below the ground where the man stood. Into the earth, the stalk became a root and entwined an unopened box where mysteries lay enclosed. Reaching from the sky were scissor handles at the top end that became flesh at the bottom as a hand reaching toward the earth. Upper left were numerous red hooded figures populating the sky in wait for what transpired below.

"I think the naked man has a choice to make. He has to make decisions. He chooses which way to go, but God is in charge of circumstances," interpreted Izzy.

"And if he makes the wrong choice?" asked Janine.

"I hope he gets a second chance."

"Like you and your father?"

Izzy looked down and nodded, then said, "Freedom to choose again."

"Does that mean you hope God won't give up on those who are his?" Janine asked.

"Yes, and like *2 Chronicles*, if we seek God's face and turn from our wicked ways, then God will forgive and heal our land."

"Izzy, what does that mean for you, and now for me," asked Janine.

Ezra Freedom Jr. thought for a minute, and said to his new wife, "For one, we are to do the counseling with Adam and have a proper wedding. Two, we are to restore Blair House. Three, Blair House should become a beacon for God's kingdom shining from under this tree to the valley below."

"I take it your previous sin and decisions neither excused you nor disqualified you from working to build God's kingdom," illuminated Mrs. Ezra Freedom Jr.

"Yes," Izzy said softly. "I get to… with you and my father at my abba daddy's direction," whispered Izzy.

"Izzy, my dear, do we have to do that now?" murmured Janine.

"Not right now. We need to get dressed and eat a hearty breakfast," answered Izzy.

"Dear Izzy, do you want me to show you where I saved the chest you lost in the pond beside the tree? It was half full of gold nuggets. Enough gold we could have a real honeymoon before school starts."

"You have the chest!" Izzy said as he embraced Janine, "I waded through every bit of water I could find looking for that chest of gold, in the creek in Rock Creek, the pond below the waterfall on north 403, and in the ponds here below the tree. Yes, I want to see the chest and the gold!"

"Then carry me back to bed," Janine whispered then touched her nose to Izzy's ear.

Izzy scooped her up into his arms to carry her down the hill and said, "One thing more, I'm to cherish you more than the gold," Izzy paused… then said, "We can restore Blair House Monday."

Book Club Discussion Guide

1. The book begins with Karen's arrival through a canyon to the town of Rock Creek. How is the valley presented as a Canaanite city and culture?
2. Is Izzy a prodigal? How or why? Why not?
3. How are women depicted in *Freedom's Tree*?
4. What does the author seem to be saying about marriage? About life in a small town?
5. Adam is compared to the Lone Ranger story. How is Adam both a lone ranger and kinsman redeemer like Boaz in the book of Ruth? How do you characterize Adam Claymore? Izzy? Karen? What are their flaws? How are they bruised?
6. Thursday noon those responding to the newspaper ad meet at John Law's office. The author states six concepts from the Arthurian legend as a code of conduct. What are they and how are they represented in the text?
7. What are the roles of the church and prayer in *Freedom's Tree*?
8. There are recurring themes or symbols, motifs that unify the text including "they stumble who run too fast," Lone Ranger, listening to wise counsel. What are they and how are they presented and used in the text?
9. How well did the scripture create a mindset or lens for reading each chapter that followed?
10. Compare the text to both Shakespeare's plays *Romeo and Juliet* and *Julius Caesar.*
11. What questions remain unanswered? How do you predict they will be answered in *Restoring Blair House*, the second book of the Rock Creek Trilogy?

COMING SOON!

RESTORING BLAIR HOUSE

The mystery continues with the second installment of The Rock Creek Trilogy. All are bruised. All are flawed. All have secrets. Author Ken Lippincott continues his tale of God bringing some of his people to a place to do his work. Personalities and politics get in the way as Karen Gustafson returns to Rock Creek to discover the restoration of Blair House is underway, but her personal hero has been injured and now is bedridden. Izzy and Janine lead the crew remodeling the old house on the edge of town under Freedom's tree. The small congregation of the little church in the glen in Rock Creek has already begun to take the offensive by ministering in the valley.